METHODS OF TISSUE CULTURE

METHODS
OF TISSUE
CULTURE

THIRD EDITION

Raymond C. Parker, Ph.D.

Research Member, Connaught Medical Research Laboratories,
and Professor of Experimental Cytology, School of Hygiene,
University of Toronto

With 127 illustrations

Hoeber Medical Division

Harper & Row, Publishers

THIRD EDITION
Published November, 1961

REPRINTED WITH REVISIONS, DECEMBER 1962

METHODS OF TISSUE CULTURE
Copyright © 1938, 1950, 1961 by
Hoeber Medical Division,
Harper & Row, Publishers, Incorporated
Printed in the United States of America

K-M

Library of Congress catalog card number: 61–11355

TO MY TEACHERS

Ross G. Harrison
Albert Fischer
Alexis Carrel

Preface to the Third Edition

IN THIS as in the earlier editions, descriptions are given of current methods for the cultivation of cells and tissues of birds and mammals under a wide variety of special conditions. As before, an effort has been made to trace the development of the various methods and to cite some of their uses. Many new procedures have been introduced over the past ten years. From these, a careful selection was made in order to keep the book to a reasonable size. For additional information the reader is directed to original publications and related literature in a greatly expanded list of references.

While the main features of the previous editions have been retained, many new sections, six virtually new chapters, and over sixty new illustrations have been added. Older material has been omitted, condensed, or reorganized and extended to include new material. It is hoped that the completed effort will be found useful in many areas of investigation.

I am grateful to the following colleagues in other institutions who contributed new illustrations for this edition: Drs. J. D. Biggers, P. D. Cooper, W. R. Duryee, H. Eagle, W. R. Earle, J. J. Elias, D. W. Fawcett, G. O. Gey, T. Gibson, C. Goldstein, S. Graff, R. B. L. Gwatkin, J. H. Hanks, M. Harris, T. S. Hauschka, A. S. Kaplan, J. E. Lovelock, S. E. Luria, W. F. McLimans, H. T. Meryman, A. Moscona, M. R. Murray, C. M. Pomerat, J. S. Porterfield, T. T. Puck, G. G. Rose, A. B. Sabin, B. M. Shaffer, J. T. Syverton, O. A. Trowell, E. Wolff, and J. S. Younger. The following manufacturing firms also contributed to the new illustrations: Bellco Glass, Inc., Corning Glass Works, Ertel Engineering Corporation, Fisher Scientific Company, Kontes Glass Company, Selas Corporation of America, and the Sub-Zero Freezer Company. I am grateful to the following colleagues elsewhere who made important information available to me prior to publication: Drs. W. R. Duryee, H. Eagle, T. S. Hauschka, W. F. McLimans, Catherine Rappaport, W. F. Scherer, H. E. Swim, and Charity Waymouth. I would ask those by whose labors of expression I have benefited to regard the bibliography as an acknowledgment of my obligations.

Among my colleagues and associates in Toronto, I am especially grateful to Dr. L. Siminovitch, who read early drafts of the revision and made many helpful suggestions; to Professor D. B. W. Reid, who prepared the section on the estimation of virus infectivity; to Dr. D. R. E. MacLeod, who supplied the technical information for the section on the preparation of an inactivated virus vaccine; to Dr. H. M. G. Macmorine, who supplied information on the large-scale preparation of cell suspensions from monkey kidney tissue; to Dr. A. A. Axelrad, who helped with Chapter XIX; to Mr. C. G. Smith, who made some of the new illustrations; to Dr. P. Sarkar and Mr. L. R. Whitman, who prepared Fig. 91; to Mrs. H. H. Weston, who assisted with the final manuscript; and to Miss Elizabeth Kupelwieser and other members of my laboratory, who helped in many ways. Finally, I would again thank the publisher and his staff for their continued patience and courtesy.

R. C. P.

Toronto, Canada

Preface to the First Edition

OVER the past ten years, much has been written about the methods of tissue culture. The various accounts that have appeared fall into two groups: those that have laid considerable emphasis upon the difficulties involved, without elucidating them sufficiently; and those that have minimized the effectiveness of the various procedures by treating them superficially. Furthermore, the recent accounts are quite incomplete, and the older ones are long out of date. As a result, many students and investigators have become discouraged even before attempting to utilize the methods, whereas others have been led into pitfalls that might otherwise have been avoided.

On the present occasion, an attempt has been made to describe the essential details of the more basic procedures used in Carrel's laboratory at The Rockefeller Institute. And while the presentation may seem somewhat incomplete because it deals almost exclusively with the methods followed in that laboratory, this course has been taken in the firm belief that the procedures described permit more precise standardization and a greater latitude of usefulness than any others now in existence. It is hoped that they have been presented in such manner that they may be applied directly in their present form, or else that they may serve as a basis for further elaborations to meet the special demands of individual requirements.

Since the book is intended both for those who are unacquainted with the more recent developments in tissue culture, and for others who have never had occasion to use the methods in any form, an effort has also been made to give the reader a certain degree of orientation in the extensive literature that has grown up around the use of the various procedures. In Chapter XVI may be found examples of the manner in which the methods have been applied to advantage in five major fields of investigation, namely, experimental morphology, and the study of tumors, viruses, hypersensitivity and immunity. In the classified bibliography at the end of the book, there are supplementary references to experiments in these and other fields of investigation not discussed in the text.

To my colleagues and associates, and all those who have given of their time and assistance, I am profoundly indebted and offer my grateful thanks. I refer, especially, to Dr. Alexis Carrel, for whose interest, advice and criticism I am particularly indebted; to Dr. Albert H. Ebeling, Dr. Lillian E. Baker, Miss Irene E. McFaul, Miss Augusta J. Hollender, Miss Olive M. Johnston, Miss Cesira Macri, Mrs. Walter M. Gladding, Jr., Mr. William La Rosa, and Mr. William Haratonik, all of whom have helped in numerous ways and have saved me from many an embarrassing error in technical detail; to Mr. Charles B. Spies, and his associates, of the Purchasing Division of The Rockefeller Institute, who helped greatly in describing the special equipment mentioned in Chapter III; to Mr. Joseph B. Haulenbeek, and his associates, of the Illustration Division of The Rockefeller Institute, who photographed all displays of equipment and technical procedures, and executed the diagrams; to Dr. Geoffrey Rake, who read the entire manuscript and offered many valuable suggestions; and to Miss Josephine Bates, who prepared the manuscript for publication.

I am also indebted to Dr. William Bloom for the privilege of reading, in manuscript form, his article on "Cellular differentiation and tissue culture"; to Col. Charles A. Lindbergh, for the privilege of describing, for the first time, an apparatus devised by him for the preparation of serum from coagulated plasma, and also a special flask for the continuous circulation of fluid media; to Dr. Warren H. Lewis, for permission to describe his ring-slide technique; and to Mr. R. P. Loveland and Mr. G. E. Matthews of the Research Laboratories of the Eastman Kodak Company, and Mr. E. Keller of E. Leitz, Inc., all of whom read Chapter XV.

Finally, I wish to acknowledge a debt of extreme gratitude to the late Mr. Paul B. Hoeber, of Harper and Brothers, whose interest and encouragement did much to lighten the task; and to his associate, Miss Florence Fuller, who has seen the book through the trials of actual publication.

R. C. P.

New York, N. Y.

Contents

Preface to the Third Edition   vii

Preface to the First Edition   ix

I. INTRODUCTION   I

II. THE LABORATORY   8

Special Facilities, *10*

III. SPECIAL EQUIPMENT   15

IV. CLEANSING AND STERILIZATION   25

Cleansing of Glassware by Ultrasonic Energy, *28*
Cleansing of Glassware by Other Means, *30*
Cleansing of Other Equipment, *32*
Sterilization Procedures, *34*
Filtration, *42*
Use of Antibiotics, *47*
Disinfection of Floors, Walls, Bench Tops, and Other
     Objects, *48*
Use of Masks and Gowns in Culture Rooms, *49*
Antibacterial Treatment of Hands, *50*
Preparation of Dakin's Hypochlorite Solution, *51*

V. BALANCED SALT SOLUTIONS AND pH CONTROL   53

pH Control, *59*

VI. CHEMICALLY DEFINED MEDIA   62

Preparation of a Chemically Defined Medium (CMRL-1066), *77*
Preparation of Chemically Defined Media from Mixed Ingredients Stored in Solid Form, *80*

VII. MEDIA CONTAINING NATURALLY OCCURRING INGREDIENTS   81

Blood Plasma, *82*
Blood Serum, *91*
Tissue Extracts, *99*
Bovine Amniotic Fluid, *108*
Complex Media Containing Naturally Occurring Ingredients, *109*

VIII. PREPARATION OF CELLS AND TISSUES FOR CULTIVATION   115

General Considerations, *115*
Preparation of Tissues by Chopping or Careful Dissection, *117*
Cells Released from Tissues by Various Enzymes, *119*
Preparation of Cell Suspensions with Trypsin, *121*
Preparation of Cell Suspensions with Collagenase, *130*
Cells Released from Tissues by Chelating Agents, *131*
Albumin-Flotation Method of Separating Malignant Cells from Serosanguineous Fluids, *131*
Separation of Leukocytes from Peripheral Blood, *134*

IX. COVERSLIP CULTURES   138

Preparation of Single-Coverslip Cultures with Plasma, *139*
Preparation of Subcultures from Single-Coverslip Cultures with Plasma, *141*
Preparation of Single-Coverslip Cultures without Plasma, *144*
Ring-Slide Cultures, *145*

Double-Coverslip Cultures, *145*
Perforated-Slide Cultures, *151*

X. FLASK AND TUBE CULTURES WITH PLASMA   152

Preparation of Plasma Cultures in Carrel Flasks, *154*
Subsequent Treatment of Plasma Cultures in Flasks, *155*
Preparation of Subcultures from Plasma Cultures in
     Flasks, *157*
Preparation of Roller-Tube Cultures with Plasma, *158*
Continuous Cultivation of Fibroblasts in Plasma, *161*
Cultivation of Epithelial Cells in Plasma, *164*
Cultivation of Blood Leukocytes in Plasma, *165*
Cultivation of Tissues in Heterologous Plasma, *166*
Use of Antitryptic Agents to Prevent Digestion of
     Coagulum, *168*
Cultivation of Tissues in Fibrinogen, *169*
Sponge-Matrix Cultures with Plasma, *170*
Reconstituted Rat-Tail Collagen as a Substitute for
     Plasma, *172*

XI. STATIONARY CULTURES WITH FLUID MEDIUM   174

Fluid Medium Cultures in Tubes, Flasks, Bottles, and
     Petri Dishes, *179*
Methods of Harvesting Cells and Tissues in Fluid
     Medium, *187*
Blood Leukocytes in Fluid Medium, *190*
Discrete Tissue Fragments in Fluid Medium, *193*
Perforated-Cellophane Cultures, *195*
Sponge-Matrix Cultures with Fluid Medium, *195*

XII. SUSPENDED-CELL CULTURES   197

Cultivation of Cells in Suspension, *199*
Estimation of Number of Cells Capable of Division in
     Suspended-Cell Cultures, *207*

XIII. CELL CLONES   209

Isolation of Cell Clones, *211*

Removal of Selected Colonies (Clones) from Plates, *218*
Estimation of Growth Rates in Clones, *218*
Use of Plating Procedures in Biological Assays, *219*

XIV. CULTURES NOURISHED BY PERFUSION 222

XV. CULTIVATION OF ORGAN RUDIMENTS AND AGGREGATES
OF DISSOCIATED CELLS 227

Cultivation of Organ Rudiments on a Plasma Coagu-
lum, *234*
Cultivation of Organ Rudiments in Chemically Defined
Media, *237*
Cultivation of Aggregates of Dissociated Cells, *242*

XVI. CULTURES FOR VIRUS STUDIES 245

Methods of Detecting Virus Multiplication in Tissue
Culture, *246*
Cytopathic Effects of Virus Multiplication, *247*
Virus Isolation and Identification, *249*
Virus Titrations, *250*
Isolation of Virus from Plaques, *259*
One-Step Growth Experiments, *260*
Preparation of an Inactivated-Virus Vaccine, *263*

XVII. GROWTH MEASUREMENTS 267

Measurement of the Growth of Cultures in a Plasma
Coagulum, *268*
Estimation of Cell Numbers in Cultures with Fluid
Medium, *271*
Determination of Cell Viability by Dye-Exclusion
Tests, *282*

XVIII. PRESERVATION OF CELLS BY FREEZING 284

General Features of Freezing and Thawing, *285*
Freezing and Thawing of Cell Strains, *289*
Slow Freezing at a Controlled Rate, *291*
Low-Temperature Storage Equipment, *293*

XIX. Histological Procedures   298

Fixing Reagents, 299
Fixation and Staining of Cells Cultivated in Fluid
    Media, 301
Fixation and Staining of Plasma Cultures, 310
Hematoxylin-Eosin Procedure for Sections, 318
Bodian's Silver-Impregnation Method for Nerve Struc-
    tures, 318
Preparation of Cultures for Electron Microscopy, 320

References   323
Index   351

METHODS OF TISSUE CULTURE

I

Introduction

IN 1878 Claude Bernard pointed out the importance of the internal environment (*milieu intérieur*) in regulating the activities of living tissue. According to his conception,[20] the environment is not only the product of tissue metabolism, it reacts in turn upon the tissues themselves and regulates their activity. If, then, an attempt were to be made to study the functional properties of cells and how cells affect or are affected by their immediate environment, it would be necessary to isolate them in artificial systems in which the influence of the organism could be avoided. One of the first steps in this direction was taken in 1866 by F. D. von Recklinghausen,[428] who kept amphibian blood cells alive in sterile containers under a variety of conditions for as long as 35 days. But the first culture experiments on organized tissues were carried out by Wilhelm Roux[458] in 1885. By transferring the neural plate of a developing chick embryo to a warm saline solution, he was able to prove that the closure of the neural tube is primarily a function of the constituent cells and not, as some had supposed, the direct effect of mechanical pressure exerted by adjacent structures. Two years later, Arnold[7] soaked fragments of elderberry pith in frog's aqueous humor, then planted them under the skin and in the peritoneal cavity of frogs, where they were invaded by leukocytes. Later, he removed the fragments of pith to dishes containing aqueous humor or saline solution and was able to study the activities of the cells that migrated from them.

In 1898 Ljunggren[288] made successful transplantations of human skin that had been kept alive for days and weeks in ascitic fluid. Four years later Haberlandt[203] published the first of his studies on the isolated vegetative cells of higher plants, and Leo Loeb[291] employed blocks of agar and clotted plasma in which small fragments of guinea-pig skin were embedded and placed for incubation in subcutaneous pockets of another animal. In 1903 Jolly[246] completed an extensive series of observations on the division of amphibian leukocytes culti-vated outside the body for one month. Three years later Beebe and Ewing[18] cultivated an infectious lymphosarcoma of a dog in the blood of susceptible and resistant animals. Yet it remained for Harrison[225, 226] to devise a simple and effective technique that would permit explanted parts to continue to grow and develop outside the organism. In a sense, Harrison's experiments were the logical development of micro-surgical procedures of elimination and transplantation already introduced to experimental embryology; for, if it were possible to transplant living tissues and allow them to develop further in new surroundings within the body, it should also be possible to find some external culture medium in which they would likewise grow.

Harrison published his first observations on the living, developing nerve fiber in 1907. The ingenious experiments constituting the basis of this report[225] not only gave visual evidence of the origin of nerve fibers but also demonstrated the usefulness of tissue culture in attempts to study the structural elements of higher organisms in relation to their environment. Previously, in an attempt to prove the contention of His and Ramon y Cajal that the nerve fiber is formed as the out-growth of a single cell, Harrison had transplanted fragments of the nervous system of amphibian larvae to other parts of the developing embryo. He found that nerve fibers always developed in surroundings composed of living, organized tissue. This situation was confusing, for it introduced the possibility that the latter might contribute organized material to the nerve element. In fact, one of the main opposing theories to be tested presupposed the existence of some sort of primitive structures, or protoplasmic bridges, that pervaded all parts of the embryo and later give rise to nerve fibers. Hence, it became necessary to isolate the nerve centers from the body and to determine their ability to form nerve fibers in a medium completely devoid of other cellular structures. To achieve this end, Harrison removed small fragments of undifferentiated embryonic tissue from the walls of the neural tube and suspended them in hanging drops of clotted lymph from the adult animal. His hopes were realized, for not only did the cultures show active growth, but with aseptic precautions they could be kept in good condition for several weeks. It now remained only to make the decisive observations, which indicated clearly that the nerve fiber was actually formed by the spinning of a

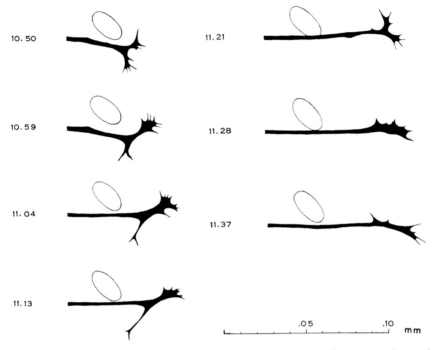

FIG. 1. Camera lucida sketches of the growing end of a nerve fiber in a culture of nerve tissue from a frog embryo, after 4 days in clotted lymph. Total length of the fiber at that time was 800 μ. Red blood cell shown in outline served as a fixed location. (R. G. Harrison.[226])

thread of neuroblastic protoplasm into a filament at the free end of the process (Fig. 1). Thus, the cell alone was shown to be concerned in the formation of the axon.

Harrison worked exclusively with amphibian material. He had an urgent problem to solve, and when he had solved it he put his cultures aside and went on with his important studies of amphibian morphogenesis. Burrows,[40] who studied with Harrison, adapted his culture procedures to warm-blooded animals and discovered the usefulness of blood plasma as a culture medium. Later, in association with Carrel, Burrows[42,53,54] laid the foundation for the continuous cultivation of tissues from many sources.

For the development of more precise techniques from these early procedures of Harrison, biologists are mainly indebted to Carrel, who promptly saw in them the possible means of realizing to a fuller extent than ever before the exacting precepts laid down by Claude Bernard. Carrel had been engaged in applying the principles of surgery to the physiological study of mammalian organ systems. His extensive experience in this field had thoroughly convinced him that the greatest hope of arriving at a clearer understanding of the laws of growth and organization rested in the study of such structural units as could be isolated from the organism and cultivated under carefully controlled conditions. Thus, with the gradual improvement in techniques and the progressive elaboration of suitable media, it soon became possible to derive thousands of cultures in pedigree fashion from the progeny of one. A strain of connective-tissue cells from the chick that served as the test material for much of Carrel's work[44,50] was kept in a state of active multiplication for 34 years (Fig. 2.)* This and other cell strains developed in many laboratories have provided an abundance of uniform material for studies of many sorts, and as a result a great deal has been learned concerning the true nature of cells and their specific requirements. Cells and tissue fragments isolated from almost any part of the body can now be cultivated and studied under a wide variety of special conditions, many of which will be described in the following chapters.

In addition to the developments made in Carrel's laboratory, the original procedures of Harrison were elaborated and improved along somewhat different lines by W. H. and M. R. Lewis, A. Maximow, G. Levi, C. Champy, and T. S. P. Strangeways. As a result, three main types of culture work have been developed, which may be described as tissue culture proper, cell culture, and organ culture. Tissue culture proper deals with the growth of cells that are integrated into a tissue, and under suitable conditions such cultures may show histiogenetic changes. Cell culture, which owes its origin mainly to the efforts of Earle and his associates, makes it possible to perform quantitative experiments with established cell lines, including clonal populations from single cells. In organ culture, which has

* Ebeling, A. H. Personal communication.

been developed to a high state of usefulness by Fell and her associates, organ rudiments are cultivated with the minimum of outgrowth and enlarge and develop as a whole.

Among the various animal cell types that have been cultivated for longer or shorter periods *in vitro* are: epithelial cells, connective tissue cells, cartilage and bone cells, nerve cells, muscle cells, reticular cells

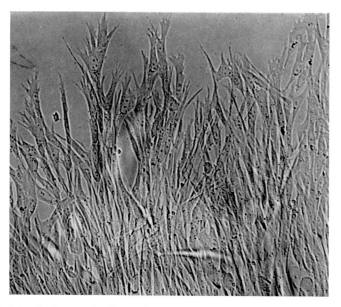

FIG. 2. Marginal area of a D-3.5 flask culture of Carrel's strain of chick-embryo fibroblasts after strain had been propagated for 26 years in homologous plasma and embryo extract. (A. H. Ebeling, unpublished data, 1938.) × 230.

from bone marrow, lymph nodes and spleen, and leukocytes from the blood, all of which may be derived either from the embryo or the adult. Depending on their origin, some of these cells can be cultivated continuously, whereas others multiply slowly or not at all. In addition, many established cell lines have been developed, and some of these cannot readily be identified with any cell type existing in the animal body. The tissue-culture techniques have also been used for the cultivation of explanted fragments of complex tissue structures, consisting of a variety of cell types; of parts of mature organs, in which the component tissue structures have already assumed definite form; of developing structures, in which the growing complexity may be studied under controlled conditions; of cell suspensions prepared by treating tissue and organ fragments with enzymes and other agents; and of malignant cells from many sources. Although cells and tissues for cultivation are usually taken either at biopsy or soon after death, it is not uncommon to initiate cultures from refrigerated material several days after death.

The combined effect of all of these efforts has been the gradual development of a system of procedures that has been used to advantage in almost every field of experimental biology and medicine, particularly in cytology, histology, embryology, cell physiology, cell pathology, bacteriology, immunology, and in the study of tumors and viruses. It has been possible, for example, to study the structural and functional characteristics of the various cell types that comprise the individual; the potencies of embryonic regions and organ rudiments; the food requirements of various cell types and the nature of substances required in chemically defined nutritive media; mitotic mechanisms; the nature of cell movement; the fine structure of cells by electron microscopy; protoplasmic constituents such as mitochondria, microsomes, and other inclusions; the action of physical forces such as irradiation, temperature, gravity, and magnetism on cells; the use of cultures in the diagnosis of certain diseases; the preparation of tissues for grafting; the origin of blood and blood diseases; the utilization of radioisotopes; reactions of cells to toxic substances; cellular responses to bacterial infection; cellular parasites; the origin of immune substances; the comparative biochemistry of cells; the elaboration and action of hormones and other cellular products; the action of medical reagents such as antiseptics, antibiotics, narcotics, and other substances on cells; the kinetics of viral multiplication; the nature and occurrence of viral mutations *in vitro;* contrasting stabilities and variabilities in cell lines; detailed mechanisms of cellular transformations; the changes that occur in clonal populations of cells during cultivation; and similiarities and differences between normal and malignant cells.

In the present account of the methods of tissue culture, an attempt will be made to outline the essential details of the more basic techniques and practices that have been developed in many laboratories. It should be remembered, however, that the tissue-culture techniques, like all others that serve a wide variety of special purposes, are undergoing constant change and revision; and some of the procedures described here will almost certainly be outmoded by the time the book appears. It should also be remembered that tissue culture is not in itself a science or even a special field of investigation. Instead, it is but one method of approach to innumerable problems in experimental biology and medicine. The effectiveness of the various techniques can be measured only by the uses to which they are put.

II

The Laboratory

BEFORE the advent of antibiotics, it was customary in most tissue-culture establishments to work in small rooms that were protected as far as possible from the air of the outer laboratory. The first laboratory of biology in which surgical cleanliness could be maintained was probably that of Pavlov.[389] The principle was simple: It provided for a series of four connecting rooms, each of which served its own special purpose and gave additional protection against the penetration of dust into the last and most important, the operating room. This feature of Pavlov's scheme was followed by Carrel in 1920 in arranging new, enlarged laboratories at The Rockefeller Institute in New York. These laboratories contained two complete suites of connecting rooms in which two operating teams could work simultaneously. Like Pavlov's, each suite consisted of four rooms, but between the two suites, and serving both of them, were the general preparation and sterilizing rooms. In the first room of each series, the animal was anesthetized and shaved; in the second, the site of operation was cleansed and the animal draped. The third was the scrub-up room; the fourth, the operating room. After an operation, animals were returned to the first room of the series where they were left to recover in special cages supplied with a continuous circulation of warm air. The second and fourth rooms of each series were also used as culture rooms.

To-day, with filtered air conditioning, it is no longer necessary to construct an architectural maze in order to protect the air of a single room. But Carrel's operating rooms had other interesting features. In all of his rooms, an unusual softness was achieved by painting the walls and ceilings gray and the floors black and by using black table coverings and animal drapes and black gowns and hoods. Because all reflected light was suppressed in these rooms, delicate anatomical structures and semitransparent culture material could be seen and handled with relative ease. It will be remembered that this was the era of "hospital white" not only for surgeon's operating theaters but also for restaurants that wished to emphasize cleanliness. But Carrel saw no reason why surgical cleanliness could not be achieved without the harsh glare and eyestrain that always accompanies all-white surroundings, and, quite typically, he went the whole way, to black and gray, as a means of demonstrating his point. Now, thanks largely to his efforts, fewer and fewer men and women in white are working in white-walled operating rooms. Carrel's rooms were lighted with skylights but only because the only alternative at the time would have been hot, incandescent lamps in rooms that could not be cooled. It is also of interest to note that just before the rooms were prepared for an experiment in animal surgery or for culture work any dust was settled by means of finely sprayed water, which was forced in through large atomizers placed in the walls. Also, all pipes and heating appliances were built into the walls, to reduce the accumulation and dissemination of dust. Wall areas that enclosed them were covered by metal plates, which were flush with adjacent areas and easily removable in emergency.

The manner in which present-day tissue-culture procedures are carried out depends partly on laboratory arrangements, i.e., whether the cultures are to be prepared and cared for in air-conditioned, "dust-proof" rooms, in safety cabinets or hoods, or on open benches in general workrooms. With the help of antibiotics and certain minimal precautions, it has become possible in many laboratories to do effective work with nothing more elaborate than a few feet of general-purpose bench space and the sort of equipment that may usually be found in any bacteriological laboratory. Other laboratories make excellent use of safety cabinets. These cabinets require relatively little floor space and can be located in almost any part of the laboratory suite where there is not too much traffic.

In any one laboratory, it is often difficult to strike a reasonable balance between the minimal precautions required for some types of work and the maximal precautions required for others. Minimal precautions are usually sufficient in working with cell strains that can be propagated in suspension like bacteria. But more elaborate precautions are required in experiments involving long and tedious dissections, in experiments that cannot be repeated because of the unusual nature of a particular component, or in complex experiments in which antibiotics cannot be used. Interesting cell strains are still being lost to antibiotic resistant organisms or before effective antibiotics can be selected by making sensitivity tests on the offending organisms (*see* p. 48). In the author's laboratory, a strain of cells that has been propagated for over four years by repeated subculture in unsupplemented chemically defined media is particularly susceptible to microbial contaminations and has not yet survived low-temperature storage (*see* p. 284). It would seem, therefore, that in laboratories where a considerable variety of work is in progress it might be safer and easier to follow a reasonably uniform routine for all operations than to try to decide, several times a day, which things can be poured through the air with abandon and which things deserve more careful handling. If a continuous effort is made to simplify procedures, it will usually be possible to devise a smooth routine that will take care of the more exacting efforts without adding appreciably to the time required by the more casual ones.

Special Facilities

Needless to state, the quality of the work done in any laboratory bears little relationship to the physical conditions under which it is performed. Much valuable information has come from tissue-culture work done in secluded little cubicles quite devoid of ventilation, and many investigators have managed to do excellent work without any special facilities whatsoever. Nevertheless, the following recommendations are made for those who are planning new accommodations for general work with explanted cells and tissues. For a laboratory to accommodate ten or more workers, including technicians, students, and senior investigators, it is suggested that there should be three or more dust-proof rooms, two or more safety cabinets, and at least 100 linear feet of general-purpose bench space that can be kept free of permanent equipment. Other special requirements, such as facilities for biochemical, cytologic and photographic work, and washing and sterilizing, would depend entirely upon the nature of the projects contemplated and upon special facilities that may be available in other, nearby sections of the organization. Research equipment has become so costly and so short-lived in basic design that it should never be duplicated within the same organization except when absolutely necessary. Research groups that can manage to share today's equipment and facilities have a better chance of sharing tomorrow's improvements without long delay.

Each "dust-proof" *culture room* should be supplied with forced filtered ventilation, fluorescent lighting, and a sliding door. If the rooms are not supplied directly with filtered air or if the air supply is inadequate, it will be necessary to draw air into them by means of a fan placed near the ceiling. In any event, the inner end of the air duct should be fitted with a removable air filter that can be changed at frequent intervals. The only outlet for escaping air should be around the sliding door; all other outlets should be sealed. Windows in the door and side walls are always an advantage for the staff and for casual visitors. The floors, walls, and ceilings should be washable.

In the author's laboratory, two culture rooms (7×10 and 8×12 ft) that are supplied with filtered air, warmed at its source during cold weather, are further conditioned by means of ceiling-mounted, fin-type evaporator coils of sufficient size to maintain a comfortable temperature at all times (designed by Livingstone Refrigeration Company, Toronto 4, Canada). Because these coils produce a gravity-type circulation, no fans are required, and there is a minimum of air disturbance. The coils also control the relative humidity; the accumulated moisture, with dust particles that come to rest on the coils as air flows over them, drips into a framework of aluminum troughs slung beneath the coils and is carried away. The coils of both rooms are connected with a remotely situated refrigeration condensing unit, but the temperature of each room is controlled by its own thermostat and solenoid valve. Germicidal lamps, located above the coils but not visible from the floor, are operated continuously to lessen the danger of microorganisms developing on the moist surfaces of the coils.

There are two main sources of bacteria in the air of culture rooms: (1) the organisms that are forcibly expired by the culture-room personnel (*see* p. 49), and (2) dust scuffed from the floor or brushed from clothing. The rooms must be kept scrupulously clean with soap and water. Dry mops and brooms should never be used. Cleaning should be done at the end of the day so that there is ample time for dust to settle before the rooms are used again. Unpolished wood floors and those covered with linoleum can be treated with spindle oil to allay dust.[525] Spindle oil is a crude, heavy, petroleum product used extensively in the cotton industry as a lubricant. One gallon of this oil is sufficient to cover 800 to 1000 sq ft of floor space. The oil is noninflammable and odorless, and the floors are not slippery when dry. Applications should be made two to five weeks after the initial oiling, thereafter at intervals of six to seven weeks. Oil is deleterious to rubber-tile floors and is ineffective on ceramic floors. Germicidal lamps can be fixed to the walls and operated overnight and when the rooms are not in use. (The switches for such lamps must always be located outside the rooms.) In some laboratories, yeasts and molds are more common air contaminants than bacteria.

If the culture room is large enough, it should be furnished with a long, narrow operating table (e.g., 18 × 60 in.) and one or more auxiliary tables, all of proper height for seated workers and so arranged that two people may work facing each other. Although most culture operations can be performed by individuals working alone, many procedures can be carried out more efficiently by two people working together. For general purposes, stools are more satisfactory than chairs.

When the utmost protection is desired, all air movement in the room should be reduced to a minimum while the work is in progress and for a considerable period beforehand. Thus, for example, if a critical experiment is to be performed just after the luncheon break, it is always best to assemble and place in the room before lunch all of the glassware and other paraphernalia that will be required. Later, while the experiment is in progress, all traffic to and from the room and all unnecessary movement within the room should be avoided.

Safety hoods or cabinets are used in many laboratories for the protection of cultures during their preparation and subsequent treatment and also for the protection of the staff during work with pathogenic materials. The hoods may be of any size and are usually provided with fluorescent lights, germicidal lamps, gas and electric outlets, and sometimes with filtered exhaust vents fitted with fans and high-temperature heaters designed to kill any microorganisms that may be present. In all vented hoods, warm air will rise and outside air will be drawn in and over the work, unless special precautions are taken. To reduce this hazard, a removable front panel can be provided with armholes that are fitted with elastic diaphragms with small central openings through which the bare arms are inserted; special discs may be provided to close these openings entirely when they are not in use. This arrangement reduces the volume of air that is drawn into the hood while work is in progress. If a gas burner is used in a vented hood, it is not lighted until the ports are closed, at least partially, by the arms of the operator. Touch-O-Matic Bunsen burners reduce the heat load.

A *general preparation room* should be provided in close proximity to the culture rooms. The preparation room should have facilities for washing, drying, and packing the glassware, instruments, and other materials. Here or elsewhere there should be enclosed cabinet and drawer space for the storage of sterile materials and other supplies. This is a feature of particular importance. Even though materials are wrapped in paper and cloth prior to sterilization, they must be well protected until used; otherwise any dust that may accumulate on the outer coverings will be scattered in the culture room when the packages are opened.

A *sterilizing room* should be provided to house the hot-air and steam sterilizers. Because of the heat usually generated by sterilizers, this room is likely to be unfit for more general purposes.

A *constant temperature room* (37° C) should be provided, with ample shelf space for stationary cultures as well as bench and floor space for special equipment. It is important that the room be also large enough for workers seated at microscopes, for photographic equipment, and for culture manipulations that cannot be carried out at room temperature.

The room can be heated by a battery of several strip heaters placed over an electric fan that is located in a strategic position, for example, over the door. Directional fins placed over the heaters may serve to distribute the heat more evenly. It may be necessary, however, to place a second fan in a particular spot in order to achieve even temperatures throughout the room.

Tight-fitting doors are never necessary. One of the constant-temperature rooms in the author's laboratory has a loose-fitting sliding door; the other room has a light, hinged door with adjustable louvers in both its upper and lower sections. Unless these louvers are open, constant temperatures cannot be maintained in the room. Any room in the laboratory can easily be converted to a constant-temperature room without special insulation (except over existing windows), provided the inner walls are of hollow-tile construction.

III

Special Equipment

MUCH of the equipment listed in this chapter is in common use in biological laboratories or is easily obtainable from laboratory supply houses. Some of the articles may be constructed by local craftsmen. Reliable sources are given for the more highly specialized items, but no effort is made to list all of the sources for any one of them. The present chapter includes only a partial listing of the special equipment mentioned in the book. Other items of equipment, too numerous to include here, are described in subsequent chapters.

The following supply houses, which are mentioned more than once in the present chapter, are identified by abbreviated designations after the first reference to them: Bellco Glass Inc., Vineland, N.J.; Corning Glass Works, Corning, N.Y.; Kontes Glass Co., Vineland, N.J.; and Microbiological Associates, Inc., Bethesda 14, Md.

Autoburets (Pyrex), for cold-room storage of filtered medium for particular sets of cultures and for dispensing measured samples of the medium without reopening the containers; available in liter and half-liter sizes (Fig. 3). A less elaborate unit can be assembled by connecting a pinchcock buret, with a filling tube at the side, to the bottom outlet of a storage bottle by means of nontoxic flexible tubing.

Blocks, wood, drilled with holes at a 45° angle for supporting glass tubes being filled with media consisting of two or more components

15

in various proportions. The oblique angle lessens the danger of contamination from falling dust particles while the tubes are open.

Blocks, wood, drilled with vertical holes for storing and transporting
media contained in glass tubes. The blocks may be about 1 ft long,
2 in. thick, and wide enough to accommodate two rows of tubes.

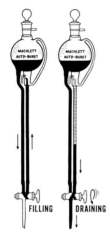

FIG. 3. Diagrams of Machlett auto-
burets (Pyrex), which are useful in
storing filtered medium and dispensing measured samples without reopening storage chamber; available in
liter and half-liter sizes. (Fisher Scientific Co., Pittsburgh, Pa.)

Cellophane, perforated, for the protection of cells and tissues in fluid
media in flasks[132] and on slides (Fig. 34). Also, a small square of
perforated cellophane placed in a flask or bottle before sterilization
can be used later as a "mop" to remove cells from the glass during
harvesting (*see* p. 188). (Microbiological Associates, Inc., Bethesda
14, Md.; Standard Scientific Supply Corp., New York 3, N.Y.)

Coverslip ring supports, glass, for careful, light microscopy; 32 mm o.d.,
3 mm thick. (Ward's Natural Science Establishment, Rochester 9,
N.Y.)

Coverslips, glass: 24 × 24 mm or 24 × 50 mm (0.13 to 0.17 mm
thick), of noncorrosive glass, for small hanging-drop cultures to be
observed, either living or fixed, under the higher magnifications
of the light microscope; 45 × 45 mm, of various thicknesses, for
use with perforated slides and large depression slides; 11 × 35 mm
for use in Leighton culture tubes; round covers, 22 mm in diameter,
for double coverslip preparations. Gold Seal (Clay-Adams Co., Inc.,
New York 10, N.Y.) or Corning (Corning Glass Works, Corning,
N.Y.) coverslips are preferred.[393]

Coverslips, mica: 24 × 50 mm for hanging-drop cultures not intended
for study at high magnifications; 41 × 41 mm for use with large

depression slides, particularly double coverslip preparations. Mica covers are unbreakable and may be used repeatedly before they become too badly mutilated for further use.

Culture bottles, prescription, flint glass, available presterilized in 1-, 2-, 3-, 4-, 6-, 8-, 12-, 16- and 32-oz sizes, plain or graduated, with screw caps (Fig. 76). These bottles are relatively inexpensive and can be discarded after using if it becomes difficult to recondition them. (Brockway Glass Co., Inc., Brockway, Pa.)

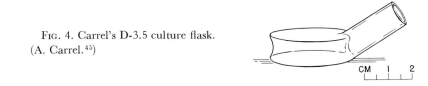

FIG. 4. Carrel's D-3.5 culture flask. (A. Carrel.[45])

Culture bottles, Pyrex, milk dilution, 1¾ in. square, 5½ in. high, with neck to accommodate No. 3 stoppers. The necks may be enlarged to accommodate West's No. 28 stoppers (see Table I) and to permit the introduction of 3 × 1-in. microscope slides for cytological studies. (Corning.)

Culture dishes, Petri, Pyrex, 60 mm and 100 mm in diameter. The smaller dishes are useful for clonal isolations; the larger dishes will accommodate two 3 × 1-in. microscope slides for cytological studies. To prevent evaporation of medium, Petri-dish cultures are incubated in a humidified atmosphere. (Corning.)

FIG. 5. Carrel's "micro" culture flask.

Culture dishes, sealable,[526] with flat bottoms: The upper edge of the dish and the under margin of the cover are ground to permit a tight seal when these surfaces are lightly coated with a silicone grease. Large or small arms may be provided for insertion of pipettes or syringe needles, respectively. Dishes are greased before sterilization and after use may be cleansed by rinsing in kerosene and washing with a metaphosphate detergent. Sizes (i.d.): 30 × 12 mm, 40 × 15 mm, 50 × 15 mm, and 65 × 15 mm. (Bellco Glass Inc., Vineland, N.J.)

Culture flasks, Carrel,[45] Pyrex: Type D-3.5 is 35 mm in diameter, 11 mm high, with an oblique neck 10 mm in diameter (Fig. 4); Type D-5 is 50 mm in diameter, 12 mm high, with an oblique neck 10 mm in diameter; Type "micro" is 35 mm in diameter, 10 mm high, with a straight neck 7 mm in diameter (Fig. 5). At the union of the neck with the chamber of the micro flask, there are slight constrictions that prevent the culture fluid from running into the neck; the extreme thinness of the top and bottom renders it possible to study the cells with oil immersion lenses. (Kontes Glass Co., Vineland, N.J.)

Culture flasks, Carrel, with optical windows: same as types D-3.5 and D-5 except with two optically ground and polished windows, approximately 0.75 mm thick, for careful microscopic observation. (Kontes.)

Fig. 6. Earle's T-15 culture flask, with a floor area of approximately 15 sq cm. (W. R. Earle and F. Highhouse.[119]) (Kontes Glass Co., Vineland, N.J.)

Culture flasks, Earle,[119] *Pyrex* (Fig. 6): Type T-15 (culture area 15 sq cm): height 14.5 mm, width 32 mm, length 100 mm; stopper size No. 00. Type T-60 (60 sq cm): height 29.5 mm, width 72 mm, length 165 mm; stopper size No. 1. Other sizes: 9 and 30 sq cm. (Kontes.)

Culture flasks, Pyrex, Eagle's modification[101] *of Earle's T-15 flasks,* in which the neck is placed on the triangular rather than on the blunt end of the flask. This change makes it easier to harvest the cells mechanically. (Kontes.)

Culture flasks, Pyrex, Porter's modification[404] *of Carrel's D-3.5 flasks,* in which the neck is larger, longer, and horizontal. This flask may be accommodated in a roller drum. (Kontes.)

Culture flasks, Swim,[502] *Pyrex:* Types S-10 and S-20 with culture areas of 10 and 20 sq cm, respectively. Made from square precision-bore tubing (2 cm i.d.). (Euclid Glass Engineering Laboratory, Cleveland 6, Ohio.)

Culture slides, micro: 76 × 25 mm, with spherical concavity 22 mm in diameter and 2 mm deep, for hanging-drop preparations; 76 × 25 mm, with oval concavity 44 mm long, 14 mm at widest portion, and 2 mm deep, for washing fresh tissues and cultures; 75 × 45 mm, with spherical concavity 36 mm in diameter and 5 mm deep, for double-coverslip preparations and cultures to be transferred to large perforated slides. (Arthur H. Thomas Co., Philadelphia 5, Pa.)

Culture slides (Romicron), Pyrex: 75 × 45 mm, with a ground and polished flat depression 35 mm in diameter, for phase microscopy. Depth of depression, 2.5 mm; thickness of bottom, 1.0 or 2.5 mm. Some slides provided with channels for fluid drainage and uptake. (Paul Rosenthal, New York 17, N.Y.)

Culture tube observation track, of two parallel metal bars, for supporting culture tube on microscope stage. The track is slightly elevated at one end to keep medium away from stopper during observation. One type of track can be fitted to a mechanical stage. (Wedco, Inc., Silver Spring, Md.)

FIG. 7. Leighton tube, with flat surface well, for stationary cultures. (J. Leighton.[269])
(Bellco Glass, Inc., Vineland, N.J.)

Culture tubes, Pyrex, Leighton,[269] with flat surface well, for stationary cultures (Fig. 7). Sizes: 16 × 125 mm; 16 × 150 mm. Well has surface area of 13 × 37 mm and accommodates 1 ml of medium. May be used with coverglass inserts (11 × 35 mm). (Bellco; Kontes.)

Culture tubes, Pyrex, screw capped, 16 × 150 mm, with plastic caps and silicone or Teflon liners.

Gas burner, micro, of a type easily handled in flaming apparatus placed on any part of the working area. The flame should be small and vigorous in its burning.

Incubators, the number and size depending upon individual requirements. When the incubator is large enough, or when a constant temperature room is available, eggs for chick embryo extract can be incubated together with the cultures. Rotating devices should be installed in separate incubators or in a constant-temperature room large enough to absorb the heat of the motors. Special incubators have been designed to provide Petri-dish cultures with a controlled atmosphere. (Labline, Inc., Chicago 22, Ill.; Johns Glass Co., Ltd., Toronto 8, Canada.)

Instruments for culture work: iridectomy scissors (Fig. 8*A*) for making fine dissections under the microscope; fine, sharp-pointed scissors; fine and medium-fine forceps, both straight and curved; platinum needles made by fitting short lengths of platinum wire into screw-

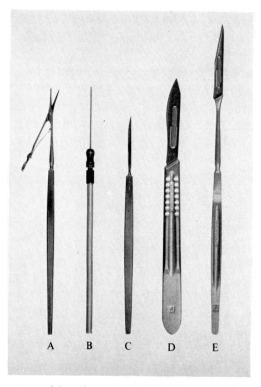

FIG. 8. Instruments used in culture work: (*A*) iridectomy scissors for making fine dissections under the microscope; (*B*) platinum needle in screw-clamp, aluminum holder; (*C*) cataract knife; (*D*) Bard-Parker holder No. 4 fitted with a No. 23 blade; and (*E*) Bard-Parker holder No. 7 fitted with a No. 11 blade. Almost ½ actual size.

clamp holders (Fig. 8*B*); cataract knives (Fig. 8*C*); and replaceable blade scalpels (Fig. 8*D* and *E*) for use in preparing explants from fresh tissues. Full-length fragments of double-edged razor blades, held securely in surgical needle holders, provide fair substitutes for cataract knives for culture work. Many useful instruments can also be made from glass, as required.

Jars (dressing), of metal, in various sizes, for dry sterilization of culture tubes and flasks. In selecting such containers, thought should be given to the relative toxicity of various metals.[182] Copper and its alloys, Monel and brass, are extremely toxic for cells; and aluminum is also toxic, although less so than copper. It is not even safe to assume that stainless steel is nontoxic, although most formulations are.

Paper, nontoxic, for wrapping materials for dry heat or steam sterilization: Steriroll made from crinkled Patipar parchment, No. 27-44, in 6-in. rolls 18 in. wide. (A. J. Buck & Son, Baltimore 13, Md.)

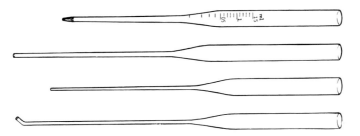

FIG. 9. Culture pipettes: 1.5-ml pipette, graduated in 0.1-ml intervals to extreme tip; coarse, ungraduated pipette; fine, ungraduated pipette; and bent pipette used to manipulate tissue fragments cultivated in tubes.

Pipettes (Pasteur): 1.5 ml, graduated at 0.1-ml intervals to extreme tip, which is sturdy and ground to a bevel; ungraduated, of approximately the same capacity, with coarse tips; ungraduated, of the same capacity, with fine tips; ungraduated, with bent tips, for tube cultures (Fig. 9). The graduated pipettes are made from Pyrex tubing by an experienced glass blower (Kontes); the others are drawn in the laboratory from flint glass tubing (e.g., Kimble) as required. For the fine pipettes, 8-mm tubing is used, and 10-mm tubing is used for the coarse ones. In addition, larger hand-drawn pipettes (from 12-mm tubing) are used for tube and bottle cultures. The shorter pipettes are plugged with nonabsorbent cotton and sterilized in large test tubes (2 × 9 in.; 2 × 11 in.), the longer ones in metal containers.

Pipettes (serological), of appropriate sizes (e.g., 10 ml), with rubber suction bulbs to fit. The pipettes are plugged with cotton and sterilized in metal containers (with flat sides). Small numbers of pipettes may be enclosed, individually, in paper cover tubes (Stone

Paper Tube Co., Washington 17, D.C.). The open end is folded over and closed with a stapling machine.

Plates, glass, about 3¼ × 4 in., cut from ordinary sheet glass, to serve as sterile surfaces (Fig. 38) in dissecting tissues and in subdividing plasma cultures removed from flasks. Several of them are packed for sterilization between single sheets of paper in a Petri dish, the cover of which can be used to protect the plate on the table.

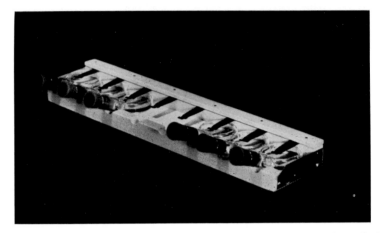

Fig. 10. Rack (wood) for D-3.5 Carrel flasks. Flexible metal clips keep flasks in place. (Modified from W. R. Earle.[114])

Platform, movable, ¾ in. thick, 8 in. wide, and extending the full width of the culture table. This platform, placed in front of the operator, facilitates many types of culture procedures, particularly fine dissections and the preparation of flask, slide, and bottle cultures. If wood is used, it may be painted or covered with a black, washable plastic material.

Rack, aluminum, for pipettes and instruments (Fig. 29). The top part of the rack forms a 45° angle with the lower part and is made with a series of deep grooves to accommodate glass tubes for holding pipettes. This arrangement protects both the pipettes and the compartment beneath from falling dust particles. The lower section may be used in emergency for the accommodation and protection of sterile instruments used in culture work. It can be flamed at frequent intervals.

Rack, for stationary tube cultures: (1) of plywood, in any convenient size (Fig. 46); (2) of metal, in small units that may be stacked and incubated at any desired angle, with the tubes held firmly in place if it is desired to drain them at fluid change without removing them from the racks (Fig. 47); and (3) commercially available (Microbiological Associates) metal racks designed either for 90 ordinary test tubes or for 90 Leighton tubes.

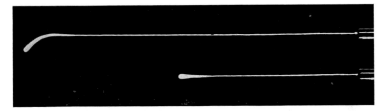

Fig. 11. Platinum spatulas: for orienting tissue fragments in flask or tube cultures (bottom); for harvesting fluid or plasma cultures from flasks or bottles (top). Only small portions of handles are shown. About ¾ actual size.

Rack, wood, for D-3.5 Carrel flask cultures, with flexible metal clips for holding flasks in position (Fig. 10).

Rack, wood or metal, for double-coverslip and perforated-slide cultures (Fig. 31).

Rubber bulbs, for pipettes: of 2-ml capacity for 1.5-ml graduated pipettes (Fig. 9); of 10-ml capacity for somewhat larger hand-drawn pipettes; of 60-ml capacity for 10-ml serological pipettes.

Spatulas, platinum, for manipulating cultures grown in flasks, bottles, and tubes. They are made from heavy platinum wire (gauge 19, Brown & Sharpe's U.S. Standard Wire Gauge) and either fused into glass rods or fitted into shortened Kolle needle holders. The tips are hammered flat (but not too thin) and polished to extreme smoothness (Fig. 11). One foot of wire weighs 4–5 Gm.

Stoppers, rubber or silicone, for culture tubes and flasks. Some years ago, certain white rubber stoppers (formulation: West S-124) were found[382] to be virtually nontoxic for cells in protein-free medium, in contrast with some other types of stoppers that were violently toxic. Stoppers made from pure silicone are preferred for cells in protein-free medium. When protein is present, the nature of the stopper is less important. Size specifications for West stoppers (The West Co., Phoenixville, Pa.) are given in Table I.

Trypsinization flasks, Rappaport,[123] for the release of cells from tissues by means of trypsin (Fig. 25). Designed for use with magnetic stirrers; fluted sides provide maximum turbulence. A more elaborate model provides for the continuous separation of trypsin-released cells before they are damaged too greatly by enzyme action. (Bellco; Microbiological Associates)

TABLE I

SIZE SPECIFICATIONS OF WEST LABORATORY STOPPERS*

(*in millimeters*)

Item	Top Diameter	Length	Bottom Diameter
0	17.0†	25.0	13.0
00	15.0	25.0	10.0
000	12.7	21.0	8.2
S-1	6.3	10.1	4.9
S-35	10.1	14.5	7.7
S-40	8.5	29.2	4.8
S-41	17.5	25.4	12.5
S-43	13.0	17.7	10.0
S-45	12.3	12.0	10.3
S-99	9.4	14.8	6.3
S-100	20.0	31.5	14.1
S-101	15.7	20.3	12.0
S-103	19.1	23.3	15.2
S-106	24.1	25.5	19.0
# 12	66.8	31.8	54.1
# 24	30.1	31.5	24.1
# 26	31.1	25.4	26.4
# 28	40.7	26.0	30.5

* The West Co., Phoenixville, Pa.

† With the exception of items 0, 00, and 000, all stoppers made from silicone are approximately 4 per cent smaller than specified.

IV

Cleansing and Sterilization

DURING the past several years, it has become increasingly evident in many laboratories that glass surfaces may be clean, as cleanliness is usually defined, and yet be completely unsuitable for tissue culture procedures that depend upon the attachment and growth of cell populations on glass. It has long been known that the quality of glass surfaces affects, in some way, the ability of cells to become attached and to multiply on them. Even when cells are propagated in media containing serum and other fluids that provide protective layers of protein on the glass and on the cells, it is often difficult to prepare glass surfaces that are suitable for cell attachment and cell multiplication. When cells are cultivated in chemically defined media, without serum and other protein, the problem of glassware becomes still more critical.

In the author's laboratory, many cleaning procedures have been tried over the past several years, often as the result of suggestions made by colleagues elsewhere who were encountering similar difficulties. Some of these procedures involved the use of new detergents; others involved the use of sodium hydroxide, warm sodium carbonate, and various combinations of these and chelating agents, with or without previous treatment with hot nitric acid (*see* p. 31). But none of these procedures was found to be completely dependable for the preparation of Pyrex surfaces for use with chemically defined media.

Often, cells would multiply abundantly on certain areas of a glass surface but die on neighboring areas; sometimes, the "toxic" areas did not affect the cells until after the cells had become attached and started to multiply. And, since these were L cells belonging to a subline that had become "adapted" to continuous multiplication in unsupplemented CMRL-1066,[377] it was not a matter of the differential susceptibility of particular parts of the population.

Recently, Rappaport and her associates[427] have made a new and more direct approach to the problem by comparing the attachment and growth of various types of cells, in defined media, on glass surfaces of different composition. They have shown that the ability of cells to become attached to glass and to multiply on it is very dependent on the physical properties of the glass surfaces, particularly the total negative charge and the amount of sodium in the glass; and, for these same reasons, soft glasses are more suitable than Pyrex glasses (*see* Table II). The attachment of HeLa cells to the various surfaces

TABLE II

ATTACHMENT OF HeLa CELLS IN CHEMICALLY DEFINED MEDIUM TO DIFFERENT GLASS SURFACES AFTER 24 HOURS*

Exper. No.	Inoculum (× 10⁵)	Corning 7900 (Vycor)	Corning 7740 (Pyrex)	Kimble N-51-A	Brockway Flint (Sani-Glas)	Kimble Standard Flint	Demuth Flint
1	5.2	<0.2	2.0	1.1	1.1	4.9	5.0
		<0.2	<0.2	0.6	3.8	3.7	4.2
			0.9	1.2	2.1	2.1	4.7
		0.9	1.1	2.1	2.3	1.5	2.6
					1.7		
2	3.8	<0.2	<0.2	0.5	2.0		2.5
			0.9	0.2	1.5		4.0
			<0.2	1.1	1.0		1.5
			1.0				1.8

* From C. Rappaport *et al.*[427]

correlated well with the amount of Na^+ in the glass, i.e., with the amount of charge and proton-exchange capacity of the glass. A similar correlation was found for the attachment of L cells; but in the latter case, probably because these cells excrete fewer protons than HeLa cells, surfaces with lower proton exchange capacity were satisfactory.

Rappaport and her associates[427] have produced suitable surfaces for cell attachment by treating soft-glass prescription bottles (Brockway; Fig. 76) with Versene (ethylenediaminetetraacetic acid tetrasodium salt) and sodium carbonate (Na_2CO_3) as follows: The culture surface of new 1-oz bottles was covered with 3 ml of a 0.01M solution of Versene made alkaline by adding, just before use, 1.0 ml of 10 per cent NaOH per 100 ml of Versene solution. The bottles were autoclaved for 30 min at 122° C with steam generated from distilled water. The Versene solution was decanted and the bottles rinsed once with triply distilled water that had *not* been passed through an ion-exchange column. (The surface of a bottle treated in this manner with Versene stained an intense lavender purple after a 1-minute contact with 0.005 per cent solution of crystal violet.) The surfaces treated with Versene were then covered with 3 ml of 0.2M Na_2CO_3 that also contained Versene at a concentration of about 2×10^{-4}M, and the bottles were autoclaved for 30 min at 122° C. The pressure was released slowly, the Na_2CO_3 solution was decanted, and the bottles rinsed three times with distilled water. The rinses were done in groups of four or five by filling the bottles with water and decanting immediately. After draining, the bottles were reautoclaved for 15–20 min in order to stabilize and sterilize the surfaces. The optimal amount of Versene to be used with a particular batch of Na_2CO_3 was determined by titrating for the concentration that gave a surface that was free, or almost free, of undesirable microcrystals and stained uniformly with crystal violet. Concentrations of Versene greater than this caused breakdown of the surface leaving unaltered areas that could not be stained. This treatment greatly improved the surfaces for the attachment and growth of various types of mammalian cells.[426]

In view of these findings, it is not surprising that most efforts to prepare glassware, especially Pyrex, for tissue culture have not been uniformly successful, for the composition of the glass is often more important than the efforts made to condition it. Many tissue culture workers have long known that once a glass surface is suitable for cells, the less that is done to it the better. Among those things that drastically alter the surface chemistry of the glass are detergents and autoclaving, particularly autoclaving in the presence of certain antiseptics. It is also common experience that new glassware is often quite refractory to cells but improves with continued use. In fact, Rappaport[425] was able to improve the surfaces of Brockway bottles simply by incubating cell-free medium in them for several days before they were used for cultures. Under these conditions, the surfaces were hydrolyzed sufficiently by the medium to acquire the negative charge required for cell attachment.

Because of the efforts of Rappaport's group and collaborating glass manufacturers, it may soon be possible to obtain glassware that has been especially compounded and conditioned for tissue culture. Also, it is almost certain that such glassware will be distributed sterile and ready for use at prices low enough to permit investigators to discard ordinary, machine-made items after one use. Disposable, wettable, plastic containers have also been developed (Falcon Plastics Division of Becton, Dickinson, and Co., Rutherford, N.J.) to meet the special requirements of tissue culture.

For over a year, in the author's laboratory, all glassware has been cleansed by ultrasonic energy, with satisfactory results; the procedures followed are described on page 29. But because other methods of treatment are also successful, at least most of the time, a description will be given of the methods in use in this laboratory before the ultrasonic procedures were adopted. In subsequent sections, attention will be given to the sterilization of materials, to filtration, and to methods for safeguarding sterility while actual culture work is in progress.

Cleansing of Glassware by Ultrasonic Energy

In the author's laboratory, all glassware is now being cleansed with ultrasonic energy generated by Narda SonBlaster equipment (Narda Ultrasonics Corp., Westbury, Long Island, N.Y.). The ultrasonic energy originates in a high frequency (40-KC) generator and is transmitted to the contents of a 5-gal treatment tank by transducers, which are ceramic devices that are attached to the underside of the tank and convert the output of the generator into sonic energy. The intensity of this energy is sufficient to cause a rapid formation and collapse of bubbles (cavitation) within the enclosed liquid and on all surfaces, and this cavitation provides the cleansing action. Sufficient time must be allowed during the rarefaction half of the transducer cycle to permit the bubbles to grow to a usable size, then collapse completely. At too high frequencies the bubbles cannot reach a size that will supply any appreciable energy upon collapse. Within certain limits, then, the lower the frequency, the better the cleaning action. In a sonic field vibrating at a frequency of 40 KC there are 40,000 cavitations per second, but this level of activity is not achieved until the cleansing liquid is freed of entrapped air, which acts as a sonic barrier. Also, cavitation is more vigorous in the presence of wetting agents and detergents.

According to the present procedure, all used glassware is first rinsed in tap water and is then completely submerged in a treatment tank in warm (45° to 50° C) tap water containing Alconox (1 tbsp. per gal of water). After the generator has been activated, a few minutes may be required before the bath is degassed sufficiently for maximum cavitation to develop. After maximum cavitation has developed, pipettes, tubes, bottles, Petri dishes, and other items of general glassware are treated for 15 to 20 min. Pipettes are then rinsed 10–15 times in warm tap water and are transferred immediately to automatic rinsers, as described on page 32. Other items of glassware are removed from the tank, rinsed with warm tap water, and placed in a second treatment tank (attached to the same generator) that is filled with warm tap water without detergent. Again, they are subjected to ultrasonic energy, as before; and the first tank is reloaded with a second batch of glassware to be treated with detergent. After the second period of ultrasonic treatment, the glassware is rinsed again with warm tap water, passed through three vats of freshly distilled (Barnstead) water, several minutes in each, then through a vat containing freshly distilled water that was subsequently passed through a mixed-bed, ion-exchange Barnstead Bantam Demineralizer (Barnstead Still and Sterilizer Co., Boston 31, Mass.). Finally, the glassware is dried and prepared for sterilization. Carrel flasks, Leighton tubes, and fritted filters are treated in the same manner except that they are suspended in a stainless-steel rack a couple of inches above the floor of the treatment tank, the energy output is reduced to about 70 per cent of maximum, and the time of exposure is also reduced. After the second ultrasonic treatment, in warm water without detergent, fritted filters are flushed with distilled and deionized water in the manner described on page 32. New, unused glassware is treated in the same manner except for preliminary, overnight treatment in a bath of dilute HCl (about 1 per cent) to remove free alkali.

Occasionally, the bottoms of Carrel flasks (and, less often, the tops) subjected to ultrasonic treatment become fractured in the central areas. Also, some pieces of glassware become pitted after many cycles of cleaning. While it is hoped that these difficulties will be overcome as more experience is gained with the method, it is felt that it would take considerable breakage to justify a return to the hazards of hot acid.

Cleansing of Glassware by Other Means

In most laboratories, tissue-culture glassware is either boiled with alkalis or moderately alkaline detergents or treated with hot oxidizing acids, depending upon the nature of the items to be cleansed. The preferred acid is nitric. The alkalis most commonly used are soap, sodium carbonate, or the combination of sodium metasilicate and a hardness-sequestering polyphosphate (e.g., Calgon), recommended by Harding and Trebler.[213]

Soap, which is still used in some laboratories, aids in wetting, acts as an emulsifying agent for immiscible liquids, and as a dispersing agent for solid particles, but it has the disadvantage that it combines with the calcium, magnesium, and metallic ions of so-called hard water to form insoluble compounds. A solution of pure, white soap, e.g., Ivory, may be prepared either from a powder (100 ml per gal of water) or from solid cakes reduced to a jelly. To prepare the jelly, two large cakes are cut into fragments and dissolved by boiling in water. The solution is diluted to a final volume of 16 to 20 qt. It is then ready for use; on cooling, it will form a gel. Before the glassware is added, the soap should be redissolved in warm water.

Moderately alkaline detergents usually contain sodium carbonate, sodium metasilicate, one or more phosphate compounds, and a wetting agent. Among the detergents, *Haemo-sol* (Meinecke & Co., Inc., New York 14, N.Y.), *7X* (Linbro Chemicals, New Haven, Conn.), *Micro-solv* (Microbiological Associates, Inc., Washington 14, D.C.), and *Alconox* (Alconox, Inc., New York 3, N.Y.) are widely used in tissue culture laboratories on this continent.

Although the cleansing procedures for glassware to be described on the following pages are recommended with the reservation that they may not always work, they are nevertheless the procedures that we ourselves would return to in the event of temporary failure of our ultrasonic equipment (*see* p. 28).

Used glassware is discarded immediately into a vat or pail containing tap water. If microorganisms are likely to be present, the tap water should contain an antiseptic (e.g., Wescodyne; *see* p. 48). Eventually, the glassware is rinsed with warm tap water to dislodge all solid matter, then boiled for 10 min in water with soap or detergent. It is again rinsed with warm tap water and boiled with soap or detergent. After a third rinsing with warm tap water, it is passed through three Pyrex vats of distilled water (several minutes in each), then through a vat containing distilled water subsequently passed through a mixed-bed, ion-exchange column (*see* p. 29), and is left to drain in the drying oven. The distilled-water vats are emptied and dried at the end of each day; and no water is stored from one day to the next. *New, unused glassware* is treated in the same manner except that it is first placed in dilute HCl (about 1 per cent) overnight to remove any free alkali.

Glassware too fragile to be boiled (e.g., Carrel flasks and Leighton tubes) is rinsed with warm tap water, immersed in equal parts of nitric acid (HNO_3) and distilled water, and heated to 90° C, after which the cleansing action is allowed to continue overnight at room temperature. On the following day, the articles are rinsed with tap water, placed for 3 hr in a solution consisting of 1 Gm of disodium Versenate (Dow Chemical Company's disodium ethylenediamine-tetraacetic acid; renewed each week) per liter of deionized water, to complex any metals that may be present. The glassware is then rinsed very thoroughly with warm tap water, is passed through three vats of distilled water and one of ion-exchange water (as described in the preceding paragraph) and is dried in an oven.

A simple arrangement for the hot acid treatment might consist of a large enamelware stockpot (about 11 in. high, 14 in. in diameter, with side handles) with an ample quantity of sea sand under and around the Pyrex acid bath ($8\frac{3}{4} \times 10$ in.), to avert disaster in the event of breakage during heating. The procedure should be carried out in a forced-draft chemical cabinet; and the stockpot should be replaced when it begins to show signs of wear. Also, because the use of hot acid is always hazardous, every item of the heating and ventilating equipment should be inspected regularly to guard against deterioration.

Used pipettes are discarded immediately into a pail of tap water (containing antiseptic, if they are contaminated), are rinsed eventually under the tap, and placed overnight at room temperature in a bath of 50 per cent nitric acid in distilled water. They are then washed for several hours in an automatic siphon rinser, passed through three vats of distilled water (several minutes in each), and dried in an oven.

Fritted glass filters (Fig. 15) are cleaned by immersing them in a bath of 50 per cent nitric acid in distilled water, which is then heated to 90° C for 1 hr and allowed to cool to room temperature overnight. They are then rinsed with distilled water, flushed with a small quantity of NH_4OH (1:1, with water) to neutralize the acid, and then with 1 l of distilled water followed by 1 l of demineralized water. To facilitate the latter procedure, filter funnels are fitted by means of their standard tapers to a one-piece, all-glass manifold located over a sink and connected to a water suction pump. A separate distilled water line, from a second manifold, leads to the funnel of each filter and is regulated by means of a screw clamp. Although fritted discs may be rinsed from the reverse side with water under pressure, the maximum pressure should never exceed 15 p.s.i. Used filters must not be allowed to dry at any time until they have been completely cleaned. Also, a cold damp filter should never be subjected to a sudden temperature change, since the evolution of steam may set up sufficient pressure within the filter to crack it. After six to eight cycles of use, the filters should be baked for 1 hr at 350° C to reduce the swelling of the discs that often results from repeated autoclaving.

Clean glassware should not be touched with bare fingers while it is still wet, for at this stage the entire effort can be defeated by contaminating the culture surfaces with oils from the skin.[437] If tongs or stainless steel baskets cannot be used, clean rubber gloves should be worn. Clean glassware should be perfectly wettable and may be tested with a few drops of balanced salt solution. The slightest trace of nonpolar compounds on glass surfaces may prevent cells from becoming attached, spreading, and multiplying.

Cleansing of Other Equipment

New Selas filters (Figs. 12 and 13) are thoroughly flushed with a hot solution of 1 part hydrochloric acid to 3 parts of distilled water to remove adsorbed impurities. A thorough flushing with distilled water should follow to remove all traces of acid. Imperfections in the filter may be discovered by making the "bubble pressure" test. In making this test, the filter is soaked in water until all the air has been removed and all the pores filled with fluid. Then, a gradually increasing air pressure is applied to the inner surface and the minimum pressure at which bubbles just break through the filter is the bubble pressure of the candle. Selas 03 filters, with a maximum pore diameter of 1.2μ, should have a bubble pressure of 35 p.s.i. If the bubble pressure is much lower, the filter is probably defective.

Used Selas filters must not be allowed to dry out until they have been reconditioned for use. Preliminary cleaning (and the *only* cleaning usually required for filters used in sterilizing salt solutions and chemically defined media) is accomplished by soaking and reverse flushing with not less than 2 l of distilled water. Reverse flushing may be achieved by arranging a suction flask and a water trap in such a manner as to draw the water through the filter in the direction opposite to that of normal use. If the filter contains protein material, it should be soaked in concentrated nitric acid or 10 per cent hydrochloric acid overnight. It should then be flushed with distilled water until acid free. If more thorough cleaning is required, the filter element (after thorough drying) may be placed in a muffle furnace, at room temperature, and heated to 1250° F at the rate of approximately 300° per hr. Then, after 1 hr at high heat, the furnace is cooled to room temperature before the filter is removed. The filter is then thoroughly flushed with distilled water to remove all ashed material.

Instruments are cleansed immediately after use, to prevent any organic material from drying on their surfaces. They are washed with soap and warm water, thoroughly rinsed with running water, placed in 95 per cent alcohol, and dried in an oven. If it is necessary to scour them, it should be done with the finest nonabrasive material.

Mica coverslips are treated according to the procedures described for glassware and dried with a linen towel. Mica is never placed in cleaning fluid.

New unused rubber stoppers are boiled in dilute sodium hydroxide (about $N/2$), rinsed in tap water, then boiled in dilute hydrochloric acid (about $N/2$), and finally rinsed very thoroughly in tap water. This treatment removes sulfur "bloom" and other surface impurities.

New rubber tubing that might come in contact with culture media is boiled in dilute sodium hydroxide (about $N/2$), rinsed in tap water, then boiled in dilute hydrochloric acid (about N/2). During the process of boiling, the hot fluids are circulated through the tubing with a syringe. This is done several times. After washing the outside of the tubing with hot tap water, the tubing is attached to a faucet and flushed with tap water for 30 min. A funnel is then attached to one end of the tubing and a generous quantity of distilled water is passed through it.

Used rubber tubing is washed thoroughly in warm tap water, then attached to a faucet and flushed with tap water for 30 min. Finally, a funnel is attached to one end of the tubing and not less than 1 l of distilled water is run through it.

Sterilization Procedures

As a rule, sterilization is accomplished by heat (dry or moist), filtration, or chemicals. Dry heat is furnished by a gas or electric oven; moist heat, by an autoclave providing steam under pressure.

Before discussing the principles of *sterilization by moist heat*, it must be stated that the quality of the steam is just as important in tissue culture as the manner in which it is used. It is futile to worry about a few harmful ions that may come to rest on glass surfaces if these same surfaces are finally sterilized in steam that may be heavily contaminated with all manner of impurities. The larger the institution, the more likely it is that new dirt is being introduced into the steam lines quite often, as repairs and alterations are made between the central supply and the laboratory autoclave. The ideal arrangement is one in which the steam used for sterilization is generated by house steam or by some other heat source from distilled water that is introduced by the laboratory staff into a special heater attached to the autoclave. Otherwise, the house steam may be cleansed by filtration. In the author's laboratory, a low volume Selas Liqui-Jector (Selas Corporation of America, Dresher, Pa.) is incorporated in the house-steam line near its point of entry into the autoclave. This compact unit, which takes only a few inches of space, is designed to provide a flow of clean, dry, sterile steam containing less than 1 p.p.m. total solids and is capable of removing condensate and dirt from steam at a rate of 75 lb of steam per hr, at a maximum pressure of approximately 125 psig.

Although the principles of *sterilization by moist heat* are well known,[392, 525] they are often disregarded in practice, sometimes with disastrous results. A frequent cause of trouble is the failure to realize that the sterilizing efficiency of steam under pressure depends entirely upon the moist heat that is present and not at all upon pressure. Steam that is saturated with moisture condenses on objects cooler than itself and, by giving up its latent heat, quickly raises them to its own temperature. When air is mixed with steam, this process is considerably less efficient because hot air sterilizes only by the slower action of heat absorption. The temperature developed in the sterilizing chamber of an autoclave is directly dependent, therefore, on the degree of air elimination from the chamber. When air is present, it results in the substitution of air under pressure for part of the steam under pressure, and heat penetration is especially poor at the bottom of the chamber where the air becomes concentrated.

For many years the performance of most steam sterilizers was measured by a pressure gauge and a thermometer mounted on top of the sterilizing chamber. This method, which is now obsolete, has been replaced by the use of a mercury thermometer placed in the discharge line. In nearly all modern sterilizers the steam enters the chamber at the back end, floats to the top of the chamber, compresses air in the bottom areas, and forces the air from the chamber through an opening at the front end. This system assures movement of steam from one end of the chamber to the other and from top to bottom. Air, being heavier than steam, tends to stratify beneath the steam and will move downwards, rapidly or slowly, depending on the density of the packing; and steam will follow as the air escapes. In order that the pressure shown on the gauge may actually represent the steam under pressure and not the air that has been compressed by the steam, the front drain valve of the autoclave must be left open one full turn for a period of 5 min to evacuate the air. Then the drain valve should be nearly, but not completely, closed and left so during the entire period of exposure. This procedure will permit a slight discharge from the chamber that will release the condensate and the pockets of air that gravitate from the load.

Certain modern steam sterilizers lack a hand-controlled discharge system but have thermostatic valves that are supposed to control automatically the discharge of air and condensate from the chamber. These valves are of the general type commonly known as steam traps.

Unfortunately, however, they often become clogged. And serious mishaps can develop unless careful attention is given to a mercury thermometer that is located in the discharge line. Under the obsolete pressure system of control, exposure was usually timed as beginning when pressure had reached 15 lb. Under temperature control, the period of exposure should be timed as beginning when the thermometer in the discharge line indicates 115° C.

In a properly designed and operated steam pressure sterilizer, it is safe to assume that effective sterilization is achieved very shortly after the material reaches a temperature of 115° C. In practice, most articles sterilized by steam are exposed for 30 min at 15 to 17 lb. But rubber gloves and solutions contained in small flasks should not be exposed for more than 15 min.

TABLE III

TEMPERATURE OF SATURATED WATER VAPOR IN DEGREES
CENTIGRADE AND DEGREES FAHRENHEIT CORRESPONDING
APPROXIMATELY TO GAUGE PRESSURE IN POUNDS

Gauge pressure lb per sq in.	Temp. °C	Temp. °F
0	100	212
5	108	227
10	115	239
15	121	250
17	123	253
18	124	255
20	126	259

The proper way to cool down an autoclave after sterilization is to regulate the valve in the discharge line so that the pressure will be reduced to zero at a uniform rate in not less than 6 or 7 min and not more than 10 min. This procedure will give any fluids that may be present time to lose their heat at the same rate as the surrounding steam, without violent ebullition.

By placing *sterilization indicators*[392] inside the actual packages, vessels or containers to be sterilized and by making a series of trial runs with many different types of packing and loading, the operator will learn what temperatures should be indicated on the thermometer in order to achieve adequate sterilization of the entire load. Once the necessary temperature has been obtained, care must be taken to ensure a full period of sterilization. For greater efficiency, sterilizers should be equipped with automatic temperature-recording devices. In any event the time of sterilization should be noted in a special *record book* showing the sterilization number (the next in a series from 1 to 100, one number for each load), the date, and a few words indicating the general nature of the load. At the conclusion of the run, a metal tag should be placed on the door of each sterilizer. This practice will prevent other members of the laboratory from removing articles from a cold sterilizer without definite assurance that they have been sterilized. Also, the sterilization number should be written on each article *as it is removed* from the sterilizer.

In *preparing the load for a steam sterilizer* the operator must make sure that adequate spaces are provided between packs to assure the passage of steam to the lower areas. It is best to place heavier packs on edge in the bottom tier and to make certain that they are not pressed tightly together.

If *sterilizing drums* are used, the supplies should never be compressed into a tight mass, nor should the drum be loaded to full capacity so that pressure is required to close the cover. There should always be free space in the top of the drum when the cover is closed. Gowns, towels, and such should be placed in the drum lying flat so that when the drum is placed in the sterilizer on edge the load will also rest on edge to promote steam circulation. Drums should be lined with a double thickness of closely woven cloth (unbleached muslin). This covering of muslin surrounding the drum load serves as an air filter to eliminate dust as air is drawn in when the drum is removed from a warm sterilizer.

Dry heat is to be recommended only when direct contact of the materials with most steam under pressure is impractical or when excessive heat can do no damage. Glassware is almost always sterilized by dry heat except when rubber fittings are present or when the items are unusually large (4-, 10-, and 20-l bottles, which are autoclaved with a small quantity of water within them, to generate steam). Dry heat is also used for such materials as paraffin wax, oils, petroleum jelly, and talcum powder, none of which can be sterilized properly in the autoclave because the moisture of steam cannot penetrate them.

Dry heat is most difficult to control; even in a well-designed and properly loaded oven, some materials may receive too much heat.

Dry heat of 160° C for 60 min is roughly equivalent to moist heat of 121° C for 10 to 15 min. But because dry heat penetrates slowly and unevenly, exposures of at least 90 min (after the load has come to temperature) are preferred. Also, the heating elements should be so arranged that a whole hour is required to attain a temperature of 160° C. A shorter time may result in damage to glassware owing to uneven heating. Although prolonged exposures to 160° C are not injurious to glassware, rapid changes in temperature are most destructive. For this reason, the oven doors should not be opened until the contents have cooled. And care must be taken to pack the oven in such a way that there is free space on all sides of the various items making up the load. Electric heat is preferred to that of gas, which is more difficult to control. Forced circulation of the air in a hot-air oven, by means of a blower, hastens heating and assures uniform conditions throughout.

The *wrapping and packing* of materials to be sterilized requires the utmost care. If materials are improperly wrapped and packed, sterilization may be incomplete or, if it is complete, they may become contaminated again by outside air even before they are removed from the sterilizer. As the materials cool, any air that is trapped within them or within the coverings will contract, and outside air will move in. For this reason, all containers and packages must be closed and covered in such a manner that the incoming air will be adequately filtered.

Except for items packed in closed containers, articles to be sterilized by dry heat are covered with one or two layers of paper that can withstand 170° C without charring. Articles to be autoclaved are usually covered with a double thickness of unbleached muslin, though paper may be used if it is strong enough to withstand moisture. There is now available (*see* p. 21) a crinkled, parchment-type autoclaving paper, Patapar, that is sulfur free, hydroscopic, of high wet strength, and withstands repeated sterilizing even in dry heat. Cellophane and other materials impervious to steam must never be used to cover articles to be autoclaved.

Care must also be taken to prepare articles to be autoclaved in such a way that no air will be trapped within them, for air that is trapped cannot be replaced by steam. Pans, jars, and all other deep containers must be left at least partially open, wrapped in a double thickness of muslin, and placed on their side in the sterilizer. Rubber stoppers are arranged between gauze pads in uncovered Petri dishes that are wrapped securely in a double thickness of muslin or paper and sterilized on edge. Rubber tubing is sterilized vertically or arranged in a vertical spiral around rolled towels or an improvised cylinder, so that air can escape and steam can enter.

Gauze pads (surgical sponges), about 3 × 4 in., have many uses in tissue culture. For example, they are placed beneath and above rubber and silicone stoppers placed for sterilization in Petri dishes wrapped in cloth or paper; they are used to protect sterility when culture stoppers have been inserted too deeply to be removed easily and aseptically with bare fingers; they are used under paper to cover the open ends of glass tubes in which short pipettes are sterilized and to provide a clean area on which to support the end of the tube once it is opened. The pads are made from 8-in. squares of surgical gauze so folded that there is an open side but no loose threads.[525]

Glassware is sterilized by dry heat (in a gas or electric oven) for $1\frac{1}{2}$ hr at 160° C. Medium tubes and test tubes used only occasionally are fitted with corks and wrapped in paper, four or five to a package. Culture tubes are sterilized open end down, without closures, in stainless-steel containers with tight-fitting covers. Pasteur-type pipettes are plugged with cotton and placed in large test tubes 2 in. in diameter and 9 or 11 in. long. Strands of cotton extending beyond the ends of the pipettes are burned off before they are placed in the tubes. A ball of glass wool covered with glass cloth (Fiberglas) is placed in the bottom of each tube to protect the tips of the pipettes. The tops of the tubes are closed with gauze pads and wrapping paper tied with string. Serological pipettes are sterilized in stainless-steel cans. They may also be sterilized individually in commercially available paper cover tubes (*see* p. 21). Small depression slides (25 × 76 mm) are sterilized, depression side down, over a layer of paper, in 6-in. Petri dishes. The covers of these and other dishes may be employed later to protect depression slides and glass plates placed on the table for use. Large depression slides (45 × 76 mm) are arranged, layer upon layer, with paper between them, in wire baskets that are packed, sterilized, and stored while lying on one side, this arrangement to facilitate the eventual withdrawal of the slides one by one as required. Glass plates are packed for sterilization (between sheets of paper of the same size) in 6-in. Petri dishes and wrapped in paper. Glass and mica coverslips are sterilized in smaller Petri dishes, wrapped in paper. Watch glasses are also sterilized in Petri dishes. Erlenmeyer flasks and large culture bottles are closed with paper tied on with string, but if the paper is not heavy enough, corks may be needed to support the paper and prevent tearing. In the author's laboratory, Patapar paper (*see* p. 21) is used, without corks. Carrel flasks and Earle's T-flasks are packed, with their open necks down, in stainless-steel boxes.

Instruments are sterilized by dry heat for 1½ hr at 160° C. The temperature should be as uniform as possible and the instruments should be kept well removed from the heating elements. Delicate instruments must never be overheated. If, under exceptional circumstances (in emergency only), instruments are sterilized by boiling, they are protected above and below with layers of gauze, covered with water and boiled for 10 min. But they should be removed from the water while they are still hot and dried in a sterile container, to prevent rusting. The sterilization of instruments by holding them in a flame often leaves a layer of oxidized metal and inevitably dulls any cutting edges. In some laboratories, it is common practice to immerse instruments in alcohol, which is then burned off in a flame. Under these conditions, the heat is derived from the burning vapor, and any heating of the metal results from the heat of combustion that is conducted through the thin liquid layer.

Cataract knives, with their blade tips inserted in gauze pads, are sterilized, two or three together, beneath other gauze pads in flat metal boxes. Forceps and syringes are sterilized individually in glass tubes. Syringe needles are sterilized either in groups in Petri dishes, with their points buried in gauze, or individually in small test tubes with restrictions to hold the needle in place. The restrictions are made by flattening one side of the tube in a Bunsen flame.

Instruments for bleeding are assembled and packed for sterilization in a special container in the manner described on page 85. In laboratories where certain animal operations requiring a variety of instruments are performed at frequent intervals, it is well to have the instruments in a separate metal box, assembled layer upon layer, in the order of use, between gauze pads. If the boxes are large, their walls should be perforated. In any event, they should be wrapped in two thicknesses of paper.

Cloth goods (masks, gowns, animal sheets, towels, etc.), *rubber goods* (stoppers, tubing), and *silicone stoppers* are sterilized in the autoclave for 30 min at 121° to 123° C (15 to 17 pounds pressure). Rubber gloves (and nail brushes) are autoclaved for 15 min at 121° C.

Solutions not denatured by heating are autoclaved at 121° to 123° C for 30 min or less, depending upon the size of the flasks. Flasks with a capacity of 1000 ml or less should not be sterilized for longer than 15 min; 50- to 250-ml flasks should not be sterilized longer than 10 min. During the actual period of exposure to steam, the solutions will not boil because of the pressure. Violent boiling and considerable loss of fluid will occur, however, if the pressure is reduced too rapidly. But if it is reduced too gradually the period of exposure may be too greatly prolonged. The flasks should never be filled more than two-thirds full and should be closed with loose-fitting cork stoppers that are covered with gauze pads and two layers of strong paper held in place with string. When the flasks are removed from the sterilizer, the corks should be inserted more firmly.

A more satisfactory means of sterilizing fluids by steam is provided by Pour-O-Vac flasks and closures (The MacBick Co., Cambridge, Mass.), which eliminate the danger of contamination by intake of laboratory air. This type of flask is provided with a heat-resistant rubber collar that fits securely over the neck of the container and provides a closure between the glass and an outer plastic hood. The collar has a bead that makes a tight seal with the inside of the plastic hood; and the distal portion of the collar, which could serve later as a sterile pouring lip, is protected from contamination. As the sterilizer pressure drops, pressure within the flask is reduced by the escape of steam through a vent in the plastic hood. As steam within the flask cools and condenses, a considerable vacuum forms; and the vacuum pulls the hood against the lip of the collar, closes the air vent, and effects a hermetic seal. Anytime after the flasks have cooled to room temperature, the "water-hammer" effect gives audible assurance that they are properly sealed. The Pour-O-Vac closure also provides a dustproof seal for the protection of fluids that are to be used more than once without resterilization.

Solutions that cannot be heated are sterilized by filtration (*see* p. 42). These solutions include balanced salt solutions, chemically defined media, and all solutions containing proteins and other heat-labile substances.

Seitz, Selas, Ertel, and fritted glass filters are autoclaved for 45 min at 121° to 123° C (15 to 17 pounds pressure). *Millipore (white) filter discs* are autoclaved at 121° C for 15 min.

When Erlenmeyer flasks containing sterile fluids are to be stored and opened more than once, the necks and stoppers may be covered with Fiberglas pads to protect them from dust. The pads are made from Fiberglas cloth hemmed with glass thread. The cloth can be cut into squares with scissors, without fraying, if the lines of cutting are brushed lightly beforehand with glue. The pads are autoclaved in packages of six or more. When they become soiled, they can be cleaned in acid; and acid removes the glue.

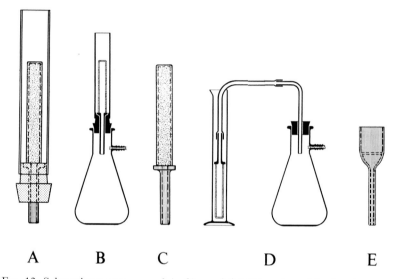

A   B   C   D   E

Fig. 12. Selas microporous porcelain filters: (*A*) VFA series, with glazed-on porcelain connector, a Pyrex glass cylinder, and a rubber adapter for a standard vacuum flask (*B*). (*C*) FPS series, with glazed-on porcelain connector for attachment to rubber or plastic tubing (*D*). This type may also be used for pressure filtration (see Fig. 13). (*E*) FMB series, micro Buchner funnel (10 ml), glazed inside and out, with a thin porous disc fitted to inside wall. (Selas Corp. of America, Dresher, Pa.)

Filtration

Filters used in tissue culture are of four main types: (1) porcelain filters (Selas); (2) asbestos filters (Seitz, Ertel); (3) sintered glass filters (Pyrex); and (4) Millipore filters.

Selas microporous porcelain filters (Figs. 12 and 13) are fine grained and smooth surfaced with the individual particles bonded together

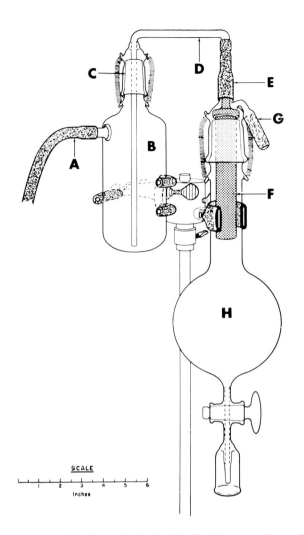

SCALE

| | | | | | |
1 2 3 4 5 6
Inches

FIG. 13. Selas pressure-filtration unit devised by Earle's group for small quantities of medium: (A) heavy-walled rubber tubing from gas tank; (B) 500-ml Pyrex pressure reservoir (surrounded by metal safety shield when in use); (C) Pyrex ground joint, standard taper, with glass hooks; (D) heavy-walled Pyrex tubing; (E) two rubber sleeves (surgical latex), one joining tube (D) to the filter connector, the other holding sleeve of ground joint to filter connector; (F) Selas filter candle, No. 03 porosity; (G) cotton air filter connected with collecting flask (H). (J. C. Bryant *et al.*[37])

43

so that no loose material is present. Selas filters are available (Selas Corp. of America, Dresher, Pa.) in various shapes, sizes, and grades of porosity (the 03 grade is recommended for culture work) and can be incorporated into vacuum-type or pressure-type equipment, either as discs, candles or open-end cylinders. They can be cleaned by ignition or washed with a wide variety of acids or solvents.

FIG. 14. Ertel stainless-steel, pressure-type filter (No. 10), which accommodates EO (ultrafine) asbestos discs of low calcium and iron content. Equipped with Pyrex glass cylinder (1.3-l capacity) and pressure gauge (maximum pressure recommended 25 p.s.i.). (Ertel Engineering Corp., Kingston, N.Y.)

Seitz filters are made of asbestos and are available in pads of different grades and sizes that are held in special vacuum-type or pressure-type metal containers, the joints of which can be tightened sufficiently to prevent leakage. The E.K. (Entkeimung) or ST (sterilizing) grade has a rated pore size of 0.1 μ; the S-3 grade, 0.01 μ. Because the pads are used but once, they present no special cleaning problem. But they do shed fibers continuously into the filtrate. Also, they are strongly adsorptive and should not be used for small quantities of fluid.

Ertel filters are pressure-type devices consisting of a heavy-walled, Pyrex glass cylinder with stainless-steel end sections for the accommodation of an asbestos pad and the necessary openings. In the author's laboratory, the 1.3-l size (Fig. 14) is used with a pad of EO (ultrafine) porosity, $4\frac{1}{8}$ inches in diameter, for the filtration of 1–4 l of medium. The filter is equipped with a pressure gauge that aids in keeping the pressure below 20 p.s.i., which is as much as the glass cylinder is supposed to withstand, with a margin of safety. The first 100–200 ml of medium passed through the filter is always discarded.

Sintered (fritted) glass filters of UF (ultrafine) porosity are made from glass that has been ground to very fine particles of uniform size, molded in the form of a disc or tube, and heated to the sintering point (just below fusion) without the addition of other substances. Unlike most filters, they can be chemically cleaned before sterilization. There are three types in common use: (1) Morton type (Fig. 15), for

FIG. 15. Morton-type, fritted glass filter for use with suction. Diameter of ultrafine (UF) disc, 40 mm. (Corning Glass Works, Corning, N.Y.)

use with suction; diameter of disc, 40 mm; capacity of interchangeable receiving flasks (fitted with standard joints), 250 ml or larger. (2) Bush type, for use with positive pressure; diameter of disc, 40 mm; capacity of chamber into which disc is fused, 150 ml. (3) Tubular type, for use with either positive pressure or suction, with glass connector for attachment to rubber tubing. The bottom of the tubular filter is clear, to allow inspection of the inner surface. Fritted glass filters, unlike most others, can be chemically cleaned before sterilization. Morton-type filters as used in the author's laboratory for the filtration of small quantities of material and for less than a liter of finished culture medium.

Millipore MF discs, for highly exacting filtration procedures, are approximately 150 μ thick and consist of cellulose esters. They are supplied in many sizes, and in highly uniform pore sizes ranging from 10 mμ (poliovirus is approximately 13 mμ) to 5 μ. The ratio of pores to solids is more than 80 per cent, which results in unusually rapid flow rates. Also, because they can easily be rendered transparent under the microscope or dissolved away, they lend themselves to many special tests and procedures (see p. 232).

Filtration under positive pressure is usually preferred to vacuum filtration, especially when loss of carbon dioxide would result in undesirable pH changes (see p. 56). Pressure filtrations may be made with nitrogen, compressed air, or a mixture of compressed air and carbon dioxide (5 per cent). When suction is used, the air in the filter flask is withdrawn by aspiration through a water pump or an electric vacuum pump; and a water trap should always be included in the vacuum line. If a mercury manometer or a vacuum gauge is used, it is easily possible to observe and regulate the pressure during filtration. Filtration should be carried out as rapidly and at as low a pressure as possible. It is best not to use a greater pressure than that represented by 35 to 50 cm of mercury. And regardless of the type of filter that is used, one should not filter too much material through one filter at a given time or continue the process too long. If the volume to be filtered is large or the rate of filtration is slow, it is better to use several filters instead of one. If bacteria are left in contact with a filter long enough, they will pass through. Before filtering, it is advisable to remove coarse materials such as blood or tissue cells, precipitates, fibrin strands, and other large particles, by centrifugation.

Bryant and his associates[37] have designed a special filter assembly for Selas candles, illustrated in Fig. 13, which is self-explanatory. When relatively large volumes of medium (e.g., 6 l) are to be processed, four filters are operated simultaneously.* The medium is placed in a large, unstoppered supply bottle enclosed in a metal

* Bryant, J. C. Personal communication.

pressure tank. A glass tube that extends from the bottom of the supply bottle and passes through a rubber collar in the lid of the tank is connected with a glass manifold to which the filters are attached. The pressure (18 lb) is provided by 5 per cent CO_2 in nitrogen, introduced through an inlet in the metal tank.

Use of Antibiotics

Although antibiotics provide a convenient means of preparing cultures from tissues that are likely to be contaminated, they should not be used continuously in the propagation of established cell strains. It has been found that tissue-culture media to which penicillin and streptomycin are added provide an ideal environment for pleuropneumonia-like organisms (PPLO) and some L forms of bacteria, all of which are filterable and may not be revealed by routine bacteriological sterility tests.[79,357,454] If antibiotics are used in propagating established cell lines, they should be withdrawn at frequent intervals in order to discover if these or other contaminating organisms are present. During the withdrawal period, the media should be tested for the presence of PPLO and L-form bacteria according to methods that are now well established.[357] According to Robinson and her associates,[447] many strains of PPLO are sensitive to antibiotics of the tetracycline series; and Chang[62] succeeded in eliminating PPLO from some of his strains by treating them with 50 u of tetracycline per ml for about two weeks. Hayflick[230] decontaminates cultures infected with PPLO by taking advantage of the differential heat lability of the contaminating organisms and the culture cells. He found that various cell lines contaminated with PPLO could be decontaminated by holding them at 41° C for about 18 hr. Although various cell lines show different degrees of tolerance to this temperature, the most of them will probably survive.

When penicillin and streptomycin are used in culture work, they are usually combined with the media at levels of 50–100 u and 50–100 μg per ml, respectively. Penicillin, which is relatively unstable, should be added to medium just before it is used; streptomycin remains active in media that are stored for long periods. In the author's laboratory, all chemically defined media contain n-butyl parahydroxybenzoate (0.2 mg per l), which offers protection from certain molds.

Various kits of antibiotic sensitivity discs are now generally available. Although these kits are designed primarily for clinical work, they are often useful in tissue culture as a means of determining the relative sensitivity of a contaminating microorganism to various concentrations of some of the more commonly used antibiotics.

If and when yeasts or molds appear in cultures that seem too valuable to discard, nystatin (Mycostatin, Squibb) may be added at a concentration of 100 u per ml of nutrient medium. One milligram of the sterile powder is approximately equivalent to 2,500 u of nystatin activity, so that 1 mg of the powder in 25 ml of medium gives the equivalent of 100 u per ml. Although Mycostatin is practically insoluble in water, the small particle size of the sterile powder permits the preparation of a very fine suspension with excellent antifungal properties. Although Mycostatin is moderately soluble in the lower aliphatic alcohols and glycols, the solutions are not as stable as the suspensions, which may be stored for one to two weeks at $4°$ C or for longer periods in dry ice (if the vials are sealed to exclude CO_2).

Disinfection of Floors, Walls, Bench Tops, and Other Objects

All surfaces that require disinfection and contaminated objects that cannot be autoclaved immediately or at all should be treated with one or another of the stable antiseptics that have been found effective in medicine and surgery. One of these, Wescodyne (West Chemical Products Inc., Long Island City 1, N.Y.), consists of iodine complexed with surface active agents that have detergent properties. This complex not only enhances the bactericidal and virucidal activity of iodine but also renders it nontoxic, nonirritating, stable, and water soluble. When used in dilutions recommended by the manufacturer, the solutions are rich amber in color. As the color fades, their activity diminishes. For the disinfection of floors, walls, bench tops, and skin, the recommended concentration is 75 p.p.m. available iodine, which may be achieved by combining 4.5 ml of the concentrate with 1 l of water. For instruments, a solution of 20 ml of Wescodyne and 6 Gm of sodium nitrite per liter of water inhibits corrosion, protects personnel, and facilitates subsequent cleaning.

In the author's laboratory, as a means of obtaining minimal, routine protection against the possible spread of yeasts, molds, bacteria, and viruses, whether real or suspected, all discarded culture pipettes and containers are immersed immediately in polyethylene buckets containing Wescodyne, 4.5 ml per liter of water. This procedure not only kills most microorganisms within a very few minutes, but it helps in reconditioning the equipment for subsequent use.

Use of Masks and Gowns in Culture Rooms

Carrel gave careful concern to the design of gowns and masks for experimental surgery and tissue culture. Because his operating rooms at The Rockefeller Institute were conditioned mainly by the intensity of the sun that streamed through overhead skylights (see p. 9), he chose light-weight, loose-fitting gowns of sateen with snap fasteners down the back. Also, because tight-fitting cotton masks are highly uncomfortable and after a few moments of wear more of a hazard than none at all, Carrel designed hoods of the finest muslin to cover the entire head. These hoods were loose and fell to the shoulders, and most of the exhaled air escaped downwards instead of through the hood and into the work. It must be remembered, however, that in those years all culture media contained blood serum or blood plasma, which gave considerable natural protection from bacterial contaminants.

When "dust-proof" culture rooms are used, the work is usually carried out on open tables or benches. Under these conditions, sterile gowns should be worn to reduce the introduction of dust from the outer laboratory. Although a cap or kerchief should be worn on the head, for the same reason, the use of face masks depends on the circumstances. In most instances, it is probably safer for solitary workers to remain unmasked than to wear the same cotton masks for extended periods. An unmasked individual breathing through the nose or mouth expels only a few bacteria into the air. As soon as he talks or coughs, large numbers of organisms are expelled forcibly, chiefly in the form of droplets of saliva and bits of mucus. A cotton mask catches the direct spray and accordingly reduces the number of bacteria in the air for the moment. As the droplets evaporate, the bacteria are deposited in the mask and are subsequently distributed in the room during quiet expiration. Unfortunately, cotton masks have scarcely any bacteria-trapping efficiency when moist, and moisture collects as breathing proceeds. Thus, the air expired through a cotton mask that has been worn for a few minutes carries more bacteria than that from an unmasked person who is breathing quietly.[227,525]

Two or more persons working together should always be masked if they wish to converse, but if cotton masks are used they should be changed at frequent intervals. Cotton masks are boiled in mild soap and water before autoclaving. When dry, they are packed in a suitable container that is placed in the autoclave on its side with a cloth or paper covering tied around the top. When they are set out for use, the container is closed with its own cover that has been sterilized separately.

An important new development in face masks for surgery has been the introduction[1] of a fitted, filter-type mask that can be autoclaved repeatedly. These masks (available from Apasco Corporation, Wolfeboro, N.H.) consist of two layers of 20-mesh bronze screen enclosing a spun glass filter that removes particulate matter down to 0.5μ. A comfortable, easily adjustable, adapter ring prevents leakage at skin surfaces, rests free of the compressible part of the nose, fits beneath spectacles, and may be laundered as often as necessary. This type of mask is useful in highly critical tissue culture undertakings, especially those in which antibiotics cannot be used. With care, the filters last for several months.

Antibacterial Treatment of Hands

In preparing for animal operations or for the surface sterilization and gross dissection of animal organs too large to be handled with instruments (*see* p. 116), the hands should be thoroughly scrubbed with a sterile brush and tincture of green soap (e.g., Saponin) under running water. The soap is then rinsed off and the hands dried with a sterile towel. Next, they are soaked for a few seconds in Dakin's solution (*see* below) or some other antiseptic that is nontoxic for tissues and dried again with a sterile towel. If gloves are to be worn, the hands are powdered with sterile talc. Finally, as an added precaution, the gloved hands are immersed in the antiseptic. If gloves are not to be worn, a drop or two of 7 per cent tincture of iodine should be applied around the finger nails. In either case, it is wise to rinse the hands in the antiseptic at frequent intervals during the operation.

As an alternative procedure, the hands may be scrubbed with a 10 per cent tincture of Wescodyne (*see* p. 48), prepared as follows:

Wescodyne	10 ml
95 per cent ethyl alcohol	50 ml
Distilled water, to make	100 ml

Whether or not gloves are worn, the hands may be immersed from time to time in an aqueous solution of Wescodyne containing 75 p.p.m. available iodine (made by adding 4.5 ml of the concentrate to one liter of water).

Preparation of Dakin's Hypochlorite Solution

The antiseptic properties of sodium hypochlorite have been known for many decades. But the hypochlorite found in commerce not only has an extremely variable composition, it also contains free alkali and often free chlorine. Consequently, it is irritating when applied to living tissues. In 1915 Dakin[*] discovered a means of obtaining a solution free from caustic alkali and one in which the content of hypochlorite did not vary beyond 0.4 and 0.5 per cent. In preparing this solution, Dakin took advantage of the double decomposition of calcium hypochlorite and sodium carbonate. Later, even more uniform results were achieved by the electrolysis of a sodium chloride solution;[†] and Cullen and Austin[‡] succeeded in making the solution from

---

[*] Dakin, H. D. *Brit. Med. J.* 2: 318, 1915.

[†] Carrel, A., Dakin, H., Daufresne, M., Dehelly, G., and Dumas, J. *Presse méd.* 23: 397, 1915.

Keen, W. W. The Treatment of War Wounds, 2nd ed. W. B. Saunders Company, Philadelphia, 1918.

[‡] Cullen, G. E., and Austin, J. H. *Proc. Soc. Exper. Biol. & Med.* 15: 41, 1917–18.

chlorine and sodium carbonate. Eventually, however, there appeared on the market various commercial concentrates of sodium hypochlorite prepared for use in homes and laundries and in the chlorination of water. It is easily possible* to prepare Dakin's solution from one or another of these concentrates.

From the standpoint of the present techniques for achieving and maintaining sterility, Dakin's solution, if properly prepared, has many advantages. It may be used frequently without rendering the skin rough or uncomfortable. Because it breaks down very readily in contact with protein materials, it causes no lasting damage to normal body tissues but destroys immediately isolated, and hence more vulnerable, bacterial organisms. During the course of an operation it may be used freely on the most delicate tissues without killing the constituent cells. In short, whenever and wherever applied, it affords the utmost protection from contaminating organisms, with the least damage to the tissues.

Definition. Dakin's solution contains not less than 0.4 per cent and not more than 0.5 per cent sodium hypochlorite ($NaOCl$). If the percentage of sodium hypochlorite is less than 0.4 per cent, the antiseptic power of the solution is too low; if it is greater than 0.5 per cent, the solution is irritating. Dakin's solution is weakly alkaline (pH about 8.5 to 9.0). If the solution is alkaline to powdered phenolphthalein, it is irritating; if it is acid to an alcoholic solution of phenolphthalein, it is too unstable.

In the author's laboratory Dakin's solution is prepared from a commercial concentrate containing approximately 12 per cent $NaOCl$. The procedure is as follows: 144 ml of concentrated solution are added to 1–2 l of water; 4 ml of 6N HCl are added to a small volume (400 to 500 ml) of water; and 32 gm of $NaHCO_3$ are added to another small volume of water. Finally, the three solutions are mixed and sufficient water is added to make 4 l. The resulting Dakin's solution has a hypochlorite concentration of 0.4 per cent and a pH of 8.8.

Only small quantities (e.g., 1 gal) of the commercial 12 per cent concentrate should be stored in the laboratory (4° C), in amber-glass jugs. Because $NaOCl$ causes glass to become brittle eventually, the jugs should be renewed once a year.

* Gault, P. S., and Ozburn, E. E. *U.S. Nav. M. Bull. 38:* 528, 1940.

V

Balanced Salt Solutions and pH Control

THE balanced salt solutions that are used in tissue culture have three main functions: (1) to serve as diluting and irrigating fluids, while maintaining tonicity with the cells; (2) to provide buffers to bring the medium to and maintain it in the physiological pH range (7.2–7.6); and (3) to provide the water and those inorganic ions needed for normal cell metabolism. Most balanced salt solutions include glucose as an energy source.

In the preparation of culture media, it is important to keep them approximately homogeneous in salt content with the tissues and hence with the serum of the animal from which the tissues are taken. Cells are so organized that their food must be brought to them in solution. The transportation of materials in solution depends upon diffusion, and diffusion is very closely related to osmotic pressure. If cells are maintained in a medium with a greater osmotic pressure than their own contents, they tend to shrink. If the osmotic pressure of the surrounding medium is too low, they swell and burst.

Solutions with the same osmotic pressure have a number of properties in common and are said to be isotonic. Although the osmotic pressure of a solution may be measured directly, it is usually determined indirectly by measurements of vapor pressure, boiling point, or freezing point, all of which properties are possessed by isotonic solutions to the same relative degree. Of these, the determination of

53

the lowering of the freezing point is the most satisfactory method. The presence of corpuscles, colloidal suspensions, and emulsions has little or no effect on the results. Hence, the determinations can be made not only on blood plasma and blood serum but also on whole blood. The osmotic pressure of Tyrode's solution, as interpreted by its freezing point ($-0.62°$ C), lies within the range of most normal sera. The freezing point of chicken serum usually varies from $-0.60°$ to $-0.65°$ C, according to the individual. Rabbit serum has a lowering of from $-0.55°$ to $-0.66°$ C; human serum, from $-0.48°$ to $-0.65°$ C. If, in addition to Tyrode's solution, other substances are used in the medium, the osmotic pressure of the final mixture must be kept isotonic with the serum of the species providing the tissue.

The early salt solutions were developed by physiologists as perfusion fluids for the study of heart function, muscle contraction, and peristalsis. The English physiologist, Sydney Ringer,[438] in a series of classical papers published between 1880 and 1895, showed that an excised frog's heart would continue to function normally for a considerable period if perfused with a fluid containing sodium, potassium, and calcium, these three cations being used in proportions similar to those existing in sea water and in the blood of higher animals. Since then, it has been found that these same three cations, acting separately or in combination with one another, help to regulate such vital phenomena as osmotic pressure, the permeability of cell membranes, the quickness of response to cell stimulation, and the adhesiveness of cells that makes for tissue integrity.

Before Ringer began his investigations it had been known that the isolated heart of the frog would cease to beat if placed in 0.75 per cent sodium chloride. But Ringer found that if a small amount of calcium chloride was added to the solution, the heart beat recovered to a degree, though not for long. If, however, a little potassium chloride was added, the heart action remained normal for a much longer period. It was further found that, although each cation was toxic when present alone, the toxic action of any one of them, even when present in excess, was neutralized by the presence of the correct physiological concentration of one of the others. These observations led Ringer to formulate the principle of a "balanced" salt solution, in which one cation is able to antagonize or neutralize the toxic effects of another. It is important to note, however, that ions that are antagonistic to one another in relation to one biological process may not be antagonistic in relation to another biological process.

In addition to the chlorides of sodium, potassium, and calcium, Ringer's solution finally came to include sodium bicarbonate, which served as a buffer. Ringer tried to substitute other salts of calcium and potassium for the chlorides but found that, in the presence of sodium chloride, the other anions produced the same effects. The composition of Ringer's solution for frog's heart is usually given as follows: sodium chloride (NaCl), 6.5 Gm; potassium chloride (KCl), 0.14 Gm; calcium chloride (CaCl$_2$), 0.12 Gm; sodium bicarbonate (NaHCO$_3$), 0.2 Gm; water, to make 1000 ml.

In 1901 Locke,[290] who worked with the excised hearts of dogs, cats, and other laboratory animals, increased the salt concentrations of Ringer's solution to make it correspond with the higher osmotic pressure of the blood of these animals. The Ringer-Locke solution most commonly used has the following composition: sodium chloride (NaCl), 9.0 Gm; potassium chloride (KCl), 0.42 Gm; calcium chloride (CaCl$_2$), 0.24 Gm; sodium bicarbonate (NaHCO$_3$), 0.2 Gm; glucose, 1.0 Gm; water, to make 1000 ml.

In 1910 Tyrode[521] modified the Ringer-Locke solution by adding magnesium and monobasic sodium phosphate (Table IV). He found magnesium to be effective in maintaining the contractions of mammalian intestine, and sodium phosphate improved the buffering capacity of the solution. Since the early days of tissue culture, Tyrode's solution has been widely used as a diluting fluid for the protein materials included in natural media and for the organic constituents of chemically defined media. The preparation of Tyrode's solution and modifications of it will now be described.

TYRODE'S SOLUTION

In Tyrode's original publication,[521] it is not stated whether the calcium chloride, the magnesium chloride, and the sodium phosphate were anhydrous, though it is unlikely that they were. In any event, Tyrode did not indicate the number of molecules of water that may have been present. While it is possible, therefore, that the amounts given in Table IV may not correspond exactly with the amounts used by him, this formula is the one most frequently followed.

In the preparation of Tyrode's solution, only reagent salts should be used. Approximately 850 ml of glass-distilled water are placed in a 1000-ml graduate, and the various ingredients are added to the water, one at a time, in the order designated. Each substance is dissolved completely and distributed throughout the entire volume of the solution before the next is added. This precaution is necessary in order to avoid high local concentrations of any one ingredient. When the mixture has been completed, water is added to make 1 l of solution and the pH is then tested with a pH meter.

The pH of Tyrode's solution should range from 7.4 to 7.8. If the pH is higher, it is probably because the sodium bicarbonate contains some sodium carbonate. Sodium bicarbonate originally free from carbonate may form the latter upon standing, particularly if exposed to the air. This change does not, however, render the salt unfit for use. By the addition of dilute hydrochloric acid, the pH may be adjusted after the solution has been made up. But this adjustment may be made before the solution is completed if the sodium bicarbonate is dissolved separately in about 100 ml of water and carbon dioxide gas is bubbled through it. This process reconverts the carbonate into bicarbonate. The adjusted material is then added to the other ingredients.

In some laboratories, the calcium and magnesium salts are dissolved in a separate quantity of water (e.g., 100 ml) to avoid precipitation of calcium and magnesium carbonate and phosphate. Then, after the other ingredients have been dissolved in about 800 ml of water, the first solution is added slowly, with vigorous stirring.

A balanced salt solution of double strength is sometimes required. Such a solution can be mixed with an equal volume of the water solution of a substance to be used in the culture medium and will still give an isotonic mixture. It is made in the usual manner, except that twice the amount of each ingredient is added to the original volume of water.

A balanced salt solution with extra glucose is useful when large quantities of tissues are cultivated in small volumes of media. If the glucose is increased to 3 or 4 Gm per l, the sodium chloride should be reduced correspondingly, to give an isotonic solution.

Balanced salt solutions containing bicarbonate are sterilized by pressure filtration (*see* p. 46). If vacuum filtration is used, CO_2 will be drawn off, and the solutions will become abnormally alkaline.

After filtration, the solutions are stored in the refrigerator in closed containers. When small quantities of a solution are required at infrequent intervals, it is recommended that it be stored in 50-ml tubes or flasks so that only small samples need be unstoppered as required. Each time a sample is opened sterility is endangered, and the loss of CO_2 increases the alkalinity.

Cell suspensions or cells cultivated directly on glass should never be exposed to unsupplemented, balanced salt solutions for more than a few minutes. Thus, for example, Tyrode's solution alone is exceedingly harmful to cells; but the addition of 14 mg per ml of crystalline serum albumin (a protein concentration roughly equivalent to that of 20 per cent whole serum) to Tyrode's solution, adjusted to pH 7.4 with 0.1N sodium hydroxide, preserves the normal appearance of the cells for at least 10 hr.[437] It has also been found[278,418] that the amount of cellular P^{32} leaking out into the culture medium is considerable when the cells are washed with protein-free saline.

MODIFIED TYRODE'S SOLUTIONS

Table IV shows the composition of Tyrode's solution and three modifications of it now in common use. In all three of these modifications, the phosphates are at more nearly physiological levels than in Tyrode's solution. In addition, Earle's[114] and Hanks's[212] solutions

TABLE IV
BALANCED SALT SOLUTIONS CONTAINING GLUCOSE
(grams per liter)*

	Tyrode's Solution[521]	Earle's Solution[114]	Gey's Solution†	Hanks's Solution[212]
NaCl	8.00	6.80	8.00	8.00
KCl	0.20	0.40	0.38	0.40
$CaCl_2$	0.20	0.20	0.13	0.14
$MgCl_2 \cdot 6H_2O$	0.10		0.21	
$MgSO_4 \cdot 7H_2O$		0.20		0.20
$Na_2HPO_4 \cdot 12H_2O$			0.30	0.12
$NaH_2PO_4 \cdot H_2O$	0.05	0.14		
KH_2PO_4			0.025	0.06
$NaHCO_3$	1.00	2.20	0.25	0.35
Glucose	1.00	1.00	1.00	1.00

* Phenol red is usually added at 1 to 5 mg per cent (w/v).
† Bulletin of the Tissue Culture Association, March 16, 1949.

provide sulfates. Earle's solution contains more bicarbonate than the others and has therefore a higher buffering capacity. Because Earle used anhydrous salts, the amounts given by him for magnesium sulfate and sodium phosphate have been adjusted for the use of hydrated salts.

Stewart and Kirk[490] have calculated the "particle" concentration (total molarity of molecules plus ions) of various salt solutions as an index of their relative tonicity (0.9 per cent NaCl—0.308M; Tyrode's solution—0.314M; Earle's solution—0.307M; Gey's solution—0.303M). These "particle" concentrations compared favorably with a similar calculation on the inorganic salt values for human plasma (0.307M).

To simplify pH control, sodium bicarbonate is often omitted from balanced salt solutions when they are prepared and is added later to the medium, as required. If less than the full amount of bicarbonate is added to new cultures or to cultures with small cell populations, it will be easily possible to adjust the pH to 7.2, without gassing (*see* p. 60), by adding graded amounts of bicarbonate to the medium at times of fluid change. For this purpose, a solution of 3 per cent bicarbonate is pressure-filtered (to retain the CO_2) and stored in tightly stoppered tubes. For new cultures, 1.0 to 2.5 ml of this solution is included in each 100 ml of finished medium. For older cultures with greatly increased cell populations, as much as 7.0 ml of the solution may be used for each 100 ml of medium. This amount would give a bicarbonate level equivalent to that of Earle's solution (*see* Table IV).

PHOSPHATE-BUFFERED SALT SOLUTION

Dulbecco and Vogt[93] devised the following solution (PBS) for use in irrigating tissues and cultures and in preparing cell or virus suspensions: (1) NaCl 8.0 Gm, KCl 0.2 Gm, Na_2HPO_4 1.15 Gm, KH_2PO_4 0.2 Gm, water 800 ml; (2) $CaCl_2$ 0.1 Gm, water 100 ml; (3) $MgCl_2 \cdot 6H_2O$ 0.1 Gm, water 100 ml. Solutions (1), (2), and (3) are autoclaved separately and mixed when cool. Alternatively, all of the salts may be dissolved in 1000 ml of water and the solution sterilized by filtration.

PHOSPHITE-BUFFERED SALT SOLUTION

Gifford and his associates[184, 445] have used a sodium-hydrogen, phosphite-buffered salt solution to provide additional buffering capacity in short-term respiration studies with HeLa cells. A 0.2M stock solution of phosphorous acid (H_3PO_3) is prepared from reagent-grade, 30 per cent solution or C.P. crystalline H_3PO_3, and checked acidimetrically. One hundred milliliters of this stock solution, adjusted to pH 7.6 with sodium hydroxide and diluted to 200 ml with distilled water, yields an isotonic 0.1M solution of NaH_2PO_3-Na_2HPO_3. It is sterilized by passage through an ultrafine, sintered glass filter. The finished phosphite buffered salt solution has the following composition: 0.1M NaH_2PO_3-Na_2HPO_3 solution 200 ml, glucose 1.0 Gm, NaCl 6.25 Gm, KCl 0.4 Gm, $MgSO_4 \cdot 7H_2O$ 0.2 Gm, $CaCl_2$ 0.14 Gm, $NaHCO_3$ 0.35 Gm, KH_2PO_4 0.06 Gm, Na_2HPO_4 0.06 Gm, and water to make 1000 ml. The final concentration of phosphite (0.02M) does not interfere with the respiration of HeLa cells nor reduce their capacity to synthesize polio virus.[184] Swim and R. F. Parker[502] prepare a stock solution of 1M sodium phosphite which is stored at $-20°$ C until just before use; and the final adjustment in pH is made on the completed culture medium after the addition of phosphite (at 0.02M).

SOLUTIONS FOR DILUTION OF DIGESTIVE ENZYMES

Moscona[344] found that elimination of calcium and magnesium from the dispersing medium enhanced the dissociation of cells of early embryonic rudiments treated with trypsin (see pp. 120 and 242). Puck and his associates[413] omitted calcium, magnesium, and phosphates from Hanks's solution (Table IV) to provide a fluid (saline A) for the irrigation of tissues and cultures and a diluting agent for trypsin.

Rinaldini[437] devised the following solution as a diluting agent for digestive enzymes: NaCl 8.0 Gm, KCl 0.2 Gm, $C_6H_5Na_3O_7 \cdot 2H_2O$ (sodium citrate) 1.0 Gm, $NaH_2PO_4 \cdot H_2O$ 0.05 Gm, $NaHCO_3$ 1.0 Gm, glucose 1.0 Gm, water to make 1000 ml.

pH Control

For many years, the pH of cultures has been regulated by means of a buffer system modeled after the naturally occurring CO_2-bicarbonate system present in blood plasma. The bicarbonate is added to the medium as part of the balanced salt solution, and the pH that is achieved is dependent on the amount of carbonic acid that is formed in the medium. When media containing bicarbonate are sterilized by vacuum filtration, there is loss of CO_2 and the medium becomes correspondingly alkaline. Carbon dioxide may be restored to the medium by introducing it from a cylinder, or the cultures may be gassed at the time they are made and as often as necessary thereafter with 5 or 8 per cent CO_2 in air. Cells cultivated in a closed system usually provide enough respiratory CO_2 to keep the pH at a satisfactory level.

Blood serum and plasma, when present in the medium, have a weak buffering action that is greatly augmented by the presence of a balanced salt solution. But when the rate of cell multiplication is high, there is a tendency for the medium to become abnormally acid. If an appropriate indicator, such as phenol red, is incorporated in the medium, it is possible to determine the approximate pH of the cultures by comparing them with a set of standards made up with phosphate buffers containing the same indicator in the same concentration. Phenol red, used in a concentration of 0.001 to 0.005 per cent, is not toxic.

Carbon dioxide in air or any combination of O_2, CO_2, and N_2 may be obtained commercially. The gas mixture is bubbled through a saturation flask containing about 1 per cent copper sulphate, to suppress molds, then passed through a cotton filter (about $3\frac{1}{2} \times \frac{3}{4}$ in.), to render the mixture sterile, and introduced into the culture container by means of a sterile glass pipette. The gas is allowed to flow into the culture very gently at the rate of about 250 ml per min; the free end of the pipette is kept well above the surface of the medium. The sterile filter is replaced daily; the glass pipettes are changed as often as there is doubt of their sterility and are always changed between cultures that are not of the same origin.

Lacking all other means, one may adjust the pH of the cultures by treating them with exhaled air. As a rule, this contains about 4 per cent CO_2. The exhaled air is blown into them through a sterile pipette, the large end of which is plugged with cotton to serve as a filter.

If the medium becomes too acid, one or more drops of isotonic sodium bicarbonate (1.4 per cent) may be added to the medium every day or so to maintain the pH in the physiological range.

Hanks[210] makes the interesting point that since 0.3N HCl and 0.3N NaOH yield isotonic NaCl, these are ideal concentrations for neutralizing other solutions without changing the osmotic pressure. The HCl solution could contain the usual concentrations of KCl, CaCl₂, MgSO₄, glucose, and phosphates (as phosphoric acid), so that ionic balance would be maintained.

Because gassing is always time consuming and because it is impossible to prevent the loss of CO_2 from certain types of cultures without continuous gassing (see p. 184), many attempts have been made in recent years to find a nontoxic, nonvolatile buffer. Swim and R. F. Parker[499] replaced the sodium bicarbonate of their media with tris-(hydroxymethyl)aminomethane[189] or with glycylglycine. The Tris buffer was used at concentrations of 2.0 to 3.6 Gm per 1; and the pH was adjusted by the addition of hydrochloric acid. The growth of some strains (HeLa and L) was somewhat inhibited with higher levels of Tris, and the cells were more granular than otherwise. Glycylglycine seemed to be less toxic than Tris for HeLa cells, but foreskin cells did not proliferate as well in glycylglycine as in Tris. McLimans and his associates* have used various mixed buffers for cells propagated in suspension (see Chap. XII). These mixed buffers included phosphate together with orthophosphite or Tris or both; and the concentration of each was usually 0.01M. In the author's laboratory, Tris has always proved toxic to cells after prolonged cultivation.

More recently, Gwatkin and Siminovitch[199] developed a medium in which animal cell-colony counts can be made in the absence of bicarbonate buffer. Chemically defined medium lacking bicarbonate was supplemented with bicarbonate-free serum and 1–2mM oxalacetic acid. Small numbers of cells (e.g., 100) were added to Petri dishes containing this medium and incubated at 37° C in an atmosphere of humidified air but with no extra addition of CO_2. The plating efficiencies (see p. 217) obtained with L and HeLa cells were as high as those achieved in bicarbonate-buffered medium. This method is successful because the few cells involved in a plating experiment do not produce enough acid to require extensive buffering capacity. It was felt by the authors that the oxalacetic acid served to satisfy the CO_2 requirements of the cells. A neutralized 0.25M solution of oxalacetic acid in bicarbonate-free CMRL-1066 was stored frozen and added directly to the Petri dishes.

* W. F. McLimans. Personal communication.

VI

Chemically Defined Media*

UNTIL recent years, the nutritive media employed for the cultivation of animal cells *in vitro* were derived almost exclusively from the organism and consisted of blood plasma, blood serum, other body fluids and exudates, and extracts of tissues and organs. But the complexity and variability of these naturally occurring materials made it difficult to use them in experiments designed to determine the nutritive substances required by the cells and the effect of particular substances upon them. The first attempts to devise chemically defined media were made by Lewis and Lewis, Baker and Carrel, and Vogelaar and Erlichman. In 1911, Lewis and Lewis[279] found that chick-embryo tissues survived for a time in Locke's solution supplemented with amino acids and polypeptides and that media containing glucose or maltose were more sustaining than balanced salt solutions alone. Carrel's[43] discovery in 1912 that extracts of embryonic tissues contained an abundance of growth-promoting substances made it possible for the first time to propagate animal cells indefinitely and stimulated

---

* For a more detailed account of the earlier work on animal-cell nutrition, the reader is referred to an exhaustive review by Waymouth.[528] Pertinent reviews of various aspects of the subject have also been published by Stewart and Kirk,[490] Biggers *et al.*,[22] Morgan,[334] Harris,[219] and Swim.[497] Day and Grace[86] have reviewed recent work on the cultivation of insect tissues, and Wolf, Quimby, Pyle and Dexter (Science *132:* 1890, 1960) have reported the cultivation of cells from six species of fresh-water bony fishes, a frog, and a turtle, in media consisting of commercially available components.

the search for the particular substances responsible, a search that has not yet ended (*see also* p. 99). In 1926, Carrel and Baker[52] reported that Witte's peptone, proteoses, and other protein degradation products, when used with serum or plasma, provided essential nutrients for fibroblasts, epithelial cells, and blood monocytes. In 1929, Baker[10] found that rat sarcoma cells grown in a washed plasma coagulum supplemented with peptic digest of casein, glycine, thymus nucleic acid, ash of liver, glutathione, and hemoglobin behaved almost as well as sister cultures cultivated in whole plasma and embryo extract. In 1933 Vogelaar and Erlichman[524] reported a feeding solution consisting of irradiated beef plasma, Witte's peptone, hemin, cystine, insulin, thyroxine, glucose, and the salts of Tyrode's solution. In this medium they were able to keep a strain of fibroblasts from human thyroid in a state of active proliferation for three months. Using the mixture of Vogelaar and Erlichman as a basis, Baker[11] then devised a medium for fibroblasts and epithelial cells by adding vitamin A (containing some vitamin D), ascorbic acid, glutathione, and 10 per cent serum; the relative proportions of these substances were altered somewhat and certain B vitamins added to provide a medium for blood monocytes (Table V). Eventually, Carrel and his associates[55] used some of these substances to advantage in preparing large quantities of medium for the cultivation of organs from adult animals.

TABLE V

COMPOSITION OF BAKER'S MEDIUM FOR MONOCYTES*

	per 1000 ml	
Witte's peptone	850.00	
Cysteine hydrochloride	11.25	
Hemin	0.0045	
Thyroxine	0.00113	mg
Glucose	2000.00	
Glutathione	3.40	
Vitamin C	0.85	
Vitamin A (containing vitamin D)	1000.00	
Vitamin B_1	0.053	
Vitamin B_2	0.001	units
Insulin	0.12	
Serum	150.00	ml

* This medium also included the salts of Tyrode's solution.

Fischer and his associates[124,154] followed the analytic approach of Carrel and Baker and used basal media consisting of dialyzed plasma, serum, and chick-embryo extract, each of which were dialyzed separately against a Ringer-glucose solution to remove all or nearly all low-molecular-weight components. These basal media supported neither cell multiplication nor survival, but, when supplemented with chemically defined nutrients and with substances prepared by controlled digestion of biological materials, they provided a means of studying the low-molecular-weight growth factors lost by dialysis. Thus, it was established[158] that the dialyzable components of embryo extract were essential for cell multiplication and survival and that the growth promoting qualities of such crude extracts could be approximated over short periods by a solution containing the salts of Tyrode's solution, glucose, fructosediphosphate, glutamine, cystine, glutathione, and certain other amino acids (Table VI). The essential

TABLE VI

COMPOSITION OF FISCHER'S SUPPLEMENTARY MEDIUM, V-614*

	Mg per 1000 ml		Mg per 1000 ml
Glucose	2000	DL-Isoleucine	20
Fructosediphosphate	200	DL-Threonine	24
L-Lysine·2HCl	30	DL-Phenylalanine	14
L-Histidine·HCl	10	L-Tryptophan	4
L-Arginine	4	Cystine	10
DL-Valine	28	Glutathione	10
L-Leucine	18	Glutamine	250

* This medium also included dialyzed plasma, dialyzed embryo extract, and certain inorganic salts.

amino-acid mixture of Rose,[451] as determined for whole animals, proved considerably less beneficial than the mixture of Bergmann and Niemann,[19] which is based on an analysis of fibrin and contains lysine, arginine, tryptophan, methionine, histidine, glutamic acid, aspartic acid, proline, and cystine.[154] Cystine was found to be the most important single amino acid, and, while it could not be replaced by methionine, it could be replaced by glutathione.[156] Also, a medium lacking both lysine and glutamic acid was less adequate than one in which only one of them was omitted. Fischer's data further suggested that different cell types may have different amino-acid requirements.

Thus, osteoblasts were more sensitive than myoblasts to lysine deficiency. It was also found[124,156] that mixtures of amino acids in the proportions present in lactoglobulin and bovine serum albumin were less effective supplements than peptic or tryptic digests of these proteins; that any phosphate source, together with glucose, could replace fructosediphosphate; that sorbose or sorbitol and rhamnose, but not ribose, could replace the fructose moiety of fructosediphosphate; that alanine and glycylglycine could replace glycine; and that asparagine could replace glutamine. The work of Fischer and his colleagues made it clear that animal tissues cultivated outside the body may require certain nutrients not required by the intact animal.

In 1952, Harris[216] found that the failure of Fischer's Ringer-dialyzed media to support cell multiplication resulted from a loss of bicarbonate during dialysis, with a consequent fall in pH, and not from a nutritional deficiency. When the pH was adjusted to physiological levels with bicarbonate, Harris obtained a stable and continuing outgrowth of chick-heart fibroblasts. Harris then developed methods for the aseptic dialysis of media at constant pH and buffer strength and was able to show that, under these conditions, dialysis reduces but does not suppress the growth-promoting properties of the media. Harris also evaluated the relative importance of the various nondialyzable components for cell growth. An initial outgrowth of chick-heart fibroblasts was obtained in a medium consisting of dialyzed plasma alone plus a balanced salt solution containing glucose, without serum or embryo extract; this represented a minimal response. When dialyzed horse serum was added, the response was not improved. The deficiency was eliminated, however, by adding the dialyzable fraction of chick-embryo extract. In later publications,[215,217] Harris reported that the active agents in a dialysate of 12-day chick embryos were nonprotein, insoluble in lipid solvents, partially heat stable, but were destroyed by acid hydrolysis. Kutsky[258] then isolated a nucleoprotein fraction from chick embryo extract that yielded a significant growth response when added to cultures containing undialyzed chicken plasma and horse serum. (*See* Chap. VII for further details.)

White[538] made the first serious attempt to cultivate animal tissues in a complex solution of known composition. In 1946, he reported a feeding solution of 20 ingredients of known composition that supported relatively large masses of chick-embryo heart tissue in a state of functional survival for several weeks. In later experiments,[539] he treated smaller amounts of tissue with a feeding solution slightly more elaborate than the first, though the culture that lived for the longest period (over 80 days) received embryo extract at about the eighth week, by which time the medium had been renewed only four times.

In 1950, Morgan, Morton, and Parker[339] published the composition of a more adequate medium, No. 199 (Table VIII), that included an almost complete complement of amino acids and vitamins as well as several nucleic-acid constituents and certain intermediary metabolites and accessory growth factors. Glutamine was included because of the importance placed upon it by Fischer's group, and Tween 80 was used as a water-soluble source of fatty acid (in this instance, oleic acid) and as a means of dissolving the fat-soluble vitamins and cholesterol in a minimal concentration of ethyl alcohol.[342,381] The medium also contained the salts of Earle's balanced salt solution, glucose, ferric nitrate, and phenol red. In the early work, the assays were made in roller tubes containing chick-embryo skeletal muscle cultivated directly on glass. Each culture was prepared from the least amount of tissue that would provide adequate growth areas. The media were renewed three times and, later, twice a week.[343] The cultures were examined frequently under the microscope and promising combinations of ingredients were detected by testing two or more solutions in the same experiment and comparing their effect on cell survival. Under these conditions, medium 199 supported cell life for an average period of 33 days, though odd cultures that chanced to contain even minute fragments of bone or cartilage continued to live for as long as 170 days;* and, for this reason, heart tissue was substituted for skeletal tissue. Eventually, the roller-tube method was abandoned as a routine means of screening new compounds. As the media were improved, these assays took longer and longer to complete and were finally replaced by an elaborate system of short-term replicate culture procedures devised by Earle and his associates (see p. 184). According to these procedures, as modified for use with chemically defined media,[378] the number of cells placed in each of a series of cultures was estimated by counting the cell nuclei in representative samples of a washed and continuously stirred cell suspension used as inoculum. After 7 and 12 days' incubation, the nuclei were freed from the cells of representative cultures comprising the replicate series and counted as before. Fluid renewals were accomplished twice a week by allowing any loose cells to settle to the

---

* Bensley, S. H., and Parker, R. C. Unpublished experiments.

tip of the culture flasks (Earle's T-flasks) and by replacing measured quantities of the cell-free medium. In addition to making nuclear counts, the size of the cell population was estimated by making deoxyribonucleic acid phosphorus (DNAP) determinations[231] on the cultures. Because good correlations were found between nuclear counts and DNAP determinations for cells cultivated both in natural and in defined media, the two methods could be used interchangeably, and one or the other was chosen, in advance, for each experiment.

When it was observed that medium 199 had an unusually high oxidation-reduction potential, Healy and his associates[232] attempted to bring it nearer the physiological range by increasing very considerably the levels of the three reducing agents already present in the medium, namely, cysteine, glutathione, and ascorbic acid. When these substances were tested separately at the higher levels, the two containing —SH groups increased the rate of cell multiplication and improved the appearance of the cells, whereas ascorbic acid had no apparent effect. When it was found that cysteine and glutathione could be used interchangeably, cysteine was incorporated at 2600 times and glutathione at 200 times their previous levels. Then, ascorbic acid was added at 1000 times its original level, in the hope that it would help maintain the —SH compounds in the reduced state. This medium was designated No. 612. Next, in order to study the effect of certain nucleic-acid constituents, a new basal medium (No. 635) was devised by omitting from solution 612 all the purines (adenine, guanine, xanthine, and hypoxanthine), the pyrimidines (thymine and uracil), as well as adenosinetriphosphate, adenylic acid, ribose, and deoxyribose. This medium gave a much better growth response than solution 612, but although a three- to four-fold increase in the cell population of replicate L-strain cultures was observed in one week, the cultures rarely survived longer than 40 days. The medium was used to advantage, however, in testing individual purines and pyrimidines (adenine, guanine, thymine, and uracil were toxic; cystosine was nontoxic), ribosenucleosides (only adenosine was toxic), ribosenucleotides (all nontoxic), and the deoxyribose nucleosides and nucleotides (all growth stimulating except those containing purine derivatives). Neither intact RNA nor its enzymic hydrolysate showed any effect on cell multiplication. In contrast, highly polymerized calf-thymus DNA, or oligonucleotides resulting from an enzymic hydrolysate of thymus DNA, gave four- and five-fold increases in the cell population of replicate cultures in one week. Eventually, the five deoxyribonucleosides (deoxyadenosine, deoxyguanosine, deoxycytidine, thymidine, and 5-methyldeoxycytidine) were added to the medium.[233]

In a study of certain coenzymes, preliminary tests[232] were made with Armour's porcine-liver coenzyme concentrate over a wide range of concentrations. Cultures of L-strain cells in solution 635 to which the concentrate was added at levels of 1 and 2 mg per cent yielded five- and six-fold increases in their cell population in seven days. When the active coenzymes known to be present in the crude concentrate (coenzyme A, diphosphopyridine nucleotide, and triphosphopyridine nucleotide) were tested individually, they had no effect; when they were tested together at levels of 36 μg, 78 μg and 42 μg per cent, respectively (for medium 703), they caused approximately the same rate of cell multiplication in short-term replicate culture assays as was obtained with the crude concentrate. Eventually, these and three additional coenzymes (cocarboxylase, flavin adenine dinucleotide, and uridinetriphosphate) were added to the medium.[233]

Because skeletal-muscle cultures that happened, accidentally, to contain bits of bone or cartilage lived much longer in medium 199 than those without, an attempt was made to discover the particular substance or substances responsible. When assays were made with various defined media that were supplemented with certain commercially available cartilage constituents, none was effective in lengthening the survival of chick-embryo tissues or in increasing the rate of proliferation of L cells. Nor were the cultures improved by adding crystalline calcium chondroitinsulfate prepared from beef tracheal cartilage. Eventually, a commercial preparation of crude chondroitinsulfuric acid (70 per cent purity) was found to be effective. Because this product had been prepared from cartilage by extraction with strong alkali, it seemed possible that the active material might be a degradation product. In any event, chondrosin, chondrosamine, and glucuronic acid were prepared from the commercial preparation, and of these glucuronic acid gave the same improvement in the cultures as had been obtained with the crude material. Similar results were obtained also with glucuronic acid prepared from 1-naphtholglucuronide and synthetic sodium glucuronate. Finally, after it seemed clear from other tests that were made[233] that the active material was indeed glucuronic acid, sodium glucuronate was incorporated in the medium at its most effective level.

Apart from the inclusion of the five deoxyribonucleosides, the six coenzymes, and sodium glucuronate, medium 858 (Table VIII) differed from earlier media in that only L-form amino acids were used. Also, five B vitamins (thiamine, riboflavin, niacin, niacinamide, and calcium pantothenate) present in medium 703 were omitted from medium 858 because they are constituents of the coenzymes that were added. Medium 858 yielded ten-fold increases in the population of L-strain cultures in seven days. Under the same conditions, medium 858 supplemented with 10–20 per cent horse serum yield 20- to 30-fold increases in seven days. In the meantime, it had been found[234] that the addition of more and more components to a medium may raise the level of trace metals, many of which are highly injurious to cells.

Before medium 858 was reported, a subsequent variation, No. 866, was being tested by ourselves and by interested investigators in other laboratories. Medium 866 was medium 858 supplemented with the three fatty acids, linoleic, linolenic, and arachidonic. But at the levels tested (1 gamma per ml), these substances did not improve the medium for L cells. Later, medium 858 was modified to give medium CMRL-1066,[377] which is now being distributed by the Connaught Medical Research Laboratories as a special service. CMRL-1066 is identical with medium 858 except that the fat soluble vitamins (A, D, E, and K), ferric nitrate, and sodium bicarbonate ($NaHCO_3$) included in medium 858 have been omitted from CMRL-1066; also, five B vitamins (thiamine, riboflavin, niacin, niacinamide, and sodium pantothenate) that were present in earlier media but omitted from medium 858 have again been added. To facilitate pH adjustments, a solution of 3.0 per cent $NaHCO_3$ (in a good grade of distilled water) is pressure filtered and stored in convenient aliquots. For new cultures, 2.5 ml of this solution is included in each 100 ml of finished medium. For older cultures with greatly increased cell populations, as much as 7.0 ml of the solution may be used for each 100 ml of medium (to provide the level of bicarbonate present in medium 858). CMRL-1066 contains 0.02 mgm per cent n-butyl parahydroxybenzoate, which offers protection from certain molds. When other antibiotics are required, they are added to the medium just before use. Detailed directions for the preparation of CMRL-1066 are given on page 77.

Medium 199 contained an almost complete supplement of amino acids and vitamins that were added at physiological levels without knowing how many of them were definitely required. Since then, Eagle[100, 101] has found that 12 amino acids (arginine, cystine, histidine, isoleucine, leucine, lysine, methionine, phenylalanine, threonine, tryptophan, tyrosine, and valine) are essential for the growth of both L-strain and HeLa-strain cultures, even in the presence of small quantities of whole or dialyzed serum. Although glutamine is re-

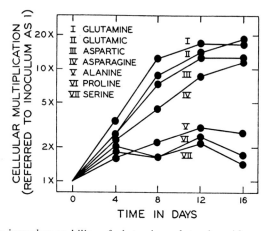

FIG. 16. The interchangeability of glutamine, glutamic acid, aspartic acid, and asparagine in supporting the growth of monkey-kidney cells in primary culture, and the failure of alanine, proline, or serine to substitute for glutamine. The basal medium, less glutamine, was supplemented with 3 per cent dialyzed serum, 0.1mM glycine, and the indicated amino acid at 1mM concentration. (H. Eagle et al.[109])

quired by both types of cells, it can be replaced by glutamic acid for HeLa cells but not for L cells.[111] Monkey-kidney cells in their first culture passage, 24 hr after explantation, required the same amino acids for survival and growth as cell lines propagated in cultures for years. With the established cell lines, glutamic acid substituted for glutamine only at extremely high levels. In monkey-kidney cell cultures, however, glutamic acid and glutamine were interchangeable, mole for mole; and aspartic acid and asparagine were also effective as glutamine substitutes (Fig. 16). More recently, Swim and R. F. Parker[501] have found the same amino acids to be required by a strain of human uterine fibroblasts (U12) propagated in a defined medium supplemented with 2.5 per cent dialyzed, chick embryo extract and 5 per cent dialyzed horse serum. In addition, a strain of rabbit fibroblasts (RM3) requires serine,[204] and the Walker rat carcinosarcoma

256 requires asparagine (in addition to glutamine).[358] On the other hand, Morgan and Morton[338] reported that glutamine and isoleucine are not required for the survival of chick-embryo heart tissues that had been depleted of nutritional reserves by a preliminary period of cultivation (3–4 days) in balanced salt solution. Morgan and Morton[336, 337] also reported that chick-heart fibroblasts have an absolute requirement for L-cystine that cannot be satisfied by any other sulphur compound tested, with the exception of L-cysteine. The requirement for methionine, however, could be demonstrated only in the presence of L-cystine. Under these conditions, L- and D-methionine were equally effective. The amino acid levels of five defined media are listed for comparison in Table VII.

Recent attempts have also been made to determine the vitamin requirements of cells cultivated in chemically defined media containing dialyzed serum. Eagle and his associates[102, 110] working with strain HeLa and Swim and R. F. Parker[500] working with their U12 strain have shown that specific vitamin deficiencies can be created in cultures when choline, folic acid, inositol, nicotinamide, pantothenic acid, pyridoxal, riboflavin, and thiamine are withdrawn. In fact, inositol was found to be most essential for 20 out of 21 cell lines examined by Eagle's group. But all of these cell lines survived and multiplied if the medium was supplemented with a small volume (5 per cent) of serum ultrafiltrate. Of the nine isomers of inositol that were tested, only myoinositol was effective. HeLa and U12 resemble other strains of human cells in their requirements for inositol.[110, 180] But Haff and Swim[205] found that strain RM3 (rabbit) does not require inositol and choline under comparable conditions. Although inositol does not appear to be required by L cells,[110] the other vitamins required for U12 and HeLa are essential for L.[102] Inositol is also required by mouse Sarcoma 180 in culture.[110] Moreover, as demonstrated by Eagle and his associates,[107] a strain-L culture can serve as a "feeder" that permits the sustained "parabiotic" growth of a culture of inositol-dependent cells (e.g., HeLa) separated from the feeder culture by a cellophane membrane (see also p. 76). Strain-L cells synthesize inositol from D-glucose, and minute amounts are released into the medium. Whatever the significance of these findings may be, they do emphasize the nutritional differences that exist between different strains of cells.

Glucose is generally added to tissue-culture media as an energy source, but other carbohydrates have also been tested. Harris and Kutsky[222]

have shown that chick-heart fibroblasts can utilize D-fructose or
D-mannose as well as D-glucose, whereas L-glucose, pentose, sucrose,
and lactose are inert for these cells. Essentially similar results have been
reported for HeLa cells, although these cells can utilize D-galactose as

TABLE VII

CONCENTRATION OF AMINO ACIDS IN MILLIMOLES
IN VARIOUS CHEMICALLY DEFINED MEDIA

Amino Acids	CMRL-1066 (Healy and R. C. Parker)	NCTC-109 (Evans et al.)	Eagle's Medium	MB 752/1 (Waymouth)	S-103 (Swim and R. F. Parker)
L-Alanine	0.28	0.35			0.3
L-α-Aminobutyric acid		0.05			
L-Arginine	0.33	0.15	0.6	0.36	0.8
L-Asparagine		0.06			
L-Aspartic acid	0.22	0.07		0.45	0.15
L-Cysteine	1.48	1.65		0.57	
L-Cystine	0.08	0.04	0.01	0.06	0.05
D-Glucosamine		0.02			
L-Glutamic acid	0.51	0.06		1.02	
L-Glutamine	0.68	0.93	2.0	2.39	2.0
Glycine	0.67	0.18		0.66	0.15
L-Histidine	0.10	0.13	0.2	0.78	0.05
Hydroxy-L-proline	0.08	0.03			0.15
L-Isoleucine	0.15	0.14	0.4	0.19	0.2
L-Leucine	0.46	0.16	0.4	0.38	0.2
L-Lysine	0.38	0.21	0.4	1.31	0.2
L-Methionine	0.10	0.03	0.1	0.34	0.1
L-Ornithine		0.06			
L-Phenylalanine	0.15	0.10	0.2	0.30	0.1
L-Proline	0.35	0.05		0.43	0.15
L-Serine	0.24	0.10			0.2
L-Taurine		0.03			
L-Threonine	0.25	0.16	0.4	0.63	0.4
L-Tryptophan	0.05	0.09	0.05	0.20	0.05
L-Tyrosine	0.22	0.09	0.2	0.22	0.1
L-Valine	0.21	0.21	0.4	0.55	0.4

well;[64] and Chang[61] has described the isolation of variant HeLa
strains that can grow on D(+)xylose, D-ribose, or sodium lactate as a
source of carbohydrate. Eagle and his associates[108] have found that
the amounts of glucose, mannose, fructose, and galactose metabolized
by various human cell strains vary according to substrate and its con-

centration but not in relation to the type of cell or the amount of growth obtained.

Interesting studies have also been made of the inorganic requirements of cells *in vitro*. Harris[218] found that CO_2 is beneficial for the outgrowth of cells from explanted chick-embryo tissues; and Swim and R. F. Parker[502] found that CO_2 was essential for six established strains of mammalian fibroblasts propagated in a chemically defined medium containing phosphite buffer (*see* p. 58) in place of bicarbonate and supplemented with dialyzed horse serum and dialyzed chick embryo extract. Under these conditions, the cells began to degenerate within five to ten days when the flasks were not stoppered. When the flasks were stoppered, sufficient CO_2 was produced by the cells to promote maximum proliferation. In fact, the rate of proliferation was the same whether the basal medium was supplemented with 0.02M sodium phosphite, or 0.02M sodium phosphite plus 0.005M sodium bicarbonate, or 0.02M sodium bicarbonate in the presence of a gas phase containing 5 per cent CO_2. Geyer and Chang[181] came to the same general conclusions after making HeLa experiments in which the CO_2 was absorbed by KOH. Eagle[104] has shown that Na^+, K^+, Mg^{++}, Ca^{++}, Cl^-, and $H_2PO_4^-$ are essential for the survival of L and HeLa cells, but neither cells required added CO_2 (as $NaHCO_3$). When Tris buffer at a concentration of 5mM was added as a partial buffer replacement, there was rapid acidification that necessitated daily changes of medium, but the cells multiplied at a normal rate. The results of these studies are not in accord with the conclusion of Harris[218] that the principal function of bicarbonate is in the maintenance of the appropriate intracellular pH. As suggested by Swim,[497] many mammalian cells resemble microorganisms in that sufficient CO_2 is produced metabolically to satisfy their nutritional needs; in any event, the multiplication of cells in closed flasks is unaffected by the omission of bicarbonate.

In recent years, defined media of considerable complexity have also been devised by Earle and his associates[38,131] and by Waymouth[531] for Earle's L cells; and somewhat less elaborate media have been devised by Rappaport[323] and Trowell[519] for short-term experiments and by Scherer,[510] Eagle,[105] Swim and R. F. Parker,[503] and Puck and his associates[414] for experiments in which protein supplements are added. The ingredients of ten defined media, all intended for mammalian cells, are listed in Table VIII.

TABLE VIII. Composition of Some Recently Developed Chemically Defined Media (*milligrams per liter*)

	199[339]	858[233]	NCTC-1098[38,131]	CMRL-1066[377]	Scherer's[510] MS*	Rappaport's[323] SM-2 Medium	Stáim's[503] S-103	Eagle's[205] Basal Medium†	Troxell's[519] T8	Waymouth's[531] MB 752/1
L-Alanine	50‡	25	31.48	25			27		21	75
L-α-Aminobutyric acid			5.51							
L-Arginine·HCl	70	70	25.76§	70		60§	168	105§		60
L-Asparagine			8.09							
L-Aspartic acid	60‡	30	9.91	30			20		47	90
L-Cysteine·HCl		260||	259.90	260||		100	14¶		
L-Cystine	20‡	20	10.49	20				24		15
L-Glutamic acid	150‡||	75	8.26	75		280	292			150
L-Glutamine	100	100	135.73	100		150	11	292		350
Glycine	50	50	13.51	50		10	10||			50
L-Histidine·HCl	20	20||	19.73§	20||			20	31§	10	150
Hydroxy-L-proline	10	10	4.09	10						
L-Isoleucine	40‡	20	18.04	20		300	26	52	26	25
L-Leucine	120‡‡	60	20.44	60		200	26	52	26	50
L-Lysine·HCl	70	70	30.75§	70		60§	37	58§	36	240
L-Methionine	30‡	15	4.44	15		12	15	15	15‡	50
L-Ornithine·HCl			7.38							
L-Phenylalanine	50‡	25	16.53	25		90	16	32	33‡	50
L-Proline	40	40	6.13	40			17			50
L-Serine	50‡	25	10.75	25			21			
L-Taurine			4.18							
L-Threonine	60‡	30	18.93	30		60	48	48	48‡	75
L-Tryptophan	20‡‡	10	17.50	10		5	10	10	4	40
L-Tyrosine	40‡	40	16.44	40		145	18	36	18	40
L-Valine	50‡	25	25.00	25		170	47	46	23	65
p-Aminobenzoic acid	0.05	0.05	0.125	0.05	0.01	0.15			35	
Biotin	0.01	0.01	0.025	0.01	0.01	0.1				0.02
Calcium pantothenate	0.01	0.50	0.025	0.50	0.4	1.00	1.2	1		1.0
Choline chloride	0.50	0.01	1.25	0.01	1.4	8.00	1.4	1		250
Folic acid	0.01	0.05	0.025	0.05	0.01	3.50	2.2	1		0.4
Inositol	0.05		0.125	0.05	1.4	0.15	2.15	2		1.0**
Niacin	0.025		0.125	0.025	0.4					
Niacinamide	0.025	0.025	0.062	0.025	0.4			1		1.0
Pyridoxal·HCl	0.025		0.062	0.025	0.4	0.115	0.6	1		
Pyridoxamine·2HCl			0.062			0.15				
Pyridoxine·HCl	0.025	0.025	0.062	0.025		0.15	1.0			1.0
Riboflavin	0.01		0.025	0.01	0.4	0.015	0.38	0.1		1.0
Thiamine·HCl	0.01		0.025	0.01	1.0		1.7	1	17	10.0
Vitamin B12			0.1							0.2
Vitamin A	0.10	0.10	0.25							
Ascorbic acid (vit. C)	0.05	50.0	49.90	50.0		50.0				17.5
α-Tocopherol phosphate (vit. E)	0.01	0.01	0.025							
Calciferol (vit. D)	0.10	0.10	0.25							
Menadione (vit. K)	0.01	0.01	0.025							
Adenine	10.0									
Guanine·HCl	0.3									
Hypoxanthine	0.3									25.0

Thymine	0.3									
Uracil	0.3									
Xanthine	0.3									
Adenylic acid	0.2									
Deoxyadenosine		10.0	10.0	10.0						
Deoxycytidine		10.0	10.0¶	10.0						
Deoxyguanosine		10.0	10.0	10.0						
5-Methylcytosine			0.1							
5-Methyldeoxycytidine		0.1		0.1						
Thymidine		10.0	10.0	10.0						
2-Deoxy-D-ribose	0.5									
D-Ribose	0.5				0.4					
Cocarboxylase		1.0	1.0	1.0						
Coenzyme A		2.5	2.5	2.5						
Diphosphopyridine nucleotide		7.0	7.0	7.0						
Flavin adenine dinucleotide		1.0	1.0	1.0						
Triphosphopyridine nucleotide		1.0	1.0	1.0						
Uridinetriphosphate		1.0	1.0	1.0						
Lecithin						25				
Tween 80 (oleic acid)	5.0	5.0	12.5	5.0						
Cholesterol	0.2	0.2		0.2		10				
Glucose	1000.0	1000.0	1000.0	1000.0	2000	1000	1000	1000	4000	5000
D-glucosamine·HCl			3.2							
Glucuronolactone			1.8							
Glutathione	0.05	10.0	10.1	10.0						15
Sodium acetate	50.0	50.0	50.0	83.0††	500††					
Sodium glucuronate		4.2‖	1.8	4.2‖						
Sodium pyruvate					500	400				
Adenosinetriphosphate	10.0									
Insulin									50	
Ethanol (as diluent for fat-soluble constituents)		16.0		16.0		394				
NaCl	6800	6800	6800	6800	8000	8000	6800	6800	6100	6000
KCl	400	400	400	400	400	400	400	400	450	150
$CaCl_2$	200	200	200	200	140	400	200	200 (0)	220	120**
$MgCl_2 \cdot 6H_2O$						100		200		240
$MgSO_4 \cdot 7H_2O$	200	200	200	200	200	100	200		250	200
NaH_2PO_4	140‖	140‖	140‖	140‖		60	140‖	150 (1500)**	450**	
Na_2HPO_4					60**	60				300
KH_2PO_4					150					80
$NaHCO_3$	2200	2200	2200	2200	1050	1100	2200	2000	2820	2240
$CoCl_2 \cdot 6H_2O$						0.05				
$CuSO_4 \cdot 5H_2O$						0.1				
$Fe(NO_3)_3 \cdot 9H_2O$	0.1	0.1				0.4				
$MnCl_2 \cdot 4H_2O$						0.1				
$(NH_4)_2MoO_4$						0.2				
$ZnSO_4 \cdot 7H_2O$						1.0				

* Medium also contains 300 mg/l Parenamine (Winthrop-Stearns, Inc., New York 18, N.Y.), which is an acid hydrolysate of casein supplied as a 15 per cent solution fortified with DL-tryptophan. Revised composition supplied by W. F. Scherer (personal communication).

† Medium is supplemented with 5–10 per cent whole or dialyzed serum. For cells propagated in suspension, amounts in parentheses are used.

‡ DL-form. § Free base. ‖ 1 × H_2O. ¶ 1 × HCl. ** 2 × H_2O. †† 3 × H_2O.

Since the last edition of this book appeared, various sublines of Earle's L cells have been propagated indefinitely, with regular subculture, in at least three defined media, namely, CMRL-1066 (Fig. 17), NCTC-109, and Waymouth's MB 752/1. Thus, it has finally become possible, 50 years after the pioneer experiments of Lewis and Lewis, to make long-term nutritional experiments with at least a few types of cells under conditions that can be rigidly controlled without

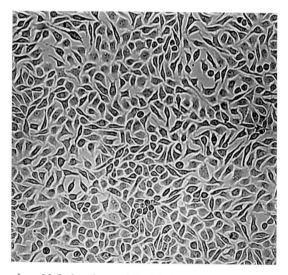

Fig. 17. Two-day-old flask culture of Earle's L-strain cells from mouse 32 months after subline had become established in unsupplemented chemically defined medium CMRL-1066, with regular subculture. (R. C. Parker, unpublished data, 1959.) × 100.

plasma, serum, or embryo extract. A defined medium that is generally adequate for all types of cells has not yet been devised; and media that are adequate for certain cell types in stationary cultures (Fig. 18) are seldom satisfactory for the same cells in agitated suspensions (*see* Chap. XII). Recently, Eagle[106] found that human (HeLa, HeLa-S3, KB) and mouse (L-929) cells can be propagated regularly in suspension in a protein-free basal medium if the culture is equilibrated across a cellophane membrane with medium containing 1–5 per cent dialyzed serum and a dialyzed pancreatic extract (Viokase, Viobin Corp., Monticello, Ill.). Because only occasional and relatively slow growth was obtained when the enzyme preparation was omitted from the "feeder" compartment containing protein, it was suggested that the primary role of serum protein in suspension cultures of mammalian cells is to provide essential growth factor(s) of small molecular weight, either initially bound to the serum protein or formed from it on proteolysis. When the factor or factors so provided have been identified, it should become possible to devise special media for particular cell types and to foster or suppress at will the conditions that promote normal cellular differentiation.

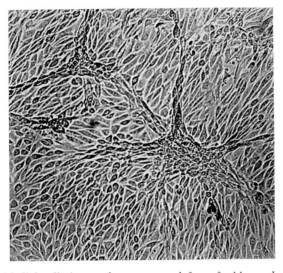

FIG. 18. Epithelial cells in a culture prepared from freshly explanted monkey-kidney tissue and maintained for 91 days in unsupplemented chemically defined medium 858.[232] During this period, the cells had been subcultured twice. (R. C. Parker *et al.*[377]) × 100.

Preparation of a Chemically Defined Medium (CMRL-1066)

The ingredients of solution CMRL-1066 are obtained commercially and employed without further purification. Aqueous stock solutions are prepared with water passed through a Barnstead still and then through a mixed-bed, ion-exchange Barnstead Bantam Demineralizer (see p. 29). All stock solutions except No. 1 are stored in convenient aliquots at $-20°$ C, without filtration. A fresh lot of solution 1 is made up each time a new batch of medium is prepared. The various stock solutions are prepared as follows:

SOLUTION 1

To 400–450 ml of water stirred continuously and heated to about 80° C are added the following: phenol red (water soluble), 20 mg; L-alanine, 25 mg; L-arginine hydrochloride, 70 mg; L-aspartic acid, 30 mg; L-cysteine hydrochloride hydrate, 260 mg; L-glutamic acid, 75 mg; glycine, 50 mg; L-histidine hydrochloride hydrate, 20 mg; hydroxy-L-proline, 10 mg; L-isoleucine, 20 mg; L-leucine, 60 mg; L-lysine hydrochloride, 70 mg; L-methionine, 15 mg; L-phenylalanine, 25 mg; L-proline, 40 mg; L-serine, 25 mg; L-threonine, 30 mg; L-tryptophan, 10 mg; L-valine, 25 mg; ascorbic acid, 50 mg; cystine, 20 mg; and L-tyrosine, 40 mg. After the solution has cooled to room temperature, the following are added: sodium acetate trihydrate, 82.9 mg; L-glutamine, 100 mg; dihydrostreptomycin sulfate (if required), 100 mg; sodium glucuronate monohydrate, 4.2 mg; deoxyadenosine, 10 mg; deoxyguanosine, 10 mg; deoxycytidine, 10 mg; thymidine, 10 mg; and glutathione, 10 mg. The ingredients of Earle's balanced salt solution are then added, as follows: sodium chloride, 6.8 Gm; potassium chloride, 0.4 Gm; calcium chloride, 0.2 Gm; magnesium sulfate heptahydrate, 0.2 Gm; sodium dihydrogen phosphate mono-hydrate, 0.14 Gm; sodium bicarbonate, 2.2 Gm; and glucose, 1.0 Gm. Finally, the volume of the solution is adjusted to 500 ml with water.

SOLUTION 2

The following partially purified coenzymes are dissolved in a final volume of 10 ml of water: 70 mg diphosphopyridine nucleotide (DPN); 10 mg triphosphopyridine nucleotide (TPN); 25 mg coenzyme A (CoA); 10 mg cocarboxylase (TPP); 10 mg flavin adenine dinucleotide (FAD); 10 mg uridinetriphosphate (UTP). When large volumes (e.g., 4 l or more) of medium are prepared, the coenzymes are weighed directly into solution 1.

SOLUTION 3

The following B vitamins are dissolved in 200 ml (final volume) of water: thiamine hydrochloride, 10 mg; riboflavin, 10 mg; pyridoxine hydrochloride, 25 mg; pyridoxal hydrochloride, 25 mg; niacin, 25 mg; niacinamide, 25 mg; calcium pantothenate, 10 mg; choline chloride, 500 mg; *i*-inositol, 50 mg; and *p*-aminobenzoic acid, 50 mg. The stock solution consists of a 1:50 dilution of this solution with water.

SOLUTION 4

Ten milligrams of D-biotin and 10 mg of folic acid are dissolved in 100 ml of Earle's balanced salt solution. The stock solution consists of a 1:100 dilution of this solution with water.

SOLUTION 5

An alcoholic tincture of cholesterol, 10 mg per ml in 95 per cent ethanol, and a 5 per cent aqueous solution of Tween 80 are prepared. Two milliliters of the tincture of cholesterol is placed in a 100-ml volumetric flask followed by 20 mg of *n*-butyl parahydroxybenzoate and 10 ml of the Tween 80 solution. The mixture is brought to a final volume of 100 ml with water and warmed under the tap, if necessary, to bring the cholesterol into complete solution. The final stock solution consists of 10 ml of this solution adjusted to 100 ml with water.

SOLUTION 6

Ten milligrams of 5-methyldeoxycytidine are dissolved in 100 ml of water.

To prepare one liter of solution CMRL-1066, the various constituents of the final medium (as also the ingredients of solution 1) are mixed in a 5-l distillation flask with a large central and a small vertical side neck. The large central neck accommodates a bent glass stirring rod attached to a small motor, and the ingredients are added through the side neck. The stock solutions are combined as follows: solution 1, 500 ml; solutions 2 and 6, 1 ml each; solutions 3, 4, and 5, 10 ml each. The final volume is adjusted to 1 l by the addition of water, and the completed medium is sterilized by passage through UF fritted glass filters (Corning) or Ertel (model 10) EO ultrafine asbestos pads and stored at 4° C. Just before use, 1 µg per ml of sodium penicillin G may be added. (If protein supplements are required, they are added before filtration.)

Preparation of Chemically Defined Media from
Mixed Ingredients Stored in Solid Form

Swim and R. F. Parker[503] prepare chemically defined media from ingredients that are weighed, mixed, and stored in solid form. This procedure prevents the rapid deterioration that often occurs when substances are stored in solution, even at 4° C. It also simplifies the storage problem and makes it possible to carry out long term experiments with media of constant composition. Thus, if the ingredients for 200 l of medium are mixed and stored in convenient aliquots, fresh batches of the medium can be prepared at frequent intervals.

In the preparation of medium S103 (see Table VIII), all of the ingredients for 40 l, with the exception of cystine and glutamine, are placed in a porcelain ball-mill jar of 1.25-qt capacity, which is then filled to about one-third its volume with flint pebbles 0.5–1 in. in diameter. (A jar of 1.3-gal capacity will accommodate sufficient chemicals for 200 l of S103.) The jar is placed overnight in a vacuum desiccator evacuated to approximately 0.005 mm of mercury by means of a suitable pump. (As a safety measure, glass desiccators must always be covered with an adequate guard.) Following desiccation, the jar is rolled overnight, after which the powder is separated from the pebbles by passage through a stainless-steel sieve. Appropriate quantities of the powder are then dispensed immediately into a series of screw-cap reagent bottles (widemouthed, amber color) that are stored in a desiccator at 4° C or −20° C. Alternatively, the bottles may be sealed with plastic tape or with caps fitted with polyethylene liners. It should be emphasized that the cover of the ball mill must be fitted with a rubber gasket, and every precaution must be taken to remove all water from the chemicals before grinding and to protect the finished powder from moisture. In preparing the medium, the powder is added stepwise to an appropriate quantity of water agitated by a magnetic stirrer. When the powder is completely dissolved, cystine is added (from a 5mM stock solution in 0.025N hydrochloric acid that is stored at room temperature), the pH is adjusted with 5 per cent CO_2 in air, and the medium is sterilized by filtration. Because glutamine is unstable in solution, it is added to the medium, just before use, from a 200mM stock solution that is stored at −20° C. Fat soluble vitamins, ethanol, and Tween 80 are always omitted from powdered mixtures.

VII

Media Containing Naturally Occurring Ingredients

ALTHOUGH certain cell lines have become adapted to continuous multiplication in chemically defined media (*see* p. 76), it is still necessary in most undertakings to depend on naturally occurring substances derived from the organism. In any event, it is not yet possible to place freshly explanted cells and tissues in defined media with any assurance that they can be propagated in these media indefinitely. At best, and with the exceptions just noted, chemically defined media serve either as maintenance media for studies in which vigorous cell multiplication is not required or as basal media that are rendered more adequate by the addition of protein supplements.

Today, many laboratories supplement balanced salt solutions containing glucose and antibiotics with enzymatic protein hydrolysates, yeast extract, peptones, blood-serum fractions, and other materials, almost all of which may be obtained commercially. Other laboratories add protein supplements of one sort or another to chemically defined media of considerable complexity. And still other research groups continue to make excellent use of the traditional three-part mixture of blood plasma, embryo-tissue extract, and balanced saline. In the present chapter, attention will be given to some of these naturally occurring nutrient materials and some of the methods used in their preparation. Descriptions will also be given of some of the more generally useful complex media containing naturally occurring ingredients.

Blood Plasma

The first tissue cultures were made by Harrison[225] in clotted frog lymph. Burrows[40] substituted a coagulum prepared from chicken plasma (whole blood minus the corpuscles). For many years, however, it was assumed that blood plasma provided only a supporting structure for cells that were nourished by other materials added to the medium, notably embryo extract (*see* p. 99). Eventually, it was found[285,372,374] that plasma (or serum) provided a complete nutrient in which cells could survive and multiply slowly for extended periods under conditions that resembled in many respects those found in the body. Today, plasma is still being used to advantage for the following purposes: (1) to provide a nutritive substrate and a supporting structure for many types of cultures, just as it also provides a matrix for new cells during the repair of injury in the body; (2) to provide a means of conditioning the surface of glass for better attachment of cells; (3) to provide a means of protecting cells and tissues from excessive traumatic damage during subculture; (4) to provide some degree of protection from sudden changes in the environment at times of fluid change; and (5) to provide localized pockets of conditioned medium around cells.

PREPARATION OF ADULT CHICKEN PLASMA

For culture work, plasma from the adult chicken is preferred to mammalian plasma because it forms a clear, solid coagulum even when diluted several times. As a rule, mammalian plasma is either too opaque for good optical work or else it fails to produce solid clots. Except in experiments in which all protein-containing materials (cells and the constituents of naturally occurring media) must be derived from the same species, it is rarely necessary to use homologous plasma. Moreover, when plasma is combined with homologous serum and tissue, there is a greater tendency for clot liquefaction than when heterologous systems are used.

Blood that has been drawn without an anticoagulant tends to coagulate spontaneously if allowed to stand for a time in plain glass tubes. If coagulation occurs before centrifugation, it is too late, of course, to prepare plasma, but the serum may be separated. Mammalian blood and chicken blood drawn with a syringe coagulate almost immediately after withdrawal unless an anticoagulant (e.g., heparin) is used or unless they are collected in chilled tubes lined with a thin layer of paraffin or in tubes treated with silicone. Chicken blood that is taken from the carotid with a glass cannula, without an anticoagulant, may be drawn in plain glass tubes, provided the plasma yield is transferred immediately after centrifugation to paraffined or siliconed tubes for final storage. Both plasma and serum may be stored indefinitely after they have been dried from the frozen state.

Depending upon the quantity of plasma or of serum required, one of two procedures may be employed in drawing the blood: (1) bleeding from the carotid artery; or (2) bleeding from the wing vein. In the first instance, it is desirable to bleed the chicken to death at one operation. It is suggested that cockerels be used exclusively for this purpose; since they are larger than pullets, they give a greater yield, their vessels are easier to locate, and, being more hardy, they are less likely to die under anesthesia. Also, as Hanks[209] has pointed out, plasma from laying hens, which contains higher levels of calcium and phosphorus than plasma from cockerels, may lead to calcification of the clot in culture systems in which mammalian serum and high levels of embryo extract (more than 5 per cent) are also present. The cockerels should not be more than one year of age. To reduce the serum lipids they should be starved for about 36 hr before they are bled. Cockerels bled from the carotid artery give from 140 to 160 ml of blood. The plasma yield varies from 40 to 60 per cent of the whole blood. Generally, over 95 per cent of the plasma may be recovered as serum (*see* p. 91).

In the second instance, when relatively small quantities of plasma or serum are required at infrequent intervals or when it is necessary to have a constant supply of plasma or serum from one bird, it is advisable to bleed from a wing vein. From 20 to 25 ml of blood can be taken from a chicken as often as once a week without seriously impairing its health.

The details of these procedures are given on the following pages.

Preparation of Paraffined Storage Tubes for Plasma

Cork stoppers to fit the tubes to be paraffined are packed for sterilization in such a way that they may later be removed from their container one by one with the fingers, without touching any of those that remain. If only a few are required, certain types of sheet-metal, test-tube racks will accommodate them during sterilization. Otherwise, a large box of sheet metal (without a lid) is fitted with a set of removable trays, each of which is perforated with a series of holes just large enough to receive the base of the cork and spaced far enough apart to allow each cork to be removed separately. The box is wrapped with two layers of paper and sterilized by dry heat. A pair of long test-tube forceps (10 to 12 in. long) are also sterilized by dry heat. Six or more cotton hand towels are sterilized by autoclaving.

A quantity of paraffin (melting point, 56° to 62° C), the amount depending upon the number of tubes to be prepared, is melted in a large, covered, enamel container. The tubes (18 × 100 mm) are submerged in the paraffin in such a manner that no air will be trapped within them. The container, with heavy wrapping paper tied over the top, is then sterilized in the hot-air oven for one hour at 160° C.

After the paraffin bath has cooled to the point where it is no longer fuming, it is placed on an electric stove located on a table in a dust-proof room. Sterile towels are spread out elsewhere on the same table. With long forceps, the tubes are then removed from the melted paraffin, drained over the container and allowed to stand, open end down, on a sterile towel, for further draining. As soon as the paraffin coating begins to congeal, the tubes are transferred to an unused part of the towel. By the time all of them have been taken out of the bath, those earliest removed will be hard enough to cork. But first, to prevent particles of paraffin from breaking off and falling into the tube, the rim of each is heated very slightly over a small flame. At no time during these operations should the tubes be held open end up, in a vertical position. After the tubes have been corked, they are wrapped in two thicknesses of sterile towels, for storage in the refrigerator.

Bleeding a Chicken from the Carotid Artery

Only minimal sterility precautions need be taken if the blood is to be processed immediately for plasma or serum that is to be used together with antibiotics or for serum that is to be filtered. The procedure to be described here is designed for those who may require relatively large quantities of plasma that is to be used as part of a culture medium that does not contain antibiotics.

MATERIALS REQUIRED

(a) *Articles packed in a dressing drum for sterilization in the autoclave* (*see* p. 37):

Mason jar, containing irrigator (large rubber bulb with special irrigating pipette attached) and saline solution

2 small enamel bowls (for saline and Dakin's solution) wrapped in unbleached muslin

gauze sponges and pads (packed separately in muslin bags)

neck sheet for chicken, of dark sateen, 1 × 1½ yd, with narrow, oval opening in center, about 5 in. long

100 ml beaker for tincture of iodine

4 hand towels

scrub-up bag (at top of drum) containing materials for hand sterilization.

(b) *Instruments packed in a metal box for sterilization by dry heat.* (They are arranged layer upon layer in order of use; each layer is protected with a black sateen pad filled with nonabsorbent cotton. The box is wrapped with paper before sterilization— *see* p. 40):

curved suture needles

suture silk, cut in 4-in. lengths

1 pr. medium-sized scissors for cutting sutures

2 pr. very fine, straight scissors for cutting into the vessel

2 very small Dieffenbach's serrefines; swivel construction; straight (in gauze sponge)

1 pr. fine, straight forceps

1 pr. fine, curved forceps

1 pr. curved, mosquito forceps

1 pr. straight, mosquito forceps

6 hemostats

2 scalpels

4 pr. towel forceps

1 pr. sponge forceps holding sponge for iodine (at top of box)

(c) *Glass bell cannulae:*

Although various types of metal cannulae are on the market, excellent ones can be blown from glass. A simple cannula of this sort (Figs. 19 and 20) was devised by Carrel. The tip is very fine, smooth, and ground off at an angle. Just back of the tip, there is a slight constriction in the glass, at which point a ligature may be applied after the cannula has been inserted in the vessel. The cannula is about 10 cm long. Its outlet is surrounded by a bell-like hood large enough to cover completely the mouth of the bleeding tube and, thereby, to furnish pro-

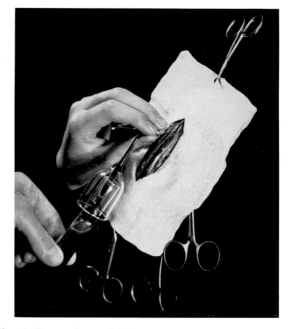

FIG. 19. Glass bell cannula used in bleeding a chicken from the carotid artery. The apron protects the collecting tube from falling dust particles.

tection from falling dust particles. For sterilization, the cannulae are enclosed in gauze pads and packed over gauze-covered cotton pads in a metal container.

(d) *Bleeding tubes:*

Measuring 18 × 100 mm and fitted with cork stoppers, these tubes are wrapped in paper, in lots of four or five, and sterilized by dry heat. Before the bleeding is started, they are set upright in a bowl of cracked ice. These tubes are not paraffined. The length of the tubes is important; when they are packed in ice for centrifugation, they should extend far enough beyond the carrier of the centrifuge head to protect their tops from water.

(e) *Paraffined storage tubes for plasma:*

Paraffined storage tubes are set upright in a separate bowl of cracked ice. They are described on page 83.

(f) *Two additional bowls of cracked ice:*

One bowl is provided to receive the filled bleeding tubes, the other to provide ice for packing the tubes in the centrifuge carriers.

(g) *Chicken board:*

A board measuring about 13 × 17 in. with canoe cleats at the corners is useful in attaching the wings and legs. Each wing is held down with a sandbag (about 5 × 14 in. weighing from 6 to 7 lb).

PROCEDURE

Two tables are used: The chicken is placed on one, the instruments and materials on the other. As soon as the operator has put on a sterile mask, the dressing drum, instrument box, and other materials are set out, as well as iodine, saline and Dakin's solution. The scrub-up materials are removed from the dressing drum and placed in the scrub-up room. The operator then cleanses his hands in the usual way (*see* p. 50), puts on a sterile gown, and arranges the operating materials.

In the meantime, the chicken, ventral side up, has been strapped to the operating board by the anesthetist, and the feathers have been plucked from the neck and upper breast region. It is then covered securely with a towel and transferred to the operating room, where it is etherized very slightly (from a small metal cone), just enough to keep it fairly quiet. Whenever possible the operator should have three assistants: one to anesthetize and to support the neck of the chicken, one to handle the bleeding tubes, and one to centrifuge the blood as it is taken and to draw off the plasma. The bleeding can be accomplished with fewer assistants, but it takes considerably longer.

As soon as the chicken is ready the operator swabs the plucked area with iodine and arranges the neck sheet so that the opening lies over the place of incision. Each end of this opening is clamped to the skin with towel forceps. A medium, ventral incision is made through the skin of the neck with one of the scalpels, and the skin is clamped back to the neck sheet with hemostats. A median incision is then made through the subcutaneous tissue with the second scalpel. With the curved mosquito forceps and the fine, straight forceps, one of the carotid arteries is now freed from the surrounding musculature and all adherent subcutaneous connective tissue. (The carotid arteries, of which there are two, lying side by side, are fairly deep.) The freed portion of the artery should be about 4 cm long. The distal end is now ligated, and the proximal end clamped with a serrefine. After the vessel has been cleansed with saline solution by means of the irrigator, a small, clean incision is made in its wall midway between the serrefine and the ligature. The serrefine is then opened for a moment to enable the blood to flow freely and to flush out any clots that may have formed between the serrefine and the incision. These clots, containing traces of tissue juice from injured cells, may, if collected in the first tube, induce further coagulation. Before the glass cannula is inserted, the incision is thoroughly washed with saline solution, and a sterile gauze pad, with a slitlike opening, is placed over the field of operation. If necessary, a ligature may be applied to hold the cannula in place.

The blood is now collected in bleeding tubes that are held under the bell of the cannula until they are about three-quarters full (Fig. 19). After filling each tube, the outflow may be controlled by means of the serrefine or preferably by pressing the forefinger on the vessel, so as not to produce injury. For a long bleeding, e.g., 16 to 18 tubes, it is generally wise to change the cannula, especially if the blood begins to come slowly.

As soon as a few tubes of blood have been drawn, they are centrifuged in ice-packed carriers for 6 min at 3000 r.p.m., or for 7 min at 2800 r.p.m. After centrifugation, the clear, supernatant plasma is withdrawn with a large bulb pipette capable of holding 100 ml. This pipette is fitted with a mouth tube and operated by suction. In removing the plasma, extreme care is taken not to disturb the underlying blood cells. The plasma from five or six tubes may be drawn off at one filling and then distributed into the paraffined storage tubes, with about 6 ml in each.

If any part of the plasma is to be processed for serum, the plasma is pipetted into unparaffined tubes, a drop or two of embryo tissue juice is added to each, and the tubes are left in the incubator overnight to ensure complete coagulation (*see* p. 93).

If the chicken has been only partially bled and is to be used again, a ligature is placed at the proximal end of the artery, just above the incision, and the serrefine is removed. After all of the exposed tissues have been thoroughly washed with saline solution, the outer skin is brought back into place and sutured. A few weeks later, the neck may again be opened and the chicken bled to death from the other carotid.

Bleeding a Chicken from the Wing

The blood is withdrawn by means of a 20-ml syringe and 2-in. Luer needle (gauge No. 18 or 19) previously sterilized in dry heat and cooled in the refrigerator. After a few feathers have been plucked from the inner part of the wing, the bird is laid on its side and the wing is supported on a sandbag. The surface is swabbed with iodine, and the needle inserted into the large vein quickly, with the least possible degree of injury to the tissues, against the direction of flow, that is, towards the tip of the wing. In withdrawing the blood, the plunger must not be pulled with too much force. If the needle has been properly inserted, the blood will flow freely into the syringe.

When the desired amount of blood has been taken, the needle is removed from the syringe and the blood injected slowly into chilled paraffined storage tubes. The tubes are then centrifuged in ice-packed carriers for 4–5 min at 3000 r.p.m. After centrifugation, the clear supernatant plasma is transferred to fresh tubes. These tubes must be paraffined and thoroughly chilled, if the yield is to be retained as plasma.

PREPARATION OF CHICKEN PLASMA WITH
AN ANTICOAGULANT

When heparin is used in bleeding a fowl for plasma, sufficient heparin for 100 ml of blood (e.g., 1 ml of saline containing 1 mg of heparin) is placed in a graduated 250-ml centrifuge bottle fitted with a glass filling bell and a glass or metal cap, as shown in Fig. 20. (At the time of bleeding, the protective cap is removed from the tube of the filling bell and the bleeding cannula, with its own bell-like apron, is inserted.) A second centrifuge bottle, without heparin, is prepared in the same manner for whatever blood is drawn in excess of 100 ml. If 100 ml of blood is collected in the first container, the plasma that is prepared from it will therefore contain a known amount of heparin (i.e., 1:100,000). The blood that is collected in the second container, without heparin, may be allowed to coagulate for the preparation of serum (see p. 93). As an alternative, the balance of the yield may be collected in plain glass tubes and centrifuged in ice-packed carriers for the preparation of plasma without heparin.

If sodium citrate is used, it may be prepared as a 10 per cent solution in saline. For 100 ml of blood, 2 ml will be required.

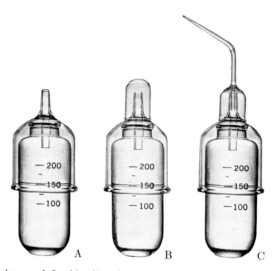

FIG. 20. Device used for bleeding from the carotid artery of a chicken directly into a 250-ml centrifuge bottle, when an anticoagulant is present: (*A*) centrifuge bottle fitted with a large filling bell; (*B*) tube of filling bell protected by glass cap; and (*C*) glass cap removed and outlet of bleeding cannula (*see* Fig. 19) inserted into tube of filling bell.

PREPARATION OF MAMMALIAN PLASMA

Small animals (rats, mice, and guinea-pigs) may be bled either from the heart or from the aorta. Unless an anticoagulant is used, the first means should not be employed, for when the heart is punctured, the entire yield may coagulate before centrifugation. As the needle pierces the skin, the muscles, and the mucous membranes, it collects a certain amount of tissue juice that is drawn up into the syringe along with the blood. Larger animals, such as rabbits, cats, and dogs, are usually bled either from the jugular vein or from the carotid artery.

In bleeding small animals from the heart, only a small amount of ether is given. The animal is placed in a battery jar, with a piece of cotton soaked in ether. As soon as the animal is unconscious, it is removed from the jar and stretched on a board, ventral side up. The hair is clipped from the area over the heart. After the skin has been prepared, the point at which to insert the needle is determined by palpation, and the region is painted with 7 per cent tincture of iodine. Then, with a 1½-in. Luer needle (gauge No. 19), fitted to a 20-ml Luer syringe, the skin is pierced, and the needle is pressed downwards very gently, through the anterior wall of the heart. The posterior wall should not be punctured. Ordinarily the pressure of the blood flow will force back the plunger. Once the blood has been obtained, it is transferred to chilled paraffined tubes and centrifuged for 3–4 min in the manner described on page 88.

In bleeding small animals from the aorta, a median ventral incision is made in the abdomen of the anesthetized animal, the internal organs are gently pushed aside, and the aorta is exposed. For a mouse, a 2-ml Luer syringe will be adequate; for larger animals a 10- or 20-ml syringe is necessary. Usually, a gauge No. 23 needle, ⅝ in. long, may be used. The syringe itself must be well chilled. In addition, for such small quantities of blood, it is usually safer to use a solution of heparin. As an alternative the wall of the syringe and the piston may be lubricated with sterile olive oil of good quality. After the vessel has been exposed, it is washed with warm saline solution. Because of limited space, a serrefine cannot easily be used. Instead, a little pressure may be applied with the finger at the proximal end of the aorta. The distal end is clamped off with a mosquito clamp, and the aorta is punctured close to the proximal end. The moment the needle has been inserted, the finger pressure is released. At first, no force should be used in withdrawing the plunger; towards the end, a very slight pressure may be necessary. The blood is placed immediately in small, well-chilled paraffined tubes, 10 × 75 mm, and centrifuged for 2–3 min at 3000 r.p.m.

Blood Serum

Blood serum (plasma minus fibrinogen), with or without other nutritive substances, may be used either as the entire culture medium or as the fluid phase of a medium consisting partly of a plasma coagulum. For many years, it was assumed that all serum was toxic, that plasma was useful only as a supporting structure, and that the nutritive requirements of the cells were supplied by the embryo extract that was usually added to the medium. Eventually, however, it was found possible to cultivate tissues in serum alone, without plasma or extract. In 1928, des Ligneris[285] reported the successful cultivation of many mammalian tissues in diluted serum; and later, Parker[373,374] cultivated chick tissues for extended periods both in heparinized plasma and in serum. Carrel[51] described a method for the cultivation of blood monocytes in diluted serum (see p. 190); and Baker[12] reported that chicken serum and embryo extract provided a complete medium for the continued proliferation of chick fibroblasts, whereas extract alone was insufficient. By that time, many investigators[113,179,280] were already using serum in addition to embryo extract in their culture media. Simms,[483] and Simms and Sanders[484] introduced an ultrafiltrate of serum that was used as a basal medium for many purposes, including the propagation of viruses;[379,380] and Fischer and his associates,[158] who worked extensively with dialyzed media, also stressed the importance in cell nutrition of the low-molecular-weight growth factors provided by serum. Eventually, Sanford and her associates[470] used the Cohn low-temperature fractionation procedures[71] to prepare a variety of horse-serum fractions that were tested on L cells. Although all fractions isolated were found to promote growth, the gross-globulin fraction could be substituted for the large molecular portion of horse serum to yield comparable increases in cell population. After removal of the γ-globulins from the gross-globulin fraction, the remaining globulins could also be substituted for whole serum with only slight decrease in cell numbers. In the meantime, as some of the more elaborate, chemically defined solutions were developed (see Chap. VI), it was found that they had to be supplemented with 10–20 per cent serum to provide completely adequate media for the continuous propagation of established cell strains and for the propagation of freshly explanted tissues for extended periods.[455] Quite recently, Harris[221] concluded that medium 199 and NCTC-109, as well as the simpler basal medium of Eagle,[103,110] are all deficient in one or more factors that occur in serum dialysate and are essential for the growth and maintenance of chick skeletal-muscle fibroblasts in monolayer cultures. Also, Eagle[106] has found that serum does, in fact, contain one or more small, molecular-weight growth factors, either bound to serum protein or formed from it on proteolysis (see p. 76). It seems clear, therefore, that blood serum does provide some of the growth factors or some of the physical conditions,[22] or both, that are presently lacking in synthetic media.

Preparation of Chicken Serum

Though it is possible to prepare chicken serum from whole blood that is allowed to coagulate spontaneously, it is generally prepared from coagulated plasma. Because the clot that forms during the coagulation of chicken blood is unusually firm, many red cells become enmeshed and destroyed with the result that the serum is often hemolytic. This is particularly true of blood taken with a syringe, which clots rapidly because of the presence of tissue juices resulting from injury. On the other hand, blood taken from the carotid by more gentle procedures often coagulates too slowly and unevenly to yield uniform serum samples unless thromboplastic material (embryo tissue extract or thrombin) is added to it and it is allowed to stand for several hours at room temperature.

In the preparation of chicken serum from fluid plasma, the latter should be coagulated as completely as possible before it is processed for serum. Otherwise, what is assumed to be serum may coagulate again after it has been placed on the cultures. To guard against this possibility, fluid plasma should be coagulated deliberately by adding to each tube a drop or two of embryo tissue extract (or an equivalent amount of thrombin) and leaving the tubes to incubate for several hours at 37° C. Also, quite regardless of the method of preparation, a small test sample of what is assumed to be serum should always be incubated together with generous amounts of extract (or thrombin) to make certain that all the fibrinogen has been converted to fibrin. If the test sample coagulates, thromboplastic material must again be added to the main sample prior to further incubation and a second processing.

There are various methods for the preparation of serum from coagulated chicken plasma. In Carrel's laboratory, prior to 1933, coagulated chicken plasma was broken up into fragments and ground in a mortar with sterile quartz sand. To guard against contamination from the air, the mortar and pestle were protected by a canopy of moist, sterile cellophane (previously cut to size, folded, and autoclaved in Mason jars filled with water). After thorough grinding, the serum was separated from the sand by centrifugation.

A more direct method[271] involves the use of a syringe and needle to draw 30 ml of blood from a wing vein (*see* p. 89). The syringe and needle are prepared for sterilization by rinsing in 4 per cent mineral oil in ether to provide a thin film of oil on the inner surfaces. The blood is transferred in 10-ml quantities to screw-cap tubes that already contain 0.1 ml of 20 mg per cent heparin. Each tube is capped, inverted to mix

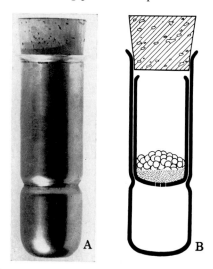

FIG. 21. Double centrifuge tube for the preparation of chicken serum from coagulated plasma: (*A*) tube constructed from sterling silver; (*B*) cross-sectional diagram. For description, see text. (C. A. Lindbergh, unpublished experiments.)

the contents, and centrifuged for 20 min at 2500 r.p.m. After the plasma has been withdrawn from the tubes, aliquots of 10 ml each are drawn into separate 20-ml syringes followed in each instance by 0.1 to 0.5 ml of chick embryo extract to coagulate the plasma and several milliliters of air. The contents of the syringe are then mixed and allowed to clot, the needle is removed, and the coagulated plasma is forced out into a suitable tube for final centrifugation (3000 r.p.m. for 20 min).

In 1933, Lindbergh* contrived a special device for obtaining serum from coagulated chicken plasma by centrifugation. This device consists of two silver-plated tubes, one of which fits loosely inside the other (Fig. 21). The outer tube is made with a slight constriction in its wall about two thirds of the way down from the top. This constriction supports the inner tube, which is loose enough to be removed easily and short enough to allow the outer tube to be corked. Several holes, each approximately 0.5 mm in diameter, are drilled in the bottom of

* Lindbergh, C. A. Unpublished experiments.

the inner tube. These holes are covered with a layer (5 to 10 mm thick) of fine quartz sand and are small enough to prevent the grains of sand from passing through during centrifugation. Above the quartz sand is placed a layer (6 to 8 mm thick) of glass beads, each having a diameter of approximately 3 mm. A sufficient number of beads must be present to cut the plasma clot into fine fragments as it is forced through during centrifugation, whereas the layer of sand must be thick enough to prevent fibrin from passing through with the serum.

The volume of the outer tube below the constriction must not be less than the volume of coagulated plasma to be placed in the inner tube. The centrifugal force required for operation is approximately 1000 times gravity. The time required for centrifugation at 2200 r.p.m. (International centrifuge, size 2, type B, with No. 239 head) varies from 7 to 10 min, according to the size of the tubes, the centrifugal force and the amount and firmness of the coagulum. The apparatus is assembled as for use and wrapped securely in paper before sterilization. It should be sterilized in an upright position.

When the plasma left to coagulate in plain glass tubes is firm enough, the mass is dislodged, broken up by a large pipette and transferred to the inner tube of the apparatus, which is then corked and centrifuged in one of the standard 250-ml centrifuge cups. After centrifugation, the cork is removed, the inner tube withdrawn, and the serum pipetted from the lower compartment.

If it is desired to prepare chicken serum directly from whole blood that is taken without an anticoagulant, the blood is collected in a 250-ml centrifuge bottle (*see* p. 89) and allowed to stand for an hour at room temperature until coagulation is complete. After centrifugation, the serum is pipetted off and stored in tubes fitted with rubber stoppers.

PREPARATION OF MAMMALIAN SERUM

When mammalian plasma prepared from blood drawn without an anticoagulant is allowed to coagulate, the serum may be separated by removing the fibrin mechanically. This procedure is extremely simple for human plasma and plasma from most laboratory animals, which tend to coagulate spontaneously if left for a time in plain glass tubes at room temperature. In these instances, the fibrin clot is broken up with a glass rod and the material is centrifuged. Most of the fibrin will adhere to the glass rod during the agitation and may be withdrawn.

Centrifugation, however, may cause a second deposition of fibrin, in which case the process is repeated until no more fibrin is brought down by centrifugation. The serum is then ready for use.

It is also possible to prepare mammalian serum from whole blood that has been left for an hour or so at room temperature until it has coagulated. Then, after the clot has been freed from the wall of the tube with a glass rod, the serum is separated by centrifugation (30 min at 3000 r.p.m.). Some investigators[271] place freshly drawn mammalian blood in flat-sided Pyrex bottles that are placed for a time in a horizontal position. After the blood has coagulated, the bottles are placed upright in the refrigerator and the serum is drawn off on the following day.

Syverton and his associates[510] draw 500 ml of human blood into a Baxter (suction) bottle. After the bottle has stood for 30–60 min at room temperature, the clot is broken up with a glass rod. The bottle is kept at 4° C overnight, and on the following day the serum is withdrawn and centrifuged for 30 min at 3000 r.p.m. When pooled serum is required, the serum from each donor is distributed in aliquots that are mixed with equal quantities from each of several other donors.

Many mammalian sera are toxic for cells. Toxic sera can usually be rendered nontoxic by heating for ½ hr at 55° C; otherwise, the toxicity tends to diminish during storage at 4° C.

Preparation of Horse Serum

Earle's group[469] obtain serum from the blood of six- to ten-year-old geldings of approximately 1500 lb weight. At bleedings, the jugular vein is punctured with a 4-mm o.d. trocar, and the blood is drawn into 9-l Pyrex cylinders (6 × 18 in.) that are kept cooled in crushed ice. Usually, 8 l of blood are obtained from each horse. The blood is defibrinated immediately by continuous stirring with a ½-in.-diameter glass rod, the lower end of which is flattened into a 1-in. disc. The fibrin collects on this rod. The defibrinated blood is stored overnight at 3° C. On the following day, the clear serum is siphoned from each cylinder, centrifuged at 3° C to remove cells, and its pH is reduced to 7.1 by means of CO_2. Until needed, the serum is stored in sealed flasks at −18° C. Eventually, it is thawed, recentrifuged at 3° C, and sterilized by passage through an 03-porosity Selas filter under pressure of a gas mixture of 5 per cent CO_2 in air.

Parker and Swim* defibrinate horse blood, as it is being drawn, with a heavy-duty stirrer fitted with a ½-in. aluminum rod. A slot about ½ in. deep and ¼ in. wide is made in the end of the rod; and a piece of stiff rubber tubing, about 4 in. long, is slit lengthwise near the middle and fitted onto one of the stirrer prongs to serve as a paddle that can be passed through the neck of the 12-l bleeding bottle. The stirrer motor is operated slowly before the bleeding commences to accustom the horse to its noise, but as the blood begins to flow the stirrer speed is gradually increased to about 500 r.p.m. and maintained at this speed for 15 min after the bleeding has been terminated. The stirrer is then removed from the bottle, the cells are allowed to settle, and the serum is aspirated and stored overnight at 4° C. On the following day, the clear serum is again aspirated and is transferred to tightly covered polyethylene pails for final storage at −20° C.

In the author's laboratory, horse serum is prepared by centrifuging freshly drawn blood after it has been allowed to coagulate. The blood, supplied by the Connaught Laboratories Veterinary Section, is drawn in 250-ml centrifuge bottles from one or another of several regular donors. Before animals are chosen as regular donors, samples of their sera are tested on cultures to eliminate any that may be toxic (*see* p. 187). Not more than 4 l of blood are drawn from any one donor each week and not more than 1 l on any one day. After the serum has been separated and sterility tests have been completed, the serum is combined with other ingredients of the culture medium and filtered before use.

Preparation of Placental-Cord Serum

Some investigators make considerable use of human placental-cord serum, which is available in most general hospitals. A glass cylinder 3 to 4 cm in diameter and 15 to 20 cm long, with a loose-fitting cap, provides a convenient receptable for placental blood.[351] It is doubly wrapped in cloth before autoclaving in order that it may be handled by a sterile nurse in the delivery room. Blood is collected only from Wasserman-negative patients having uncomplicated deliveries. After the baby is delivered and the umbilical cord cut, the maternal end of the cord is unclamped and allowed to bleed into the tube until the blood clots or the placenta is delivered. Later, in the laboratory, the

---

* Parker, R. F. Personal communication.

clot is allowed to harden at room temperature for about 1 hr and is then loosened from the walls of the tube with a glass rod or pipette, and the tube is refrigerated (4° C) overnight. The following day, the supernatant serum is drawn off. Sterility tests are made on the individual samples, and those that are contaminated or hemolytic are discarded. The remaining samples are pooled and filtered.

Preparation of Serum Albumin

Chang and Geyer[63] found that 20 per cent human and equine serum albumin, in Eagle's basal medium (see Table VIII) plus mesoinositol, provided a satisfactory medium for the propagation of several established strains of human cells as well as freshly explanted human-kidney and -amnion cells.

The serum albumin was prepared by dissolving 22 Gm of sodium sulfate in 100 ml of whole serum at 37° C and allowing the mixture to stand for 1 hr; the 22 per cent sodium sulfate portion was dialyzed against running water for about 16 hr and then against several changes of distilled water until the dialyzing fluid failed to show a visible precipitate with an equal volume of 5 per cent barium chloride. The material was then dialyzed against Eagle's basal medium for about 1 hr, after which it was frozen at −60° C until used. Two batches of human serum albumin prepared by this method were still effective after storage for six and nine months, respectively.

Some investigators supplement chemically defined media with small amounts (e.g., 0.5 per cent or less) of bovine serum albumin, Fraction V.[72]

Preparation of Serum Fractions Promoting
Attachment of Cells to Glass Surfaces

Lieberman and Ove[284] isolated from calf serum a partially purified protein that was reported to be effective in promoting the attachment and stretching of human appendix cells (a clonal derivative of Chang's strain[60]) on glass surfaces. The active material was not dialyzable, was insoluble in water but soluble in salt solutions, and was heat labile. Electrophoretic analysis revealed two components that appeared to move as α-globulins.

Fisher and his associates,[160] working with a clonal derivative of strain HeLa, reported that they had achieved a similar flattening effect with fetuin,[87,391] a glycoprotein that represents about 45 per cent of the protein of fetal-calf serum. But they were also able to separate the active factor in lesser amounts from adult-beef serum. Moreover, its activity was found to depend upon the presence of divalent cations and could be inhibited by 10^{-3}M Versene. Magnesium in a concentration of 3×10^{-4}M was highly active as a cofactor, calcium was less active, while zinc, cadmium, cobalt, and copper were ineffective. The material was also active as an inhibitor of proteolysis by agents like trypsin.

More recently, Lieberman and his associates[283] have made further purification studies on fetuin and find that the most highly purified fetuin fractions are lacking in flattening-factor activity. They suggest that the cell-flattening effects observed by Fisher and his associates may have resulted from contamination of fetuin with the flattening factor.

Tissue Extracts

In 1912, when Carrel's strain of connective-tissue cells from embryo-chick heart was in its first year of cultivation, it was discovered[43] that embryo tissue extract had remarkable powers of promoting cell growth and multiplication. Until this time, the subcultures were becoming smaller and smaller with each subsequent transfer. While blood plasma was adequate as a basic nutrient, it did not stimulate the cells to divide fast enough to compensate for those lost in trans-planting the fragments to new media. With the addition of tissue extract, however, this situation was remedied, and the strain (Fig. 2) was maintained for 34 years (see p. 4) in a combination of fowl plasma and chick-embryo tissue extract, diluted with Tyrode's solution.

Since Carrel's early experiments, there have been many attempts to determine the chemical nature of the substances responsible for the stimulating effect of embryo extract. Baker and Carrel[13] obtained active fractions of the extract by precipitation with carbon dioxide and found that the activity was concentrated largely in the protein portion containing nucleoproteins and glycoprotein. It was further observed[52] that proteoses and higher molecular weight protein degradation products also had very potent growth promoting properties. Fischer and his associates[153,158] prepared an active growth-promoting factor from beef embryos by isolating the nucleoproteins, but repeated reprecipitation of this material resulted in loss of potency. Growth-promoting activity appeared to be associated particularly with fractions containing predominantly nucleoproteins of the ribonucleic acid type. Fractions relatively high in deoxyribonucleic acid were much less active. These results were confirmed by Davidson and Waymouth,[83] who worked with the nucleoprotein from dried, sheep embryo extract. In an extension of this work, Waymouth[527] found that the content of ribonucleic acid seemed somewhat more important than that of deoxyribonucleic acid, but no absolute correlation existed between the growth-promoting activity of the material and the relative proportions of the two types of nucleic acid. Details of these investigations may be found in various reviews.[22,155,219,490,497,528,544]

More recently, Kutsky[258] isolated a ribonucleoprotein fraction of high activity from chick embryos by selective precipitation with streptomycin from saline extracts, and Harris and Kutsky[223] reported that this fraction exerted a synergistic action with the dialysate of embryo extract. Subsequently, Kutsky and associates[261] showed that active nucleoprotein fractions could be isolated from a variety of embryonic tissues and that cartilage was the richest source. But, when newer methods[259] were used to separate the nucleic-acid fraction from the protein fraction, the potency of the latter was found to be similar to that of the nucleoprotein fraction, whereas the nucleic-acid moiety was inactive. In the meantime, Sanford and her associates[469] found that in the presence of horse serum the ultrafiltrate of embryo extract was more effective for L cells than the extract residue and compared favorably with whole extract; and Rosenberg and his associates[452,453] isolated from chick embryo-extract ultrafiltrate a fraction that possessed the major activity of the original material. Also, Earle's group[118] found an ultrafiltrate of whole, unincubated eggs to be as growth stimulating as chick embryo extract. It might be, as Kutsky[259] suggests, that the activity of his protein fraction is due to tightly adsorbed or complexed large or small molecules, chemically dissimilar from the majority of the proteins in the fraction.

Growth stimulation by adult tissue extracts has also been reported by various investigators.[89,90,260,308,520] Kutsky and Harris[224,260] obtained active nucleoprotein fractions from adult-chicken brain, liver, heart, and spleen. No indications of organ specificity were observed, and the activity of the fractions did not depend on their total nucleic acid content or on the age of the individuals from which they were prepared. The adult-spleen nucleoprotein fraction induced rapid multiplication of newly explanted skeletal-muscle fibroblasts when added to a basal medium containing chicken serum and medium 199 (Fig. 22), and the cultures could be maintained for a number of serial

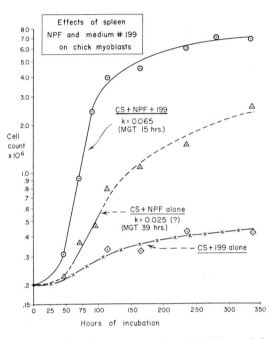

FIG. 22. Relative effects of nucleoprotein fraction (NPF) from adult-chicken spleen and medium 199 on growth of fibroblasts from chick-embryo skeletal muscle. Basal medium: chicken serum (CS), 10 per cent; solution 199 (supplemented with 1 mg/ml fresh glutamine), 50 per cent; and balanced salt solution (Earle's), 40 per cent. (M. Harris and R. J. Kutsky.[221])

passages in this medium with no decrease in growth rate. But growth did not occur in the unsupplemented basal medium alone or in serum-free 199 supplemented with the nucleoprotein fraction. Although omission of 199 from the complete medium did not prevent cell multiplication, it reduced its rate. As Harris[219] points out, these observations suggest that serum proteins and cellular proteins are not equivalent in growth-promoting properties and indicate an interaction of protein and crystalloidal growth factors.

Jacoby, Trowell, and Willmer,[245] working with fibroblast-like cells, have shown that the concentration of embryo extract present in the medium is a more important factor in determining the number of mitoses produced than is the time during which it acts and that it is not necessary for the embryo extract to be present in any appreciable amount during the actual division process. The only necessity is that the cells shall have been treated with extract 10 to 12 hr previously, but it makes little difference whether the extract is applied for 1 or for 10 hr. If the extract remains on the culture for more than 10 hr, it is possible for the cells produced at the first division to give rise to a second generation. It would seem, then, that if a sufficient quantity of embryo extract is present in the medium when the cell divides, the cell can divide again; if not, the cell has very little chance of undergoing a second division unless more extract is subsequently added. The same investigators have also shown[545] that cells do not divide just because they have reached a certain size. Cells divide only when stimulated to do so by special substances present in the medium; when these substances are absent, the cells become, and remain, larger.

The utilization of amino acids by explanted tissue was studied by Winnick and his associates,[165] who found that increases in the protein of chick-heart fibroblasts could be accounted for by corresponding decreases in the protein and amino acids contained in the medium when all were appropriately labeled with C^{14}. During the first few days, tissue protein was synthesized chiefly from the amino acids, but later more than half of the tissue protein was derived from the soluble protein of the embryo extract, apparently without hydrolysis to the amino-acid level.[297,547] (The embryo extract was labeled by injecting labeled amino acids into the eggs eight days before harvesting the embryos.) In contrast, Eagle and Piez[112] have shown for HeLa cells that the serum protein in the medium served to only a negligible degree as a source of cell proteins; at least 94 to 97 per cent of the latter was derived from free amino acids of the medium.

PREPARATION OF EMBRYO TISSUE EXTRACTS

Although chick embryo extract is used more extensively than embryo extract from other species, its very nature precludes the possibility of universal standardization. But each individual can arrive at a certain degree of uniformity in his own material by establishing a strict order of routine in caring for the eggs and preparing the extract. Then, if he ascribes a certain biological effect to the presence of a given amount of extract in the medium, he is in a better position to reproduce his results at some future date when the original sample is no longer available. It is important that the eggs should show a high percentage of fertility, that is, they should be of the grade sold expressly for breeding purposes or for laboratory use. Under no conditions should they be procured by random selection in the public market. Because antibiotics have come to be used quite extensively in poultry diets, the investigator must decide whether their presence in the embryos will effect his results. There is also the ever-present danger of virus contaminants.

Before incubation, the eggs may be stored in a cool room or refrigerator, but they must not be allowed to freeze. The temperature of incubation should lie between 37° and 39° C. Plenty of moisture should be provided in the incubator, and both the incubator and the eggs should be well ventilated. Wire racks provide more adequate ventilation than paper trays.

It is recommended that chick embryo extract be made from 10- or 11-day-old embryos (before the calcifying mechanisms have become too active). To remove the embryo from the egg, the shell is first cracked on one side with a suitable metal object. Then, while the operator holds the egg in an upright position over a waste pan, the shell is completely removed from the upper half of the egg, and the escaping fluid is allowed to pour off over the side of the lower portion without displacing the embryo. The embryo is now grasped around the neck with a pair of curved forceps and removed to a sterile container. The extract is prepared according to one of the procedures now to be described.

Embryos from small laboratory mammals (e.g., mice, rats, guinea pigs, and rabbits) are removed aseptically after the abdomen of the dead animal has been shaved and sterilized by swabbing first with tincture of iodine and then with 70 per cent alcohol and allowed to dry. The gravid uterus is removed intact and placed in a sterile, covered container. The embryos are then released one at a time by cutting through the uterine wall and separating them from the placenta.

PREPARATION OF TISSUE EXTRACTS IN
MOTOR-DRIVEN HOMOGENIZERS

In the author's laboratory a Pyrex homogenizer (Fig. 23) was devised in which TenBroeck's design[512] was used for the outer tube and Potter and Elvehjem's design[409] for the pestle. The outer tube has an outward flare at the top to facilitate loading. Just below the flared portion, there is an enlarged section that serves to lessen the danger

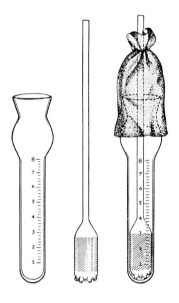

FIG. 23. Motor-driven Pyrex homogenizer for preparation of tissue extract from six to eight chick embryos. For complete description, see text.

of the tissues and diluent overflowing during the grinding. Below the enlargement the tube has a capacity of 85 ml when the pestle is removed; with the pestle in place, its capacity is 45 ml. The pestle rod is made from a piece of 8-mm capillary tubing and is about 230 mm long. One end is sealed to a thick-walled cylindrical bulb, which is about 65 mm long and rounded at the tip to fit the bottom of the outer tube. The sides of the bulb are straight and parallel to the sides of the outer tube for a space of about 40 mm. Bits of glass to form 12 or more toothlike protrusions are fused into the tip of the pestle bulb and ground down until their edges are sharp and fit the contours of the outer tube. The clearance between the pestle bulb and the outer tube is so slight that the pestle, falling by its own weight into the tube when both are dry, descends very slowly. The pestle is rotated by a cone-drive stirring motor at a speed of 80 to 90 r.p.m. To reduce the danger of breakage a short length of rubber tubing is used to connect the pestle with a glass chuck attached to the stirrer.

During the grinding process, the tube is moved up and down while the pestle is revolving. The tissue is torn apart by the protrusions on the end of the pestle, and the fragments remain below the pestle bulb until they are small enough to pass along the straight sides of the bulb, where additional grinding takes place. To protect the material

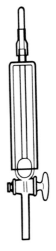

FIG. 24. Tissue homogenizer in which 100 ml or more of tissue may be ground at about 400 r.p.m., through three or four up-and-down cycles. The pestle is of glass or Teflon, and the grinding tube has a protective glass shield. (J. C. Bryant et al.[37]) (Kontes Glass Co., Vineland, N.J.)

from bacterial contamination during the grinding, a canopy of Fiberglas cloth (sewn with glass suture material) is arranged over the mouth of the tube. The canopy, which is sterilized with the apparatus and can be cleaned in acid, fits closely around the pestle but is not permitted to rotate with it.

In this apparatus, six to eight chick embryos and a measured quantity of balanced salt solution (e.g., 2.0 ml per embryo) may be processed at one time. After centrifugation (10 min at 2500 r.p.m.), the material is further diluted to give an extract consisting of one part tissue and 10–20 parts diluent.

Bryant and his associates[37] use a larger Potter-Elvehjem-type grinder (Fig. 24) that is described on page 107.

Beef embryos are usually homogenized in Waring-type blenders. Embryos from 4 to 5 in. long are preferred. They are transported to the laboratory in the intact uterus shortly after removal from the animal. According to the method reported by Robbins and his associates,[444] the muscle and connective tissue are dissected from the bones, combined with the brain, heart, lungs, and kidneys, and minced in the blender for about 30 sec. An equal quantity of balanced salt solution containing 100 u of penicillin and 100 μg of streptomycin per ml is then added and the mixture again minced for 30 sec. The suspension is incubated at 37° C for 30 min in a water bath and then centrifuged at 2000 r.p.m. in a horizontal head of an International No. 2 centrifuge. The supernatant fluid is removed, a portion cultured for sterility, and the remainder stored in convenient aliquots at −15 to −20° C. If a precipitate develops during storage, it is removed by centrifugation. It is suggested, however, that caution should be observed in using Waring-type blenders for the preparation of tissue extracts for highly critical purposes. It is possible that important substances, e.g., enzymes, may be lost as the result of the violent disruption of cells and the forces released during the bursting of bubbles.

When it is necessary to prepare large quantities of extract from tissues that are unusually tough and fibrous, the material may be passed through a grinding device of the type designed by Latapie (supplied by Arthur H. Thomas & Co., Philadelphia, Pa.). With this apparatus, tissue fragments are fed into a cylinder through an opening in the top and are gradually forced against cutting discs by turning a hand wheel. The discs are operated by means of a hand crank or motor.

Embryo extract may be stored indefinitely after it has been dried from the frozen state.

Preparation of Chick Embryo Extract in Luer Syringes

Chick embryo extract is frequently prepared in 20- or 30-ml Luer syringes. Scherer[474] inserts a close-fitting, 28-gauge, stainless-steel screen in the bottom of the syringe barrel before sterilization, and the embryos are reduced to a pulp as they are forced through the screen. Waymouth and White[532] prepare a good grade of extract without resorting to screens. According to their method, the tissue pulp from eight to ten 10-day-old embryos is forced from the barrel of a 20-ml syringe into 15-ml conical centrifuge tubes, with about 5 ml of pulp per tube. An equal quantity of Earle's balanced salt solution is added, and the material is mixed and refrigerated (5° C) overnight. The following day, the extract is separated by centrifuging the pulp for 10 min at about 3000 r.p.m. The extract is used immediately in the preparation of filtered medium containing other ingredients or is stored temporarily at $-15°$ C. To aid in filtration, hyaluronidase is added (*see* below).

FILTRATION OF EMBRYO EXTRACT
TREATED WITH HYALURONIDASE

Embryo extract and other body fluids should be filtered before use to eliminate viable cells. Bryant and his associates[37] have devised a method for the filtration of chick embryo extract after treatment with hyaluronidase, which depolymerizes the hyaluronic acid and related compounds and facilitates their passage through filters. Briefly, their method consists of freezing (in CO_2 ice) and thawing the embryos, triturating them in a tissue homogenizer, diluting and separating the pulp by centrifugation, treating the supernatant with hyaluronidase, and clarifying it by ultracentrifugation. The finished extract is then combined with other ingredients of the medium and filtered.

In more detail, ten-day-old chick embryos are placed in thick walled, 3×28 cm, Pyrex test tubes to a height of about 10 cm. The tubes are then packed in powdered CO_2 ice to retard chemical changes and partially disrupt the cells. After the entire lot has been collected and frozen, the tubes are thawed in a 37° C water bath. The embryos are then ground in a large Potter-Elvehjem tissue grinder, with a barrel about 3.4 cm in diameter and 24 cm long (Fig. 24). The grinding is done at a speed of 400 r.p.m., through three or four up-and-down cycles. A homogenizer of this size has a maximum capacity of about 45 ten-day-old embryos (about 125 ml volume); the cylinder is then about two-thirds full. The pulp is poured into a glass-stoppered cylinder and is diluted by adding 1.25 vol of Earle's balanced salt solution. The mixture is then centrifuged at 2300 r.p.m. (1600g) in a refrigerated centrifuge, and the supernatant is pipetted into a fresh cylinder. A solution of hyaluronidase (lyophilized; Worthington Chemical Sales Company, Freehold, N.J.) containing 1 mg per ml is prepared, without filtration, immediately before use and is added to the supernatant in the amount of 2 ml per 100 ml. The treated extract is mixed thoroughly and transferred to 120-ml Lusteroid tubes for ultracentrifugation in a Spinco Model L preparative centrifuge at 18,000 r.p.m. (33,000g) for 90 min, at 2° C. (The Lusteroid tubes are held overnight in the refrigerator in distilled water to lessen the danger of their collapse during centrifugation.) At the end of the run, the supernatant is poured off without disturbing the pellet and is either mixed with the other ingredients of the final medium (e.g., horse serum and balanced saline) and filtered immediately or is frozen for two to six days before being thawed and combined with the other materials for filtration (through an 03 porosity Selas filter under pressure of a gas mixture of 5 per cent CO_2 in nitrogen).

Waymouth and White[532] have also reported the use of hyaluronidase as an aid in the filtration of media containing chick embryo extract. But their extract is prepared without preliminary freezing with CO_2 ice, without trituration in a tissue grinder and without ultracentrifugation. The embryos are reduced to a pulp by forcing them through the barrel of a syringe. When the finished extract has been separated from the diluted pulp by centrifugation (*see* p. 106), it is decanted and stored temporarily at −15° C. Eventually, it is mixed with the other ingredients of the medium (e.g., 2 vol of horse serum and 7 vol of balanced salt solution, to 1 vol of extract), about 10 mg of hyaluronidase are added to each 100 ml of finished medium, and the whole is filtered through a Selas candle of 03 porosity. With vacuum provided by a water pump or a conventional vacuum pump (and kept below 250 mm of mercury by means of a bleeder valve), 150 ml of medium are passed through a 2-in. filter with almost 100 per cent yield in about 10 min. Although the filtration of the diluted extract can be carried out without hyaruronidase, its addition speeds up the process enough to justify its use.

Bovine Amniotic Fluid

Enders[129] used bovine amniotic fluid in combination with horse serum, bovine embryo extract, and balanced salt solution for the cultivation of chick and human cells (*see* p. 110). It is prepared in the following manner. The gravid uterus is conveyed to the laboratory and suspended from a support by a cord. After the entire surface of the organ has been cleansed and dried, an appropriate site near the embryo and close to the dependent area is lightly cauterized with a flame. A special trochar (bore 1.5 mm, length 22.5 cm; the MacBick Co., Cambridge, Mass.) is then passed through this portion of the uterine wall into the amniotic cavity, care being taken not to pierce the embryo. The clear fluid, which usually runs freely, is collected in sterile flasks. The yield varies from about 0.5 to 1.5 l, depending upon the size of the embryo. Fluids that are contaminated with blood, presumably because of injury to the embryo by the trochar, are discarded. Embryos about 7.5 to 25 cm long are selected. After withdrawal of the fluid, the embryo may be used for the preparation of embryo tissue extract (*see* p. 105). To the fluid withdrawn from each amniotic cavity, sufficient penicillin and streptomycin are added to give a final concentration of 50 u and 50μg, respectively, per ml. Portions of the fluid (0.1 ml) are then added to thioglycollate broth and incubated for 48 hr to determine the presence or absence of bacteria insensitive to the antibiotics. In the meantime, the fluids from each embryo are kept in an ordinary refrigerator in tightly stoppered flasks. Eventually, a pool is made of the fluids from several embryos. Sufficient phenol red solution (0.4 per cent) is added to the pooled fluid to give a final concentration of 0.002 per cent. The material is stored in the refrigerator. If the fluids become too alkaline during storage, the pH is adjusted to 7.5–7.6 by gassing with a mixture of 5 per cent CO_2 in air just before use.

Complex Media Containing Naturally Occurring Ingredients

During the 1930's, Carrel and his associates[55] made considerable use of Witte's peptone, casein, and enzymatic digests of various protein materials (e.g., fibrin, casein, crystalline egg albumin, edestin, liver, and whole ox blood), in combination with blood serum, vitamins, hormones, and other substances, to provide large batches of media for the continuous perfusion of whole organs. Twenty years later, as vast quantities of tissue culture media came to be required for large-scale virus studies, many laboratories made excellent use of various protein materials and bacteriological preparations that were commercially available, inexpensive, and completely free of contaminating viruses and natural antibody. Thus, in 1952, Melnick and Riordan[325] used

0.5 per cent lactalbumin enzymatic hydrolysate, serum ultrafiltrate (*see* p. 92), and balanced saline, for the propagation of polioviruses in monkey testicular tissue. Three years later, Robertson and his associates[446] used 0.1 per cent Difco dehydrated yeast extract and 4 per cent chicken or monkey serum, in Hanks's saline with extra glucose but without bicarbonate, for poliovirus assays with HeLa cells; and Cooper[75] combined 0.5 per cent lactalbumin hydrolysate, 0.1 per cent yeast extract, and 0.1 per cent Armour's crystalline bovine albumin with Earle's saline that was modified by replacing the bicarbonate buffer with 0.3 per cent Tris (*see* p. 61). The composition of a few of these complex media will now be given.

Supplemented Hanks-Simms Medium

In their early work with polioviruses, Weller and his associates[535] made excellent use of a combination of 3 parts Hanks's balanced salt solution (*see* p. 57) and 1 part Simms's ox serum ultrafiltrate (*see* p. 92). For Erlenmeyer-flask and roller-tube cultures of various human and animal tissues (embryonic, infant, and adult), the complete medium consisted of *Hanks-Simms solution* (85 per cent), beef embryo extract (10 per cent), horse serum inactivated at 56° C for 30 min (5 per cent but increased to 20 per cent for mature tissues), penicillin (50 u per ml), and streptomycin (50 μg per ml). The roller tubes were prepared with a substrate of chicken plasma that was clotted with embryo extract after the tissues fragments had been implanted.

Supplemented Bovine Amniotic Fluid Medium

For virus studies involving trypsinized suspensions of chick embryo and human amnion cells (*see* p. 127), Milovanic and his associates[251,330] used the following medium during the initial period of cell outgrowth: *bovine amniotic fluid* (37.5 per cent), horse serum inactivated at 56° C for 30 min (20 per cent), bovine embryonic extract (5 per cent), Hanks's balanced salt solution (37.5 per cent), streptomycin (100 mg per ml), penicillin (100 u per ml), and Mycostatin (100 u per ml). When confluent cell layers had been established and viruses were to be introduced, the first medium was replaced by one of the following composition: *bovine amniotic fluid* (45 per cent), inactivated horse serum

(5 per cent), bovine embryonic extract (5 per cent), Hanks's balanced salt solution (45 per cent), and antibiotics, as before.

MEDIUM FOR HUMAN "EPITHELIOID" AND "FIBROBLASTIC" CELLS

Puck and his associates[413] devised a medium for normal human "epithelioid" cells that consisted of a chemically defined solution supplemented with serum. But single, dispersed "fibroblastic" cells from the same organs almost never produced colonies with high plating efficiency (*see* p. 217) unless this medium was further supplemented with embryo extract or a cell "feeder" layer. Also, media that differed mainly in the presence or absence of embryo extract favored the multiplication of either "fibroblastic" or "epithelioid" cells, respectively, from trypsin-dispersed cell suspensions (*see* pp. 121 and 217) prepared from the same tissue. Unfortunately, the terms "fibroblastic" and "epithelioid" referred only to the superficial appearance of the cells after attachment to glass and bore no relationship to their origin or function. The *medium for "fibroblastic" cells* was comprised of a chemically defined solution (consisting essentially of amino acids, vitamins, and inorganic salts), 10 per cent; human serum, 17 per cent; embryo extract (1:1), 4 per cent; and Hanks's balanced salt solution, 69 per cent. The *medium for "epithelioid" cells* consisted of: the same chemically defined solution, 10 per cent; human serum, 10 or 20 per cent; horse serum, 0 or 10 per cent; and Hanks's balanced salt solution, 60 to 80 per cent.

SKIM MILK AS A SUPPLEMENT FOR SYNTHETIC MEDIA

Although animal sera have been included in many tissue-culture media used in virus studies, it is highly desirable to replace serum with materials that do not contain virus inhibitors or antibody. To this end, Baron and Low[17] have investigated the nutritive value of skim milk, with interesting results. Pet instant, nonfat, dry milk was reconstituted in distilled water according to the instructions on the container and either boiled for 5 min or autoclaved at 7 lb press. for 15 min. The pH was adjusted to 7.2 with sterile 5 per cent sodium bicarbonate, and aliquots were frozen at $-20°$ C. This material was designated as 100 per cent skim milk. A final concentration of 20 per cent skim milk in medium 199 (at pH 7.3–7.6) was used successfully to maintain Salk's monkey-heart cells, Eagle's KB cells, and rhesus-monkey kidney cells for periods up to four weeks, with renewals of medium at seven-day intervals.

SERUM-SUPPLEMENTED LACTALBUMIN HYDROLYSATE MEDIUM

In 1958, Madin and Darby[303] used a modification of Melnick's medium[321,325] for the cultivation of bovine and ovine cells in 65-ml Blake bottles. The medium is prepared from three stock solutions: *Solution I* (modified Earle's balanced salt solution): NaCl, 70 Gm; KCl, 4.0 Gm; $CaCl_2$, 2.0 Gm; $MgSO_4 \cdot 7H_2O$, 2.0 Gm; $NaH_2PO_4 \cdot H_2O$, 1.4 Gm; dextrose, 10 Gm; penicillin (potassium G), 2 Gm; streptomycin sulfate, 1 Gm; polymixin B, 1 Gm; phenol red (0.2 per cent stock solution), 10 ml; distilled water, to 1000 ml. Sterilize by filtration, and dispense in 100-ml amounts. *Solution II:* Lactalbumin enzymatic hydrolysate, 50 Gm; distilled water, to 1000 ml. Dispense in 100-ml amounts and sterilize by autoclaving at 10 lb for 10 min. *Solution III:* Sodium bicarbonate, 75.0 Gm; distilled water, to 1000 ml. Sterilize by autoclaving at 15 lb for 15 min. The complete medium is prepared as follows: Solution I, 100 ml; solution II, 100 ml; solution III, 6–12 ml; lamb serum (filtered), 100 ml; distilled water (sterile) 800 ml.

SERUM-SUPPLEMENTED YEAST-EXTRACT MEDIUM

Syverton and McLaren[508] attribute the successful establishment of various human cell lines and strains from other species to the use of a yeast-extract medium (Robertson *et al.*[446]) and a thin plasma layer for primary cultures and clonal isolations. The *yeast-extract medium* consists of a 1 per cent solution of Difco's Yeastolate (10 parts), 10 per cent glucose solution (2.5 parts), and Hanks's balanced salt solution (87.5 parts). When increased buffering capacity is desired, 0.113 Gm per cent sodium acetate and 0.064 Gm per cent sodium pyruvate are added to Hanks's balanced salt solution. The complete fluid medium consists of *yeast-extract medium* (76 parts), human serum (20 parts), and 1.4 per cent sodium bicarbonate (4 parts). When it is desired to maintain the cells in a low state of metabolic activity, 3–5 parts of human, monkey, calf, or chicken serum are combined with 5 parts of

1.4 per cent sodium bicarbonate and 90 parts of the *yeast-extract medium*. Penicillin and streptomycin are added to all media at levels of 100 u and 100 μg per ml, respectively.

SERUM-SUPPLEMENTED LACTALBUMIN HYDROLYSATE AND YEAST-EXTRACT MEDIUM

In 1957, Fogh and Lund[162] reported a medium for the cultivation of human-amnion cells that consisted of Earle's saline containing lactalbumin hydrolysate (0.5 per cent), yeast extract (0.1 per cent), and human or ox serum (10 or 20 per cent). The glucose was increased to 0.4 per cent and in sebsequent modifications to 0.6 per cent. For HeLa cells, ox or horse serum gave better results than swine or lamb serum.

MEDIA CONTAINING OTHER BACTERIOLOGICAL PREPARATIONS

In addition to the products already mentioned, numerous other materials that are prepared commercially have been tested as possible substitutes for blood serum and tissue extracts in cell nutrition and virus studies. Several of the earlier semisynthetic media[11,14,524] contained peptones, usually Witte's peptone, a product of the incomplete digestion of fibrin. Later, Hanks[207] found a rapid increase in cell population in cultures from chick-embryo muscle when Witte's peptone (at 1 mg per ml) was added to a serum ultrafiltrate medium. In 1956, Waymouth[530] supplemented synthetic media with Difco Bacto-peptone (0.5 per cent) and Armour's bovine albumin, fraction V (0.05 per cent), which contain predominately high-molecular peptides or albumins, respectively, and only traces of other substances. When peptone was present, the addition of albumin increased only slightly the proliferation of L cells. When peptone was absent, the albumin fraction had no effect. Mayyasi and Schuurmans[312] found that L cells can be propagated in 0.1 per cent Difco Bacto-yeast extract and 0.1 per cent Difco proteose-peptone No. 3, in Hanks's balanced salt solution supplemented with 10 or 20 per cent horse serum. Ginsberg and his associates[186] reported that Difco tryptose phosphate broth (15–25 per cent) in combination with chicken serum (7.5 per cent) and Scherer's maintenance medium (*see* p. 74) kept HeLa cells alive for at least ten days. Morgan and his associates[335] supplemented medium 199 with various naturally occurring materials and found that whole liver extract (Sigma Chemical Co.), beef extract, horse serum, and yeast extract (all from Difco Laboratories, Inc.), and liver fraction L (Nutritional Biochemicals, Inc.) each increased the survival time of chick-embryo, heart-muscle cultures by about 50 per cent, as compared with an increase of 300 per cent when chick embryo extract was used. More recently, Harris[221] found that proteose-peptone (Difco) at 0.1 per cent restored to dialyzed chicken serum (10 per cent) in medium 199 the factor or factors required for the growth and maintenance of chick fibroblasts in monolayer cultures. Pumper[420] propagated mouse-lung cells in 1 per cent Bacto-peptone (Difco) and 100 mg per cent glucose, in medium 199.

VIII

Preparation of Cells and Tissues for Cultivation

THERE are three methods in general use for the preparation of freshly isolated tissues and organ fragments for cultivation: (1) by chopping tissues and organs with scissors or knives; (2) by making careful dissections resulting in discrete tissue fragments; and (3) by treating the tissues with enzymes and chelating agents to disperse the cells. The cellular population of body fluids and exudates and leukocytes from the blood are isolated and concentrated for cultivation (1) by ordinary centrifugation, (2) by the albumin-flotation method, or (3) by the phytohemagglutinin method. All of these various procedures will be discussed in the present chapter. In Chapter XV, special attention will be given to the preparation of embryonic parts that are to be cultivated *in toto*.

General Considerations

Small organ or tissue fragments that are to be cultivated in their entirety, without loss or wastage of bulk or constituent parts, should be kept moist from the moment of extirpation, preferably with the medium in which they are to be cultivated. Care should also be taken not to allow the fluids in which the tissues are stored, even temporarily, to become too acid or alkaline. It is also helpful to have the medium warmed to room temperature before use. In short, all of the procedures used in preparing tissues for cultivation should be designed to lessen, by every conceivable means, the physical and chemical shock that the cells are likely to encounter before being placed in an artificial environment that is still far from optimal.

Murray[351] makes helpful suggestions regarding tissue specimens obtained from surgery. It is assumed, of course, that the cooperating surgeon is aware of the exact nature of the material that is desired. He arranges to have the laboratory informed of operations that may provide such material, preferably on the preceding day. The operating room maintains a stock of sterile Petri dishes (60 or 100 mm in diameter) prepared in such a way that they can be placed on the instrument table and handled by the sterile nurse. The surgeon selects the material at a convenient moment and places it in the dish. An assistant notifies the laboratory that the specimen is available. For most favorable results, the specimen should be fresh, aseptic, moist, cellular (that is, meaty rather than fibrous or mucinous), well vascularized, nonnecrotic, subjected to a minimum of trauma by handling, and selected from a site at least 1 cm distant from a cauterized area. It should not be wrapped in gauze, the fibers of which would adhere to it.

Adult tissues from food-producing animals[302] are usually obtained from a local slaughterhouse as intact organs. Organs such as kidneys and testicles are removed and brought to the laboratory with the capsule intact. When lung or liver is required, suitable portions are selected and brought to the laboratory. The tissues and organs should be transported in sterile containers, and care should be taken to keep them moist. Embryonic tissues are prepared in the laboratory by removing the entire foetus from the intact uterus. Sterile instruments are then used to remove the desired parts. If antibiotics are not to be used in the culture medium or if it is desired to take additional precautions against microbial contaminations, the tissues or organs may be washed in two changes of Dakin's solution (*see* p. 51), 1 min in each, and then immersed in a great excess of buffered saline to dilute the Dakin's solution. If the organ is too large to be handled with forceps (e.g., a horse kidney), rubber gloves may be used in washing the surface with Dakin's solution, in cutting away the fatty tissue, and in transferring the organ from one container to another. Finally, the organ is placed in a sterile pan for the dissection of the tissues that are required.

If it is desired to explant adult mammalian skin for cultivation, one may decide to rely entirely on antibiotics as a means of obtaining sterile cultures, or one may attempt to sterilize it. There are many ways, of course, to *attempt* to sterilize skin, but because of its complexity none is always successful. In the author's laboratory, Dakin's solution (*see* p. 51) is used for this purpose, partly because it is easy to prepare and is always on hand and partly because it affords maximal protection with minimal injury to the constituent cells. After the area has been shaved, it is scrubbed with a soft brush and mild soap, then with water alone, and finally with Dakin's solution applied with a gauze sponge held in forceps. The area is then covered with a gauze sponge saturated with Dakin's solution. After a few minutes, the wet sponge is removed, the area is swabbed with dry gauze, and the dissection is made. The dissected tissues are then washed by immersing them in liberal quantities of phosphate buffered saline (*see* p. 58), in balanced salt solution without bicarbonate (*see* p. 58), or better, in the medium in which they are to be cultivated. Finally, they are cut with knives to the desired size and the cultures are prepared.

If the skin itself is not to be cultivated but only to be sterilized as a means of reaching underlying parts aseptically, iodine and alcohol may be used, or any number of other preparations now preferred by surgeons. There are also available on the market stable preparations of modified Dakin's solution (for example, Abbott's Chlorazene tablets and Wampole's Hygeol). Because Dakin's solution and alcohol are incompatible, they are never used to sterilize the same area.

Preparation of Tissues by Chopping or Careful Dissection

Cell cultures are often made from tissues by chopping them to extreme fineness with scissors or knives, but enough fluid should be added during the chopping to keep the fragments well moistened. It is only necessary to wash the tissues when it seems desirable to free them of excess blood. Under these conditions, the washing (in buffered saline solution) should be done while the majority of the fragments are still 3 to 4 mm in diameter. The chopping may then be continued until the suspension is fine enough for the preparation of the cultures.

Small quantities of tissue may be chopped on a glass plate protected from above by a large Petri-dish cover. Soft tissues are chopped most effectively with cataract knives that are thin, sharp, and flexible (Fig. 8). Inexpensive substitutes for cataract knives (for culture purposes) can be made from full-length fragments of double-edged razor blades, held securely in surgical needle holders. The knife or blade is held at a 45° angle, away from the operator, and is worked evenly and progressively through the mound of tissue from right to left by a series of short, firm shearing motions. The fragments are then scraped together and chopped again, as before. These operations are repeated several times or until the tissue has been reduced to a suspension of minute fragments that can be taken up into a hand-drawn pipette having a tip 2–3 mm in diameter. Tough, fibrous tissues may first be reduced to relatively small fragments by means of small, sturdy scissors with curved blades. The final chopping should then be done with knives. McIlwain and Buddle[313] developed a mechanical chopper, which has been adapted to sterile work by Rinaldini.[436]

Large quantities of tissue, e.g., a monkey kidney, may be chopped in a 250-ml centrifuge bottle with 8-in., straight, uterine scissors. With practise, two pairs of scissors may be operated simultaneously in the same bottle. The tissue should be covered with about 2 vol of buffered salt solution and reduced to fragments approximately 1 mm in diameter. The fragments are washed with a few changes of saline while the majority of them are still large enough to settle rapidly. If the washing is delayed until the larger fragments have been reduced to final size, vast numbers of smaller cell aggregates will be lost when the washing fluids are removed.

Pomerat and his colleagues[368,398,400] use a variety of freshly explanted tissues for coverslip preparations in the testing of drugs (see p. 138). The cultures are prepared from fragments of leg muscle, frontal bone, or ventricular wall of the heart of 10- to 12-day-old chick embryos, transverse sections of intestine of 8- to 10-day embryos, or spleen fragments from 18- to 20-day embryos. Intestine provides compact sheets of epithelial cells, and fragments of spleen cultivated in plasma produce symmetrical colonies suitable for areal measurements. Transverse sections of spinal cords from nine-day embryos are used for testing the toxicity of nerve stimulants and depressants on the growth of nerve fibers. When human material is required, fibroblast-like cells are obtained from subcutaneous, areolar, or mesenteric tissue derived from healthy areas of surgical specimens. Tonsils, lymph nodes, and skin left over from grafting procedures are also used; and ganglia from the lower thoracic and upper lumbar sympathetic trunks, as well as celiac, splanchnic, and stellate ganglia provide material for studies on adult nerve cells. It always takes considerably longer for migrating cells to emerge from adult tissue fragments than from embryonic material.

Pomerat's group[398] have worked out a useful technique for the preparation of cultures from the spinal cord of nine-day chick embryos. The necks of the embryos are severed at the base with scissors or knives. The spinal cord is expelled from the neural canal by compressing the tissue in the mid-dorsal line with two pairs of forceps that are moved alternately in the direction of the severed vertebral column. In this way, both a cervical and a thoracolumbar segment of cord is obtained. The segments are washed in balanced salt solution and are cut into transverse sections with sharp knives. Each knife is made from a thin fragment of razor blade that is soldered into the broken eye of a sewing needle. Transverse sections varying from 0.25 to 0.5 mm in thickness can be cut by moving the tips of two of these knives in opposite directions at right angles to the cord segment.

For projects involving the careful dissection of particular parts, it cannot be emphasized too strongly that they should be kept moistened at all times with a protective fluid of optimal pH. When possible, the protective fluid should contain serum protein of some sort. In any event, it should be similar to, if not identical with, the medium in which the tissues are to be cultivated. In making the dissections, it is often helpful to have a low-power, binocular, dissecting microscope provided with an attached light source and a flexible, free-swinging supporting arm. There are also available various types of simple magnifying lenses of large area that are mounted together with shielded lamps in plastic frames attached to flexible supporting arms.

Cells Released from Tissues by Various Enzymes

Enzymes are commonly used to separate cells from tissues when it is desired (1) to prepare cultures having a uniform layer of cells, (2) to prepare cultures from cell suspensions of particular population densities, (3) to obtain populations from individual cells, and (4) to obtain the greatest possible yield from a given quantity of tissue. Enzymes are also used occasionally as a means of selecting particular cell types that may be more resistant than others to certain enzymes (see p. 130).

In 1916, Rous and Jones[457] treated tissue cultures with trypsin for 1 hr at 37° C and were able to prepare subcultures from the dispersed cells. Good results were obtained with both avian and mammalian tissues including spleen, connective tissue, endothelium, and malignant tumors; but epithelial sheets were not readily broken up. In 1941, Medawar[317] used trypsin to obtain viable cells from chick-heart cultures and to separate the epidermal layer of human skin from the dermis. In 1952, Moscona[344] reported cultivation experiments (see also p. 242) in which the cells of embryonic rudiments were dispersed with trypsin in a saline solution lacking calcium and magnesium. Since the beginning of the century,[236] these divalent cations had been known to increase the stability of the intercellular matrix; and Chambers and Cameron[58] succeeded in separating epithelial cells in cultures by treating them with calcium-free saline alone. Zeidman[554] found, however, that the lack of both calcium and magnesium proved more effective in lowering adhesiveness than lack of either cation alone. In 1952, Dulbecco[92] introduced the trypsin procedure to virology by demonstrating macroscopic virus lesions in cultures of chick-embryo cells prepared with the aid of trypsin. He also found that more uniform culture populations could be obtained by using as the inoculum cells released from the glass of existing cultures by means of trypsin.

Rinaldini[436, 437] has studied the effect of several enzymes, including trypsin, pancreatin, elastase, and papain, on various chick tissues. For study, each enzyme was included in a calcium- and magnesium-free Tyrode's solution containing 0.1 per cent sodium citrate. Powdered trypsin preparations were found to vary greatly in their ability to disintegrate a given tissue. It was also found that liver yields more easily to tryptic digestion than skeletal and cardiac muscle, which in turn are more readily digested than skin. Crystalline, salt-free trypsin (Armour) in concentrations of 1 to 5 mg per ml only partially disintegrates heart, skeletal muscle, and liver and leaves behind a viscous mucin-like residue, which binds together the undigested collagen and elastic fibers. But although crystalline trypsin will not dissociate intact tissues, it is useful in digesting a plasma clot and in detaching cells from glass. Crude pancreatin is more damaging to cells than trypsin, presumably owing to the presence of lipases and other enzymes that attack cell membranes. Although the residues of digestion with crystalline trypsin yield to crude pancreatin, they do not appear after digestion with pancreatin alone. It was concluded, therefore, that the ability of some noncrystalline trypsin preparations to carry tissue digestion up to the free-cell stage was due to other enzymes present as impurities. Crude elastase, a complex of enzymes extracted from pancreas, is capable not only of hydrolyzing the mucoid residue remaining after digestion with crystalline trypsin but also of producing by itself discretely isolated cells in high yield from chick-embryo heart, breast muscle, liver, and unkeratinized skin. Elastase, like trypsin, is strongly inhibited by blood serum.

Cultures prepared from trypsinized organ tissues from adult animals usually yield mixed cell populations consisting of epithelial or parenchymal cells and fibroblasts. According to Madin and his associates,[302] kidney cultures yield tubular epithelium and fibroblasts. Testicle cultures yield Sertoli cells and fibroblasts. Bladder cultures consist of pure transitional epithelium, while cultures of skin and cervix appear to be stratified squamous epithelium. Lung cultures yield fibroblasts and cells from the alveolar walls. Liver cultures produce pure liver parenchyma cells.

Lasfargues[265] and Hinz and Syverton[237] have used collagenase successfully in the dispersions of cells from organs rich in connective tissue. Details of their procedures are given on page 130.

Preparation of Cell Suspensions with Trypsin

The preparation of trypsin-dispersed cell suspensions from freshly explanted tissues may be carried out in three ways: (1) by treating the cells with trypsin in ordinary flasks or bottles, with manual agitation; (2) by using a special trypsinization flask[423] and a magnetic stirrer; and (3) by using a special trypsinization flask and magnetic stirrer, with continuous, automatic addition of trypsin and removal of dispersed cells.[423] Trypsin-dispersed cells from certain adult tissues may remain dormant in cultures for many days, perhaps even for a week. Usually however, cell multiplication begins within 48 hr.

Because the most efficient trypsinizing procedures have been devised for monkey-kidney tissues, as a means of obtaining maximal yields of viable cells for use in poliovaccine programs, these methods will be described first and will be followed by descriptions of other, less elaborate procedures suitable for small quantities of tissue.

FROM MONKEY-KIDNEY TISSUE

In 1954, Dulbecco and Vogt[93] used trypsin for the preparation of cell suspensions from monkey-kidney tissue. The tissues from two kidneys were cut into small discrete fragments that were transferred to a 250-ml flask or centrifuge bottle, washed several times in phosphate buffered saline, and suspended in 50–60 ml of prewarmed (37° C), 0.25 per cent trypsin (1:250 or 1:500) solution in phosphate buffered saline. After 10 minutes' incubation at 37° C, the trypsin solution was discarded and replaced with about 20 ml of fresh, prewarmed trypsin. The tissue was pipetted back and forth 10 to 15 times with an automatic pipette, and, after the large fragments had settled, the turbid supernatant was poured into a centrifuge bottle. Again, warm trypsin was added to the remaining tissue fragments, and the dispersed cells were collected as before. This procedure was repeated several times or until the fragments had lost their brownish color and become whitish masses of connective tissue. The entire yield was then washed three times by centrifugation (2 min at 600 r.p.m.) in phosphate buffered saline, and each time the packed cells were resuspended in one-half the previous volume of saline. Finally, the packed cells were resuspended in 10 to 20 times their volume of the culture medium to be used, a hemocytometer count was made, and cultures were prepared having a final population density of 3×10^5 cells per ml. The procedure of Dulbecco and Vogt was soon modified by Younger,[553] who used a Waring-type blender to agitate the tissues during digestion with trypsin; but both methods were later refined by Rappaport,[423] who developed more efficient procedures that are now widely used for relatively small quantities of tissue.

Rappaport found that the manual method giving the highest cell yield was one that alternated periods of incubation with trypsin with periods of stirring during which the fluid was changed every 3 to 10 min. To facilitate this, 250- and 500-ml Erlenmeyer flasks were modified for use with a magnetic stirrer by indenting the sides at right angles to the bottom surface at four equally spaced points (Fig. 25). The indentations extended about two thirds of the height of the flask, and each cut into the bottom surface about 2.5 cm. This modification permitted satisfactory mixing with cavitation at certain critical volumes. Maximum mixing over a wider range of volumes was obtained by accentuating the curvature between the bottom and the sides of the flask. A side arm for decanting was placed so that the tissue tended to be trapped in the bottom when the flask was tilted for pouring. The

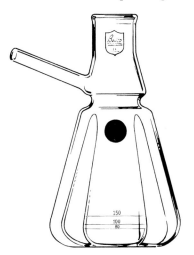

FIG. 25. Trypsinizing flask (Rappaport[123]) designed for use with magnetic stirrer. Four fluted sides provide maximum turbulence during stirring. Dam in neck prevents tissue from being poured off with cells in suspension through side arm. (Bellco Glass Inc., Vineland, N.J.)

efficiency of trapping was increased by enlarging the flask just under the side arm.

It soon became obvious that trypsin-dispersed cells are unusually fragile and should be removed from the trypsinizing chamber as soon as they are released from the tissues so as to protect them from mechanical damage or excessive digestion with trypsin. In fact, the favorable effect of incubation and of frequent fluid changes during stirring suggested an automatic system in which the tissue would be stirred gently for many hours with a continuously renewed trypsin solution and continuous withdrawal of the cell suspension. For this purpose, Rappaport designed a glass mixing chamber made from a 500-ml Kjeldahl flask with the side walls indented as before but without the side arm. The chamber was closed by a ground glass joint with two openings. Through one, trypsin was admitted from a reservoir kept at 37° C; the other opening admitted air when needed. In the bottom center of the mixing chamber, which was placed over a magnetic stirrer, holes were drilled so that cells and fluid could drain from the mixing chamber through a collecting channel into a receiving jar kept chilled with ice water. In this system, the flow of trypsin is controlled by a pinch clamp on the tube leading into the mixing chamber. When tissue fragments and trypsin are stirred in the mixing chamber, the motion of the magnet sweeps the fragments from the draining area and permits only the dispersed cells to pass through into the receiving jar, which is placed at a lower level. If the trypsin-inlet tube is opened and the magnet is not turning, the tissue will settle and clog the outlet holes. If this happens, the cells are not recovered as soon as they are released from the fragments and may be lost by excessive digestion with trypsin. If it is desired to tap the trypsinizer for cell suspension during the run, a bell cap can be used on the outlet tube of the mixing chamber.

The 500-ml flask is marked on the outside at three levels indicating a total volume of 60 ml, 100 ml, and 150 ml, which have been found suitable for loads of up to 13, 30, and 50 Gm of tissue, respectively. When the flask is operated at a working volume of 60 ml, a rate of flow of one to two drops per second is usually satisfactory. At the beginning or end of the run, when cells are released slowly, the rate of flow may be considerably reduced. Rappaport found that large fragments (1 cm) of tissue disintegrate more quickly after incubation with trypsin and with a greater yield of free cells than smaller pieces. The size of the magnet was also important. For 500-ml flasks, a 9 × 40 mm magnet (Teflon covered) was suitable for 30 Gm of tissue or less. The inside, bottom surface of the flask is flat, but the diameter of the flat portion is only about 6 mm greater than the length of the magnet. Thus, if the magnet is displaced during stirring, it will automatically return to the center. The self-regulating capacity of the flask is not sufficient, however, to withstand marked changes in the rate of stirring due to fluctuations in line voltage or to large accumulations of connective tissue.

In a typical run, the tissue is incubated with gentle stirring in pre-warmed trypsin solution for 30 to 45 min. This operation may be carried out in an ordinary Erlenmeyer flask that is kept warm in a water bath and agitated occasionally by hand, after which the entire contents may be transferred to the automatic trypsinizing flask; or, the trypsinizing flask may be placed at 37° C before it is attached to the other vessels. After incubation, the speed of stirring is increased until there is rapid swirling of tissue up and around the sides of the mixing chamber. There should be slight cavitation but no foaming. At this time, with the air valve closed, the drain valve is opened slowly. Trypsin will flow from the mixing chamber into the receiving jar and will prime the siphoning of trypsin from the reservoir. When trypsin starts flowing into the mixing chamber, the inlet valve should be closed gradually until, with the drain valve completely open, the rate of flow through the flask is regulated by the pinch clamp on the inlet from the trypsin reservoir. The rate of flow cannot be regulated by a pinch clamp on the drain valve, for this will cause clogging. Two or three liters of trypsin are sufficient for four kidneys; but considerable trypsin can be saved by using a 250-ml mixing chamber for less than 30 Gm of tissue.

Bishop and his associates[26] trypsinize monkey-kidney fragments in a 1-l measuring cylinder provided with two side arms near the bottom. By means of silicone tubing and a peristaltic pump, the kidney fragments (up to 35 Gm) are circulated for an hour or more at $37°$ C, during which time the cell aggregates that are released float up through the fluid in the cylinder and are thereby removed from further mechanical damage. Eventually, the suspension is harvested through a side arm inserted in the pump line.

In the Connaught Laboratories' poliovaccine section, five to ten pairs of monkey kidneys are usually processed together. After the capsule has been removed and the medulla cut away and discarded, the tissue is chopped (with 8-in., straight, uterine scissors) in a 250-ml centrifuge bottle until the fragments are about 4–5 mm in size. The fragments are washed repeatedly both during and after chopping, until the fluid is clear. They are then immersed in 0.25 per cent trypsin solution in phosphate buffered saline in a 1-l, round-bottom flask (with indentations similar to those of a Rappaport flask) and incubated at $36°$ C for 1 hr. The fluid is then decanted and discarded, 10 ml of prewarmed trypsin solution per gram of tissue are added, and the tissue is agitated with a magnetic stirrer for 4 hr at $30–32°$ C. After the cell suspension has been passed through a cheese-cloth strainer (to remove connective tissue) into an Erlenmeyer flask provided with a protected bottom outlet, it is transferred to centrifuge bottles and sedimented at 700 r.p.m. for 10 min. The supernatant fluid is then discarded, a known volume of nutrient medium is added, and cell clumps are broken up by vigorous pipetting. The cell yield runs as high as 80 per cent of the original tissue. Cells from ten pairs of kidneys are sufficient to inoculate 80 to 100 Povitsky bottles, each containing 500–700 ml of chemically defined medium supplemented with 1 per cent serum. Confluent layers of cells are obtained in six to seven days.

FROM SLAUGHTERHOUSE MATERIAL

Although monkey-kidney cells have been used extensively in recent years because they were readily available in certain centers, many investigators rely almost entirely on cells from domestic animals. Thus, Madin and his associates,[302] who have made excellent use of slaughterhouse material for virus studies in veterinary medicine, prepare swine-kidney cells in the following manner. The kidney capsule is removed with forceps and scissors. A portion of the cortex is excised (10 to 25 Gm) and minced into pieces (3 to 5 mm) with scalpels. To 1 part of tissue by weight (in an Erlenmeyer flask) 3 parts of trypsin solution (0.25 per cent) by volume are added and maintained at 37° C. For preliminary extraction, the kidney-trypsin mixture is agitated with a magnetic stirrer until the kidney tissue begins to liberate tubules (approximately 30 min). This stage is determined by occasional low-power microscopic examination of the supernatant fluid. The supernatant fluid is then discarded and fresh trypsin is added. The mixture is then stirred by a magnetic stirrer for about 10 min. The supernatant fluid is decanted and centrifuged for 2 min at 600 r.p.m., and the packed cells are resuspended in 10 vol of nutrient medium at room temperature. These processing cycles are continued until the desired volume of cells is obtained or until the tissue is exhausted. The cells harvested from each extraction are collected in a 50-ml, graduated, conical centrifuge tube. When a sufficient quantity has been collected, they are recentrifuged for 2 min at 600 r.p.m. The supernatant fluid is discarded and the cells resuspended in 4 vol of nutrient medium. The cells are then dispersed throughout the fluid by gentle mixing with a pipette. The mixture is again centrifuged, the volume of packed cells is measured, the supernatant fluid is discarded, and the cells dispersed in 4 vol of nutrient fluid. The dispersed cells are transferred to a large Erlenmeyer flask that contains the volume of medium necessary to complete a 1:200 dilution. The cells are then dispensed into culture tubes or bottles; during the dispensing procedure, the flask containing the cells is agitated repeatedly to minimize settling or clumping.

FROM HUMAN AMNION

Wherever available in sufficient quantity, human amniotic membranes are definitely preferred[88,533,556] as a continuous source of primate epithelium for the preparation of cultures for virus studies, mainly because they are usually free from simian viruses, some of which are infectious for man. Human placentas and membranes are collected in 2-l, sterile beakers containing about 300 ml of Hanks's balanced salt solution without bicarbonate (*see* p. 57). Material from Caesarian sections or normal deliveries can be used, but, because care must be taken to avoid contamination with antiseptics, the placenta is taken directly from the patient into the beaker and is stored at room temperature not longer than 10 hr before use. In the laboratory, the placenta is suspended by the umbilical cord from a retort stand, with hemostats. The amnion is carefully separated from the chorion, starting from the base of the cord; with forceps and scissors, it is gradually pulled down over the placenta and collected in one piece. Because of the high hyaluronic-acid content of the cord, parts of the membrane immediately adjacent to it are not saved.

Before a membrane is chosen to initiate cultures, small fragments from various parts of it are spread on a slide and examined microscopically.[2] Only those membranes showing finely granular cells with distinct boundaries are used. Membranes with coarsely granular cells or cells with indistinct boundaries are rejected. After the membrane selected for cultivation has been washed several times in regular Hanks's solution to remove blood and debris, it is transferred to a 250-ml centrifuge bottle containing 100 ml of prewarmed 0.25 per cent trypsin in phosphate buffered saline at pH 7.4–7.6. After three quarters of an hour at 37° C, this solution is discarded and replaced with fresh, prewarmed trypsin. After 1–2 hr at 37° C, with occasional vigorous agitation, most of the cells are released into the solution. The membrane is then placed in a beaker and the cell suspension is transferred to a 250-ml centrifuge bottle. The undigested portion of the membrane is rinsed, with vigorous agitation, in two to three changes of balanced salt solution to increase the cell yield. These rinsing fluids are pooled and added to the centrifuge bottle, and the cells are sedimented at 1000 r.p.m. for 20 min. The supernatant fluid is drawn off and discarded, and the packed cells are resuspended in 7–8 ml of 0.5 per cent lactalbumin hydrolysate in Hanks's solution and transferred to a graduated 15-ml centrifuge tube. Cell clumps are broken up by mixing the suspension eight to ten times with a pipette. After the volume of the suspension is adjusted to 10 ml, a cell count is made, and the suspension is diluted with propagating medium (20 per cent human or ox serum and 0.5 per cent lactalbumin hydrolysate, in Hanks's balanced salt solution) to give a population density of 3.5×10^5 cells per ml. The cultures are prepared directly from this suspension. Whenever possible, however, antibiotics (pencillin, streptomycin, and Mycostatin) should also be included. The membranes from one delivery yield approximately the same quantity of cells as the kidneys of one monkey.[556]

Puck and his associates[413] follow a more gentle procedure in preparing trypsin-dispersed cell suspensions from human tissues. After the tissues have been minced to fine fragments, they are washed twice with saline A (see p. 59), covered with 0.05 per cent trypsin (1:500, in saline A), and placed in a 38° C bath for 15–45 min. Trypsinization is usually sufficient when the solution has become faintly cloudy and the edges of the tissue appear transparent and gelatinous. If one part of this suspension is diluted with several parts of nutrient medium containing serum protein, the action of the trypsin will be stopped automatically and the cultures can be prepared directly.

FROM WHOLE CHICK AND MOUSE EMBRYOS

In 1952, Dulbecco[92] prepared trypsin-dispersed cell suspensions from minced chick embryos. Five nine-day-old embryos were decapitated, washed in balanced salt solution, and pressed through a 24-mesh, stainless-steel grid that had been fitted to the bottom of a 50-ml syringe. The tissue pulp was collected in a 40-ml centrifuge tube containing 15 ml of balanced salt solution. After gravity sedimentation, the supernatant fluid was discarded and replaced with 15 ml of a 0.5 per cent solution of trypsin in balanced saline. The tube was placed in a water bath at 37° C for 10 min and then stirred vigorously by repeated pipetting. The pieces of tissue that remained intact were eliminated by straining the cell suspension through a platinum-gauze sieve unit.[133] The suspension was then washed twice by centrifuging at 1000 r.p.m. for 2 min and resuspending the sediment in 15 ml of balanced saline. Aliquots of the suspension were introduced into large Carrel flasks (80 mm i.d.) that contained a final volume of 11 ml of medium. Two such flasks could usually be made from one embryo.

Trypsin-dispersed cell suspensions from seven- to nine-day-old chick embryos were prepared by Medearis and Kibrick[318] and by Katz and his associates[251] without mincing. The embryos were washed with phosphate buffered saline (see p. 58) after removal of the eyes, incubated for 1 hr at room temperature (or for 30 min at 37° C) in 0.25 per cent trypsin solution adjusted to pH 7.8, and then agitated (magnetic stirrer) for 1 min. The released cells were separated from the remaining coarse debris and centrifuged at 1000 r.p.m. for 10 min, after which they were washed once and resuspended in nutrient medium. Sufficient cells were usually obtained from a single embryo to provide about 100 stationary-tube cultures. Cultures initiated with 2–4 × 10⁵ cells per ml were usually ready for use after 48 to 72 hr. When the medium was changed at appropriate intervals, the cultures remained suitable for virus inoculation for at least one month. Suspensions of chick-embryo cells have yielded satisfactory cultures after storage at 4° C for periods up to one week, although growth under these conditions was somewhat delayed.

Cooper[76] prepared suspensions of whole chick embryos either by forcing the embryos through a syringe and digesting the resulting pulp with trypsin[459] or by coarse mincing and digestion with trypsin. The latter method gave three or four times as many cells as the former, but the cell layers that were achieved seemed to be identical.

Medearis and Kibrick[318] also prepared trypsin-dispersed cell suspensions from mouse embryos. Six to eight 12- to 15-day-old embryos were treated with trypsin for 1 hr at 37° C and agitated for 1 min over a magnetic stirrer. Stationary tube cultures prepared with 6–8 × 10⁵ washed cells per ml were ready for use after five to seven days.

FROM NEWBORN-MOUSE BRAIN

Trypsin-dispersed cell suspensions were prepared by Medearis and and Kibrick[318] from the brains of newborn mice. Ten milliliters of 0.25 per cent trypsin solution adjusted to pH 7.5 were added to a brain mince prepared from four to eight anesthetized animals. After 1–2 min at room temperature, the trypsin was replaced and allowed to act for 5–10 min with occasional shaking. The cells were separated by centrifugation in the cold for 30 min at 300 r.p.m., washed once, and resuspended in nutrient medium at a concentration of 10^6 cells per ml. Stationary tube cultures prepared with 1 ml of this suspension were ready for use in four to five days.

Preparation of Cell Suspensions with Collagenase

Lasfargues[265] used collagenase to separate ducts and acini of the mammary gland of mice from the adipose tissue surrounding them. The enzyme preparation was of sufficient strength to hydrolyze 25 mg of collagen in 18–24 hr at a concentration of 0.02 mg per ml. Mammary glands from mice in an early stage of pregnancy were minced in a collagenase solution that was ten times as concentrated (0.2 mg per ml). It was found that the degree of dissociation depends upon time and agitation. Simple contact of the fragments for 1 hr at 37° C loosens the cells well enough to favor an epithelial migration. Moderate agitation is usually necessary to bring about the mechanical separation of the adipose tissue from the glandular stroma and the epithelium. A longer period of treatment (1½ hr) has injurious effects on the connective tissue that has remained attached to the epithelium; almost pure epithelium can then be obtained. A wrist-action shaker giving 120 agitations per min was used. After 10 min centrifugation at 1200 r.p.m., most of the fat could be separated and discarded. The sedimented cells were then washed and resuspended in culture medium.

More recently, Hinz and Syverton[237] have used commercially prepared collagenase (Worthington Biochemical Corp., Freehold, N.J.) in the preparation of cultures from human-, swine-, and rabbit-lung tissue. Because the enzyme was believed to be unstable in phosphate buffer, it was diluted with a solution of glucose, potassium chloride, and sodium chloride, at the levels used in Hanks's solution (*see* p. 57). An 0.1 per cent stock solution was stored at 5° C and used at a final concentration of 0.01 per cent. The lung tissue was minced into 1–2 mm fragments, washed repeatedly with Hanks's solution to remove erythrocytes, transferred to a screw-capped flask containing a Teflon-covered, magnetic stirring bar, covered to an approximate depth of 30 mm with collagenase solution, and incubated for 10 min in a water bath at 37° C. The contents of the flask were then agitated with a magnetic stirrer for 2 hr in a 37° C incubator. To prevent cell damage from heat, an inverted, Petri-dish plate was placed between the flask and the magnetic stirrer. The cells were then filtered through four layers of sterile gauze, centrifuged (20g for 6 min), separated from the supernatant fluid, and resuspended in nutrient medium.

Cells Released from Tissues by Chelating Agents

Considerable use has also been made of chelating agents as a means of dispersing animal tissue cells. In 1953, Anderson[3] dispersed rat-liver cells with various chelating agents including sodium citrate and Versene (ethylenediaminetetraacetic acid; distributed by Versenes, Inc., Framingham, Mass.). A year later, Zwilling[558] reported the use of Versene, together with Ca-Mg-free saline, for dissociating cells from chick embryos. Rinaldini,[436] who prepared a comprehensive review of the various methods of dissociating animal tissue cells, feels that more information on the permeability of the cell membrane to these substances is desirable before they are used routinely in culture work. Rinaldini found that citrate, Versene, and glycine, in concentrations of 0.1 and 1.0 per cent were much less effective than proteolytic enzymes for disintegrating minced embryonic heart and liver. Chelating agents, unlike proteolytic enzymes, are not inhibited by serum, and unless they are washed away they may do lasting damage to the cells.[436]

Albumin-Flotation Method of Separating Malignant Cells from Serosanguineous Fluids

In studies on malarial blood, Ferrebee and Geiman[147] described the separation of parasitized erythrocytes from normal erythrocytes by a method that took advantage of the difference in their specific gravity. Malarial whole blood was layered onto a solution of plasma albumin of high specific gravity. After centrifugation, the normal red cells, with a specific gravity greater than that of the albumin, were packed at the bottom of the tube while the lighter infected cells remained suspended at the interface between the plasma and albumin. A modification of this technique (Fig. 26) was employed by Fawcett and his associates[136,137] to separate and concentrate malignant cells from serosanguineous fluids, as follows:

(1) Two round-bottomed centrifuge tubes each containing 40 ml of serous fluid were centrifuged for 5 min at 2000 to 2500 r.p.m.

(2) The cellular sediment from both tubes was resuspended in 8 ml of normal saline solution to give a tenfold concentration of the cells.

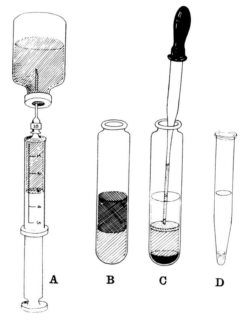

FIG. 26. Diagram showing principal steps in separating and concentrating leukocytes from whole blood or cancer cells from sanguineous body fluids, by albumin-flotation procedure: (A) Drawing 3.4 ml of 35 per cent bovine plasma albumin into syringe in which it will be diluted to 5 ml with saline; (B) Cell suspension layered on surface of albumin solution before centrifugation; (C) After centrifugation, erythrocytes are packed at bottom; lighter cells remaining at surface of albumin are transferred to small centrifuge tube; (D) Packed cells ready for study in smears and cultures. (D. W. Fawcett and B. L. Vallee.[136])

(3) Because the results of pilot experiments[137] had shown that 35 per cent crystalline bovine plasma albumin (Armour Laboratories, Chicago, Ill.) with a specific density of approximately 1.10 would give satisfactory results if diluted with normal saline to give a solution with

a density of about 1.06, such a dilution was made up as follows: A 5-ml syringe fitted with an 18-gauge needle was used to aspirate the 35 per cent albumin solution from its rubber-capped bottle up to the 3.4-ml mark. After the needle was removed, the syringe was immersed in saline solution and the plunger withdrawn to the 5-ml. mark. The saline and albumin were then mixed by inverting the syringe several times, after which the mixture was transferred to a 50-ml centrifuge tube.

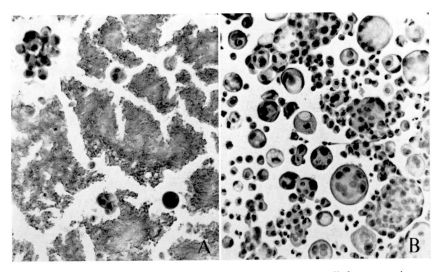

Fig. 27. Use of albumin-flotation method in separating cancer cells from sanguineous pleural fluid of a patient with adenocarcinoma of the lung; Papanicolaou stain. (*A*) Direct smear of pleural fluid showing cancer cells between dark masses of blood; (*B*) Smear of concentrated cancer and mesothelial cells after elimination of blood cells by albumin flotation. (D. W. Fawcett and B. L. Vallee.[136]) × 205.

(4) The saline suspension of cells was gently layered onto the albumin solution with a capillary pipette, great care being taken to prevent mixing.

(5) The tubes were then centrifuged 20–25 min at 2000 to 2500 r.p.m.

(6) After centrifugation, the erythrocytes were found at the bottom of the tube, and a thin, buffy layer containing malignant cells, mesothelial cells, and macrophages was found at the saline-albumin interface. This layer was pipetted off into a 15-ml conical centrifuge tube, and saline was added to the 15-ml mark.

(7) The cells were centrifuged 5 min to pack them, the supernatant was decanted, and the cells were ready for cultivation. It was also found useful to prepare a smear of the cells for immediate fixation and staining (Fig. 27).

Separation of Leukocytes from Peripheral Blood

BUFFY-COAT METHOD

In cultures, blood monocytes mature into macrophages that re-semble the wandering histiocytes of the body tissues. Since other types of leukocytes either do not persist *in vitro* or else become transformed to cells resembling macrophages, it is easily possible to obtain uniform cultures of macrophages by centrifuging the blood and isolating the buffy-coat layer of leukocytes and platelets that forms at the surface of the red cells, beneath the plasma layer. When fragments of buffy coat are cultivated in a plasma coagulum, the persisting cells invade the medium at a uniform rate from all sides of the explanted fragments. Within an hour after the cultures have been prepared, the original fragments become surrounded by a dense corona of cells, and colonies supplied with substances that stimulate cell migration are much larger than those without them. These differences become more pronounced during the next few days. When fragments of buffy coat are cultivated in fluid medium, they provide a convenient system in which one may study the special properties of blood cells and blood serum, just as they also provide a uniform source of test material. If the medium contains 20 to 50 per cent serum or its equivalent in a balanced salt solution, the monocytes will become attached to the glass and multiply with great rapidity for several days.

If the blood is taken without an anticoagulant, it should be centri-fuged in ice-packed carriers (*see* p. 88). Otherwise, it may coagulate during centrifugation. In withdrawing the plasma from each tube of centrifuged blood, a capillary pipette is used to remove the plasma as completely as possible. A drop of chick embryo extract (or thrombin) is then deposited on the surface of the leukocyte layer and spread by rotating the tube. These operations must be carried out gently so as not to disturb the leukocytes and cause them to mix with the under-lying red cells. After the embryo extract has been added, the tubes are set aside at room temperature for a half hour or so to await the coagulation of the leukocyte layer. With experience, the investigator will be able to judge from the general appearance of the layers when they may be removed. Otherwise, they are tested from time to time by sliding a platinum spatula around the periphery of the layer in order to loosen it from the wall of the tube. If the leukocytes are firm enough, the entire layer may be folded over the spatula and transferred to a glass plate for cutting or else placed temporarily in phosphate buffered saline (*see* p. 58). If by this time, however, the underlying red cells have also coagulated, the leukocytes may still be salvaged by loosening the entire coagulum from the tube and shaking it out into a Petri dish. A knife is then used to cut the leukocyte layer from the red cells. After the discoid layers have been washed several times in buffered saline, they are cut into strips and fragments for the preparation of the cultures. As the fragments are cut, they are placed in fresh saline and washed several times before preparing the cultures. Each fragment should be clean, firm, and 1–2 sq mm in surface area. If a quantitative experiment is to be made, the fragments should be of approximately equal size. It is not always possible, however, to obtain suitable fragments from certain samples of blood. Although this requirement is not important for cultures in which it is desired only to obtain a representative cell population, it is most important if the cells are to be cultivated in plasma for quantitative estimates of the size of colony formation. If populations of comparable size are required for fluid cultures, it is desirable to separate and concentrate the leukocytes by the albumin-flotation method described in the following section.

ALBUMIN-FLOTATION METHOD

Vallee and his associates[522] and Weiss and Fawcett[534] adapted the albumin-flotation method of Ferrebee and Geiman[147] to the separation of leukocytes from whole blood (Fig. 28). This method takes advantage of the difference in the specific gravity of leukocytes and erythrocytes. Thus, when whole blood is layered onto a solution of crystalline, bovine plasma albumin with a specific density of approximately 1.079, which is intermediate in density between leukocytes and erythrocytes, subsequent centrifugation causes the leukocytes to collect at the plasma-albumin interface whereas the erythrocytes are thrown to the bottom of the tube (Fig. 26). When the specific density of the albumin solution is higher (e.g., 1.09), many erythrocytes remain suspended in the albumin layer, and some are intermingled with the leukocytes. When the density is lower (e.g., 1.07 to 1.06), the leukocytes are brought down with erythrocytes and in increasing numbers as the density is decreased. Because the physical properties of

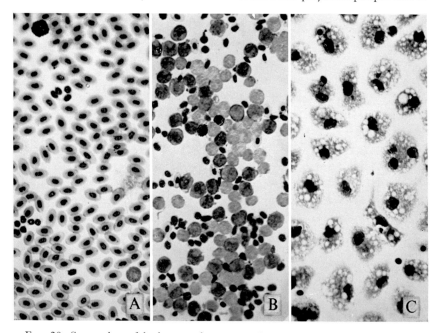

FIG. 28. Separation of leukocytes from normal peripheral blood of chicken by albumin-flotation method. (A) Smear of freshly drawn blood showing two leukocytes and several clusters of thrombocytes; Wright's stain; × 400. (B) Smear of leukocytes separated from blood by albumin-flotation; Wright's stain; × 400. (C) Macrophages that developed after leukocytes had been cultivated *in vitro* for three days; May-Grünwald-Giemsa stain; × 490. (D. W. Fawcett and B. L. Vallee.[136])

different batches of albumin vary slightly, it is best to prepare a somewhat more concentrated solution than is ordinarily required for leukocyte flotation, and this solution can be diluted after appropriate pilot tests have been made.

In practice, leukocytes may be separated from fowl blood as follows: Into a syringe containing 0.05 ml of heparin (100 mg per cent), 10 ml of blood is drawn from a wing vein and delivered into a sterile tube. With a second 10-ml syringe and an 18-gauge needle, sterile 35 per cent albumin solution is drawn up to the 8.4-ml mark. The needle is then withdrawn from the bottle of albumin, immersed in normal saline solution, and the syringe filled to the 10-ml mark. The albumin and saline are mixed by inverting the syringe several times. Five milliliters of this diluted albumin solution (with a specific density of approximately 1.079) are delivered into each of two 15-ml conical centrifuge tubes. With a capillary pipette, 5 ml of the heparinized blood are carefully layered onto the albumin in each tube, and the tubes are stoppered and spun for 12 to 14 min in an SB No. 1 International centrifuge at 2000 r.p.m. The leukocyte layer is then found floating at the plasma-albumin interface with 5 mm or more of clear albumin separating it from the erythrocytes. A pipette is introduced through the supernatant plasma and the leukocyte layer is taken up in about 1 ml of fluid without contamination by erythrocytes. The leukocytes from each of the tubes are then combined, gently resuspended in 10 ml of saline solution containing 4 per cent albumin, and centrifuged for 5 min at low speed. The washing solution is then discarded and the leukocytes are resuspended in 10 ml of the final culture medium for distribution to ten culture flasks. Thus, each culture is seeded with the leukocytes from 1 ml of blood. Otherwise, a hemocytometer count can be made from one drop of the cell suspension, and replicate cultures can be prepared with known numbers of cells.

PHYTOHEMAGGLUTININ METHOD

In 1955, Rigas and Osgood[434] reported methods for the purification of the phytohemagglutinin of *Phaseolus vulgaris* (red kidney beans), which agglutinates human erythrocytes as well as those of various laboratory animals, including frogs. Because phytohemagglutinin is nontoxic and does not agglutinate human leukocytes and nucleated erythrocytes, it is suitable for the separation of nucleated cells of blood or marrow from erythrocytes for culture purposes.

Hungerford and his associates[242, 363] draw 10 ml of venous blood into a sterile syringe wet with heparin, mix the blood with 0.2 ml of Bacto-phytohemagglutinin (Difco Laboratories, Inc., Detroit, Mich.), and allow it to stand 30–60 min in an ice bath. The blood is then centrifuged at 300–500 r.p.m. (approximately 25g) for 5–10 min at 5° C to sediment most of the erythrocytes. The supernatant plasma, which contains the leukocytes in suspension, can be combined directly with other ingredients of the culture medium (*see also* p. 193).

IX

Coverslip Cultures

COVERSLIPS were first used in tissue culture to make hanging-drop preparations over hollow-ground (depression) slides. First, a single coverslip was used; later, two were used, a small one on the inside that was made to adhere to a larger one on the outside by means of a film of moisture. After the outer coverslip was detached from the depression slide, the inner coverslip bearing the culture could be washed and supplied with fresh nutrient without otherwise disturbing the culture and with little danger of bacterial contamination. Both single- and double-coverslip preparations are still being used to advantage for many purposes. Single coverslips are used when it is desired to make short-term cultures for careful light-microscope study under optical conditions that restrict the total thickness of the preparation to a minimum (Figs. 32 and 33), and Pomerat[398] recommends single-coverslip preparations for large-scale screening studies of the effect of chemicals on cells. Double-coverslip preparations, introduced by Maximow,[311] are used when it is desired to have long-term cultures on coverslips that can be studied and photographed under the highest magnifications of the light microscope (Figs. 35 and 36). A description of some of the more basic coverslip procedures will now be presented.

Preparation of Single-Coverslip Cultures with Plasma

If the cultures are to be prepared either on a table in a sterile room or in a protective hood or cabinet, the supplies are unwrapped and placed on an auxiliary table within easy reach of the operator. Three or four large sterile tubes (e.g., 30 × 130 mm) are opened and placed flat on the working surface to the right of the operator. These tubes are for the accommodation of instruments required in preparing the tissues. The lower section of the pipette rack (Fig. 29), which may be sterilized by flaming, is also useful for the protection of instruments. A package containing several medium tubes (18 × 100 mm) is unwrapped, and the tubes are placed in a clean pan or tray within easy reach. It is important that their corks should not have worked out during handling. An unwrapped tube that has lost its cork is always discarded. Four or more of the tubes are opened, flamed about the neck, and set in the pipette rack. Two fine capillary pipettes and two or more coarse ones are removed from their container, flamed about the top, and fitted with rubber nipples. They are then flamed throughout their length and inserted in the tubes that have been placed in the rack. One of the coarse pipettes is filled with buffered salt solution or whatever fluid is chosen for washing the tissues (*see* p. 119).

The tissue to be cultivated is then transferred to a glass plate (*see* p. 22), moistened with the washing fluid, and cut into a number of small fragments not exceeding 1 mm in diameter. If it is necessary to wash the fragments to free them of excess blood, they may either be irrigated on the plate or transferred with a coarse, flat-tipped pipette to a small test tube containing the washing fluid and then to a covered depression slide or Petri dish along with a few drops of fluid. The fragments are now ready for implantation in the culture medium. Before proceeding, the working area is cleared of all instruments and glassware no longer required. Used glassware is collected in a pan or vat the moment it can be discarded. If cataract knives have been used, they are carefully dried and set aside. Cataract knives, which must never be flamed, are removed one by one as required from the boxes in which they are sterilized.

One of the capillary pipettes is partly filled with plasma, the other with embryo extract (or its equivalent). With freshly flamed forceps, four glass or mica coverslips are placed in a row on a raised platform of black plastic (or a board, ¾ in. thick, that is either painted or covered with a black, washable fabric) immediately in front of the operator (Fig. 29A). A single drop of plasma is placed near the center of each coverslip and spread with a cataract knife or a glass rod. During this operation, the coverslip is steadied with a platinum needle held

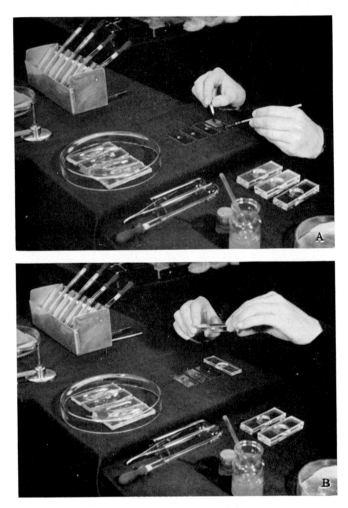

Fig. 29. Preparation of hanging-drop cultures: (A) the medium containing the tissue is spread with a circular motion of the knife tip; (B) depression slides, bearing a trace of Vaseline at each end, are placed down over the coverslips. Eventually, the preparations are inverted and sealed with paraffin.

in the other hand. The tissue fragments are then removed from the washing fluid and deposited in the plasma, one in each drop. Next, a drop of embryo extract (or its equivalent) is added, and the various ingredients are thoroughly mixed, again with a knife or glass rod. Each drop should be regular in outline and spread to cover an area of approximately equal size throughout the series. It should be neither too small nor yet so large as to come into contact with the edge of the concavity of the depression slide that is to accommodate it.

Finally, and before coagulation takes place, the tissue fragments are oriented so as to lie near the center of the medium. In the meantime, several pairs of round depression slides are prepared with Vaseline. Since an excess of Vaseline is likely to run into the culture upon incubation, only a trace is used. This is applied with a sterile glass rod to three or four slides near the area that will be in contact with the ends of the coverslip. Each of these slides is now placed face to face with an unprepared slide. The pairs are then separated and oriented, depression side down, over the coverslips (Fig. 29B).

By this time, the medium will have coagulated, and it will be possible to turn the preparations over, mark them for identification, and set them aside to be paraffined. The Vaseline will serve to keep the coverslips in place until another set has been made from the remaining tissue fragments. When the desired number of cultures have been made, they are all sealed with melted paraffin to prevent evaporation and set away for incubation. The paraffin is applied with a brush around the entire margin of the coverslip.

There are now available culture slides with flat depressions that are ground and polished for careful microscopic work (*see* p. 19).

Preparation of Subcultures from Single-Coverslip Cultures with Plasma

If it is desired to propagate cells indefinitely as single-coverslip preparations, it will be necessary to transfer them at frequent intervals to fresh coverslips and new media. Otherwise, they will soon degenerate. The frequency with which the cells should be subcultured will depend largely on their origin and on the richness of the medium. Cells from freshly explanted tissues multiply rapidly and should be transferred every few days in order to maintain active growth and multiplication.

Before transferring a set of hanging-drop cultures, one should study them under the microscope in order to determine the particular treatment they are to receive. Cultures to be divided may be so designated by making appropriate inscriptions on the coverslip with a glass-marking pencil. If any portion of a culture is to be discarded, it can be blocked out with pencil. Later, when the coverslip is removed and the culture inverted for cutting, the red or black marking is easily seen and that portion of the culture resting over it may be avoided.

A mica coverslip is nonbreakable and may easily be pried loose from a depression slide. A glass coverslip requires more delicate handling. An old cataract knife or a razor blade is useful for this purpose. The paraffin is removed as completely as possible from the surface and margin of the coverslip, in order to loosen it more easily and to ensure against an uneven surface. If the surface is not perfectly flat before the coverslip is inverted on a glass plate or a porcelain plaque for cutting, the pressure of the knife may crack it. When the paraffin has been removed, the sharp point of the knife is inserted most cautiously between the cover and the slide at various points on the margin. The lifting is done with balanced effort from all sides, for every part of the coverslip must be freed from the paraffin and underlying Vaseline before any portion of it is raised.

In subdividing a culture, it is first of all essential that the cut surfaces be clean, not ragged. Consequently it is necessary that the knives be extremely sharp and that the culture be cut by a single, quick, forward thrust of the blade, the whole length of which bears upon the coagulum, and with the back of the knife tilted slightly away from the operator. It is also important that the four marginal incisions be made well within the zone of outgrowth, at a point where the cell population is fairly dense (Fig. 30). After the culture has been entirely severed from the surrounding medium, one is in a better position than before to judge the advisability of halving it. Because each incision causes a rapid contraction of both cells and medium, an exact division is more easily approximated if the culture is freed from the surrounding coagulum before the fifth incision is made. If the halves are large enough, they may in turn be divided by a sixth incision, to give four subcultures.

It is sometimes difficult to decide if a culture should be divided at the time of transfer. Size alone is not necessarily the determining factor. If the central area of a culture intended for strain has become unusually thick, the culture should be divided, although it may be smaller than usual. Otherwise, the innermost cells may become necrotic. When the marginal areas are large enough, an even better

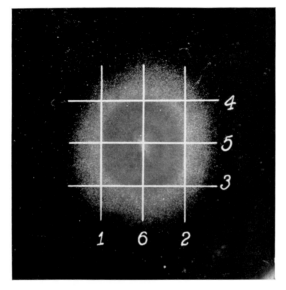

Fig. 30. Incisions made in preparing transplants of a colony of tissue cells cultivated in a plasma coagulum. The thin, marginal areas are eliminated by the 1st, 2nd, 3rd and 4th incisions. If the culture is to be divided, a 5th incision is made; if four transplants are needed, both a 5th and a 6th are made.

remedy is to cut away and discard the whole central portion. The marginal cuttings may then be embedded in the new coagulum in close proximity to one another.

Extreme care must be taken not to mutilate the culture fragments after they have been cut loose from the old medium, and the use of a needle should never be necessary. A culture fragment is transferred from the old clot to the washing fluid on the blade of the knife used in cutting it. Once in the fluid, the fragment may easily be dislodged from the knife if it is kept well back from the tip of the blade. It should never be scraped off on the edge of the concavity. Similarly, when a fragment is removed from the washing fluid, the knife (or platinum spatula, if it is being transferred to a flask) is slipped under it and the fragment caught by an upward sweep of the blade. If the culture has become folded around the edge of the knife, one may wash it loose in the plasma by rotating the knife very quickly around the long axis, taking care not to crush the cells.

Fig. 31. Rack (wood) for the accommodation of lying-drop, perforated-slide, and double-coverslip cultures; also, a small Coplin jar (Columbia staining dish) with vertical grooves to hold four coverslips during washing or staining.

Preparation of Single-Coverslip Cultures
without Plasma

It is extremely easy to prepare depression-slide cultures in which the cells are placed directly on the coverslip in a fluid medium. After the coverslip has been covered with a depression slide in the manner already described, the preparation is sealed from beneath with paraffin and allowed to incubate with the coverslip on the under side (Fig. 31). If the culture is left undisturbed in this position for 24 hr, it may then be inverted for study under the microscope. By this time the cells will have become firmly attached to the glass.

Ring-Slide Cultures

Although concave depression slides are convenient to use, they are optically poor and are never suitable for careful light microscopy or for photography. According to a simple alternative devised by Gey, hanging drop cultures are prepared on coverslips and ordinary thin slides held apart by metal rings of various sizes and thicknesses. The sterile metal ring is dipped in a warm sealing mixture (e.g., 1 part Vaseline, 6 parts paraffin), drained for a moment, and placed on the slide. The inverted coverslip bearing the culture is then pressed down over the ring, or the slide and ring are pressed down over the coverslip. This arrangement gives a preparation with good optical properties. The outside diameter of the rings should be somewhat less than the width of the slides and coverslips that are chosen.

Double-Coverslip Cultures

Because the volume of medium in the ordinary hanging-drop preparation is relatively small, it must be renewed at frequent intervals. To facilitate renewals of medium, Maximow[311] devised a double-coverslip type of preparation in which use is made of a large depression slide, 75 × 45 mm, with a spherical concavity 36 mm in diameter and 5 mm deep. The culture is prepared on a small, round or square coverslip that is kept in the center of a larger coverslip (mica or glass) by means of a drop of water. The larger coverslip covers the depression in the slide and is sealed in place with paraffin. The advantage of this type of culture rests in the ease with which the inner coverslip, which remains sterile on both sides, may be manipulated in order to wash the culture or change the fluid medium.

To wash the cultures, the inner coverslip bearing the tissue is dropped into a Columbia staining dish (provided with vertical grooves for the accommodation of four coverslips; Fig. 31) containing fresh medium or balanced salt solution and subsequently transferred from

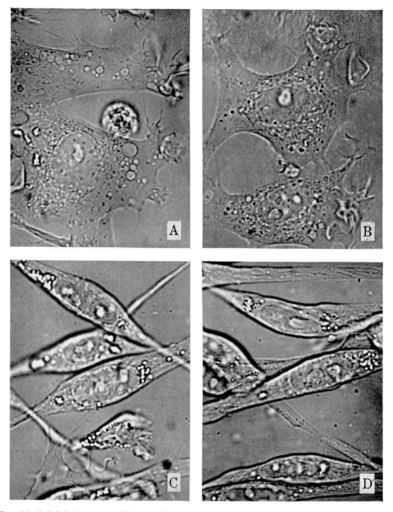

FIG. 32. (A) Malignant cells from dibenzanthracene mouse tumor C_{37} removed from an animal after three generations and cultivated for one day in a hanging drop. (Compare Fig. 32B.) × 1100. (B) Cells from a culture of the tumor shown in A but removed from an animal after 25 generations. The cells have retained their peculiar morphological features through 22 animal passages. (W. H. Lewis, unpublished data.) × 1100. (C) Malignant cells from mouse tumor PHS 1 (produced by dibenzanthracene) removed from an animal after 22 generations and cultivated for one day in a hanging drop. (Compare Fig. 32D.) × 1100. (D) Cells from a culture of the tumor shown in C but removed from an animal after 37 generations. The cells have retained their peculiar morphological features through 15 animal passages. (W. H. Lewis.[281]) × 1100.

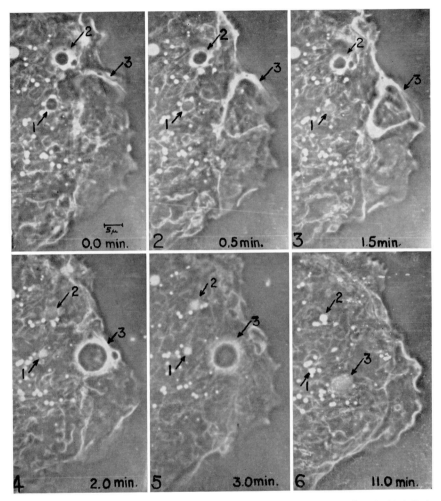

FIG. 33. Portion of a living, human chondromyxosarcoma cell (strain D-1 Re) photographed at various time intervals with phase-contrast optics. Note prominent membrane-like pseudopodium below region marked 3 (in 1) and gradual incorporation of inclusion droplets (marked 1, 2, and 3) entrapped by pinocytosis,[282] with a progressive diminution in their size as fluid is lost and protein materials become more concentrated. The numerous, smaller bright masses in the cytoplasm originated in the same manner from previously ingested fluid droplets. A.O. 1.8 mm, Bright M-phase objective. (G. O. Gey.[177])

one dish to another, if it is desired to prolong the washing. After the culture has been washed, its coverslip is attached, as before, to a fresh outer coverslip, a few drops of fresh medium are added, and the preparation is sealed to a fresh slide. Ordinarily, the cultures are incubated

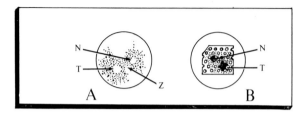

FIG. 34. Diagram of a fixed and stained culture preparation consisting of normal kidney tissue and renal adenocarcinoma, of frog. These tissues can be maintained side-by-side for several weeks on the inner coverslip (A) of a double coverslip system, under perforated cellophane (B), in a Romicron slide. The cellophane (B), to which the tissue fragments usually become attached, is peeled from the original cover lip (A) just before fixation. Note location of normal (N) and tumor (T) cells with interzone growth area (Z), which is suitable for detailed studies of cell changes. × 1. (Courtesy of W. R. Duryee.[97])

in a lying-drop position with the depression slide inverted. For this purpose a suitable rack should be provided (Fig. 31).

Duryee[97] has improved the double coverslip method very considerably by using Romicron culture slides (see p. 19) and 11-mm squares of perforated cellophane, under which the tissues are placed in a fluid medium. The Romicron slide has a ground and polished flat depression that favors high-power light microscopy. Perforated cellophane protects the tissues (see p. 16) and favors gaseous exchange, and microtool operations can be performed through the holes. Also, by cutting off a corner of the cellophane square, a convenient reference grid is provided that permits ready identification of cells and structures adhering to the cellophane. Before the culture is fixed for staining, the cellophane is peeled from the coverslip to yield a separate preparation that complements the one made from the original coverslip (Fig. 34).

Duryee[98] uses this improved method to advantage in studying virus-induced renal cancers of the frog and in comparing the sequence of nuclear events in transforming frog cells (Fig. 35) with similar situations observed in human neoplasms.[99] His medium for frog tissues* consists, approximately, of chemically defined NCTC-109, 48 per cent; calf serum, 15 per cent; chick embryo extract (frozen), 15 per cent; distilled water, 22 per cent (to make the medium isotonic with amphibian cells); and, sufficient 0.01N HCl to adjust the final

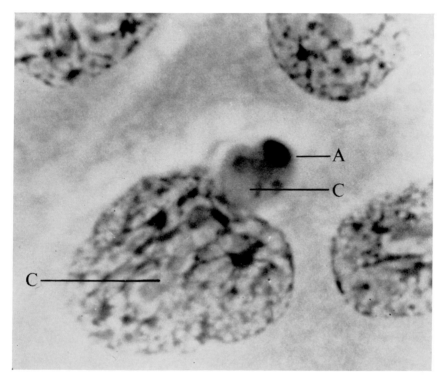

FIG. 35. Nucleus of cell from renal adenocarcinoma of the frog, showing extrusion into the cytoplasm of green-staining [RNA] nucleolar core (C) along with dark Feulgen-positive [DNA] aggregates (A), presumed to be tumor virus. Cells cultivated in fluid medium in double-coverslip preparation (Romicron slide) under perforated cellophane. Feulgen–Fast-Green stain after alcohol-formalin-acetic fixation. (W. R. Duryee.[98]) × 3600.

medium to pH 7.8. Under these conditions, frog-kidney explants maintained at 26° C yield three-dimensional, branching cords of cells that are reminiscent of the sort of growth one might expect to obtain only in a plasma coagulum, and confluent layers of cells develop on the inner coverslip and on the cellophane (Fig. 34).

* Duryee, W. R. Personal communication.

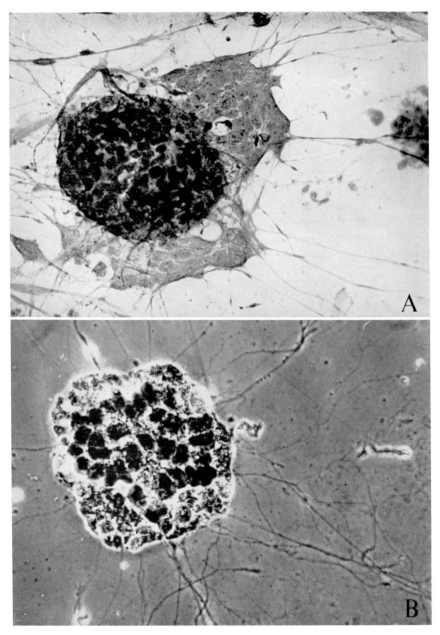

Fɪɢ. 36. Sympathicoblastoma (double-coverslip cultures): (*A*) Neurites and neuro-epithelium in 17-day-old culture from a metastatic nodule in a one-year-old child; Bodian's protargol stain; $\times$ 325. (*B*) Living, seven-day-old culture (phase-contrast illumination) from a metastasis in a three-year-old child. (M. R. Murray and A. P. Stout.[355]) $\times$ 335.

Murray and Stout[355,356] use the double-coverslip method in the classification and diagnosis of human tumor cells (Fig. 36). In general it may be said that in certain instances the use of tissue culture as a means of diagnosing tumors may (1) be quicker and more reliable than the routine section method (e.g., sympathicoblastoma[354]), (2) provide a useful supplement to the clinical and pathological findings (e.g., neurilemmoma,[350,352] lymphoma, Hodgkin's disease[193]), (3) serve to distinguish between several possible diagnoses (e.g., liposarcoma,[353] rhabdomyosarcoma,[518] and fibrosarcoma or myxoma), or (4) be of no obvious benefit in diagnosis, though useful in collecting general information.

Perforated-Slide Cultures

Excellent optical conditions are provided by a system in which glass coverslips are fixed to the two opposing sides of a thin, perforated slide. One of the coverslips bears the culture, and the space between the two coverslips is filled with nutrient fluid, at least in the central area where the culture is located. The early perforated slides were of glass and were used by Gey, Carrel, Fischer, and others for the preparation of culture material for the microcinema, where the optical requirements are most exacting. Later, Gey devised perforated slides of stainless steel. These slides (available from Microbiological Associates, Inc., Bethesda 14, Md.) are 2 × 3 in. in size, with a circular perforation $1\frac{3}{8}$ in. in diameter, and are made from sheet metal approximately 0.029 in. in thickness. Fluid-medium cultures prepared on depression slides or on ring slides (*see* p. 145) and intended for subsequent transfer to perforated slides are prepared on coverslips of the appropriate size and attached to the depression slides in the usual manner. For the first 24 hr, the cultures are incubated in the lying-drop position, that is, with the tissues resting on the coverslip. On the second day they are inverted, with the culture in the hanging-drop position. This procedure allows the cells to attach themselves to the glass during the early period of incubation and makes it possible for debris to fall away from the cells, leaving them in better condition for cytological study. Suitable racks (Fig. 31) are provided to accommodate cultures of this sort.

X

Flask and Tube Cultures with Plasma

AS INDICATED in the last chapter, the slide-coverslip methods of preparing hanging-drop and lying-drop cultures are exceedingly useful for various special purposes. But because the volume of medium that can be accommodated in these systems is relatively small, it is difficult to measure it accurately and to follow changes that may occur in its composition, and the space for air is usually less than optimal. It was in an effort to overcome these difficulties that the flask procedures were developed by Carrel.[45] During the past 35 years, these procedures have been gradually improved and modified to satisfy an almost endless variety of special conditions. Yet the underlying purpose has remained the same throughout, namely, to provide a relatively stable system in which both the effect of the medium on the cells and the effect of the cells on the medium can be studied simultaneously over long periods. In the present chapter, attention will be given to the cultivation of tissues in flasks, tubes, and bottles when a plasma coagulum is used. Subsequent chapters will deal with the cultivation of cells and tissues in fluid media.

Briefly, the flask techniques for the cultivation of tissues in plasma depend on the preparation of a two-phase system within the flask, one being a permeable, semisolid plasma or fibrinogen (*see* p. 169) coagulum in which the tissues are embedded, the other, a fluid phase that may be introduced and removed at will, according to the nature of the experiment. The frequency with which flask cultures are transferred depends on the nature of the tissue, the purpose of the experiment, and the rapidity with which the cells are allowed to multiply. The lower the rate of cell multiplication, the easier it becomes to maintain cultures in good condition without subculturing them. Many years ago, fragments of chick-embryo breast muscle were kept alive in single flasks for an entire year without being subcultured[374] (Fig. 37). The

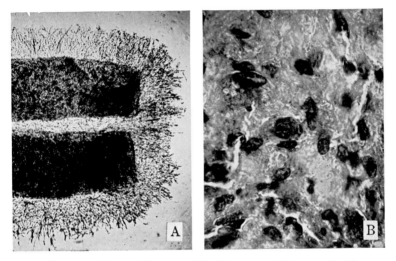

FIG. 37. (A) Fringe of new cells surrounding fragments of tissue excised from a culture of chick-embryo breast muscle that had been embedded in a plasma coagulum and treated with adult-chicken serum for one year before being transferred to a fresh flask. (B) Section through center of a tissue fragment that had been treated with adult-chicken serum for one year in a single flask. Fixed in Zenker-formol and stained according to Masson's trichrome procedure. (R. C. Parker.[374]) (A) × 21; (B) × 620.

nutrient materials were supplied by frequent applications of fresh medium consisting of chicken serum diluted with Tyrode's solution. Since then, such experiences have become commonplace.

Most tissue-culture workers have noted that the coagulum of long-continued plasma cultures tends to become more and more opaque the longer the cultures are carried with regular renewals of the nutrient fluid. Hanks[208,209] made a considerable study of this phenomenon and came to the conclusion that the coagulum adsorbs certain inorganic constituents, particularly calcium phosphate complexes, from the fluid phase of the medium and that, because of this, the fluid bathing the cells of plasma cultures soon comes to have a composition quite different from that intended. Hanks also suggested that this process may be one of the factors that causes plasma to become growth inhibitory during prolonged maintenance as a culture substrate. Some years ago,[376] however, it was observed in the author's laboratory that mouse-fibroblast cultures that had barely survived in old plasma clots that were almost opaque with precipitates and debris would suddenly burst into almost explosive activity and proceed to repopulate the entire coagulum with healthy young cells. In these instances, at least, the old clots were not inhibiting to the new cells that appeared in the cultures.

Preparation of Plasma Cultures in Carrel Flasks

For convenience in describing the preparation of plasma cultures in flasks, it will be assumed that D-3.5 Carrel flasks are to be used, although the techniques can be applied equally well to many other types of flasks and bottles now available (*see* pp. 17, 18). Carrel D-3.5 flasks are of modest proportions, particularly sturdy, and especially desirable for general purposes. Also, reasonably good photographs can be taken through them (*see* Figs. 17, 18, 44, 58, and 90).

To obtain the best optical conditions, the plasma coagulum should be as thin as the nature of the culture will allow. The original clot for D-3.5 flasks is rarely greater than 1.2 ml or less than 1.0 ml. It might, for chick-embryo tissues, consist of 0.3 ml of plasma and 0.7 ml of a mixture containing 1 part 0.01 per cent phenol red made up in Earle's balanced salt solution or its equivalent (to serve as an indicator of pH), 3 parts embryo tissue extract (1:12), and 3 parts balanced salt solution.

When everything is in readiness for the actual preparation of the cultures, two straight-tipped, platinum spatulas (Fig. 11) are heated to a glow and placed for protection in a large sterile tube to the right of the worker. (Eventually the spatulas are used alternately, so that no time is lost in waiting for one of them to cool.) Four or six flasks are next placed in a row across the table, necks to the right, and the neck of each is carefully flamed by passing an inverted burner over the entire series. With a clean, graduated pipette, 0.3 ml of plasma is measured into each flask, and each is shaken carefully in order to spread the plasma evenly over the bottom. The flasks are again flamed about the neck. To the plasma in the first flask is now added 0.7 ml of the diluting fluid, which is thoroughly mixed with the plasma by gently whirling the flask a few times. To retard coagulation the various media are kept on ice until the moment of use. But as soon as the diluting fluid has been mixed with the plasma, no time should be lost in planting the tissue fragments. Each fragment is transferred from the washing fluid (*see* p. 119) and oriented near the center of the flask with one of the platinum spatulas. This spatula is then thoroughly flamed and returned to its protecting tube. Or the tissue fragments may be placed in the flasks with a plain, ungraduated pipette (one that is neither too fine nor too coarse), provided the operator is able to transfer the tissue fragments with a minimum of fluid.

Each of the remaining cultures is prepared in the same manner. After the last one has been finished, all the flasks receive a final flaming before being stoppered. If the flasks are carefully flamed before the sterile stopper is introduced, any amount of moisture that may eventually collect around the inner surface of the stopper will not endanger the sterility of the cultures. When moisture is present care must be taken not to contaminate the culture upon withdrawing the stopper. The stopper is loosened little by little, and all moisture is carefully dried away from the opening by constant flaming. This procedure prevents moisture that has come in contact with the rim of the neck from flowing back into the medium.

If the cultures that have just been prepared are too alkaline, they may be treated before they are stoppered with a gas mixture consisting of 8 per cent CO_2 in air (*see* p. 60). The gas mixture is fed into each flask in turn by means of a sterile pipette for a period of about 15 sec. If, after 10 or 15 min the cultures are still too alkaline, they should be reopened and gassed for a longer period.

Subsequent Treatment of Plasma Cultures in Flasks

After the cultures have been incubated for 24 hr, they are "patched" by superimposing a second coagulum upon the first. Patching compensates for any digestion of fibrin that has taken place or that may be

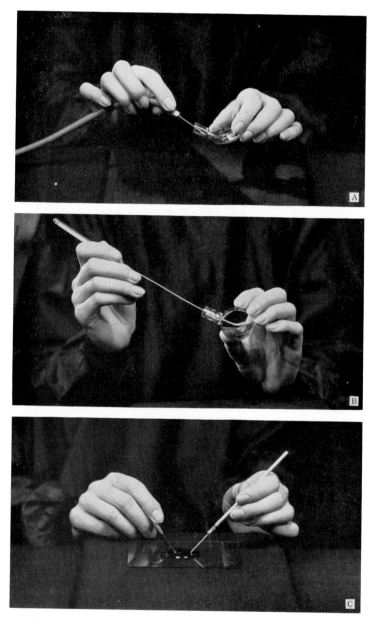

Fig. 38. (A) Removal of culture fluid from a D-3.5 flask by suction. (B) Plasma culture being freed from the bottom of a D-3.5 flask with the aid of a platinum spatula. (C) Plasma coagulum after it has been removed from the flask and deposited on a glass plate for cutting.

expected to occur upon further incubation (*see* p. 168). It is especially recommended for very active cultures, for example, those cultivated in a medium containing large amounts of tissue extract. If necessary, it may be done on the day the cultures are made but only after the first coagulum has become quite solid.

Cultures are usually patched with the same medium in the same amount as was used in the original clot. The diluting materials are added first and spread over the entire coagulum before the plasma is introduced. Once the plasma is added, it is thoroughly mixed with the other materials. Before the cultures are returned to the incubator, the pH is adjusted by gassing. On the following (the third) day, the cultures receive an additional supply of nutrient materials in the form of a supernatant fluid. Two days later, the supernatant fluid is aspirated by suction (Fig. 38*A*) and replaced with a fresh one. In certain instances, where the plasma of the coagulum has become badly digested, it must be reinforced with a second patch. Under these circumstances another supernatant fluid need not be added until later if at all. Rapidly growing cultures from which it is hoped to isolate cell strains (*see* p. 162) are usually transferred to fresh flasks on the seventh day.

Before patching a culture or a series of cultures for the second time, it is often advisable to reduce the size of the coagulum by inverting the flasks for several hours (or overnight) before removing them from the incubator. The fluid, or a measured quantity of it, may then be withdrawn to provide more space for air and additional medium. This procedure ensures a quick and easy removal of waste materials.

Preparation of Subcultures from Plasma
Cultures in Flasks

The length of time elapsing before it becomes necessary to transplant plasma culture to fresh flasks and new media depends upon both the nature of the tissue and the rapidity with which the cells have been allowed to multiply. The lower the rate of cell multiplication, the easier it becomes to maintain the cultures in good condition without transplanting them. As already indicated, fibroblasts cultivated in serum have been kept alive for a year without being disturbed in any way except by regular changes of the nutrient fluids that bathed them[374] (Fig. 37).

The evening before plasma cultures are to be transplanted to fresh flasks, they are inverted and left in this position (in the incubator) until the time of transfer. This procedure, which serves to drain the fluid from the interstices of the plasma, greatly reduces the thickness of the coagulum and makes it easier to cut the cultures into fragments of equal size.

When a flask culture is transplanted, the entire coagulum is removed from the flask, after which the culture is trimmed and subdivided in the manner already described for coverslip preparations (*see* p. 142). With a little practice, it will be found possible to remove the discoid clot from the flask in its entirety without tearing it. The flask is held in one hand, and a platinum spatula is passed through its neck. With the tip of the spatula, the coagulum is then detached from one side of the flask. The curved elbow of the spatula is used to roll the coagulum back over itself. Care should be taken to manipulate the clot evenly across the entire width of the flask (Fig. 38*B*). As the thin central area containing the cell colony is approached, the utmost caution should be exercised and only the thin, straightened edge of the spatula should be applied. This part of the clot will be found to adhere more firmly to the glass than will the adjacent cell-free areas. Finally, when the coagulum has been entirely loosened from the interior, the neck of the flask is thoroughly flamed and the contents shaken out onto a glass plate for cutting (Fig. 38*C*).

The transplants prepared for subcultures are placed in a protective solution consisting of a nutrient fluid at appropriate pH until fresh flasks are ready to receive them. A separate bath is reserved for each fragment or group of fragments taken from any one flask. It is advisable to prepare all of the fragments to be used in a given experiment before introducing any of them into the new flasks.

Preparation of Roller-Tube Cultures with Plasma

Roller-tube cultures are now being used very extensively as a means of preparing cultures with relatively small volumes of medium and insuring an even exchange of nutrients and waste products between the medium and the cells. The first practical roller-tube system was devised by Gey.[176,179] According to the technique most commonly used, the cultures are prepared in test tubes or bottles that are rotated continuously around their long axis, in a nearly horizontal rack accommodated in an incubator (Fig. 39). The rack is driven by a

FIG. 39. Motor-driven wheel for slow rotation (about 12 revs. per hr) of tube cultures during incubation. Tube carrier can be disengaged from drive shaft for transportation. (New Brunswick Scientific Co., Inc., New Brunswick, N.J.)

motor to give from 6 to 15 revs. per hr and is so tilted that the fluid bathing the cultures does not come in contact with the stoppered ends of the tubes. The cells may be cultivated in a thin coagulum of plasma (Fig. 40) or fibrinogen (*see* p. 169) or may be cultivated directly on the walls of the tubes in a fluid medium (*see* p. 179).

The preparation of roller-tube cultures embedded in a plasma coagulum may be carried out by following essentially the same techniques that have already been described for flask cultures (*see* p. 154). Four or five drops (about 0.3 ml) of pure plasma are introduced and spread with the end portion of a curved-tip pipette (Fig. 9) to cover the lower two thirds of the tube, which is kept horizontal. The tissue fragments, of which there may be 20 or more, are then selected with a curved-tip pipette, concentrated at the extreme tip of the pipette to free them of excess fluid, and deposited in the upper, plasma-free portion of the tube. After the excess fluid has been removed with a capillary pipette, the fragments are oriented in the plasma layer and the excess plasma is allowed to drain to the bottom of the tube. At

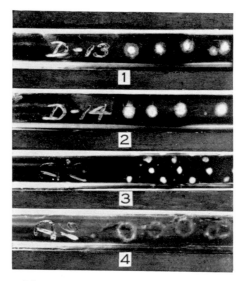

Fig. 40. Four-year-old strain of human sarcoma cells cultivated in plasma in roller tubes for 29 days (1 and 2); for 11 days (3); and for 11 days after the central portion of the cultures had been transplanted to another tube (4). (G. O. Gey and M. K. Gey.[179])

this point six or seven drops (about 0.4 ml) of diluting fluid are introduced and mixed with the plasma that has collected in the bottom of the tube. This diluting fluid may consist of 4 parts serum, 4 parts balanced salt solution, and 2 parts embryo extract; or any combination of these or equivalent nutrients may be used, depending upon the nature of the tissue and the purpose of the experiment. Once the diluting fluid has been mixed with the plasma in the bottom of the tube, it is distributed over and between the fragments that have been placed in the thin plasma layer on the walls of the tube, and any displaced fragments are quickly reoriented. If all this is done with the utmost despatch, a very thin coagulum will be obtained. But the diluting mixture, which is prepared beforehand, must be mixed with the excess plasma at the bottom of the tube and spread over the walls of the tube a few seconds after the tissue fragments are first oriented in the undiluted plasma. If a thick coagulum is required, the relative amounts of the various materials to be used should be worked out in preliminary tests, and the tubes should be rotated until the materials have begun to coagulate. The amounts will depend on the size of the tubes that are used.

The tubes are closed with stoppers and left lying on the work table until it is quite certain that the coagulum is firm enough to withstand a supernatant fluid, which may consist of 2 ml of the same materials that were used to dilute the plasma. Once the supernatant fluid has been added, it is spread over the coagulum by a gentle rolling and tipping motion, and the tubes are placed in the rotator.

Some cultures may digest the coagulum fairly rapidly and require frequent patching. If the digestion is not too extensive, fresh plasma may be introduced and spread over the coagulum after the old fluid has been withdrawn; and fresh fluid may be introduced after the new plasma layer has coagulated. Otherwise a fresh diluting mixture may be introduced, mixed in the bottom of the tube with fresh plasma, and the combined mixture spread over the old coagulum by rotating the tube until clotting occurs. If the tube is rotated beyond a certain point, however, the new coagulum will separate from the old, and the whole procedure will have to be repeated until the new coagulum remains attached.

At 37° C, the supernatant fluid should be changed two or three times a week. But if the cultures are incubated at a lower temperature (32° C, for example), cell growth will be greatly diminished and the fluid may be changed less often, perhaps as infrequently as twice a month.

Continuous Cultivation of Fibroblasts in Plasma

Strains of fibroblasts to be used in testing the stimulating or inhibiting qualities of special ingredients added to the culture medium should be reasonably homogeneous, but it is not essential that they be initiated by single-cell isolation. Over the years, innumerable strains of mixed-cell origin have been used to advantage in many laboratories. In 1912 Carrel[44] succeeded in isolating from the heart of an embryo chick a strain of fibroblasts (Fig. 1) that continued to live and multiply for 34 years, during which time it provided an abundance of uniform test material for physiological studies of every sort and description; and, as a result, a great deal was learned concerning the nature of these cells and their nutritional requirements.

After a strain of fibroblasts from chick-embryo heart or skeletal muscle has passed through several transfers, it becomes remarkably uniform, that is, if cell multiplication is kept at a maximum and if the dense, central areas of the culture are laid open by cutting each time the culture is transplanted. Under these conditions sister halves or quarters of the same parent culture can be relied upon to give an almost identical response to the same environmental conditions. Certain cell types present in the beginning are left behind and disappear either because the medium is not suited to them or because they are overgrown by more active cell types undergoing rapid, continuous proliferation. Other cell types that are capable of reversible changes or modulations (Bloom[29]) probably assume a character that is indistinguishable from the majority of the cells comprising the cultures. In any event, fibroblast cultures carried through several passages of rapid proliferation become progressively more and more homogeneous both in structure and function.

In the author's laboratory some years ago, numerous strains of chick fibroblasts were used in testing a wide variety of substances of nutritional interest in connection with the development of chemically defined media. But the strains were rarely carried for more than 15–18 passages (weeks). After 14 or 15 passages, the rate of cell multiplication usually decreased for a time and for several passages thereafter individual cultures were rarely large enough at seven days to be divided into four equal transplants, which was the procedure ordinarily followed. Because of this difficulty, new strains were isolated every few weeks; and there were always on hand strains of different ages, all of which were used to advantage from the time of isolation. During the first few passages (weeks), the cultures were used in preliminary experiments designed to test, approximately, the toxic levels of substances not previously studied. Then, as the strains became progressively older and more uniform in behaviour, they were used for more critical experiments (Fig. 41). Barring accidents, it is possible, of course, to carry most cell strains indefinitely. But every cell strain that has been isolated has, for one reason or another, shown the same fluctuations in rate of proliferation. Hence, the most practical means of providing a continuous supply of vigorous test material from newly explanted tissues is to develop a succession of strains at regular intervals.

In developing a strain of fibroblasts by the technique of gradual purification, the greater part of the original tissue explant may often be removed and discarded at the first transfer by cutting out the

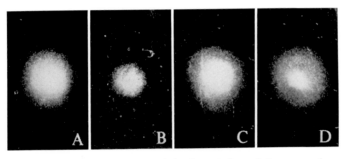

FIG. 41. The inhibition of cellular activity by cobalt and the protective action of L-histidine. Seven-day cultures prepared from four transplants cut from a single colony of fifth-passage, chick-embryo fibroblasts and placed in separate Carrel flasks in homologous plasma and embryo extract. (A) control medium; (B) medium containing 1.0 μg cobalt per ml; (C) medium containing 75 μg L-histidine per ml; (D) medium containing 1.0 μg cobalt and 75 μg L-histidine per ml. (J. F. Morgan et al.[310]) × 2.

entire colony (well within the sparsely populated peripheral zone), halving it, and dissecting out the dense central area. If the marginal pieces are too small for individual transplants, they are re-embedded in the new medium, side-by-side and in direct contact with each other. Or marginal cuttings from various sister fragments may be re-embedded together. Thereafter, the cultures may be multiplied at the time of transfer by the simple process of dividing each colony into two or four equal portions. By following the usual techniques, it is possible to derive a strain of fibroblasts from almost any part of the embryo or adult form of any bird or mammal, including the human. In practice, however, the most vigorous strains of fibroblasts usually are obtained from the breast and skeletal musculature of 10- to 12-day-old developing chick embryos. Ordinarily, these are transferred to fresh flasks and new media every seven days. A set of 10 or 12 cultures will enable one to make an elaborate experiment each week and still have enough cultures left over at each transfer for the continuation of the strain.

Cultivation of Epithelial Cells in Plasma

In the isolation of strains of epithelial cells, the problem is often complicated by the presence of fibroblasts in the cultures. Under these conditions, it is usually necessary to separate the fibroblasts from the epithelial elements by mechanical isolation at the time of subculture.

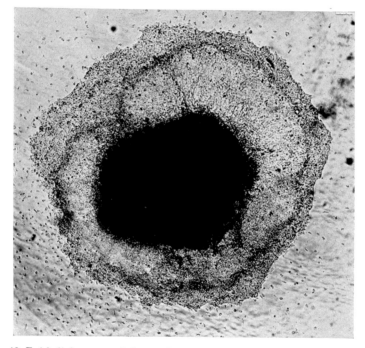

FIG. 42. Epithelial outgrowth from a fragment of spontaneous adenoma of a mouse, after four days in a Carrel flask in a washed plasma (chicken) coagulum with a superimposed fluid phase consisting of rat serum and Tyrode's solution (1:1). (L. Santesson.[471]) × 42.

Pure cultures of epithelial cells from epithelial tumors and from certain organs (e.g., kidney, intestine, lung, and skin) may often be obtained either by chopping or trypsinizing (*see* p. 121) the tissues before they are placed in the culture containers. Eventually, innumerable colonies of epithelium will appear and increase in size until they are large enough to subculture (Fig. 42). Epithelial cells can be left in their original flasks or tubes without being disturbed for long periods, provided the fluid phase of the medium is changed at least twice a week.

Quite recently, Harnden[214] has used a plasma medium to advantage as a means of initiating cell proliferation from fragments of human skin in connection with chromosome studies. Subcultures were prepared with the aid of trypsin.

Cultivation of Blood Leukocytes in Plasma

In an earlier chapter (*see* p. 134), a method was described for the preparation of leukocyte fragments from buffy coat. When fragments of buffy coat are cultivated in a plasma coagulum, the persisting cells exhibit the very convenient property of invading the medium at a uniform rate from all sides of the explanted fragments. Consequently, they provide a highly sensitive means of measuring the stimulating or inhibiting effects of substances introduced into the medium.

Once the leukocyte fragments are ready, the cultures are prepared in the manner described on page 154. In experiments designed to test the effect of substances that may be inhibiting or stimulating, the medium should contain very little, if any, tissue extract. If the cultures are left undisturbed for a few minutes after they have been made, the plasma will coagulate spontaneously without the addition of extract. Otherwise a single drop may be added.

Where the nutrient materials consist entirely of plasma or plasma and serum together, they should comprise one third to one half of the total medium. If other nutrients are present or if plasma and serum diluted with balanced salt solution are being used as a control medium for experiments designed to test the effect of other substances, the plasma content may be reduced to one fourth or one sixth, according to the particular concentration required to produce a solid coagulum.

Unless the serum is to be washed from the coagulum before the final medium is added (*see* p. 168), the coagulum should contain all the ingredients required in the experiment. It is seldom necessary to reinforce the coagulum by patching. On the second or third day, the cultures should receive a fresh supply of nutrient materials in the form of a supernatant fluid. It is always advisable that this fluid consist of the same materials as those present in the coagulum, in the same relative proportions, serum being used to replace the plasma. In Chapter XI, a description is given of the cultivation of leukocytes in fluid medium.

Cultivation of Tissues in Heterologous Plasma

In the cultivation of certain tissues, it is often desirable to prepare the supporting structure of the solid phase from the plasma of another

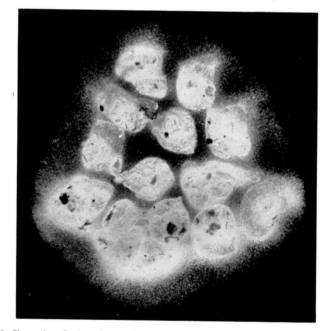

FIG. 43. Four-day flask culture of connective-tissue cells derived from the skeletal muscle of a 12-day-old chick embryo and cultivated for 16 passages (weeks) in rabbit plasma. The denser areas represent fragments cut from a culture in the preceding passage; these fragments are completely surrounded by new outgrowth. (K. Landsteiner and R. C. Parker.[262]) × 7½.

species, for any one of the following reasons: (1) The homologous plasma may be undesirable for serological reasons (Fig. 43). (2) The homologous plasma may give a coagulum that is opaque, weak, or uneven in density. (3) The homologous plasma may be difficult to obtain. (4) A particularly valuable sample of blood may coagulate before plasma can be prepared from it, or the plasma itself may coagulate spontaneously before the cultures are made; in either case, the material can be used only in the form of serum. (5) Certain combinations of plasma, serum, and tissue may result in pronounced lysis of the plasma coagulum.[187,471] In many instances of this sort, the tissues may be cultivated in a chicken-plasma coagulum containing heterologous serum and other nutrient substances compatible with the tissue (Fig. 44). Chicken plasma is well adapted for this purpose; it is easy to obtain in large quantities and provides a firm, transparent coagulum that can be treated almost indefinitely without sacrificing its rigidity.

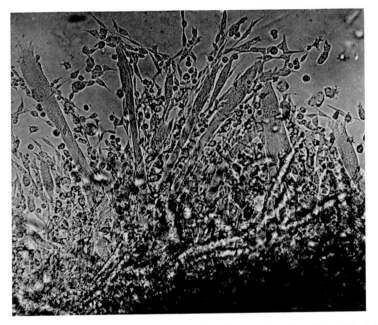

FIG. 44. Culture of rat-embryo skeletal muscle after two days in a Carrel flask in a washed plasma (chicken) coagulum with a superimposed fluid medium consisting of rat serum in Tyrode's solution (1:2). Note the development of several well-defined muscle buds. (R. C. Parker, unpublished experiments, 1933.) × 115.

For Carrel D-3.5 flasks, the plasma coagulum may be prepared from 0.5 ml of chicken plasma and 0.7 ml of a mixture consisting of 2 parts serum, 2 parts balanced salt solution, and 1 part chick embryo extract or its equivalent. A day or so later, 0.5 or 1.0 ml of the same combination of serum, saline, and extract are placed on the clot as a fluid overlay. Although horse serum is often the preferred serum, human, bovine, and ovine serum are also suitable for many purposes. If clot lysis becomes troublesome, it can often be lessened or prevented by heating the serum at 56° C for 30 min.[187]

When the use of heterologous plasma is undesirable because of the serum it contains, it is best to use a clot prepared from purified fibrinogen and thrombin (see p. 169). Otherwise, the original coagulum, once it is firm enough, may be washed for 2 hr with two changes of buffered salt solution. If phenol red is to be used in the culture medium, it should also be included in the washing fluid. After the final washing, the cultures receive from 0.5 to 1.0 ml of the actual feeding mixture. If it is not known whether the clots will withstand this treatment without losing their rigidity, appropriate blanks, without tissue, may be prepared for testing.

Use of Antitryptic Agents to Prevent
Digestion of Coagulum

The rapidity with which actively growing tissues digest the fibrin of the plasma coagulum makes it difficult to use plasma in studies in which it might otherwise be useful; and repeated attempts have been made over the years to suppress this lytic action. Substances that inhibit the action of trypsin, which is the enzyme mainly responsible, have been found in serum and plasma,[195] in egg white,[15] in navy beans and soybeans,[33] and in extracts of pancreas;[252, 257] and some of these substances have been used in tissue culture to prevent clot digestion. Thus, Fischer[157] cultivated Rous chicken sarcoma in fowl plasma to which he added crystalline soybean antitrypsin; and Morgan and Parker[341] studied the action of crude soybean antitrypsin on chick-fibroblast cultures maintained in fowl plasma and in fibrinogen-thrombin clots (see p. 169). Antitrypsin levels between 0.25 and 5.0 mg per ml completely prevented the digestion of the coagulum. High levels of the antitryptic agent were found to delay the coagulation of plasma, even in the presence of embryo extract, but this inhibition could be overcome by the addition of a few drops of diluted thrombin. Also, high concentrations of antitrypsin (1.0 to 3.0 mg per ml) retarded the rate of cell multiplication. It was observed, however, that by making repeated passages (3–5) through media containing inhibitory levels of antitrypsin, the cultures gradually acquired a tolerance to it. Weller and his associates[536] added soybean trypsin inhibitor (crystalline; 0.05 mg per ml; Worthington Biochemical Corp., Freehold, N.J.) to the fluid overlay of coagulated chicken-plasma cultures in roller tubes.

Cultivation of Tissues in Fibrinogen

Chicken plasma is particularly favored as a supporting structure for cultures because it provides a firm, transparent coagulum that is remarkably resistant to the weakening effects of fluid changes. But all plasma has certain disadvantages: It is tedious and time consuming to prepare; it sometimes coagulates during storage; and its tremendous complexity makes it impossible to duplicate exactly many types of experiments in which it is used. Different samples of plasma vary in their clotting time, in their chemical composition, and in their general effectiveness as a culture medium. Furthermore, plasma can transmit infectious agents, notably viruses. Because of these obvious disadvantages, repeated attempts have been made over the years to find a more suitable supporting structure.

The first successful attempt to use fibrinogen as a substitute for whole plasma was reported by Ebeling[122] in 1921. When the fibrinogen, which was prepared from adult-chicken plasma by acetic-acid precipitation, was used together with serum and embryo extract, it provided a medium in which fibroblasts grew almost as well as in plasma. The next attempt to substitute fibrinogen for plasma was reported by Porter and Hawn,[405] who used fibrinogen prepared by the method of Cohn and his associates.[72] It should be pointed out, however, that the fibrinogen samples thus far available are by no means pure. Certain samples contain as much as 40 per cent citrate, with fibrinogen comprising only 70 per cent of the remaining portion.

The fibrinogen most generally used is that contained in fraction I of bovine blood plasma, which is distributed as a dry powder (Armour Laboratories, Chicago 9, Ill.). A 0.5 per cent solution of fibrinogen in balanced salt solution is sterilized by Seitz filtration and stored in the refrigerator. It is used at room temperature at pH 7.6 to 7.8. If the pH of the solution is below 7.5 during coagulation or if the solutions are used while cold, the coagulum is likely to be opaque.[148] This opacity is related to the size of the fibers that are formed.[229] The thrombin used for the coagulation of fibrinogen is that contained in fractions II and III of bovine plasma and is available commercially as a sterile, dry powder designed for topical application (Parke, Davis and Co., Detroit, Mich.). The powder is dissolved in balanced salt solution to give a final concentration of 20 u per ml. It is then distributed in small containers and stored in a dry-ice box or low-temperature refrigerator. One drop of thrombin solution is sufficient to coagulate 1.5 ml of a nutrient mixture one third of which consists of fibrinogen.

Fibrinogen cultures may be prepared in a variety of ways provided ample time is left for orienting the tissue fragments after the nutrient materials and the thrombin have been added to the fibrinogen solution. To lessen the danger of clot digestion, any serum that is used should be inactivated by heating at 56° C for 30 min.[187]

Sponge-Matrix Cultures With Plasma

When tissue fragments are embedded in a coagulum prepared from blood plasma or fibrinogen, the cells migrate along the fibrin strands to form colonies whose architecture depends on the nature of the cells, the composition and consistency of the coagulum, and the degree to which it may be digested by the cells. Any structures formed in such a culture can only be studied after the material has been sectioned and stained, and, if the clot is thin, the culture must be double embedded in some way in order to preserve the relationship of its parts (*see* p. 313).

Leighton[269, 272] has overcome many of the difficulties encountered in working with plasma cultures by combining plasma with small pieces of cellulose sponge. In this system the fibrin reticulum of the plasma coagulum stretches across the interstices of the sponge, and cells and cell aggregates move into these spaces where they often produce tissue patterns remarkably similar to those observed *in vivo*. Within the interstices of the sponge the rate of diffusion of nutrients and metabolites depends in large measure on the degree of cell crowding, so that closely packed cells tend to create their own special environment. Leighton[272] suggests that the trabeculae of the sponge may serve as wicks to provide a slow, continuous exchange of substances deep in the plasma clot. When clot liquefaction occurs, the tissues remain supported by the sponge and can be preserved intact for histological study after the sponge has been fixed, sectioned, and stained. Leighton[270] has also found that transplantable animal tumors and human tumors can be cultivated in the same manner, often with the development of distinctive patterns of outgrowth.

Leighton[272] uses fine-pore, cellulose sponge (Dupont) of the type used in photography. The dry sponge is first cut into strips measuring 5×10 mm in cross section. The strips are then pressed between glass slides, and the protruding ends are sliced with a razor blade into thin fragments, 0.5 to 1.0 mm in thickness. The slices are boiled in two changes of distilled water for 1 hr, then immersed for 30 min each at room temperature in acetone, ethyl ether, and absolute alcohol successively, after which they are again boiled in two changes of distilled water. Each slice of sponge is inserted in a 16×150 mm culture tube that is plugged with cotton and autoclaved.

In preparing the cultures, the piece of sponge is oriented about 2 cm from the bottom of the tube. One to four small fragments of tissue are placed on the surface of the sponge, and one drop of chicken plasma and one of diluted, chick embryo extract are placed over and around it and are mixed and spread so as to cover the sponge and the tissue fragments and cement the sponge to the wall of the tube. After the clot has hardened, a nutrient fluid is added to the tube, and the culture is incubated either in a slow roller drum (see p. 159) or in a stationary position.

After several days, the explants become flattened and smaller, and the interstices of the sponge become filled with cells. Eventually, areas of liquefaction may appear in the plasma clot, especially in areas that are densely populated with cells. After two to four weeks, the sponge fragments may be fixed and sectioned, and the sections stained for histologic study. When dense growth is obtained in the marginal zone of the plasma clot, the clot may be removed, trimmed, and used as transplants for new cultures with or without sponge; or the sponge itself may be cut into small squares and used in preparing subcultures.

Leighton and Kline[273] used the sponge matrix method to study the infiltration of normal tissues (infants' foreskin) by malignant cells (strain HeLa[178]). Fragments of normal tissue were cultivated on a slice of cellulose sponge in the center of which a 5-mm hole was punched.

Two explants of normal tissue were placed on the margin of the hole, which became completely filled with cells after a few weeks. Then, at 35 days, small Gelfoam particles (*see* p. 195) containing the HeLa cells were placed on the margin of the hole in the cellulose sponge, and a thin plasma patch (*see* p. 155) was added. After three or four days, individual tumor cells had migrated short distances into the connective tissue. After three weeks, the connective tissue was considerably reduced and replaced by tumor tissue. In contrast, comparable tumor-cell inocula placed on slices of cellulose sponge prepared in like manner but devoid of connective tissue showed almost no proliferation during the same period.

Reconstituted Rat-Tail Collagen
as a Substitute for Plasma

Clot liquefaction and subsequent retraction and distortion of both the implanted tissues and the zone of outgrowth has always been a major hazard when tissues are cultivated in plasma. To overcome this difficulty, Ehrman and Gey[126] devised a method of preparing the walls of roller tubes with a coating of reconstituted rat-tail collagen gel as a substrate for the cells. The method was tested successfully in the propagation of 29 different cell strains, without lysis of the gel.

Collagen is prepared from rat tails that have been placed in low temperature storage while still fresh. After a tail has been thawed and cleansed with 95 per cent alcohol, it is fractured into small pieces, beginning at the tip. Each piece is pulled away to expose the tendons, which are cut free and deposited in sterile water before making the next fracture. The pooled tendons from one tail are then placed in about 150 ml of 1 : 1000 acetic-acid solution and stored for 48 hr in the refrigerator. After centrifugation for 2 hr at 2300 r.p.m. about 40 ml of collagen solution may be separated from the residue; two additional extractions are made and harvested at 24-hr intervals. The combined yield may be stored for months at low temperature.

Before use, the viscosity of the collagen solution is gradually increased by dialysis at 4° C against several changes of distilled water. After one to three days or before the material becomes too viscous to handle (as judged by the movement of entrapped air bubbles), dialysis is interrupted and the thickened solution is stored frozen until needed. To prepare a roller tube, 1–2 ml of the solution is spread over its inner surface and the collagen is allowed to gel by exposing it to the vapor of an ammonia-moistened cotton plug. The ammonia is removed from the gel by washing it repeatedly with distilled water (containing phenol red as indicator), after which it is conditioned by treating it with double-strength, balanced salt solution to compensate for the water of syneresis and, finally, with one or more changes of the medium that is to be used. Coverslips may be prepared in a similar manner, and cells may be released from the gel with collagenase. (Dried collagen and collagenase are supplied by Sigma Chemical Company, St. Louis 18, Mo.)

XI

Stationary Cultures with Fluid Medium

ALTHOUGH plasma has many properties that make it useful as a culture medium (*see* p. 82), it also has many disadvantages. Apart from its variable nature, it is tedious and time consuming to prepare, and the fibrin clot that it provides is almost always lysed by enzymes, sometimes with great rapidity. Because of these difficulties, plasma has gradually been eliminated from most tissue-culture undertakings. It was first eliminated for nutritional and optical reasons. Then, it was found that many types of cells could be cultivated directly on glass in fluid media and that cells so cultivated were even more sensitive than plasma cultures to environmental changes. But this was not always an advantage. Because diffusion is somewhat retarded in a plasma clot, as it is in the body, cells cultivated in plasma are able to develop in an environment that is partly, at least, of their own creation; consequently, many efforts have been made in recent years to include in fluid media such inert materials as perforated cellophane and cellulose sponge, in order to provide the cells with a similar means of conditioning their immediate environment.

Since the early years of tissue culture, it has been customary for various special purposes to initiate cultures from discrete fragments of tissue; and, although plasma is useful as a means of securing tissues firmly in place until they are anchored to the glass by their own outgrowth, it is usually possible to achieve this without plasma. Sometimes the attachment of tissues to glass is accomplished by leaving the cultures completely undisturbed for a few days; sometimes it is accomplished by holding the fragments in place with a thin film of cellophane (*see* p. 225); or it may be accomplished by allowing the fragments to dry onto the glass very slightly before the medium is added. In many undertakings, attachment to glass is completely unnecessary.

For many years, fluid-medium cultures have been prepared from minced and chopped tissues, first for virus studies[305,379,380] and then for other purposes.[375] Also, it has become common practice to initiate cultures from freshly explanted tissues by dispersing the cells with trypsin (*see* p. 121), and trypsin and other agents are useful in harvesting cells for subculture (*see* p. 188). All of these measures make it easy to achieve uniform populations of sufficient density to yield confluent cultures a few days after planting. Finally, there have recently been developed a great variety of established cell lines, all of which may be propagated in fluid medium.

When tissue fragments, cell strains, and cells released from fresh tissues by trypsin are cultivated on the glass surfaces of flasks, tubes, bottles, and Petri dishes in fluid medium without plasma, the cells migrate over those surfaces that are kept moistened with medium and often multiply to cover the areas with continuous sheets of cells within a few days. Under these conditions, the following precautions should be taken: (1) Fresh medium should be supplied to the cultures often enough and in sufficient quantity to provide an adequate supply of fresh nutrients and to remove waste products before they reach toxic proportions; small populations may require only partial changes of medium. (2) The depth of medium should not be so great as to interfere with the ready exchange of gasses between the cells and the atmosphere. (3) If the cultures are not gassed continuously, the air space within the container should be large enough to provide sufficient oxygen for the cultures during the intervals between fluid changes. (4) If active cell multiplication is desired, the pH of the medium should be kept between 6.9 and 7.2; at more alkaline levels, cells may metabolize without dividing. (5) Because many variables are involved, new systems of cultivation should be worked out empirically, i.e., by testing the effect of different initial population densities, different volumes of culture fluid, and different schedules of fluid change.

There is usually no difficulty in propagating the cells of established strains (Fig. 45) directly on glass in fluid media, but special precautions must be taken if freshly explanted cells are to be propagated indefinitely without undergoing extensive alterations in character. Thus, Puck and his associates,[413] in attempting to maintain explanted

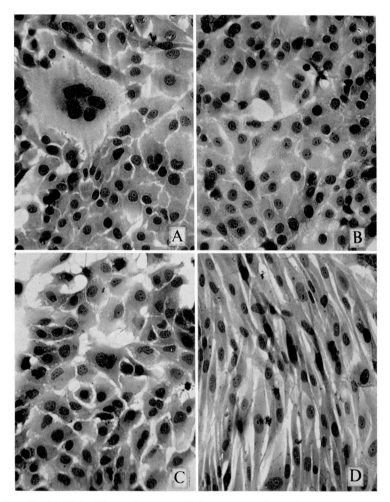

FIG. 45. Established lines of human cells four to seven days after subculture, stained with Harris's hematoxylin and phloxin. (A) Carcinoma of cervix (strain HeLa, G. O. Gey et al.[178]). (B) Pulmonary adenocarcinoma (strain Maben, A. W. Frisch et al.[169]). (C) Esophageal epithelium (No. 5), as clonal strain A2B14. (D) Palate fibroblast (No. 3), in passage 13. (J. T. Syverton and L. C. McLaren.[507]) × 160.

human cells in a healthy state for extended periods, follow the following four rules: (1) Toxic media are detected by testing aliquots of each batch of chick embryo extract and serum to determine whether, when incorporated in a special medium for fibroblasts (*see* p. 111), they will promote the growth of colonies from single fibroblasts by the plating procedures described on page 217. (2) The medium of all cultures is changed every 48 hr, to maintain optimal levels of essential nutrients. (3) The cells are not allowed to reach too high a density in each bottle but are trypsinized and subdivided when they have covered about 30 per cent of the available surface; in any event, each culture is trypsinized at least once a week. (4) Cultures are initiated with at least 10^3 cells per ml in bottles accommodating 10 ml of medium. Of these various measures, it is felt by Puck's group that the most important is the screening of successive batches of embryo extract. But even small deviations from the routine can result in an increase in the surface area and granularity of the cells, a decrease in their rate of multiplication, and their eventual death. When these or other signs of deterioration appear, cultures are trypsinized and combined, in order to achieve the original population density. In addition, Puck and his associates[411,414] claim that the addition of fetal-calf serum to the medium is useful in maintaining a stable karyotype. In this connection, it is interesting to note that Gey has used human umbilical-cord serum to advantage for many years in the cultivation of mammalian cells from many species.

When cells are handled with the utmost care and placed in media that are adequate in all respects, both physically and chemically, it is possible for single cells to live and multiply in relatively large volumes of fluid. If the medium is not entirely adequate, the smaller its volume or the larger the cell population per unit volume, the greater the chances are that the cells will survive. But some cells, particularly cells of established lines, have wonderful powers of adjusting themselves to an unfavorable environment. It often happens, for example, that L-strain cells that are placed in inadequate, chemically defined media are almost entirely lost within a few days. But if the cultures are not discarded immediately it sometimes happens that a small group of healthy cells will eventually be found, presumably derived from one or more surviving cells that remained unnoticed. The small group of cells grows, little by little, to form a compact island. For weeks, sometimes for months, the component cells will not venture away from this island, but the larger it becomes, the faster it grows. Sometimes, the distal extremities of the cells flatten out on the glass like flower petals, while their proximal parts remain firmly anchored to the mother colony. Eventually, however, there usually comes a time when the cells begin to migrate away from the colony; and this, if it happens, is an indication that the cells are present in sufficient numbers to condition their environment or that their nutritional requirements have become less exacting. In time, the cell population may increase to fill the entire bottle or flask; and all this may take place without any change having been made in the composition of the medium or in the frequency with which it is renewed. The cells that survive may do so because of genetic change or the change may be entirely adaptive. But whatever its nature, it is very real.

Except in undertakings requiring vast populations of cells for special purposes, it is seldom necessary to propagate cells at maximum speed. In fact, cells so propagated bear little resemblance to cells in the body. Though it may be comforting to know that many types of cells can, if necessary, be propagated in massive quantities, it is infinitely more important to discover the particular qualities that cells must possess or develop in order to make such performance possible. Cells multiplying at abnormally high speeds cannot perform the special functions that characterized their progenitors in the body and can seldom be identified with them.

In the present chapter, attention will be given to techniques for the cultivation of cells and tissues in fluid media on the surfaces of various types of glass containers. Procedures will be described for the preparation of replicate cell cultures, and various methods of harvesting will be discussed. Descriptions will also be given of techniques for the cultivation of cells and tissues in fluid media together with materials that are added to the culture system as a means of providing a discontinuous matrix. Subsequent chapters will be devoted to techniques for the cultivation of cells in suspension (Chap. XII), for the development of clonal populations from single cells (Chap. XIII), for the continuous perfusion of cultures with fluid media (Chap. XIV), and special procedures for the study of developing embryonic parts (Chap. XV) and of viruses (Chap. XVI). In Chapter IX, reference has already been made to the preparation of coverslip cultures with fluid media.

Fluid Medium Cultures in Tubes, Flasks, Bottles, and Petri Dishes

TUBE CULTURES

Gey[175,176] was the first to make extensive use of ordinary test tubes as culture containers (Fig. 40), and tubes are now employed by many

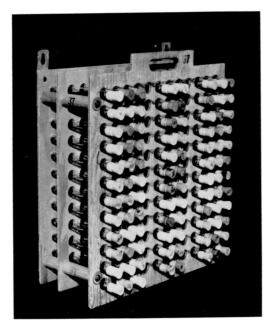

FIG. 46. Transportable rack that can be attached to wall of warm room during incubation of tube cultures without rotation.

investigators for the propagation of normal and malignant tissues and established cell strains from many sources. When test tubes (e.g., 16 × 150 mm) are used for stationary cultures with fluid media, they are incubated in an almost horizontal position in an appropriate rack (Fig. 46) at an angle just sufficient to prevent the medium (1.5–2.0 ml) from wetting the stopper and the forward end of the tube. Some racks (Fig. 47) are designed for ease in stacking, have adjustable devices for holding tubes at a slight angle, and spring clips that hold them firmly in place. All tubes in such racks can be drained simultaneously.

When freshly explanted tissue fragments are to be cultivated, they are introduced along one side of an empty tube by means of an ordinary, hand-drawn pipette or one with a tip that is bent at a slight angle (Fig. 9). Care should be taken to remove any excess fluid carried

Fig. 47. Metal rack for 20 culture tubes. Main body of rack consists of an unperforated back plate and two that are perforated. Spring retaining clips attached to rear of middle plate hold tubes firmly in place. Angle of incubation is adjustable, and racks can be stacked.

over with the tissues, or the tissues may be pushed to a dry area once they have been deposited on the glass. If the tissue fragments are then left to dry very slightly before they are flooded with medium, they will remain adherent to the glass, that is, if their first contact with the fluid is brought about with extreme caution. Usually, a 10- or 15-min drying period will suffice, and during this time it will be possible to introduce the culture medium into the tubes, adjust its pH with a gas mixture if it seems too alkaline (*see* p. 60), and close the tubes with stoppers. Before doing so, however, the tubes should be rotated through 90° in order that the medium will not come into immediate contact with the tissues. If the tissues in the first tubes prepared come loose when they are flooded with medium, the drying period should be extended until subsequent trials give satisfactory results. Morann and Melnick[333] reported experiments in which the tissue inoculum was streaked on the inner surface of tubes that had been preheated at 45° C. The tubes were then stored at 4° C for 30 min, after which the fluid was added. Finally, and regardless of the method of preparing the tubes, an inked line or some other indicator should be placed on the wall of each tube in order that it can be kept properly oriented, with the medium bathing the populated side of the tube during incubation.

The culture fluid may be renewed two or three times a week, depending upon the activity of the cells. The old fluid or any part of it may be withdrawn with an extra-long, hand-drawn pipette fitted with a rubber nipple, or with a suction device. If it is desired to prepare

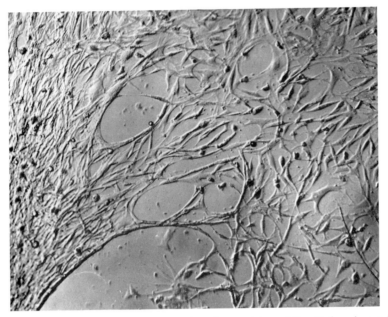

Fig. 48. Cells from an 11-day-old chick embryo cultivated for 69 days in a roller tube in a fluid medium consisting of 40 per cent horse serum, 40 per cent balanced salt solution, and 20 per cent chick embryo extract. × 75.

discrete transplants for subculture from tissues growing in test tubes, they may be scraped from the walls of the tube with a platinum spatula or a bent-tipped pipette. But if the medium is adequate, it is often possible to keep cultures of newly isolated tissues healthy and active for several months without subcultures (Fig. 48). From time to time as the density of growth increases, local areas of stress develop, and whole sheets of cells become detached from the glass. Eventually, these detached cells become lost, and new cells grow into the vacated areas.

When tube cultures are made from trypsin-dispersed cell suspensions prepared from freshly explanted tissues (*see* p. 121) or from suspensions prepared from cultures of established strains of cells, the cellular inoculum may be added to the culture medium and dispensed as aliquots to all tubes of the series (*see also* p. 184). When tube cultures are prepared from cell suspensions, the tubes must be oriented for incubation the moment the cells have been introduced, for suspended cells become attached to glass with great rapidity.

Leighton[269] has designed a special culture tube (16 × 100 mm or 16 × 150 mm) with a flat, rectangular, side window (13 × 40 mm) near the bottom (Fig. 7). The flat window not only provides a generous area that is optically suitable for microscopic work but also makes it possible to insert coverslips into the area to obtain specimens for careful cytological study. The window also provides a shallow well that reduces the volume of medium required to just the amount needed to cover it, which is a great advantage when it is desired to cultivate small quantities of tissue. In addition, the window serves to keep the tube properly oriented during incubation; special racks have been designed (Microbiological Associates, Inc., Bethesda 14, Md.) to accommodate the tubes when more than the minimal volume of medium is used.

According to Gey's original procedure, tube cultures were rotated continuously at 6 revs. per hr in a nearly horizontal rack or drum accommodated in an incubator (*see* p. 159). Because most tissues cultivated at that time were embedded in a plasma coagulum, it is quite possible that rotation was beneficial as an aid to diffusion. But rotation is not necessary and is indeed injurious for small populations of cells cultivated directly on glass in fluid media. Under these conditions, rotation prevents the accumulation of essential metabolites in the immediate vicinity of cells that may not be present in sufficient numbers to condition the entire medium. Cells of established strains can always, of course, be introduced in sufficient numbers in the beginning to insure good reproduction during rotation, and rotation does increase the area available to the growing cell population. But it is seldom necessary to line whole tubes with cells. Larger cell populations can easily be obtained in flat-bottomed, stationary bottles of any desired size (*see* p. 183) or in test tubes that are rotated fast enough (50 r.p.m.) to keep the cells multiplying in suspension (*see* p. 199).

The tube carriers that are presently being used for slow rotation are of many sizes; some are small enough to be driven by tiny, synchronous-type motors, and others accommodate many hundreds of tubes. The most useful carrier is one of medium size that is detachable from the drive shaft or spindle and can therefore be used for transporting the cultures about the laboratory (Fig. 39). If a heavy motor (e.g., ¼ H.P.) is used in a bacteriological incubator, the space may not be great enough to absorb the heat generated by the motor.

FLASK AND BOTTLE CULTURES

Animal tissue cells have been cultivated in many types of flasks and bottles, some especially designed for the purpose, others not. At present, the flasks and bottles in most common use include Carrel's D-3.5 flasks, Earle's T-flasks, Swim's S-flasks, and a vast assortment of flat-sided bottles originally designed for other purposes, some of soft glass (prescription or dispensing bottles) and some of Pyrex (milk-dilution bottles, Roux bottles, Povitsky bottles, and Kolle flasks modified to accept No. 6 stoppers). In fact, many laboratories are now using various types of prescription bottles that are distributed sterile and ready for use at such low cost that it is often more economical to discard them than it is to try to recondition them for subsequent use. More information relating to some of these containers will be found in Chapters III and IV.

The techniques for the preparation of cultures in fluid media in flasks and bottles do not differ essentially from those recommended for test-tube cultures. It is only important that the glassware be clean, the medium adequate, not too alkaline, and in proper proportion to air, and that the inoculum be sufficient. For cell suspensions, the inoculum should not be less than $1-2 \times 10^5$ cells per ml. Procedures for the preparation of replicate cultures in fluid media are outlined on page 184.

In the large-scale propagation of viruses for use as vaccines (*see* p. 263), bottle cultures are often agitated by placing them on rocking platforms. This same sort of procedure was employed in 1931 by Carrel[49] as a means of increasing the volume of medium that could be accommodated in culture flasks provided with lateral, winglike extensions. It is presently not certain, however, that there is any real advantage in agitating the media of ordinary bottle cultures, however large, provided the layer of medium is not too deep.

PETRI-DISH CULTURES

Unsealed Petri dishes may be employed as culture containers provided they are incubated in a humidified atmosphere; if the buffering

system depends upon CO_2 being retained in the immediate atmosphere of the culture, a continuous flow of CO_2 and air must be supplied (*see also* p. 60). In some laboratories, separate incubators for
Petri-dish cultures are flushed continuously with humidified air
containing 5 per cent CO_2. In other laboratories, including the
author's, Petri-dish cultures are incubated in especially constructed
stainless-steel cabinets housed in walk-in, warm rooms. Each cabinet
is 19½ in. high, 18½ in. wide, and 19½ in. deep, with a single, hinged
door closing the entire front. The cabinet accommodates a removable
water pan (2 in. deep) at the bottom and 15 shallow culture trays
(½ in. deep) upon which the cultures are placed. The culture trays,
which are spaced 1 in. apart and are removable, slide on metal strips
fixed to the side walls of the cabinet. The rate of flow of the gaseous
ingredients of the atmosphere, compressed air from the house system
and CO_2 from a high-pressure cylinder, is each indicated by a precision-bore flowmeter, and the combined flow then passes through a
wash bottle, containing a copper sulfate solution (to provide humidity
without microorganisms), and an empty bottle that serves as a water
trap, before entering the cabinet through its rear wall near the bottom.
The mixture currently employed consists of 5 per cent CO_2 in air.

Small (60-mm) Petri dishes are particularly useful in making clonal
isolations (*see* Chap. XIII), in virus studies (*see* Chap. XVI), and in
testing the plating efficiency of cell suspensions in particular media
(Fig. 60). At the termination of an experiment, the cell colonies (or
clones) may be fixed and stained for ease in counting, or individual
colonies may be selected for continued subcultivation or recloning.
These dishes accommodate 5 ml of medium. Larger (100-mm) Petri
dishes, with 15 ml of medium, are also useful for virus studies and for
cytological work. For the latter purpose, two standard microscope
slides are placed in each dish before sterilization. When the dishes are
seeded with cell suspensions, the cells settle and multiply on the slides,
which may later be removed for staining (*see* p. 305).

Replicate Cell Cultures

The first reliable procedures for the preparation of replicate cell
cultures were devised by Evans, Sanford, and their associates.[133,467]
According to these procedures, which were designed especially for L
cells, a washed cell suspension is prepared from massive cultures of

cells. Then, after the suspension has been screened through a sieve unit to eliminate cell clumps, it is transferred to a special reservoir and stirrer assembly (Fig. 49), its density is determined and adjusted to an appropriate level (e.g., 2×10^5 cells per ml), and it is dispensed eventually as replicate 0.5-ml samples into a series of flasks (e.g., Earle's T-15 flasks) to which the balance of the medium has already

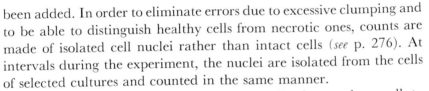

FIG. 49. Reservoir and stirrer assembly used in the preparation of replicate cell cultures. For description, see text. (V. J. Evans et al.[133]; Kontes Glass Co., Vineland, N.J.)

been added. In order to eliminate errors due to excessive clumping and to be able to distinguish healthy cells from necrotic ones, counts are made of isolated cell nuclei rather than intact cells (see p. 276). At intervals during the experiment, the nuclei are isolated from the cells of selected cultures and counted in the same manner.

Twice a week, fluid renewals are made by allowing any loose cells to settle and by withdrawing and replacing measured quantities of the cell-free medium. According to the original procedure of Evans and her associates, fluid withdrawals were accomplished by centrifuging the flasks at 300 r.p.m. for 20 min, after which the supernatant fluid was withdrawn by means of 1-ml, volumetric pipettes operated by a syringe barrel and piston connected with a special flask-centering frame and pipette-positioning clamp and shield. But Parker and his associates[378] found that flasks containing cells cultivated on glass in chemically defined media could not be centrifuged, even at low speed, without dehydrating and killing a large part of the cell population. To overcome this difficulty, fluid withdrawals were made after the flasks had been allowed to stand vertically in racks for 15 min, during which time any loose cells settled to the bottom. Before the flasks were placed in the racks, the silicone stoppers were replaced by glass caps that could be removed without agitating the flasks when measured quantities of fluid were to be withdrawn and replaced by fresh medium.

The reservoir and stirrer assembly (Fig. 49) consists of a motor-driven glass stirrer with a screw-type blade that rotates in a cylindrical reservoir designed to hold the cell suspension (80 ml) while it is being stirred and delivered as replicate samples into the culture flasks. Near the top of the reservoir, there is an inlet for gassing the cell suspension during the stirring. The reservoir has a broad base that is closely joined to a special three-way stopcock with a gas inlet and a delivery tip calibrated to dispense 0.5 ml of the cell suspension. After the delivery tip has been charged with cell suspension from the reservoir, the sample is expelled into a culture flask by means of a gas mixture introduced through the gas inlet of the stopcock. For protection against falling dust particles, the top of the reservoir is provided with a loose cap which, in turn, is surmounted by a glass sleeve held by rubber tubing to the stem of the stirrer. The delivery tip is protected by a glass bell held in place with a cork.

Syverton and Scherer[509] described a modification of this apparatus in which the stopcock assembly was replaced by a simple bottom outlet connected by a short length of flexible tubing to an automatic Cornwall syringe (Becton, Dickinson and Co., Rutherford, N.J.). The Cornwall syringe can also be used to deliver replicate samples of a cell suspension that is being agitated with a magnetic stirrer.

The close correlation between DNAP values and nuclear counts made it possible for Healy and his associates[231] to determine the efficiency of the replicate culture procedures used in our Toronto laboratory. For this purpose, a series of 48 samples (0.5 ml each) were drawn from the stirring and dispensing unit, and the DNAP per sample was determined for the entire series. The first 24 samples were remarkably uniform in cell population, as measured in terms of their DNAP values. The remaining samples of the series showed considerable variation. Also, statistical analysis showed that within sets of three consecutive samples of the series the standard deviation was 2.8 per cent of the mean, whereas it increased to 9.6 per cent of the mean when comparisons were made between different sets of three samples each. It was concluded, therefore, that smaller sets of replicate cultures provide more uniform populations at the outset and contribute less to the final variations. It was further concluded that in selecting a group of cultures from a series for nuclear counts and DNAP determinations an effort should always be made to choose pairs of cultures (if two solutions are being tested) or sets of three (if three solutions are being tested) that have received their cell inoculum in sequence and that include the two (or three) test solutions. The number of replicate cultures that may be prepared depends upon the size of the stirrer assembly and the volume of suspension that may be dispensed before the top level of the remaining portion falls too far below the upper section of the stirrer blade.

PRELIMINARY, NONQUANTITATIVE SCREENING TESTS WITH WASHED-CELL SUSPENSIONS

In many undertakings, much useful information can be obtained by means of a greatly simplified version of the quantitative procedures just described. These tests, which may be made in Carrel flasks, prescription bottles, or tubes, are designed primarily to compare the effects of various levels of a substance of nutritional interest and to eliminate all toxic combinations of substances before testing them by more elaborate procedures. This method is also used to advantage as a quick and simple means of testing new batches of medium. The tests may be made from the same washed-cell suspensions used in the preparation of replicate cultures. But the cell suspension is agitated by hand, rather than mechanically, and an ungraduated, hand-drawn pipette is used to transfer one or more drops of the agitated suspension to each of the culture containers. The effects of the various solutions are judged, not by isolating and counting the cell nuclei, but by examination of the cultures at frequent intervals under the microscope. Some experiments have to be kept for as long as 20 to 30 days or more before it is possible to detect significant differences between cultures in different solutions. Three cultures are prepared for each solution tested, and all culture fluids are renewed twice a week. No precautions are taken to guard against the loss of unattached cells at times of fluid change.

Methods of Harvesting Cells and Tissues in Fluid Medium

One means of harvesting cells propagated on glass is by scraping them free with a platinum or Teflon spatula. Cell clumps can be broken up fairly successfully by vigorous pipette action before or after the population has been removed to a test tube. With established cell strains, it is always possible to continue the line by this means, provided the population is large enough to compensate for cells that may be damaged or lost in the process. In the author's laboratory, a small fragment of perforated cellophane (about 1 in. square) is placed in all of the larger flasks and bottles before sterilization. During the preparation of the culture, the piece of cellophane is moistened with medium and brought to rest on the roof of the container, where it remains until the culture is harvested. At the time of harvesting, the cellophane may be used as a mop that is guided over the populated area of the culture by means of a pipette tip or a spatula. In this way, the cells may be freed from the glass very quickly and with less mutilation than with naked spatulas. If the cells are harvested by means of trypsin, the cellophane remains unused but does no harm. The cellophane method is particularly useful in harvesting certain strains of cells that are highly sensitive to trypsin. Additional squares of cellophane are tightly rolled and sterilized in glass tubes to be used when needed for flasks and bottles that were sterilized without it. The dry roll can easily be inserted with sterile forceps even into the small neck of a Carrel flask.

After the scraped cells and their medium have been transferred to a test tube, the cells may be sedimented by gravity or by low-speed centrifugation. If the population is unusually sparse, only half of the old medium should be discarded and replaced in the subcultures by fresh medium. If the culture is to be divided, the proportion of fresh medium that is added should depend upon the population density, which can be determined by making hemocytometer counts. For most cells in adequate media, an initial inoculum of $2-4 \times 10^5$ cells per ml will provide successful subcultures. If the utmost care is taken in handling the cells, cultures may be initiated from smaller inocula and even from single cells (*see* Chap. XIII).

A more efficient means of harvesting cells propagated on glass is to release them with trypsin, with Versene, with a combination of these, or with a mixture of trypsin and sodium citrate. Trypsin may be made up in Puck's saline A (*see* p. 59) and used as an 0.03 per cent solution (0.3 Gm trypsin, 1 : 300, in 1 l of saline). After the nutrient medium has been removed from the bottle to be harvested, the cells are washed once at room temperature with saline A, which is then removed and replaced with trypsin solution. After 10 minutes' incubation at 37° C, with occasional agitation, the tryptic action is ended by dilution with an equal volume of nutrient medium at room temperature. An aliquot of this suspension is removed for determination of cell density in a hemocytometer. Appropriate dilutions are then made in the nutrient medium, and aliquots containing the desired number of cells are used to prepare the subcultures.

Versene, a chelating agent (*see* p. 131), is also used[162,324] to harvest cells that are attached to glass surfaces. Versene is made up at a concentration of 0.02 per cent in calcium- and magnesium-free phosphate buffered saline (*see* p. 58). After the medium is removed from the culture, Versene solution warmed to 37° C is added, and the culture is returned to the incubator. If the culture has not cooled appreciably, the cells may be loosened with two quick, horizontal shakes after 10 to 20 min, depending upon the nature of the cells. If the culture has cooled, it may take longer to free the cells from the glass. After the cells have been sedimented by centrifugation, they are resuspended in a known volume of culture medium and hemocytometer counts are made to determine the density of the population.

Madin and Darby[303] remove bovine and ovine kidney cells from glass with a solution that combines trypsin and Versene, as follows: NaCl, 8 Gm; KCl, 0.4 Gm; $NaHCO_3$, 0.58 Gm; dextrose, 1 Gm; trypsin (1:250), 0.5 Gm; Versene, 0.2 Gm; distilled water to 1000 ml. The solution also contains phenol red and antibiotics. Rinaldini[436] found that, although Versene or citrate at a concentration of 1 per cent in Ca- and Mg-free Tyrode's solution was effective in detaching chick-embryo cells from glass after vigorous shaking, the cells came away in clusters. Rinaldini also warns that chelating agents, unlike proteolytic enzymes, are not inhibited by serum and may do lasting damage to the cells unless they are washed away.

Magee and associates[304] report that cells multiplying on glass surfaces may be harvested for chemical analysis by denaturing them *in situ* with a combination of alcohol and ether (3:1). The alcohol-ether solution is added to each culture, and the denatured cells are removed by scraping. The cells are then heated in the alcohol-ether solution to extract lipid materials, and the cell residue is dissolved in 1N KOH at 37° C for subsequent protein, RNA, and DNA determinations by colorimetric methods. Trypsinization was found to be less efficient as a means of obtaining material for these analyses. For protein determinations, Eagle and his associates (*J. Biol. Chem. 228:* 847, 1957) wash intact cell layers with cold balanced salt solution, then treat them with cold 8 per cent trichloroacetic acid (TCA). The coagulated cell mass is then harvested by scraping, emulsified in a tissue grinder, centrifuged, and washed with cold 8 per cent TCA. Less protein N is obtained if the cells are scraped from the glass *before* treatment with TCA.

The procedures involved in harvesting newly isolated clonal populations are discussed in Chapter XIII.

Blood Leukocytes in Fluid Medium

Blood leukocytes cultivated directly on glass in fluid media provide a convenient means of testing the effect of a variety of substances on cells, including blood serum from different sources. It is easily possible to obtain uniform cultures of monocytes (which mature into macrophages) by the simple expedient of incubating whole blood (heparinized or citrated) for several days in stationary flasks or bottles, during which time the monocytes settle out and become attached to the glass. The blood may then be removed and replaced by a suitable medium containing 20 to 50 per cent serum or its equivalent. Eventually, if the medium is adequate, active cell multiplication should be obtained. Whenever possible, however, cultures of avian and mammalian leukocytes from peripheral blood should be prepared either from the layer of leukocytes and platelets (buffy coat) that is obtained at the surface of the red cells after the blood has been centrifuged (*see* p. 134) or from leukocytes separated from whole blood with phytohemagglutinin (*see* p. 137), or by the albumin-flotation method (*see* p. 135). When comparable cell populations are required, the latter method should be used; and the procedures are the same as those followed for other cells in suspension.

If buffy-coat fragments are to be cultivated, they are prepared as described on page 134 and placed in the culture flasks (one or more to a flask) after the medium has been added. The medium may consist of serum diluted with equal parts or less of balanced salt solution containing phenol red. Or it may consist wholly or partly of chemically defined ingredients. In the incubator, the cultures are left undisturbed for two to three days, during which time the leukocytes will have spread over the entire bottom surface of the flask. On the third day, the medium is renewed and the pH adjusted. If the medium is renewed twice, the cultures should remain in excellent condition for ten days. For many purposes, however, the results may be read on the seventh day.

Monocytes cultivated in blood serum are exceedingly sensitive test objects. Their various sensitivities are expressed not only in their rate of migration and multiplication but also in their morphological appearance and mode of association with other cells. Each monocyte or colony of monocytes can be said to have its own individual aspect that distinguishes it from all others (Fig. 50). Each reflects its own innate qualities and the response of these qualities to the environment.

Carrel[51] made the interesting observation that monocytes from different sources tend to take on the same appearance in a given serum. Thus, when monocytes from one individual are cultivated in the serum of a second individual, they assume the appearance of monocytes from the second individual cultivated in their own serum. In fact, it seldom happens that the blood serum of two normal individuals of the same species gives an identical appearance to two sister cultures of the same cells. Carrel,* Draper,[91] and their associates studied the monocytes of patients suffering from various diseases. When cells of the patient and those of an appropriate control individual were cultivated each in their own serum and in serum of the other individual, striking differences were found that confirmed the earlier conclusions, namely, that the appearance of monocytes in a given sample of serum reflects at least some of the peculiarities of the individual providing the serum.

Osgood and his associates[364,365] developed an ingenious *gradient* method of determining the most suitable culture conditions for cells of the blood and blood-forming organs. According to this method, a microscope slide is inserted at a steep angle in a deep suspension of cells in a widemouthed bottle, and cells settle out on the slide. This system provides a gradient in cell numbers from the top of the slide to the bottom as well as gradients in O_2 tension, CO_2 tension, and oxidation-reduction potential. As cells mature, they migrate over the edge of the slide and drop to the bottom of the vessel. For each type of cell there seems to be an optimal depth for a particular initial concentration of cells; and appropriate counts and calculations are made to

* Carrel, A., Ebeling, A. H., and Rhoads, C. P. Personal communication.

serve as a guide for future experiments and for the treatment of sister cultures in the same experiment.

Nowell[363] used Osgood's gradient method to advantage in studying the differentiation of human leukemic leukocytes, both granulocytic and monocytic, and of the conditions under which it takes place. The

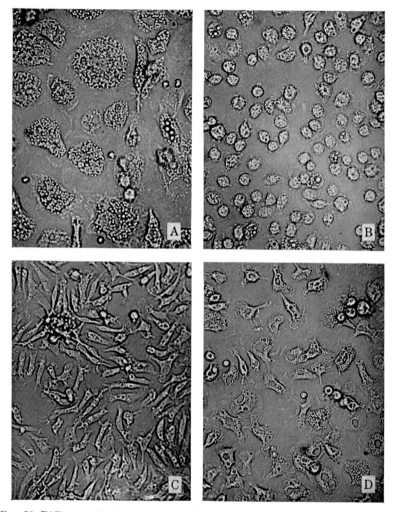

Fig. 50. Differences in the appearance of leukocytes derived from the blood of four normal chickens and cultivated for seven days in D-3.5 flasks in 50 per cent serum and Tyrode's solution. In each instance, the cells were cultivated in their own (autologous) serum. (A. Carrel, unpublished data, 1936.) × 230.

leukocytes were separated from heparinized venous blood with phyto-hemagglutinin (*see* p. 137) and planted in 2-oz, square, screw-capped bottles. The culture medium, which consisted of 30–50 ml of 10 or 20 per cent autologous plasma in solution 199, was seeded initially with $1-2 \times 10^6$ cells per ml. One or two glass slides were placed in each bottle at an angle of 50° to 60°. To study the cells, a slide was removed, rinsed with water, air dried, and stained (Giemsa). Except when slides were removed or fresh medium was added, the cultures were left undisturbed; and room air provided the gas phase. If the cultures became too acid, CO_2 could be released by loosening the caps.

Discrete Tissue Fragments in Fluid Medium

In 1936, in a study of antibody formation, the author[375] cultivated discrete fragments of adult-rabbit spleen in 50 per cent rabbit serum in Tyrode's solution containing extra glucose. For each culture, approximately 100 mg of tissue (about 75 fragments) were suspended in 2 ml of medium in modified Erlenmeyer flasks. Because demonstrable antibodies were produced by the tissues during the period of cultivation and because the tissue fragments from each culture were fixed, sectioned, and stained at the termination of an experiment, it was easily possible to correlate the degree of survival of the tissues with at least one measurable, functional activity. While it was found that spleen fragments from different animals might remain in an equally good state of preservation when cultivated in a particular serum, their antibody production might vary tremendously. But a high antibody production was never demonstrated in cultures that showed widespread necrosis of the tissue elements, particularly the lymphocytes. Certain sera were decidedly toxic, whereas others permitted the tissue to remain in an excellent state of preservation for considerable periods. Oddly enough, instances were encountered in which a serum from another animal provided a better medium than autologous serum from the animal providing the tissues. Serum toxicity could usually be reduced or eliminated by heating the serum for 1 hr at 56° C. The method was also used[262] to advantage in a study of serum protein production by tissues cultivated in heterologous media (Fig. 51); and many tissues other than spleen were likewise cultivated (Fig. 52).

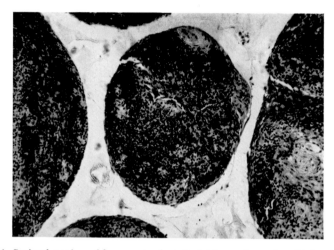

FIG. 51. Stained section of fragments of adult-chicken spleen after 20 days' cultivation in an Erlenmeyer-type flask in rabbit serum and Tyrode's solution (1:1). The medium was renewed at five-day intervals. (K. Landsteiner and R. C. Parker, unpublished data, 1938.) × 110.

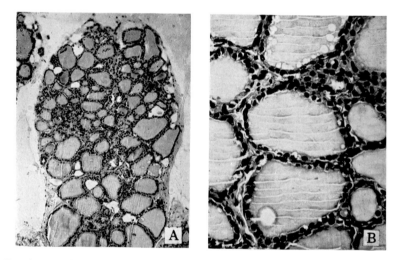

FIG. 52. *A* and *B*. Stained sections of fragments of adult rabbit thyroid cultivated for five days in an Erlenmeyer-type flask in a fluid medium containing 50 per cent rabbit serum. Approximately 100 mg of tissue were suspended in 2 ml of medium. (R. C. Parker, unpublished experiments, 1937.) (*A*) × 62; (*B*) × 230.

Perforated-Cellophane Cultures

In 1947, Evans and Earle[132] introduced perforated cellophane for the protection and support of cells and tissues cultivated in fluid media. Many cells adhere to the under surface of the cellophane rather than to the glass and become anchored to the edges of the perforations. As would be expected, better growth is obtained when the tissues are placed under the cellophane rather than over it (*see also* p. 148). Very often, the cells grow in several overlapping layers and, when the medium is adequate, continue to multiply until the whole surface of the cellophane has been covered. When the cellophane is unperforated, stresses and strains develop in the growing sheets of cells, which then break loose and are lost.

A grade of cellophane that has been found satisfactory is Dupont's PT (plain, transparent) 62, thickness about 40 μ. It is usually supplied (*see* p. 16) in rolls $3\frac{1}{2}$ in. wide and perforated in a staggered pattern of 324 holes per sq in., each hole 0.023 in. in diameter, giving an open area of $13\frac{1}{2}$ per cent. The cellophane is cut into squares to fit the thimble of a Soxhlet extraction apparatus and extracted for 1 hr with acetone to remove surface impurities. The squares are then rinsed and stored in the refrigerator in ion-exchange water (*see* p. 29). Eventually, the wet cellophane is cut to fit the culture containers, which are sterilized by autoclaving.

Sponge-Matrix Cultures with Fluid Medium

Reference has already been made on page 170 to procedures developed by Leighton and his associates[274] for the cultivation of tissues in a combined matrix of plasma and cellulose sponge. In this system, the cells are able to develop in localized environments that are partly, at least, of their own creation. Leighton's group has also devised methods for the continuous cultivation of established strains of cells (e.g., strain HeLa) on the matrix of gelatin-sponge (Gelfoam) particles in a fluid medium. After one or two days, the proliferating cells migrate into the interstices of the sponge particles and eventually cover the particles completely. At any time, some or all of the sponge particles may be removed, fixed, and sectioned for histologic study.

A small piece of Gelfoam pack (The Upjohn Co., Kalamazoo, Mich.), well moistened with nutrient medium, is minced aseptically with scissors until it has been reduced to particles about 1 mm in diameter. After the medium has been removed from an existing tube culture containing a luxurient layer of cells, moistened Gelfoam particles are introduced and gently wiped over the populated area. Alternatively, the gelatin particles may be placed in a fresh tube together with a suspension of cells. After nutrient medium (1 ml) has been added, the culture is returned to the incubator. At the time of fluid change, it may be difficult to remove the depleted medium without removing the gelatin particles as well. This difficulty may be avoided by including a piece of cellulose sponge in the tube before autoclaving. If the piece of cellulose sponge is held against the wall of the tube with a pipette and the depleted medium aspirated through it, the Gelfoam particles will be prevented from entering the pipette. The volume of fresh nutrient that is added should depend upon the pH changes that occurred during the previous feeding interval.

When subcultures are to be prepared, freshly minced Gelfoam particles are added to the donor cultures and mixed thoroughly with the older particles in the tube. On the following day, the particles are divided into aliquots that are pipetted into fresh tubes with new medium.

XII

Suspended-Cell Cultures

FOR many investigations, especially studies relating to the physiology and biochemistry of animal cell populations, it is useful to be able to remove representative samples of the population at intervals during the incubation period. It is also useful to be able to prepare subcultures by simple dilution with the least degree of injury to the cells. Both of these operations are easily possible with cells that are propagated in agitated suspension. Cells in suspension can also be used to establish stationary cultures in flasks, bottles, or Petri dishes, if it is desired (1) to obtain discrete colonies from single dispersed cells or (2) to obtain confluent layers of cells. Animal cells cultivated *in vitro* exhibit growth cycles[435] that are similar to those of microbial populations. These growth cycles, which are especially easy to demonstrate in suspended-cell cultures,[192, 255] can be separated into four main phases: (1) lag phase; (2) logarithmic growth phase; (3) stationary phase; and (4) logarithmic death phase. The cells that can be propagated in suspension most efficiently are usually derived from established lines that can be scraped from the glass mechanically, concentrated by centrifugation, and resuspended by simple pipetting.

During recent years, many systems have been devised for propagating cells in agitated suspension. One of the first of these was a demonstration by Owens, Gey, and Gey[366] that a strain of lymphoblastic mouse cells (deBruyn's MB-III strain) could be propagated with some measure of success in small glass tubes that were attached to a wheel at right angles to the axis of rotation. With each turn of the wheel, at 38 r.p.m., the cell suspension "tumbled" from one end of the tube to the other. Unfortunately, there was a tendency for a precipitate to form in the medium (which contained human serum and beef embryo extract) and a large proportion of the cells remained attached to the glass. But it was definitely established by these experiments that at least one type of cell could multiply in suspension.

The next effort was made by Earle and his associates,[120,121] who increased the speed of rotation of conventional roller-tube cultures (*see* p. 182) from less than 1 to 40 r.p.m., but the results were not entirely satisfactory. Graham and Siminovitch[192] then increased the speed of rotation of the tubes still further to 50 r.p.m. and were successful in propagating cells continuously in fluid media under simple conditions that yielded population densities as high as 5×10^6 cells per ml. Other methods that have been developed for propagating cells in suspension include: the use of rotary shakers to keep the contents of culture flasks in a continuous whirling motion (Earle and associates;[38,116,117] Kuchler and Merchant.[255,256]); the use of magnetic stirrers to agitate cell suspensions in flasks and bottles (Cherry and Hull;[68] McLimans and associates.[85,315]); Danes[81] use of an elaborate glass-stirrer unit to agitate the cells; Graff and McCarty's[191] use of a continuous flow "cytogenerator"; the use of large-scale fermenter units by McLimans's group;[316,555] and, the "chemo-turbidostat" of Cooper and his associates.[78] Some of these methods will be discussed in detail in the present chapter.

The propagation of cells in suspension presents special problems pertaining to the speed of uptake of essential nutrients. Because periodic replacements of the entire medium are seldom practicable, efforts have to be made to anticipate the nutritive requirements of the cultures when they are prepared and to add at subsequent intervals those substances that disappear most rapidly from the medium. Earle and his associates[118] increased the glucose concentration in media used for agitated cultures. Thomas and his associates[516] found that the addition of arginine (42 μg per ml) every other day greatly increased the number of cells in suspended-cell cultures of HeLa and ERK/KD cells, and other amino acids and inositol were added for human amnion cells.[85] Cooper and his associates[77] reported that reduced oxygen tension (19–17 per cent) was beneficial for the proliferation of transformed rabbit-kidney cells[537] in suspended culture and that a mixture of galactose or fructose (6 Gm per l) and glucose (2 Gm per l) allowed better pH control than glucose alone (6 Gm per l).[78]

Cultivation of Cells in Suspension

CELLS CULTIVATED IN ROTATED TEST TUBES

In 1955, Graham and Siminovitch[192] described a useful test-tube method for the continuous propagation of certain established cell lines in suspension. According to this method, cultures that are properly cared for can be sub-cultured repeatedly without an initial lag phase and often show a 100-fold increase in population density during the logarithmic phase of multiplication. To initiate such a culture from L cells, a stationary flask or bottle culture containing about 30 ml of medium is first subjected to a complete fluid change, after which the cells are scraped gently into the fresh medium (*see* p. 188). About 20 ml of the cell suspension are then transferred to a Pyrex test tube, 1×6 in. in diameter, which is then closed with a silicone stopper, shaken vigorously, and placed for incubation ($37°$ C) on a wheel rotated at about 50 r.p.m. around the long axis of the tube. The speed of rotation is rather critical; with speeds of less than 45 r.p.m. the cells tend to stick to the inner surface of the tube, and speeds greater than 55 r.p.m. result in extensive cell damage. Within a few hours after the tude has been placed on the wheel, the cells become spherical, few cell clumps are visible, and no cells are adherent to the inner surface of the tube. These conditions prevail during the entire growth cycle.

To follow the day-to-day increase in cell population, small samples (less than 0.5 ml) are removed from the tube, and the cells are counted in a hemocytometer. When roller cultures that are initiated from stationary cultures have an initial population of 5×10^4 or more cells per ml, there is little or no cell multiplication during the first 24 hr. The cells then begin to multiply rapidly. When the medium is adequate, e.g., 20 per cent horse serum in CMRL-1066, the cultures will reach densities of 10^6 cells per ml without change of medium. Cells will remain in the logarithmic phase for three to four generations. When multiplication ceases, a further increase in population can be obtained by renewing the medium; and population densities of

5×10^6 cells per ml have been obtained in this way. Renewal of the medium is accomplished by centrifuging the culture tube at 1000 r.p.m. for 10 min and by replacing all of the old fluid or any part of it with fresh medium.

If cells that are still in the logarithmic phase are subcultured into fresh, warm (37° C) medium at a concentration of 4×10^4 cells per ml or greater, multiplication begins without a lag phase. Thus, cells can be kept in the logarithmic growth phase indefinitely. The doubling time for populations of L cells in 20 per cent horse serum in CMRL-1066 varies between 24 and 30 hr. During the logarithmic growth phase, the amounts of RNA, DNA, and protein per cell remain constant.[482]

Cells Cultivated in Rotary Shaker Flasks

Earle and his associates[116] used a modified Type AV, New Brunswick rotary shaker (New Brunswick Scientific Co., New Brunswick, N.J.) to agitate suspended-cell cultures in 1.5-l containers at an operational speed of 120–180 r.p.m. The container was a spherical, flat-bottomed boiling flask modified by replacing the central neck with two off-center ports that served both for continuous gassing and as a means of introducing and withdrawing cells and medium. The swirling motion provided by the shaker caused the cell suspension to form a thin layer that extended some distance above the equator of the flask. With each fluid change, the volume was gradually increased to a maximum of 400 ml for each 1.5-l container. For L cells, the medium consisted either of 30 per cent horse serum and 20 per cent embryo extract (1:1) in balanced saline with the glucose level increased to 2 Gm per l or of 20 per cent horse serum in chemically defined medium NCTC-109 (*see* Table VIII). At one- to four-day intervals, the culture was opened and either additional nutrient was added or the cells were centrifuged out at about 900 r.p.m. (250g) and returned to the flask in fresh medium. The cultures were gassed continuously with a mixture of 5 per cent CO_2 in air, but even continuous gassing was found to be inadequate as a means of controlling the pH of heavily populated cultures. Younger cultures could be kept at fairly constant pH by flushing out the flasks twice a day with the gas mixture. By these means, large populations of L and HeLa strain cells were obtained, although the average generation time (i.e., doubling time) was usually two days or more in length, even for L cells.[38] By contrast, the generation time of L cells propagated in suspension in roller tubes at 50 r.p.m. is 24–30 hr.

Kuchler and Merchant,[255] working with 80-ml suspensions in 250-ml Erlenmeyer flasks agitated on a New Brunswick rotary shaker, found that cell multiplication proceeded at similar rates when the serum concentration varied between 5 and 40 per cent in medium 199. The maximum population density was lower at 5 per cent levels, but at 15 per cent or higher the densities were similar. Also, within certain limits, the rate of increase was independent of the number of cells in the original inoculum. Kuchler and Merchant[256] have since extended these studies with 100-ml suspensions in 500-ml flasks that are agitated on an Eberbach rotary shaker at 100 r.p.m. (Eberbach Corp., Ann Arbor, Mich.). When hemocytometer counts, estimations of packed-cell volumes and dry weights, cell-size measurements, and DNA, RNA, and total nitrogen determinations were made on aliquots of individual cultures, the following conclusions were drawn: (1) Measurements of packed cell volumes showed that cell protoplasm increases exponentially from zero time even though cell counts may indicate a lag phase. (2) The range in cell volumes, as determined by measuring cell diameters, was $1500 \ \mu^3$ to $3000 \ \mu^3$. An increase in cell size during the lag phase accounted for the increase in packed cell volume in the absence of an increase in cell numbers. (3) DNA increases were found to be related directly to increases in cell number, whereas increases in RNA, total nitrogen, and dry weight were related to increases in cell volume. In the more recent work, the nutrient fluid consisted of 5 per cent horse serum in equal parts of Eagle's basal medium (*see* Table VIII) and a medium containing Hanks's balanced saline, 0.5 per cent lactalbumin hydrolysate, 0.1 per cent yeast extract, and 0.5 per cent Bacto-peptone (*see* p. 113).

CELLS CULTIVATED IN MAGNETIC-STIRRER UNITS

Cherry and Hull[68] used a magnetic stirrer to agitate a suspension of cells in a round-bottomed flask. McLimans and his associates[315] performed the same operation in Pyrex cylinders, in each of which a Teflon-covered magnetic bar was suspended from a fishing swivel fixed beneath the stopper. The vessels were of different sizes to accommodate culture volumes ranging from 25 to 130 ml. To leave space for air, the culture volumes ranged from 12 to 65 per cent of the total volume of the containers.* Agitation of the suspension was obtained by placing the vessel with the suspended magnetic bar in the field of a magnetic stirrer. The stopper contained two ports for continuous gassing; and, to facilitate sampling, the vessel had an outlet near the base that was closed with a stopper. Successful cultures were initiated

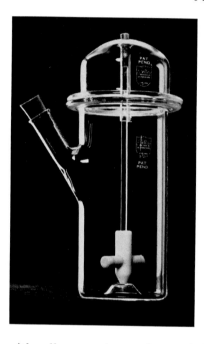

FIG. 53. Spinner flask for propagating cells in suspension by means of platform-type magnetic stirrer; sealable-type flange joint between cover and body of flask. To assure uniform agitation, the impeller has a horizontal, magnetic stirring bar mounted in a Teflon retainer with a pointed end that rides in an indentation in bottom of flask. (Bellco Glass, Inc., Vineland, N.J.)

with cell suspensions as low as 1.5×10^4 cells per ml. One culture of L cells, with a volume of from 300 to 500 ml, was maintained continuously for several months, during which time $1-3 \times 10^8$ cells were harvested every two or three days. (These larger volumes were accommodated in Mason-type fruit jars.*) The reaction of cells to trypan blue served as a useful index of the state of the culture (*see also* p. 282). It was usual to record at least 95 per cent viability. There are now available commercially improved stirrer vessels with permanently centered magnetic bars (Fig. 53). In the author's laboratory, two such vessels, each with a capacity of 1 l below the side arm, are incubated in a stainless-steel, constant-temperature water bath (12″ × 18″ × 6″ high) supported by two magnetic-stirrer units.

* McLimans, W. F. Personal communication.

Cells Cultivated in Fermenter Vessels

In an attempt to achieve even larger batches of cells, McLimans and his associates went on to the fermenter-type of culture that had been used to advantage in the antibiotic industry. Their first experiments[316] were made in 5-l, impeller-agitated fermenters, three of which were connected individually by means of flexible rubber couplings to a common variable-speed agitator drive, whose operating range was 150–750 r.p.m. The main body of the New Brunswick fermenter consists of a standard 6 × 12 in., 5-l Pyrex jar that is locked into a frame connected with a stainless-steel (#316) head. Attached to the head are four baffles, a blade impeller, an air or gas-mixture sparger, a sample line, and ports that can be used for the introduction of a gas overlay. Because the built-in sample line was not practical, samples were taken by passing a 10-in., 18-gauge syringe needle through an available port closed with a vaccine stopper. To avoid depletion of the volume of the culture from evaporation, the air mixture supplied to each tank was passed through a container of water, and glass-wool filters were inserted in both the inlet and outlet lines. The cultures were harvested by forcing the cell suspension out through the sample line by pressure.

Because the L-strain cells that were propagated did not have high oxygen requirements, the impeller speeds used were just sufficient to keep the cells in a suspended state. It was found that the inclusion of a small amount of Dow's Methocel (4000 c.p.s.) in the medium improved the efficiency of the system (*see also* Earle[118,121]). It was also found that the bicarbonate-CO_2 buffer system of Earle's balanced saline could be replaced by 1.44 Gm per l of Na_2HPO_4 combined with Earle's levels of NaCl, KCl, and $MgSO_4$ (*see* p. 57). The glucose was raised to 2.5 Gm per l, but the remaining ingredients of Earle's saline were omitted. It was stated, however, that it was necessary to add alkali to the medium from time to time to maintain the pH above 7.0; and, because the generation time of the cells varied from 24–60 hr, it was felt that the culture conditions were not yet optimal. The maximum cell population usually obtained in the 5-l fermenter was $1.0–1.5 \times 10^6$ per ml.

From the 5-l fermenter, McLimans's group[555] went on to a 20-l unit (Fig. 54). The cells that were propagated included Earle's strain L, Gey's strain HeLa, and Westwood's ERK strain.[537] The cell inoculum for the 20-l fermenters were produced in 3-l volumes in the 5-l fermenters, which, in turn, were inoculated from magnetic-stirrer cultures or from stationary cultures.

CELLS CULTIVATED IN SEMIAUTOMATIC SYSTEMS

Graff and McCarty[191] developed a "cytogenerator" (Fig. 55) in which the cells produced were retained in the growth chamber until

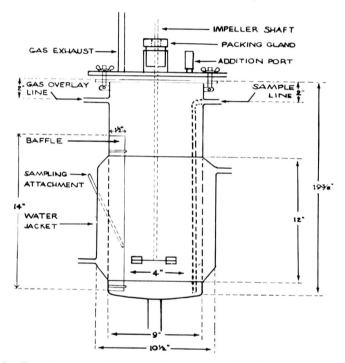

FIG. 54. Twenty-liter, stainless-steel fermenter used in the propagation of mammalian cells in suspension. (D. W. Ziegler et al.[555])

they were removed manually, but samples of medium could be separated at any time. Fresh nutrients and spent medium were exchanged through a fritted glass septum with pore size just small enough to retain the cells, and matched variable pumps kept the outflow of medium equal to the inflow. Turbulence and pH control were provided by alternate pulsations of gas pressure, which also prevented clogging of the efferent fritted glass candle.

More recently, Cooper and his associates[78] examined several methods of propagating mammalian cells in suspension and found that a system providing a continuous flow of medium ("chemostat" principle) was more efficient for large-scale operations than the "batch" culture systems described in the preceding sections. Over a period of four months, a 1.5-l culture vessel provided with a continuous flow of medium yielded an average of 10^9 cells per day in 1 l of medium. The maximum cell density was 2×10^6 cells per ml; cell viability was 90–95 per cent. The doubling time averaged 25 hr over the entire

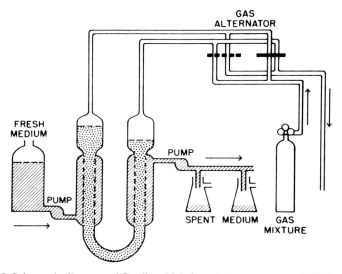

Fig. 55. Schematic diagram of Graff and McCarty's "cytogenerator."[191] For further description, see text. (S. Graff.[190])

period and was occasionally less than 16 hr. In this system, however, as in "batch" cultures, it was necessary to anticipate the needs of the culture for the following 24 hr and make the necessary adjustments. In a system providing a photoelectrically controlled discontinuous flow of medium ("turbidostat"), the control was affected by nonviable cells, size of cells, and the turbidity that forms with stirring in the absence of cells. When conditions were optimal, growth was quite rapid, but cell density tended to drift to low values. In the preferred system ("chemo-turbidostat"), the medium was added to a 20-l culture vessel (Fig. 56) regularly in small intermittent quantities (at a rate similar to growth rate) by means of a time switch that actuated a solenoid closure. A turbidimetric safety device ensured that cell density did not drop below levels that permitted growth. On occasion, doubling

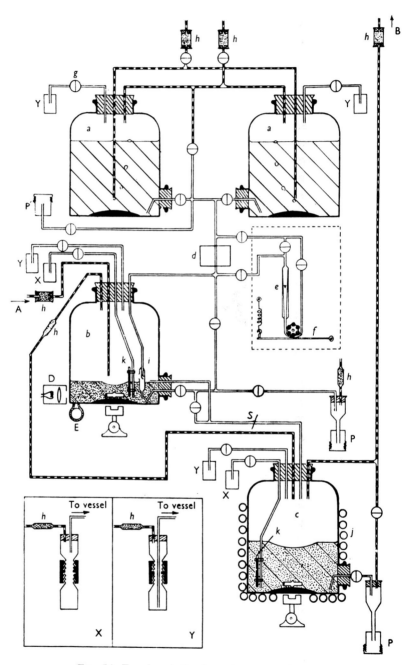

FIG. 56. For descriptive legend see opposite page.

times of 14–16 hr were obtained with ERK cells in a medium that included lactalbumin hydrolysate, yeast extract, various amino-acid and vitamin supplements, glucose, and antibiotics in Earle's balanced salt solution. But these and other automatic devices were considered uneconomical unless they could be operated continuously for at least two months. Also, it was found that the cell yield of a chemostat-type culture was greater than that of automatically controlled ones, and this increase was attributed to the greater attention required by the simpler devices.

Estimation of Number of Cells Capable of Division in Suspended-Cell Cultures

Gwatkin and his associates[200] have developed a method for determining the number of cells capable of division in cultures in which the cells are propagated in suspension. During the logarithmic phase of growth, samples are removed and cell densities are estimated from hemocytometer counts (Fig. 57). Serial dilutions of the sample are then made in a chemically defined medium at room temperature; 100 cells or more are plated in each of several Petri dishes (60-mm diameter) containing 5 ml of the defined medium supplemented with serum and previously equilibrated at 37° C in a humidified atmosphere of 5 per cent CO_2 in air. (The serial dilutions are made in serum-free medium to reduce to a minimum the number of cells that become attached to the walls of the tubes while the dilutions are being made.)

After the Petri dishes are incubated at 37° for eight to ten days, the colonies are washed with buffered saline, fixed with Bouin's solution (*see* p. 299), stained with Giemsa, and scored. While the percentage of

---

FIG. 56. Diagram of a "chemo-turbidostat" assembly for continuous cultivation of ERK[537] cells. The lines carrying air or gas are stippled; a, medium reservoirs; b, culture vessel; c, receiver; d, solenoid valve closure; e, rotameter; f, pump; g, screw clips; h, cotton filters; i, antisplash medium inlet; j, rubber tubing of cooling jacket; k, thermometers; A, gas inlet; B, gas outlet; D, light source; E, photocell; P, harvesting and P′ replenishing ports. X and Y are sampling and inoculating ports respectively, shown in detail in the inset; samples are withdrawn via X or added via Y by sucking or blowing through the cotton filters. The bar across the medium line at S indicates the position of a sterile connection made during assembly. (P. D. Cooper *et al.*[78])

cells capable of forming colonies (i.e., the *plating efficiency*) varies widely when they are plated during the stationary phase of growth, 60 to 75 per cent of the cells give rise to colonies when plated during

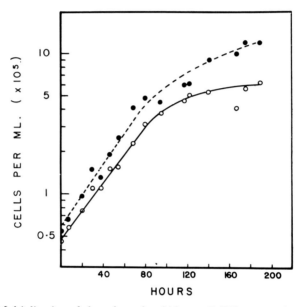

FIG. 57. Multiplication of altered monkey-kidney cells[377] in suspension. *Upper curve:* hemocytometer count; *lower curve:* colony count. (R. B. L. Gwatkin *et al.*[200])

the logarithmic phase. Almost 100 per cent of the cells in the logarithmic phase produce colonies if they are placed over feeder layers of x-irradiated cells,[416, 418] showing that nearly all of the cells are capable of multiplying if they are provided with an adequate nutritional environment (*see* p. 215). The method is particularly suitable for L cells and cells of similar nature.

XIII

Cell Clones

WHEN a cell strain has been derived from mass cultures of explanted tissue fragments, it is impossible to know which cells of the original tissue gave rise to the strain. During cultivation, the selective influences of the culture system usually operate in favor of particular cell types, though the surviving cell types may not be the ones most desired. Because of these difficulties, it is useful to isolate clonal populations from single cells as soon as possible after explanting the tissues. If clones are established early enough, it is usually possible to identify particular cell types as the clones develop. Although wide variations may be expected even in clonal populations, it would at least be known that such variations do not result from a mixture of cell types, all present in the explanted tissues. The single-cell plating techniques that have been developed[413] make it possible to define cellular genetic characteristics with considerable accuracy. Under optimal conditions, clonal stocks can be prepared from almost any cell in a population. Single cells of such stocks can be plated and, from an examination of the isolated colonies that develop, the proportion of cells that possess a given characteristic can be determined. Moreover, the persistence of this characteristic throughout many generations of cells can be tested under various conditions. If the characteristic persists with repeated cloning, the conclusion may be drawn that it is genetic in origin.

Many years ago Fischer[152] observed the multiplication of scattered, isolated Rous sarcoma cells, but he was unable to obtain colonies from isolated, normal fibroblasts. In 1935 Moen[331] followed the development of colonies of fibroblasts in cultures containing scattered exudate cells from the guinea pig and carried their progeny through repeated

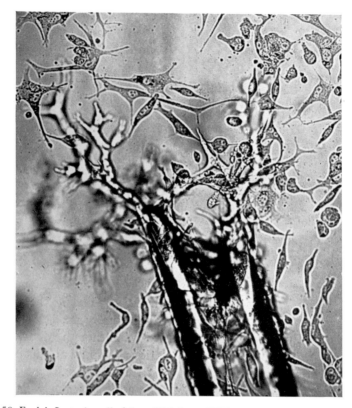

FIG. 58. Earle's L-strain cells (clone 929) from C3H mouse emerging from open end of capillary tube into plasma medium of outer culture flask 28 days after first cell had been isolated in this same capillary. (K. K. Sanford *et al.*[468]) × 145.

subcultures. He also showed that the presence of other cells in the vicinity enhanced cell division. In 1948 Sanford, Earle, and Likely[468] reported the first strain (or clone) of tissue cells derived from a single, isolated cell (Fig. 58). Their procedure was based on the theory that single cells fail to multiply when completely isolated because even the best culture medium is so inadequate as to need extensive modification that can be provided only by the cells themselves. Accordingly, they supplied their isolated cells with cell-free medium that had been conditioned by using it as the fluid phase of large plasma cultures of the cell type to be isolated. Several years later, Puck and Marcus[416] followed the same reasoning when they developed clones from isolated cells nourished by a "feeder" layer of living, metabolizing cells that had been prevented from continued multiplication by x-radiation. Eventually, by handling the cells more gently, they were able to develop clones from single, isolated cells without the use of a "feeder" layer.

It now becomes clear that cultures initiated from single cells may have special nutritional requirements. Thus, Sato and his associates[472] found that dialyzed serum that did not support the multiplication of HeLa cells recovered this capacity upon the addition of cholesterol to the medium. Neuman and McCoy[359] obtained similar results with Walker 256 cells by adding pyruvate, oxalacetate, or α-ketoglutarate to the medium. Neuman and Tytell[360] found that a number of purines (hypoxanthine, adenine, and several of their derivatives) stimulated the growth of Walker 256 cells in isolated colonies.

Isolation of Cell Clones

CLONES ISOLATED IN CAPILLARY TUBES

Sanford and her associates[468] isolated single cells from cultures of a strain (L) originally derived from normal, subcutaneous connective tissue of an adult C_3H mouse. Several individual cells were picked by hand from the floor of the culture flask by means of a fine capillary pipette, and an attempt was made to distribute the cells (in the medium in which they had been growing) along the length of the capillary. Each pipette was flushed beforehand with chicken plasma, which formed a thin clot on the capillary wall. After the cells had been introduced, a bubble of air was drawn into the pipette, and the end of the capillary was plugged by drawing up a small amount of plasma mixed with the culture fluid. The capillary was then broken from the base of the pipette, and its proximal end and then its distal end were sealed by contact with a molten glass bead. After the sealed tubes had been incubated for 15–20 hr, they were examined under the microscope, and well-isolated, healthy, single cells were selected and their exact location was recorded. Then, after the capillaries had been sterilized by immersion in chloroform, they were placed in a sterile Petri dish and broken into 4- to 5-mm segments, each of which contained a single cell (Fig. 58). The capillary segments were then inserted into Carrel flasks containing 1 ml of medium consisting of equal parts of plasma and the conditioned culture fluid already mentioned (p. 211). When the clots had hardened, 1 ml of conditioned culture fluid was added to the surface of each clot, and the flasks were incubated. The supernatant fluid was renewed every 48 hr. Only about 4 per cent of the cells survived for 48 hr after planting. Two to three days after isolation, the rate of division varied from zero to three divisions per cell per day. After three to five days, the rate was slightly higher.

It is interesting to note that in all of their preparations no single cells divided in normal, unconditioned medium, and that the only single cells to divide were those located near the center of the capillary tube. Later, when the cell density increased, the center of the capillary tube seemed less favorable, since cells in this area became necrotic and died, whereas the cells near the open ends of the capillary continued to proliferate. It was also found that, even though small clumps of cells might become established in the capillary tubes in unconditioned medium and cause successive waves of cells to migrate from the ends of the capillary into the outer plasma, the cells could not grow into a healthy colony unless the outer medium contained conditioned fluid.

CLONES ISOLATED IN MICRODROPS

Lwoff and his collaborators[301] isolated single cells by a modification of a method devised by deFonbrune.[164] The single cells are placed in small drops of medium under a layer of mineral oil. The oil, which is nontoxic, permits an exchange of oxygen and carbon dioxide between the drop and the controlled atmosphere, but evaporation is reduced to a minimum. In the author's laboratory, a slight variation of this method has been used to advantage in the development of clonal populations derived by single-cell isolation from a variety of sources.

According to this procedure, halves of standard microscope slides are cleaned and placed for sterilization in 60-mm Petri dishes. Fine pipettes are made from 8-in. lengths of 4-mm (O.D.) Pyrex tubing that are fire polished at each end, cleaned in the manner described for pipettes in general (see p. 32), plugged at each end with cotton, and sterilized in glass tubes. The finished pipettes are drawn as required over a small burner, two being made from each length of tubing. The tip is drawn out to a fine, hairlike capillary, which is broken off at an appropriate point with sterile forceps, and the pipettes are placed for protection in glass tubes lying flat on the workbench. A little practice will determine the degree of fineness that is required. In use, the pipette is operated by means of a mouth tube.

The medium is removed from a bottle containing a confluent layer of cells and is replaced with equal parts of 0.25 per cent trypsin (made up in Hanks's saline solution without calcium, magnesium, or phosphates) and 0.44 per cent sodium citrate (see p. 189). After 5 to 8 min at $37°$ C, with occasional gentle agitation, the suspension containing single cells and cell aggregates is removed to a centrifuge tube, the cell clumps are broken up by vigorous pipetting, and the cells are sedimented by centrifuging for 3 min at 800 r.p.m. After the supernatant fluid has been withdrawn, sufficient nutrient is added to give a suspension of roughly $3-5 \times 10^5$ cells per ml.

In the meantime, the mineral oil is poured to a depth of about 4 mm into all of the Petri dishes that are to be used on a given day. Then, with the mouth pipette, a drop of medium about 3 mm in diameter is deposited beneath the oil on the glass slide in 12–15 dishes. (A microscope is used for this operation and all subsequent ones.) If too many drops are dispensed at once, the medium is likely to become too alkaline before the cells have been added. With a fresh pipette, single cells are then deposited in each of four to five dishes to which medium has been added, after which a fresh pipette is taken for the next group, and so on. The pipettes are changed frequently to minimize the danger of cell clumping. As each set of 12–15 dishes has been inoculated with cells, they are placed in a CO_2 cabinet (see p. 184) before the next set is prepared. This complex procedure could be greatly simplified, of course, if a nontoxic buffering system were available.

Within 24 hr, and before any divisions have occurred, the cultures are scanned under the microscope, and only those with viable, single cells are retained. After 5 days, and twice a week thereafter, mouth pipettes are again used to withdraw and replace the medium in each drop. After a clone has grown to fill the area of a drop (Fig. 59), the medium is replaced with a drop of 0.03 per cent trypsin, and after 3 to

5 min at 37° C the cells are freed from the glass and may be transferred directly to a Carrel flask containing 1.5 ml of nutrient medium. Twice a week thereafter, until the clone is well established, only half of the medium is renewed. Once the cells have begun to multiply, complete

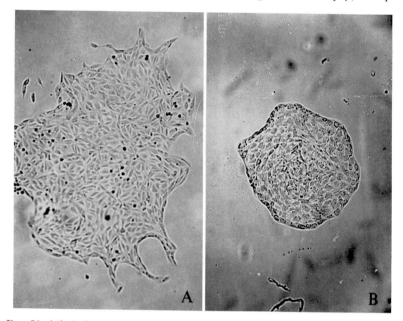

Fig. 59. (A) A clone of monkey-kidney epithelial cells eight days after a single cell had been isolated in a capillary drop of medium on a coverslip, under a layer of mineral oil in a Petri dish. The medium, which was renewed twice during this period, was CMRL-1066 supplemented with 20 per cent horse serum. (B) Another clone of monkey-kidney cells ten days after a single cell had been isolated. (R. C. Parker et al.[377]) × 45.

fluid changes are made. The nutrient medium used in this work consists of CMRL-1066 that is supplemented with 20 per cent horse serum before final filtration.

CLONES ISOLATED WITH AID OF HEAT

Goldstein[188] devised a simple cloning method that consists essentially of killing all but one of a small population of cells by applying heat from a small, electric soldering iron to the outer surface of the culture container in those areas in which cells are to be killed. The soldering iron (Ungar, with handle 776 and high-heat part 1235) is modified by replacing the soldering tip with a 3-in. length of brass rod,

$\frac{1}{16}$ in. in diameter, and with a $\frac{1}{2}$ in. 90° bend at the tip. A small piece of 18-gauge, soft copper wire is wound around the tip and filed to a fine point. This fine point, when heated, is applied to the area selected. A cell suspension is diluted to the extent that 0.1 ml contains about ten cells, which are added to D-3.5 Carrel flasks with 2 ml of culture medium. After 8–12 hours' incubation, the cultures are examined under the microscope and the location of (a) widely separated cells, (b) cells close together, and (c) occasional cell clumps, are marked with ink on the outer surface of the flasks. Cell clumps and cells that are close together are killed by applying heat to the marked areas for 15–20 sec. Because it is difficult to detect cells at the edge of the flasks, the heated rod is passed slowly around the periphery. An effort is made, however, to leave three or four isolated cells undamaged. The flasks are then incubated for an additional 24-hr period to permit any floating cells to settle to the glass surface. Finally, one cell is selected for the development of the clone, and the others are destroyed by heat.

CLONES ISOLATED WITH AID OF IRRADIATED "FEEDER" CELLS

Puck and his associates[416, 418] devised a method by which the cells to be cloned are distributed over a layer of irradiated cells (Fig. 60). Although the irradiated cells are unable to multiply indefinitely, they metabolize actively and "condition" the medium so as to permit single cells to reproduce to the point where they become self-sustaining. According to this method,[413] a bottle containing a confluent layer of cells is exposed to a dose of 2500–4000 r of 200–240 kv x-rays. The irradiated cells are then trypsinized (see p. 188) and 10^5 cells are added to each 60-mm Petri dish along with the suspension of nonirradiated cells to be cloned. Alternatively, the cells for the feeder layer can be added to each Petri dish before irradiation, which is then accomplished in situ. After irradiation, the cells to be cloned are introduced, and the cultures are placed for incubation in a CO_2 cabinet (see p. 184). Controls consisting of cultures with feeder cells alone should be included in the experiment in order to detect the possibility of colony formation arising from surviving cells in the feeder layer.

Usually, 10 to 12 days of incubation is sufficient[413] for optimal colony development, but when a feeder layer is employed it is necessary to change the medium on the sixth day. After incubation, cells from selected colonies (clones) may be harvested by the method

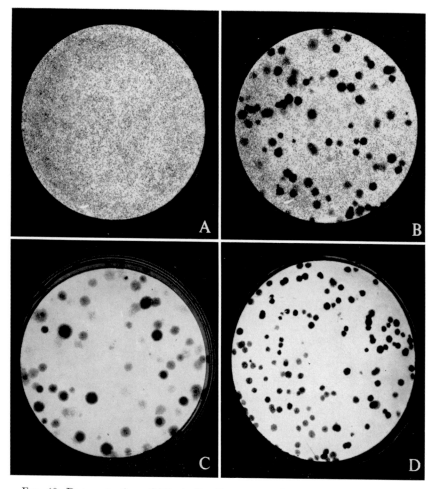

Fig. 60. Demonstration of "feeder" cell system and colonies grown from single HeLa cells. Plates were incubated for eight days, fixed with Bouin's solution, and stained with hematoxylin-eosin. (A) Plate with x-irradiated "feeder" cells alone. The granular background is due to the irradiated HeLa cells. (B) Plate with feeder cells and, in addition, an aliquot of 100 normal HeLa cells. The colony count obtained is 97. (C) Plate to which 100 gently trypsinized HeLa cells were added in an identical manner, except that no feeder layer was employed. These colonies generally show greater variation in density than do those grown over feeders. (D) Colonies developed from single cells of a pure genetic strain (S3) of HeLa cells, under conditions identical with those used in the experiment shown in C (i.e., no feeder system). The greater uniformity of the S3 cells as compared with the parent HeLa population is obvious. The observed plating efficiency was 93 per cent. (T. T. Puck, P. I. Marcus, and S. J. Cieciura.[418]) Actual size.

described in the next section, or some or all of the culture plates may be fixed and stained for ease in counting the total number of colonies that have developed. From this count, it is then possible to calculate the *plating efficiency* of the cells, which is defined as the percentage of cells set down that form colonies visible to the unaided eye within a specified time limit (e.g., eight or ten days). For HeLa cells, Puck's group reported plating efficiencies ranging from 60 to 100 per cent.

To make routine colony counts, the growth medium is poured off, the plates rinsed with saline to remove all extraneous protein, and the colonies are fixed and stained with Giemsa or hematoxylin solutions.

CLONES ISOLATED WITHOUT "FEEDER" CELLS

In their early work with HeLa cells, Puck and Marcus[416] obtained very low *plating efficiencies* unless "feeder" layers were used (*see* p. 215). But they were able eventually to improve[418] the plating efficiency by shortening the exposure to trypsin, by reducing mechanical stress, and by eliminating all unnecessary washings. According to their improved procedure, the nutrient medium was removed from a bottle culture of confluent cells, and 0.25 per cent trypsin was added to a depth of about 1 mm. The bottle was incubated at 37° C for 15 min with occasional gentle agitation and cooled immediately to room temperature, or trypsin action was stopped by adding an equal volume of nutrient medium (containing serum) at room temperature. After brief agitation by pipetting to disperse cell clumps, the suspension was either diluted directly in nutrient medium for plating or, if washing was required for some reason, the supernatant was replaced with fresh nutrient medium after a single centrifugation at room temperature for 5 min at a speed not exceeding 1000 r.p.m. (International centrifuge model SBY No. 1). The cell number was then estimated from hemocytometer counts, and any desired aliquot of the suspension was transferred to a 60-mm Petri dish containing 4.5 ml of nutrient medium and incubated in a CO_2 cabinet (*see* p. 184).

The plating procedure just described affords a quantitative method of studying the action of agents that enhance or impair cellular reproductive capacity.[418] As a means of establishing clonal populations of cells, the plating procedure is considerably more rapid than Earle's capillary technique (*see* p. 211) or the microdrop procedure of Lwoff and his associates (*see* p. 212). Its advantage is that it permits screening of large populations so that rare mutants can be isolated and developed into new strains. Its disadvantage is the danger of cells from one colony migrating to another.

Gwatkin and his associates[200] used Puck's plating techniques to determine the number of "viable" cells in suspended cell cultures (*see also* p. 207). During the logarithmic phase of growth, 60–75 per cent of the cells in a suspension were able to form colonies when placed in Petri dishes and incubated in a humidified atmosphere containing 5 per cent CO_2 (Fig. 57). Once the cells entered the stationary phase, the plating efficiency decreased. When cells in the logarithmic phase were placed on x-irradiated feeder layers, plating efficiencies close to 100 per cent could be obtained.

Removal of Selected Colonies (Clones) from Plates

Selected colonies derived from single cells in Petri-dish cultures may be subcultured and developed into clonal population[418] as follows: All but 0.5 ml of the medium is removed from the culture dish, and a sterile glass or stainless-steel cylinder (6 mm in diameter, 12 mm high, with 1 mm wall), whose bottom edge has been coated with silicone stopcock grease to provide a water-tight seal, is placed over the colony to be isolated. A few drops of weak trypsin solution are delivered into the open end of the cylinder, and the culture is incubated at 37° C for 5 min. The supernatant fluid is aspirated slowly from the cylinder and replaced by nutrient medium. With mild agitation, the cells are then detached from the glass, and the resulting cell suspension is drawn off and transferred to a new vessel. (Certain cell types may often be released from the glass within the confines of the cylinder by vigorous pipetting, without the use of trypsin.) When the new culture has developed sufficiently, it should be passed through at least two or more cloning cycles as a means of insuring genetic purity of the cell line.

Estimation of Growth Rates in Clones

Puck and his associates[418] found it possible to determine the rate of division of clonal populations. Single cells were deposited in Petri dishes in nutrient medium and incubated in a CO_2 cabinet (*see* p. 184). At various time intervals, a microscopic count was made of the cell number in one or a few clones or in an average of 10 to 20 clones chosen at random on the plate. The growth curves obtained were highly reproducible and exhibited an initial lag period followed by linearly logarithmic reproduction, as shown in Fig. 61. When the cell

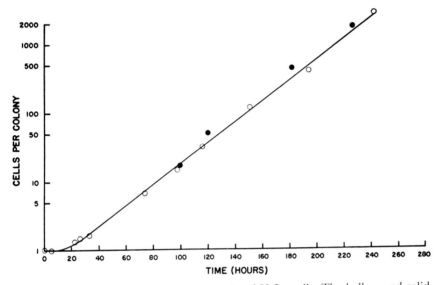

FIG. 61. Typical growth curve of S3 strain of HeLa cells. The hollow and solid circles, respectively, represent two different experiments separated by an interval of three weeks. The extrapolated lag period is 18 hr and the generation time (time taken for the population to double) is 20 hr. Each point in the experiment represented by hollow circles is the mean of at least 6 and at most 43 colonies. The standard deviation of the cell counts averaged 22 per cent and never exceeded 33 per cent. (T. T. Puck et al.[418])

number exceeded 3000, the slope of the curve tended to flatten, perhaps because of crowding of the innermost cells. When the progeny of a single cell grows up to a population of 10^7, approximately 23 generations have elapsed.[415]

Use of Plating Procedures in Biological Assays

The plating procedures just described can be used to advantage in assessing cellular responses to physical or chemical shock or to nutritional deficiencies. To cite examples from one area of investigation, Puck and his associates[412, 417, 419] have utilized cell-plating procedures in studying the effect of increasing doses of x-rays on the ability of mammalian cells to multiply and form colonies. By making duplicate or triplicate platings at various x-ray doses, x-ray survival curves were determined for the S3 HeLa strain (Fig. 62) and for various other

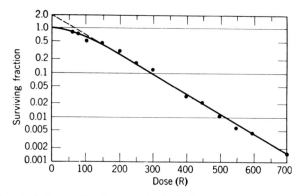

FIG. 62. Survival of reproductive capacity in HeLa cells as a function of x-ray dose. The points fit the equation $S = 1 - (1 - e^{-D/96})^2$ within the limits of uncertainty of the experimental procedure. (T. T. Puck and P. I. Marcus.[417])

aneuploid, hyperdiploid human cells, as well as for normal diploid human cells. Four radiosensitive processes were noted[417] for HeLa cells: (1) Loss of the ability of single cells to form macroscopic colonies. At doses higher than 75 r, the surviving population was reduced by a factor of 37 per cent for each additional 96 r. Cells injured fatally (by doses up to 600 r) retained their ability to multiply for one to five generations. (2) Slowing of growth among the survivors, even with doses of 100–200 r. Unfortunately, an incubation period adequate to produce well-developed colonies from all cells of a control plate was insufficient to permit identification of some slow growing survivors. (3) With doses greater than 600 r, damage to the reproductive apparatus appeared. Such cells rarely divided even once but continued to metabolize and formed giant cells. (4) With greater doses, cells tended to disappear, but giants were still formed after exposures of 10,000–20,000 r.

By means of these plating procedures, Puck and his associates[411] were able to establish mutant clones that either arose spontaneously or were induced by x-irradiation. Among these were clones with

(a) divergent nutritive requirements for colony formation, (b) altered colony morphology, (c) resistance to destruction by specific viruses (e.g., Newcastle-disease virus), and (d) difference in karyotype.

A considerable variety of evidence suggested that reproductive death was due to damage to the genetic apparatus and primarily to the chromosomes. Thus, a dose of 20–40 r was sufficient to introduce an average of one chromosome break per cell in cultures of normal diploid cells.[412] But certain differences were found between the survival curves for normal diploid cells and for hyperdiploid, aneuploid cells. The mean lethal dose for the former cells was 50 r whereas that for the aneuploid cells (e.g., HeLa) was two or three times larger.[417,419] Also, diploid cells showed one-hit inactivation curves whereas aneuploid cells showed two-hit curves. These findings led the authors to suggest[412] that strictly diploid cells are inactivated by a one-hit process because of damage to genetic loci whose sister genes are recessive lethals. In polyploid cells, the main mechanism of reproductive death "would appear to be the formation of chromosomal complexes resulting from interaction of broken ends of different chromosomes, which should largely (though not exactly) follow a two-hit process."

Puck and his group[419] found that cells whose ability to divide had been impaired by irradiation retained their ability to metabolize and to carry out complex biosyntheses of macromolecular structures, e.g., virus. In fact, Whitmore and his associates[540] have shown that even at doses of 5000 r, where the fraction of surviving cells is very close to zero, the synthesis of macromolecules such as RNA, DNA, and protein continues almost unimpaired over extended periods.

XIV

Cultures Nourished by Perfusion

THE first attempt to furnish animal cells *in vitro* with a continuous supply of fresh nutrient medium was made by Burrows[41] in 1912. By means of a cotton wick, the fluid medium was carried from a reservoir at one end of the system, through a culture chamber, and then discharged into a receiving reservoir placed at a lower level. The tissues to be cultivated were fixed with plasma to an open network of cotton fibers prepared by teasing apart a portion of the wick. Since this early work of Burrows, many attempts have been made to increase the volume of medium in relation to the mass of tissue without preventing cell respiration. The first practical step in this direction was taken by Carrel[45] in 1923, when he introduced the flask techniques. Eventually, some of the flasks were constructed with lateral, winglike extensions[49] for the accommodation of still larger amounts of culture fluid. When these flasks were rocked on platforms kept in constant motion, the fluid was caused to flow back and forth over the coagulum containing the tissues. Carrel[49] also developed a pump flask consisting of a single glass unit that was easy to clean and sterilize. But because the circulation of fluid was governed by two glass check valves that often became seized, the device was not entirely satisfactory. Several years later, Lindbergh[286] devised a more dependable flask for the cultivation of a large quantity of tissue in a thin layer of well-oxygenated medium that circulated continuously. Unfortunately,

however, neither the Carrel pump flask nor the Lindbergh flask provided for microscopic examination of tissues during cultivation.

In 1928 deHaan[202] described an apparatus for the circulation of
fluid medium through a culture chamber that could be placed under
the microscope, but the apparatus was complicated and consisted of
many parts. In 1932 Lindbergh devised a one-piece, all-glass perfusion

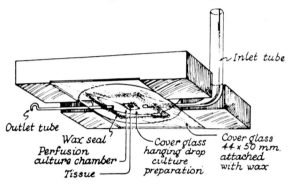

FIG. 63. Perfusion chamber (Pomerat). Stereogram showing metal supporting
frame and position of culture in relation to inlet and outlet tubes. (C. M. Pomerat.[399])

unit for microscopic work. This unit, which was illustrated in the first
edition of this book, consisted of a culture chamber with upright inlet
and outlet tubes that were connected also by means of a gas lift. The
tubes served both as reservoirs and as conducting channels for the
circulating fluid; the gas lift was actuated by a continuous flow of
control gas that served also to regulate the pH of the cultures. Unfortunately, however, the flasks were expensive to produce, rather difficult to operate, and provided for recirculation of a fixed volume of
medium rather than continuous perfusion with fresh medium.

Pomerat[399] devised a relatively simple perfusion chamber (Fig. 63)
consisting of glass coverslips and glass perfusion tubes that are sealed to
a stainless-steel frame with a mixture of equal parts of beeswax and
paraffin (melting point, 50° C). The cultures are started on coverslips
inserted in roller tubes (see p. 179) or as Maximow double-coverslip
preparations (see p. 145), and are transferred later to the perfusion
chamber for careful microscopic observations or cinematographic
recordings of the effects of particular substances added to the medium.
The chamber is filled with medium, and air bubbles are dislodged by
holding the outlet end of the metal frame in an elevated position while

rocking the chamber so as to obtain an even spreading of the fluid. A C- or S-shaped bend at the free end of the outlet tube prevents the chamber from emptying.

Rose,[448] Richter and Woodward,[433] Paul,[388] Sharp,[480] and Sykes and Moore[504] have all developed perfusion chambers in which the culture space is formed by sandwiching glass coverslips and one or more rubber or silicone gaskets between metal plates. In the device of Rose, and in some of the others, the exchange of fluids is accomplished by means of syringe needles that pierce the gasket. In Paul's chamber, a plastic insert is provided with channels that serve as ducts to and from the chamber when all the parts, including two rubber gaskets, are clamped together. The chamber is filled with medium by placing the fluid in one of two small vertical reservoirs and tilting the device so that air is removed from the system before the fluid flows through to the second reservoir. To change the medium, fluid is added to one reservoir and withdrawn from the other.

In the Rose chamber (Fig. 64) there are two stainless-steel retaining plates ($2 \times 3 \times \frac{1}{8}$ in.), a pure gum-latex (floating-stock) gasket, and two glass coverslips (50×43 mm). Each steel plate has a center hole that is 25 mm in diameter and beveled at a 45° angle. To provide for the excursion of high-power lenses, the hole on the objective side of the chamber has a $\frac{1}{16}$-in. countersink extending $\frac{1}{8}$ in. from the perimeter. Each plate has corner holes for the accommodation of four standard, flat-headed Allen bolts (0.19-in. diameter, 32 threads per in., $\frac{3}{8}$ in. over-all length) that hold the components together. On one side of the chamber, the holes are countersunk to receive the flat heads of the bolts. As the thickness of the assembled chamber is only slightly greater than $\frac{3}{8}$ in., these bolts allow for flush surfaces.

The parts are assembled after sterilization, but final tightening of the bolts is done only after a No. 25 $\frac{1}{2}$-in. syringe needle (plugged with cotton) has been inserted into the chamber through the edge of the rubber gasket to serve as an air vent. With this needle in place, cells and medium may now be introduced by means of a 2-cc syringe fitted with a No. 20 $\frac{1}{2}$-in. needle. After the chamber is almost completely filled (approximately 1.8 ml), the needles are removed. If it is desired to cultivate tissue fragments that are too large to pass through a No. 20 needle or if a plasma substrate is required, the explants must be placed in the chamber while it is being assembled. The medium is changed with the aid of two needles twice a week, or more often if it becomes too acid. If it is desired to fix and stain the cultures eventually, a syrinGe may be used to wash and fix the culture before the bolts and retaining plates have been removed, and one needle is left inserted in the chamber. If the coverslips and rubber gasket are adherent, these parts may be immersed in the fixative or in water (if compatible) for several minutes before applying gentle fluid pressure from within by

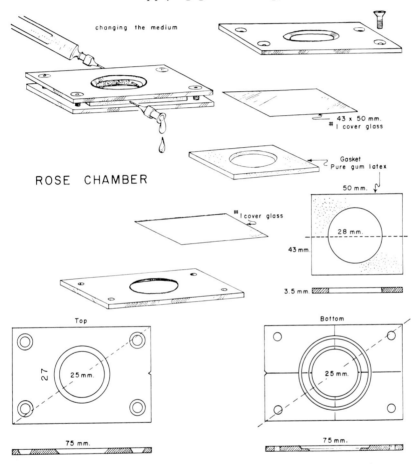

changing the medium

43 x 50 mm.
I cover glass

Gasket
Pure gum latex

ROSE CHAMBER

50 mm.

I cover glass

28 mm.

43 mm.

3.5 mm.

Top

27

25 mm.

75 mm.

Bottom

25 mm.

75 mm.

FIG. 64. Rose perfusion chamber for cultivation of cells and tissues on glass cover-slips. For description, see text. (G. G. Rose.[448])

means of a syringe. If one coverslip becomes separated, even partially, it is usually possible to lift it away from the gasket and to lift the gasket, in turn, away from the other coverslip.

More recently, Rose and his associates[449,450] have improved this culture system by adding two ¼ × 4 in. strips of thin cellophane, which serve to hold the explants in place on the coverslip and afford protection against violent fluid currents when the nutrients are replaced. After the tissue fragments have been assembled on the first coverslip, the two strips of cellophane are laid across them. The explants have just enough fluid over them to prevent air from being trapped between the glass and the cellophane. After the rubber gasket has been set in place, the chamber closed, and the retaining screws tightened, the ends of the cellophane strips are pulled tight to smooth out any wrinkles that may have formed. By this means, the explants are securely lodged against the surface of the coverslip. Two strips of cellophane are used, instead of one, to reduce the number of air bubbles that may be trapped beneath them. Rose and his associates also describe a larger culture chamber that is 4 × 4 in. in size and accommodates coverslips that are 3 × 3 in. The cellophane strips are cut from Visking dialysis tubing (1⅛-in. diameter). After the strips have been cut to size they are immersed in 95 per cent alcohol for a few minutes, then rinsed with and stored in synthetic medium.

Christiansen and associates[69] devised a chamber from acrylic-plastic sheet (polished Plexiglas) that is completed by sealing coverslips in place with paraffin and Vaseline. Fluid circulation is accomplished by a system of grooves terminating in plastic nipples and Tygon tubing. A loaded syringe is connected with the inlet tube; the outlet is connected with an empty syringe so that pressure or vacuum is not created when fluid is introduced or removed. To oxygenate the culture, the fluid is replaced periodically by air; and the chamber is housed in a warming stage.

Buchsbaum and Kuntz[39] have devised a much more elaborate perfusion system that permits of an automatic, continuous flow of medium at known rates and under known gas tensions. In this system, the medium may be changed at any time without interrupting the continuous observation of cells under study, and samples of the medium can be taken before it enters the culture chamber and after it leaves. All of the various components of the perfusion line are provided with interchangeable, ground-glass ball-and-socket joints, and one medium can be substituted for another simply by manipulating stopcocks.

Because some forms of rubber and other elastomers are violently toxic for cells,[382] *they should be tested in culture before use.* If a sample of the material is reduced to small fragments and autoclaved in a culture container, cells and medium may later be added and incubated for several days as a means of detecting any toxicity.

XV

Cultivation of Organ Rudiments and Aggregates of Dissociated Cells

TISSUES cultivated *in vitro* show two types of growth, unorganized and organized. Unorganized growth resembles wound healing. When the medium is rich in growth-stimulating substances, cells from the explant migrate into the medium with great rapidity and multiply to form broad sheets of undifferentiated cells. Organized growth, on the other hand, corresponds more nearly to normal growth in the body. When it occurs, the explant enlarges as a whole, the outward migration of cells from the explant is reduced to a minimum, the normal histological structure is preserved, and, if the explant is in an early stage of development, it usually continues to develop histologically and sometimes anatomically as well (Fell;[138] Borghese[32]).

Organized growth was first described in 1914 by Thomson,[517] who found that explants of isolated parts of the chick embryo, such as feathers and toes, increased in size without diffuse spreading of the tissues. But the modern methods of organ culture were devised by Strangeways and Fell[492,493] as a means of studying the further development of undifferentiated limb buds (Fig. 65) and eye rudiments *in vitro*. Later, the method was perfected and extended by Fell and her associates[139,141] and is currently being used to advantage in many laboratories. Under appropriate conditions, it is now possible to cultivate many other complex structures and organ rudiments, e.g., the mesonephros, metanephros, and gonads; the knee joint, sternum,

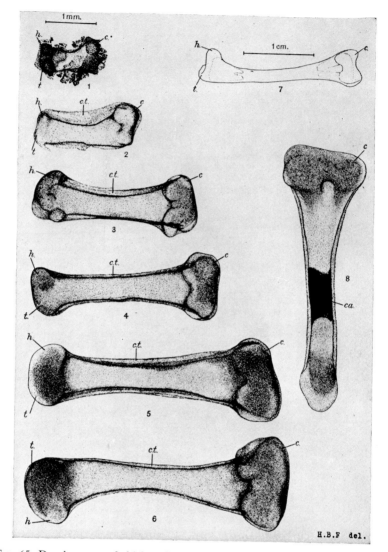

FIG. 65. Development of chick-embryo femora cultivated on the surface of a clot consisting of homologous plasma and embryo extract: (1) normal 5½-day femur as dissected for explantation; (2) after 3 days' cultivation; (3) after 9 days; (4) after 15 days; (5) after 21 days; (6) after 27 days; (7) normal femur from 21-day embryo; (8) 5½-day femur after 27 days stained by von Kóssa's silver-nitrate method. (H. B. Fell and R. Robison.[146])

and parietal bone; ear rudiments, isolated tooth germs, hair follicles, and skin; lungs, liver, intestine, and spleen; many glandular structures, including the pancreas; and a vast array of infant and adult tissues and organs. At first, organ culture was used almost entirely for morphogenetic studies. More recently, the method has been applied to a much wider variety of biological and medical problems, even including the cultivation of glandular tissues for use in postoperative therapy.[173] Organ culture offers a useful means of studying the direct effect on tissues and organs of many influences, both physical and chemical, and of analyzing many complex phenomena and situations that cannot easily be studied in the intact organism, where primary and secondary effects are often difficult to distinguish. Recently, for example, the method has been used to advantage to study such complex problems as the effect of vitamin A,[145] thyroxin,[144] and insulin[67] on developing bones, of steroid hormones and vitamin A on vaginal and uterine epithelium,[21,248,249] of ACTH and the anterior pituitary on the adrenal cortex,[473] and of carcinogens on the prostate gland.[266] Also, Sidman[481] has obtained longer survival of brown adipose tissue in chemically defined media when insulin was present, and Elias[127] maintained secretory activity in adult mammary-gland tissue cultivated in medium 199 but only after various hormones had been added (Fig. 66). Prop[410] studied the effect of hormones on whole mammary glands of infant mice.

Organ cultures and the sponge-matrix cultures of Leighton (see p. 170) are both tremendously useful as a means of studying the invasion of normal tissues by malignant cells. Wolff and Schneider[551] have found that chick-embryo organs in vitro can be invaded by cells of Fischer's mouse chondrosarcoma (S180). Of all the structures that were tested, including mesonephros, metanephros, gonads, skin, intestinal walls, liver, lungs, and long-bone perichondrium, the mesonephros (Fig. 67) was most quickly and most frequently invaded by the malignant cells. Although the normal cells were gradually replaced, mostly by inward invasion along the connective-tissue pathways, it was never clear just how they finally disappeared. Under the same culture conditions, two established lines of malignant cells, HeLa and KB, were less invasive.

In another field, Wolff and his associates[485,549,550] have found that when male and female gonads of avian embryos were explanted at the beginning of sexual differentiation, they developed normally. When

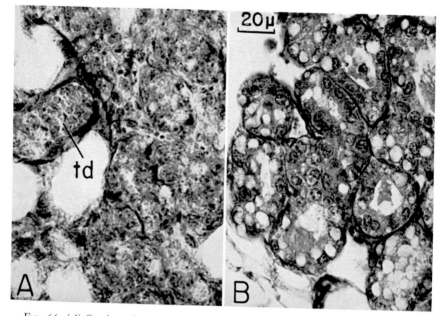

FIG. 66. (A) Section of explant from prelactating mammary gland of C3H mouse after five days in medium 199. Note degenerate alveoli and terminal duct (td). (B) Explant from same gland in medium 199 supplemented with estrone, progesterone, cortisol, growth hormone, and mammotropic hormone in "high" concentration. Note active secretory appearance. (J. J. Elias.[127])

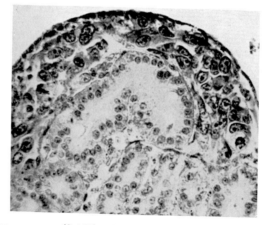

FIG. 67. Mouse sarcoma (S-180) cells cultivated together with fragment of mesonephros from seven-day chick embryo, after three days. Note invasion of tumor cells between urinary tubules and outer membrane of fragment. (E. Wolff and N. Schneider.[551]) × 450.

they were explanted before the beginning of sexual differentiation, they developed almost normally but remained sterile. When they were allowed to grow together in parabiosis, the female gonad caused feminization of the male gonad. When parabiotic unions of various types of whole embryos were made, with and without the extra-embryonic genital crescents, it became clear, as had long been suspected from histological studies of avian embryos, that the primary gonocytes from the anterior part of the extraembryonic area migrate through the extraembryonic circulation to the primordium of the gonad to complete their functional development. It is interesting to note, however, that Holyoke and Beber,[238] working with rabbit and rat embryos, have found that, in these species, the differentiation of the testis is not affected by the presence of the ovary. On the contrary, ovaries that were explanted together with testes were always retarded in development in comparison with those cultivated in the absence of the male gonads. Although their medium consisted partly of plasma from castrated rabbits, it did include chick embryo extract prepared from the anterior halves of 11-day-old chick embryos. Because of the very complexity of endocrine problems and in view of the earlier findings of Wolff, it is perhaps unfortunate that any avian material was used.

A most useful application of organ culture in the endocrine field involves the preparation of homologous grafts for transplantation. In 1934 Stone, Owings, and Gey[491] applied the method with some measure of success to the treatment of human thyroid and parathyroid deficiencies. The tissues were cultivated in the recipient's plasma and serum for about two weeks prior to implantation in the axilla. More recently, Gaillard and his associates[171,172,253] cultivated fragments of human parathyroid from newborn infants for two to three weeks and grafted the explants into patients suffering from postoperative tetany. During the culture period, the main ingredients of the medium, consisting of plasma, placental-cord serum, and fetal-brain extract, were gradually replaced by plasma and serum from the future host. Later, it was reported[173] that seven patients had responded favorably to culture grafts that had been implanted 3 to 11 years earlier. Of eight recipients between 16 and 26 years of age, four responded favorably; of ten between 26 and 36 years of age, only three responded; and there was no improvement in nine recipients between 36 and 56 years of age. Although the tissues retained their organotypic properties

for two to three weeks in cultures, the authors could not be certain
that the period of cultivation before grafting was absolutely necessary.
It did, however, provide a means of selecting healthy, sterile tissues.
It has long been the hope of clinicians that this method of treating certain endocrine deficiencies might one day become practical enough to
be of general use.

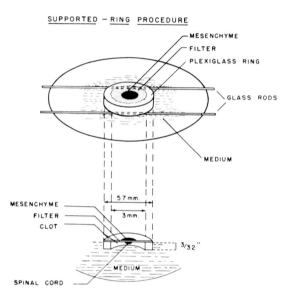

FIG. 68. Diagram of Grobstein's "supported-ring" method of testing transfilter
induction in cultures of embryonic tissues. A cellulose-ester membrane filter (cemented
to a Plexiglas ring) separates the interacting tissues (embryonic spinal cord and metanephrogenic mesenchyme of mouse). (C. Grobstein.[196])

Grobstein[196] has made interesting tissue-culture experiments on
embryonic induction and has demonstrated the interdependence of
tissues during the development of particular parts. He found, for
example, that although kidney-forming mesenchyme from 11-day-old
mouse embryos does not form epithelial tubules when isolated *in vitro*,
it does produce tubules when cultivated in close association with
ureteric-bud epithelium, salivary-rudiment epithelium, or embryonic,
dorsal spinal cord. In an effort to discover the nature of the mechanism
involved, Grobstein prepared plasma clots on opposite surfaces of
extra-thin, membrane filter discs (Millipore Filter Corp., Watertown,
Mass.), and each clot contained one of the interacting tissues (Fig. 68).

The filter discs were rim mounted on Plexiglas rings and supported on two glass rods over a well in a flat culture dish. The filter-ring assembly, with its open end down, was in contact with a nutrient fluid, consisting of horse serum, balanced salt solution, and extract from nine-day-old chick embryos (2:2:1), that was changed daily. The outer culture vessel was a round, flat dish, 4.5 cm in diameter and 1 cm

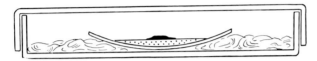

Fig. 69. Cross-sectional diagram of a watchglass culture. For description, see text. (H. B. Fell.[13])

high, with a central depression for the fluid medium that was 2 cm in diameter and of about 0.5 ml capacity. The dishes were loosely covered and incubated in a humidified atmosphere containing 5 per cent CO_2 (*see* p. 184). The usual antibiotics were used.

It was found[197] that weak inductions were produced through filters 20 to 60 μ in thickness but were almost eliminated when filters 80 μ in thickness were used. (The pore size was estimated to vary from 0.1–0.8 μ, according to type.) It was also found that the active material does not cross an interposed cellophane membrane of 20 μ thickness but does move through a fluid-filled hole in the cellophane, producing inductive effects immediately over and surrounding the hole. When electron-microscope observations[198] were made on sections of extra-thin filters that had been interposed between tissues during inductive interaction, they showed virtually no cytoplasmic penetration into the least porous type of filter that was effective. Although these results did not rule out simple diffusion on the one hand or direct cytoplasmic exchange on the other, it was felt that macromolecular material might be involved, either as a direct mediator or as a carrier.

Though some organ fragments survive for limited periods when submerged in thin layers of fluid (Figs. 51 and 52), most organs thrive best at or near the air-medium interface. This is achieved in Fell's watchglass method by growing the organ on the surface of a plasma clot (Fig. 69). But some tissues digest the clot rapidly, or invade it, or are damaged in transfer from one clot to another. Martinovitch[309] gives organs additional support and interferes with cell migration by laying them across thin glass rods resting on the clot; the explants are moved along the rods at frequent intervals. Still other investigators have given up the use of plasma entirely and support the explants on inert structures kept moistened with a fluid medium. Both methods will be discussed in the following sections.

Cultivation of Organ Rudiments on
a Plasma Coagulum

For the cultivation of organ rudiments in plasma, by Fell's watch-glass method, the watchglass is enclosed in a Petri dish carpeted with cotton wool soaked with distilled water; a hole is cut in the cotton to allow transillumination (Fig. 69). The plasma is first deposited in all the watchglasses that are to be used in an experiment. The embryo extract is then added to not more than two vessels at a time, and the medium is thoroughly mixed and spread with a glass rod and allowed to clot. The culture vessels are now ready for use. Fell[140,143] recommends that the plasma should not be used after more than a week's storage at 4° C and that only freshly prepared embryo extract be used. The explants are placed in a drop of embryo extract, sucked into a pipette, and deposited on the surface of the clot; all surplus fluid is removed from the tissue with a fine pipette. The watchglass cultures are incubated on a strip of board, which prevents heavy condensation of water on the inner surface of the Petri-dish lid. Fell uses Petri dishes that are 8 cm in diameter and 1 cm deep with watchglasses 4 cm in diameter. Observations and growth measurements are made under low-power magnification after the cover of the Petri dish is replaced temporarily by a thin glass plate free from optical defects. To avoid condensation of moisture, the glass plate may be warmed by flaming. Gaillard uses embryological watchglasses (3.5 cm square, 1.5 cm deep) covered with glass squares that are sealed in place with paraffin.

When limb bones from five- to six-day-old chick embryos are cultivated in a plasma coagulum, the clot may consist of 3 parts fowl plasma and 1 part embryo extract, with the glucose level of the balanced salt solution increased to 0.25 per cent. The higher glucose level has a beneficial effect on the explants and reduces internal necrosis.[143] This medium causes such rapid growth of the explants that it is necessary to transplant them to freshly prepared watchglasses four times a week; otherwise, they will exhaust the medium in their immediate vicinity and degenerate, sometimes quite suddenly. Because it is important, for the same reason, to have a sufficient depth of medium beneath the rudiments, they are explanted on 9 or 12 drops of medium, transferred to 15 drops at the first subculture, and finally to 20 drops, with the original plasma-extract ratio being maintained throughout.[143] Smaller and less active rudiments from other sources do well in 9 to 12 drops of medium and may often be left undisturbed for several days. The consistency of the medium is likewise important. Although many avian organs do well on a firm clot, certain mammalian structures flourish best on a soft coagulum.[141] With fowl plasma, the consistency of the clot depends mainly upon the extent to which the plasma is diluted. With mammalian plasma, it is often difficult to achieve a firm clot by any means.

Although chick embryo extract is easy to prepare, it is by no means indispensable for organ culture in natural media, either as a plasma coagulant or as a source of additional nutrients. Thrombin (*see* p. 170) can be used to coagulate the plasma, and nutritional supplements can be supplied by other means. Thus, Gaillard[173] uses fetal-brain extract for the cultivation of human parathyroids, and Moscona and Moscona[348] used adult heart extract in the cultivation of avian anterior pituitary. Also, Wolff and Haffen[550] substituted agar for embryo extract in order to prevent excessive outgrowth from embryonic gonads.

Because of the size of the usual type of container, relatively large explants can be grown. As Fell[138] points out, however, the maximum size to allow further growth and normal development *in vitro* depends largely upon the nature of the tissue. It is possible to cultivate a fragment of cartilage 3 to 4 mm in diameter provided it is not too thick, whereas an epithelial explant more than 2 mm in diameter soon becomes necrotic in the interior. Fell has also shown that when a relatively large rudiment is to be cultivated, the limiting factor of size can often be overcome by using embryos of a smaller species.

For parathyroid glands from newborn infants (*see* p. 231), Gaillard[172] uses embryological watchglasses in which four to eight fragments (0.25–0.5 mm³) are placed on top of a weak coagulum consisting of 1 part human blood plasma (heparinized), 2 parts placental-cord serum, 2 parts human fetal-brain extract, and 15 parts balanced salt solution (Gey's). The glandular fragments, which may include other structures from the thyroid region, are all cultivated until it can be determined from histological control sections which ones are truly parathyroid. Human materials are also used in Gaillard's laboratory in the cultivation of organs from other species. Thus, Schaberg and deGroot[473] cultivate adrenal and pituitary glands from newborn rats in human plasma (1 part) and human fetal-brain extract diluted 1:10 with balanced salt solution (4 parts).

Although it is often stated that mitosis and cellular differentiation are mutually antagonistic, Fell[142] suggests that in organ culture this is not a general rule. In fact, it is usually her experience that the more mitoses the better the culture and the better the differentiation. Fell points out, however, that very active mitosis should not be encouraged in organ culture, for two reasons: First, conditions that favor active mitosis also favor cell migration; and cell migration must always be suppressed in organ culture. Secondly, because organ cultures have no circulation, they must feed, respire, and excrete by diffusion; for this reason, they must not be allowed to become too large. If there is too much growth, the interior will become necrotic, and this is likely to lead to poisoning of the superficial cells and death of the explant. The ideal situation is one in which the explant reaches an optimal size with just enough mitosis to compensate for cell death.

Organ culture experiments can be performed in any clean, draft-free room, for they do not usually involve a large series of cultures made simultaneously or cultures kept for long periods. It is only necessary to attach a small glass canopy to the microscope stage to protect the material from falling dust particles. Fell makes dissections with a fine cataract knife and an ordinary fine sewing needle broken off short and mounted in a thin glass rod. The knife as it comes from the makers is useless for most experiments, and the point has to be specially ground to extreme sharpness and flexibility by the worker himself. The needle is also sharpened before use. When the instruments have been properly prepared, very fine dissections of early rudiments can be made, and explants not more than 200 μ in diameter can be excised from certain regions with almost perfect precision. The dissections are made in a drop of balanced saline in a depression slide under an ordinary wide-field, stereoscopic microscope. A magnification of 15 diameters for large structures and 24 diameters for smaller ones is usually employed.

Cultivation of Organ Rudiments in Chemically Defined Media

In order to study the effect of particular substances, e.g., vitamins, hormones, and amino acids, on developing structures, it is always helpful to cultivate them on chemically defined media without plasma. Under these conditions, the organ rudiments must be supported

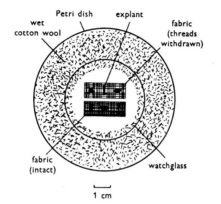

FIG. 70. Use of cellulose-acetate fabric (silicone treated) as a supporting structure for organ explants. Sometimes, threads are withdrawn to provide large gaps in the mesh. As soon as the silicone solvent has evaporated, the fabric is washed, dried, and sterilized in dry heat. (B. M. Shaffer.[479])

in some way so that they are covered by only a thin film of fluid. Trowell[519] uses a stainless-steel grid covered with a piece of lens paper that extends into the fluid on two sides. Chen[66] found a grade of lens paper that would float indefinitely on a liquid medium and serve as support for small explants. The explants become attached to the lens paper and are left undisturbed during washing and transfer to fresh medium. But because the cellulose fibers often have to be dissected away from the tissues for histological processing, Shaffer[479] supports the explants on an open-weave rayon (cellulose acetate) fabric that is coated with silicone to make it float (Fig. 70). Before the tissues are sectioned, the rayon is removed by dissolving it in acetone. Likewise, when lens paper becomes too troublesome, Trowell[519] uses a sheet of 2 per cent agar, 1 mm thick, that is made by pouring a predetermined volume of molten agar in 0.7 per cent NaCl into a stainless-steel tray of known area. When set, squares of agar are cut out with a knife. For radiation experiments, thicker (3-mm) sheets are used. For the cultivation of fragments of mature organs in chemically defined media, Trowell[519] has designed a chamber (Fig. 71) that accommodates about 20 tissue fragments in a single dish of medium. The

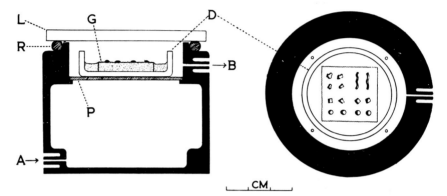

FIG. 71. Scale diagram of Trowell's Type II culture chamber: on the left, in vertical section; on the right, as seen from above and in horizontal section through gas outlet B. The solid black is aluminum. L, plate-glass lid; R, silicone sealing ring; D, culture dish; G, perforated metal grid. A, B, rubber-tube connections for gas inlet and outlet, respectively. Fourteen explants are shown in position. (O. A. Trowell.[519])

chamber is constructed mostly of aluminum and is divided by a removable Perspex diaphragm into an upper culture compartment and a lower compartment that serves as a gas reservoir. The two parts have a total gas space of about 170 ml. The chamber is not gassed continuously but is regassed for 5–10 min every third day or as often as it is opened. During incubation, several chambers are attached to a common gas line.

Recently, Biggers and his associates[23] demonstrated some of the advantages of making organ culture experiments in chemically defined media. The test objects consisted of the femora and tibiae of 6½- to 7-day-old chick embryos. At this stage, the bones are cartilaginous rudiments with only a slight degree of periosteal ossification as a collar around the diaphysis. Chen's lens-paper method[66] was used to support the bone rudiments on three types of media, as follows: solution 770, which was solution 703[232] supplemented with 0.1 per cent chondroitin sulfate; solution 858;[233] and solution 929, which was solution 858 modified by doubling the concentration of amino acids. Three responses were measured, namely, length (from camera lucida drawings), wet weight, and total nitrogen. The femur and tibia from one limb were usually kept together in the same culture dish as an experimental unit.

When the glucose was increased two and one-quarter times, growth of the bones was greatly improved. It was also found that if the medium was replaced daily, a lower concentration of glucose was required to produce a given amount of growth than if the medium was changed less often. Mannose was found to be an adequate substitute for glucose, but galactose and fructose were ineffective. The same degree of elongation was observed over a four-day period of cultivation on media 858 and 929, but growth was less in medium 770.

The growth that occurred in four days in medium 929 was compared with that in a natural medium containing serum for the same period; in both media the glucose concentration was raised to 2.25 mg per ml. When increase in length was taken as the criterion, there was no difference in growth between the chemically defined and the natural media; but when wet weight was considered, the bones cultivated in serum were consistently heavier than those in medium 929. The content of total nitrogen was closely correlated with the wet weight, and it was also noticed that the rudiments grown in serum maintained a more normal shape than those in medium 929. These results showed that more than one criterion should be used when evaluating growth in different media.

A series of experiments were made to investigate the disappearance of amino acids from the medium (Fig. 72). The total amino-acid content of the medium was estimated by means of the ninhydrin color reaction. Up to 50 per cent of the total amino acids may disappear from the medium in four days, the amount depending on the size of the bones and the original concentration of amino acids. Incorporation of glycine into the protein of the explants was shown by the uptake of radioactivity by bone rudiments cultivated in medium 929 supplemented with glycine that had been uniformly labeled with the isotope C^{14}. After 24 or 96 hours' growth, the bones were extracted with ether and then with perchloric acid; the remaining protein residue was radioactive. When it was hydrolyzed with hydrochloric acid and the amino acids were separated by two-dimensional paper chromatography, autoradiographs of the chromatograms showed that radioactivity was confined almost exclusively to the glycine spot. Activity was also present to a lesser extent in serine, indicating some synthesis of this amino acid from glycine.

It was also considered worth-while to perform culture experiments on bone rudiments analogous to the classical deficiency experiments of Rose on the whole animal. Twenty media were prepared, each deficient in one amino acid, and the response obtained with each of

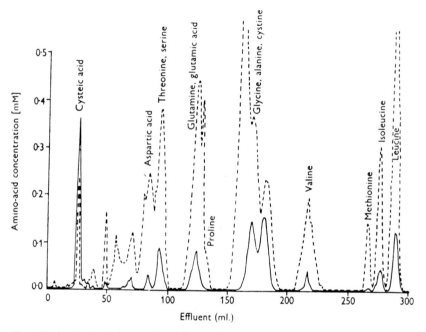

FIG. 72. Analysis of changes in amino-acid levels[332] in chemically defined medium No. 858,[333] containing double the stated level of amino acids: (1) after incubation alone for four days (broken lines) and (2) after chick embryonic femurs and tibiae (two pairs of bones per ml of medium) had been cultivated in the medium for four days. (J. D. Biggers et al.[22])

these media was compared with that of a control medium containing all the amino acids (Fig. 73). The results showed that nine of the amino acids (hydroxyproline, alanine, serine, proline, glycine, cystine, cysteine, glutamic acid, and aspartic acid) were nonessential under the conditions of the experiments, although glutamic acid and aspartic acid were on the border line (see also p. 70). The remaining eleven (tyrosine, lysine, phenylalanine, valine, isoleucine, leucine, histidine, methionine, tryptophan, arginine, and threonine) were all most essen-

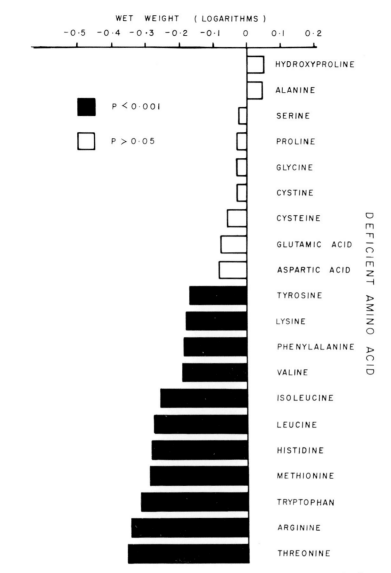

Fig. 73. Effect of individual amino-acid deficiencies on the wet weight (log treated − log control) of femora and tibiae from 6½–7-day-old chick embryos cultivated for six days in a chemically defined medium (No. 858[233]) with the glucose level raised to 2.25 mg per ml. The medium was renewed on the fourth day. (J. D. Biggers *et al.*[23])

tial. Deficiencies of some amino acids, e.g., threonine, arginine, and tryptophan, produced a marked depression of growth that appeared very early. Other deficiencies (e.g., lysine) showed up more slowly.

The fact that the omission of certain amino acids from the medium had no effect on the growth of the rudiments raised the question of the ability of the tissue to synthesize these compounds from other constituents of the medium. Since a likely source of amino acids is glucose, experiments were made in which glucose uniformly labeled with C^{14} was added to medium 858. After 24 hours' incubation, the bones were fractionated and the protein residue hydrolyzed with hydrochloric acid. The amino acids were separated by two-dimensional chromatography and the radioactive spots located by autoradiography. Areas of the paper bearing these active components were cut out and the individual amino acids eluted with water. When samples of these eluates were assayed both for radioactivity and amino-acid content, it was found that the explants had synthesized the following six amino acids in decreasing order of radioactivity: alanine, aspartic acid, glutamic acid, serine, glycine, and proline. The results showed, then, that glucose can serve as a source of all of these "nonessential" amino acids.

Cultivation of Aggregates of Dissociated Cells

Although the classical organ-culture procedures are useful in studying morphologic phenomena at the tissue level, Moscona[344,346,347] devised an ingenious means of studying these phenomena at the cellular level. After dissociating tissue and organ cells with trypsin (see p. 120), Moscona studied their ability to reconstruct a tissue fabric suitable for their continued development. When trypsin-dispersed cells from various organ rudiments of chick and mouse embryos were intermixed in the desired proportions and aliquots of the mixture were distributed into hollow-ground (Maximow) slides with 1.0 ml of fluid medium in each, the cells aggregated to form composite, chimeric tissues similar to those obtained by Wolff[348] when he cultivated heterologous rudiments in apposition (Fig. 74). The medium, warmed to room temperature, consisted of 40 per cent serum, 40 per cent embryo extract (freshly prepared from 10- to 12-day chick embryos), and 20 per cent balanced salt solution. The slides were sealed and incubated at

38° C for 24 hr, after which the medium was changed. One or two days later, the cell aggregates were transferred for further incubation to plasma clots in watchglasses contained in Petri dishes. Eventually, the cell aggregates were fixed, sectioned, and stained in a manner that made it possible to identify cells derived from different sources. Thus, when chick-mouse chimeras were stained lightly with Ehrlich's

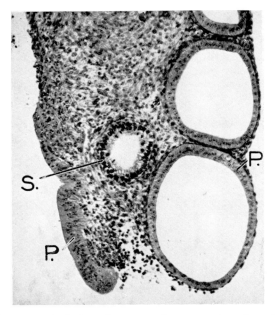

FIG. 74. Pulmonary tubule from fragment of mouse-embryo lung (S), developing in a culture that also contained bronchial epithelium (P) from fragments of chick-embryo lung. (E. Wolff.[548]) × 185.

hematoxylin and Biebrich's scarlet, the nuclei of chick cells were light purple whereas those of mouse cells were deep blue.

Moscona found that in aggregates of intermixed chick and mouse cells of the same type the cells reconstructed a tissue consisting of interspersed chick and mouse cells. In aggregates of intermixed chick and mouse cells of different types (e.g., chick nephrogenic and mouse chondrogenic cells), the cells became associated according to type and formed separate groupings (Fig. 75) that developed in accordance with the original histogenetic properties of the cells. Because it was easily possible to distinguish between the chick and mouse cells, it was certain that no transformation of one cell type to the other had occurred.

When more than one type of cell was incorporated in a cluster, they became sorted out to form tissue-specific cell groupings, regardless of their generic identities. Also, the persistence *in vitro* of cartilage chimeras beyond the embryonic age of their constituent cells suggested that the cells, although generically alien, remained histocompatible.

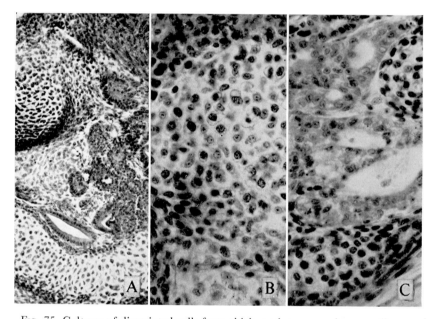

FIG. 75. Cultures of dissociated cells from chick- and mouse-embryo cartilage and chick kidney (mesonephros) mixed in various combinations: (*A*) Section through aggregate formed in seven-day culture of chick cartilage and kidney cells, showing their separate groupings. Hematoxylin-eosin. × 120. (*B*) Section through aggregate formed in three-day culture of chick- and mouse-cartilage cells, showing the chimeric structure of the cartilage. Hematoxylin and Biebrich's scarlet. × 280. (*C*) Section through aggregate formed in three-day culture of chick-kidney and mouse-cartilage cells, showing their separate groupings. Hematoxylin and Biebrich's scarlet. × 220. (A. Moscona.[345])

XVI

Cultures for Virus Studies

ALMOST since its inception, tissue culture has provided a useful means of studying viral agents. As early as 1913, Steinhardt, Israeli, and Lambert[489] demonstrated that vaccine virus retained its activity for more than a month in fragments of rabbit or guinea-pig cornea surviving in a drop of plasma. Over the next 35 years, many different viruses were propagated for longer or shorter periods in tissue culture, and in certain instances culture material was used for the production of virus vaccines. Thus, Rivers and Ward[441] produced Jennerian prophylaxis in man with a strain of vaccinia virus that was cultivated *in vitro* for several years without intercurrent animal passage. And in 1932 Haagen and Theiler[201] reported the successful propagation in cultures of chick-embryo tissue of a strain of yellow-fever virus that had been greatly modified by intracerebral passage through many generations of mice. Eventually, Lloyd, Theiler, and Ricci[289] succeeded in establishing the unmodified Asibi strain in tissue culture. Although this strain was one of the most virulent that had been isolated, both in viscerotropic and neurotropic properties, it lost much of its pathogenicity[513] in tissue culture and could be used for human vaccination against yellow fever.[514] Eventually, subcultures of this strain, designated 17D, were used as seed material for the preparation in developing chick embryos of vast quantities of living virus for use as a vaccine.[488] During this early period, the tissue-culture techniques were also used to advantage by Carrel,[46,47,48] Findlay,[149] Maitland and Maitland,[306] Hallauer,[206] and Hecke[235] in studying problems of virus specificity; by Andrewes,[4,5,6] Rivers, Haagen, and Muckenfuss,[439,440] and Sabin[460] in studying the relative importance of humoral and cellular immunity in connection with virus diseases; and by Bland and his associates[27,28] in studying the developmental morphology of virus inclusions.

In 1949, Enders, Weller, and Robbins[130] reported the propagation of the Lansing strain (Type 2) of poliovirus in cultures of nonneural tissue from human embryos. This discovery had far-reaching consequences in poliomyelitis research and led immediately to an intensification of efforts in many other aspects of virology. The discovery also came at an opportune time. With the advent of antibiotics, it had become more easily possible to maintain cultures without bacterial contaminations and to isolate viruses from clinical material in which bacteria were also present initially. Also, during this time, nutritionally adequate, chemically defined media were being developed, and these were free of contaminating viruses and antiviral-immune substances.

The discovery of the Enders group and subsequent developments had many immediate applications, including: (1) the development of tissue-culture procedures for the routine isolation and identification of viruses, some of such low pathogenicity that they could not have been propagated or even recognized by the older methods of animal inoculation; (2) the development of procedures for the propagation of viruses in established strains of susceptible cells; (3) the development of procedures for the quantitative measurement of virus-neutralizing antibodies by tissue-culture methods and the demonstration that complement-fixing antigens could be prepared from infected cultures; and (4) the demonstration that polioviruses could be propagated in tissue culture in sufficient quantity for the large-scale preparation of virus fluids that would still be effective as vaccines after inactivation with formalin.

Methods of Detecting Virus Multiplication
in Tissue Culture

The effects of virus multiplication in tissue culture may be detected in the following ways: (1) by observing degenerative changes in the cells; (2) by measuring pH changes that take place in the medium as the result of decreased metabolism; (3) by harvesting the virus fluids and inoculating serial dilutions of them into animals or developing chick embryos and calculating the percentage of survivors at each dilution; and (4) by estimating hemagglutinins or by making neutralization and complement fixation tests. Only those methods that relate directly to the cell-cultivation techniques will be described here. For descriptions of the serological procedures, the reader is referred to general textbooks on virology.

Cytopathic Effects of Virus Multiplication

In 1950, Robbins, Enders, and Weller[442] described a "cytopathogenic" effect of poliovirus on susceptible cells in tissue culture and its inhibition by a specific antiserum. This cytopathic effect is due to the multiplication of the virus, which leads eventually to the degeneration of the cells. In so-called "monolayer" cultures, the cytopathic changes can be detected microscopically, particularly if slides are placed in the culture containers when they are prepared, for eventual removal and staining. Usually, virus-infected cells become granular, round up, degenerate, and disappear. This sequence leads occasionally to the formation of holes or plaques[93,161] in what had been continuous sheets of cells (Figs. 76 and 77). It was soon found that many viruses produce cytopathic changes in tissue cultures, for example, vaccinia, varicella, psittacosis, herpes simplex, herpes zoster, equine encephalomyelitis, influenza, measles, mumps, lymphogranuloma venereum, lymphocytic choriomeningitis, Newcastle disease, fowlpox, pseudorabies, rabbit virus III, St. Louis encephalitis, simian (monkey) virus B, simian "foamy" virus, a long list of other simian viruses isolated from animals providing tissues for diagnostic purposes and for the preparation of poliovaccine, and many hitherto unknown viruses mentioned in the next section.

Different viruses affect cells in different ways.[322] In epithelial cultures, poliovirus produces a rapid rounding of cells that generally involves the entire culture within 24 or 36 hr after the first changes are noted, and relatively few cells survive. In contrast, certain "orphan" and Coxsackie viruses produce focal lesions that spread slowly over a period of nine or ten days and leave many cells morphologically unchanged. In some infections, multinucleated giant cells are formed. In other infections, distinctive inclusion bodies may appear in the cells.

Care must always be taken, of course, to ensure that cytopathic changes observed in cultures prepared from fresh tissues or from established cell lines are not due to (1) toxic substances present in the

FIG. 76. Relation between the size of poliovirus plaques and neurotropism in monkeys of Type 3 (Leon) virus. Monkey-kidney monolayers grown simultaneously in 3-oz, Brockway prescription bottles and photographed five days after inoculation with: (A) the original, highly virulent Leon virus; (B) an attenuated derivative segregated from it after many culture passages; (C) and (D) the nonparalytogenic progeny of separate virus particles that were segregated from the attenuated derivative shown in B. In these instances, the smallest plaques were produced by the most highly attenuated virus strains, but variation in size of plaques in same bottle is attributed to different day of first appearance. (A. B. Sabin.[461])

medium or in the material being tested or (2) some component of the culture system, other than the material being tested, that may carry a viral agent. If cytopathic changes are not observed, it may be (1) that the virus population is heterogeneous, with only a small portion of the population participating; (2) that the cell population is heterogeneous, with only a small portion of the cells susceptible; or (3) that the medium may have inactivated the agent believed to be present. If at first no cytopathic effect is observed, many blind passages may be required. If these fail, evidence of virus multiplication may have to depend on other virus properties (e.g., hemagglutination, complement fixation, infectivity in eggs or animals), and these latter activities must be shown to be present through many serial passages.

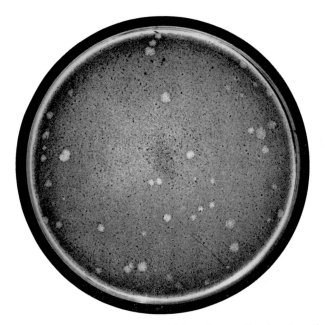

FIG. 77. Petri-dish (50-mm) culture of chick-embryo cells, showing plaques produced by vaccinia virus after five-days' incubation at 37° C; with Tris buffer in agar overlay. (J. S. Porterfield and A. C. Allison.[408])

Virus Isolation and Identification

Since the pioneer work of the Enders group,[443] tissue cultures have been used extensively in the isolation and identification of viruses. As already indicated, viruses produce characteristic cytopathic effects on susceptible cells in tissue culture. Thus, by combining tissue-culture studies with serological tests and the injection of newborn mice, it has become possible to isolate and identify an ever increasing number of viruses, many for the first time. By these means, for example, it is now possible to distinguish three major groups of *enteroviruses* derived from the intestinal tract of man: (a) *polioviruses;* (b) *Coxsackie viruses;* and (c) *enteric-cytopathogenic-human-orphan* (ECHO) viruses. The three types of polioviruses are responsible for minor subclinical illnesses, aseptic meningitis, and the various forms of nonparalytic and paralytic poliomyelitis. The Coxsackie viruses, which are also pathogenic for newborn mice, comprise 24 antigenically distinct types in two groups, A and B. Group A Coxsackie viruses are the causal agents of herpangina, aseptic meningitis, and summer febrile illnesses; the group B viruses cause aseptic meningitis, summer febrile illnesses, pleurodynia, and infantile myocarditis. The ECHO group, which includes 20 antigenically distinct types, causes aseptic meningitis, summer rash, summer febrile illnesses, and summer diarrhea in infants and children. Because some of the Coxsackie, ECHO, and polioviruses produce neuronal lesions in monkeys and because they all share such properties as size, resistance to ether, seasonal incidence, and epidemiologic pattern, they are considered to be members of a single family of viruses. According to Sabin,[461] some but not all of the Coxsackie viruses share with the ECHO group the property of being cytopathic for the usual type of tissue cultures. Also, among the ECHO group there are variants that are pathogenic for newborn mice, just as in the Coxsackie group there are variants that originally are not pathogenic for newborn mice but are cytopathic in tissue culture.

Virus Titrations

As already indicated, virus titrations may be made in animals or in tissue culture. In animals, the titrations are made by inoculating serial dilutions and computing the percentage survivors at each dilution. In tissue culture, titrations are made either by the tube method or by the plaque method. The tube method is essentially the same as the animal titration method.

TUBE METHOD

Serial half-log dilutions of virus fluids are inoculated into a series of 150 × 16 mm test tubes containing uniform layers of susceptible cells (*see* p. 179). The number of dilutions prepared from each virus sample will depend upon what is judged to be the likely concentration of virus and must cover the desired range in small increments. The dilutions are made in chemically defined medium adjusted to an optimal pH; no serum is used because of the possible presence of neutralizing antibody. At least 5 ml of each dilution is required for ten tubes. As a means of removing any serum that may have been included in the "growth" medium used in developing the cell layers, the original nutrient is removed the day before the titrations are to be made and replaced with 2 ml of chemically defined medium. On the following day, the defined medium is withdrawn and replaced with 1.5 ml of fresh defined medium together with 0.5 ml of the virus dilutions to be titrated. Ten tubes are inoculated with each virus dilution, and the cells are examined daily for cytopathic effects. For poliovirus, end points are usually computed seven days after infection, and titers are expressed in terms of the dilution of virus causing cytopathic changes in 50 per cent of the inoculated cultures (*see* next section). If the medium contains phenol red, pH changes in the alkaline direction will serve as additional evidence of cell damage. Occasionally the tubes are rotated at about 12 revs. per hr, but it is not necessary to rotate the tubes in order to achieve reliable assays. Where rotating devices are available, however, it is usually easier to place the tubes in rotation than to make certain that they are properly oriented with respect to cells and medium. Leighton tubes, with flat side windows (*see* p. 19), may be oriented with minimal effort.

Estimation of Virus Infectivity (Tube Method)[*]

The strength of virus suspensions can be judged from the extent to which they must be diluted before inoculated cell cultures fail to show signs of virus growth. In such tests, several serial dilutions of a suspension are prepared and fixed volumes of these used to inoculate different groups of cultures. From the proportion of cultures that become "positive" at each dilution, a suitable end point is estimated, generally the dilution at which 50 per cent of the cultures would be positive. This dose is called the $TCID_{50}$ ($TCID$ = tissue-culture infectious dose). The designation ED_{50} (ED = effective dose) is frequently used. The 50 per cent end point can, in most instances, be determined with greater precision than any other.

[*] This section was prepared by Mr. D. B. W. Reid, M.A., M.Sc., Professor of Biometrics, School of Hygiene, University of Toronto.

As an illustration of this type of test, some results obtained in a titration of a suspension of Mahoney (Type 1) poliovirus are given in Table IX. The ED_{50} can be seen to lie at a dilution of about 10^{-7} of the virus suspension.

TABLE IX

TITRATION OF A SUSPENSION OF MAHONEY
(TYPE 1) POLIOVIRUS

Dilution of Virus	Logarithm of Dilution	Proportion of Positive Cultures
$10^{-8.0}$	-8.0	$0/10 = 0.0$
$10^{-7.5}$	-7.5	$2/10 = 0.2$
$10^{-7.0}$	-7.0	$6/10 = 0.6$
$10^{-6.5}$	-6.5	$8/10 = 0.8$
$10^{-6.0}$	-6.0	$10/10 = 1.0$

This end point can be estimated more accurately in a number of different ways. Simple procedures used by Reed and Muench[429] and by Kärber[243] will be outlined. For these methods to be applicable, the dilutions chosen must be equally spaced on a logarithmic scale with approximately the same number of cultures at each dilution. The ED_{50} should lie somewhere in the center of a range of dilutions giving responses from 0 per cent to 100 per cent, or values close to these. Methods are available for estimating end points where these requirements are not met.[151]

TABLE X

ESTIMATION OF THE ED_{50}, REED AND MUENCH METHOD

Logarithm of Dilution of Virus	Observed Number of Cultures		Accumulated		"Percent Positive"
	Positive	Negative	Positive p	Negative n	$100 \left(\dfrac{p}{n+p} \right)$
-8.0	0	10	0	24	0
-7.5	2	8	2	14	12.5
-7.0	6	4	8*	6†	57.1
-6.5	8	2	16	2	88.9
-6.0	10	0	26	0	100

* $8 = 6 + 2 + 0$
† $6 = 4 + 2 + 0$

The *Reed and Muench method* is the one most frequently used by virologists. In this procedure a series of "percentages" based upon accumulated numbers of positive and negative cultures is prepared, and the dilution giving 50 per cent response is estimated from them. For the titration given, the tabulations in Table X can be constructed. The logarithm of the 50 per cent end point is seen to lie between -7.5 and -7.0. Simple linear interpolation places it at

$$-7.5 + 0.5 \frac{(12.5 - 50.0)}{(12.5 - 57.1)} = -7.08.$$

As a dilution of the original suspension, the ED_{50} is $10^{-7.08}$.

By the *Kärber method*, which is somewhat simpler, the actual proportion of positive cultures at each dilution is determined. The sum of these (S) is substituted into this formula:

$$\log ED_{50} = m - \Delta(S - \tfrac{1}{2}),$$

in which m is the log dilution containing the highest concentration of virus, and Δ is the difference between successive log dilutions. The $\tfrac{1}{2}$ is a constant that is used in all cases. For the data just given, S is $0.0 + 0.2 + 0.6 + 0.8 + 1.0 = 2.6$. The log ED_{50} is then estimated to be:

$$-0.6 - (+0.5)(2.6 - \tfrac{1}{2}) = -7.05.$$

In terms of a dilution of the original suspension, the ED_{50} is $10^{-7.05}$.

With the limited number of cultures used in tests of this kind, it is readily apparent that estimates of the ED_{50} will not be very reliable; that is, repeated determinations made under seemingly identical conditions will give results that vary widely. Some effort should then be made to assess the extent to which this sort of fluctuation occurs. Statistical procedures are available for determining the reliability of individual estimates.[151]

The relationship that seems to exist in some of these titrations between dilution of virus and corresponding proportion of positive cultures can be used to provide estimates of the concentration of virus. If the suspensions used are shaken before inocula are removed, the virus particles will tend to be distributed throughout their volumes. Although the average number of particles per volume of inoculum should then be about the same for all parts of a suspension, the number of particles present in individual volumes will vary in a random fashion, since the particles themselves are of negligible size.

At certain dilutions, where the average number of particles per inoculum (m) is small, some inocula may by chance contain no particles and so subsequently produce no infection. It can be shown that if the particles are actually distributed at random in the original suspension, the proportion of inocula of this kind will be e^{-m}, where $e = 2.718 \ldots$, the base of the natural logarithms.

In *certain* virus assays, the proportion of negative cultures may be related in this simple way to the average number of "infectious" particles (d) present per inoculum. The proportion of positive cultures (p) will then be equal to $1 - e^{-d}$. If so, d may be estimated from the relationship:

$$d = - \log_e (1 - p) = -2.303 \log_{10} (1 - p).$$

Values of d corresponding to certain proportions are given in Table XI. The average number of infectious particles per inoculum (d) may

TABLE XI

ESTIMATED NUMBER OF PARTICLES PER INOCULUM

Percentage Positive	0	1	2	3	4	5	6	7	8	9
0	—	.01	.02	.03	.04	.05	.06	.07	.08	.09
10	.11	.12	.13	.14	.15	.16	.17	.19	.20	.21
20	.22	.24	.25	.26	.27	.29	.30	.31	.33	.34
30	.36	.37	.39	.40	.42	.43	.45	.46	.48	.49
40	.51	.53	.54	.56	.58	.60	.62	.63	.65	.67
50	.69	.71	.73	.76	.78	.80	.82	.84	.87	.89
60	.92	.94	.97	.99	1.02	1.05	1.08	1.11	1.14	1.17
70	1.20	1.24	1.27	1.31	1.35	1.39	1.43	1.47	1.51	1.56
80	1.61	1.66	1.71	1.77	1.83	1.90	1.97	2.04	2.12	2.21
90	2.30	2.41	2.53	2.66	2.81	3.00	3.22	3.51	3.91	4.61

be less than the average number of particles per inoculum (m), since some particles may not find suitable conditions for growth.

From this relationship estimates of particle density can be obtained for each dilution of a culture assay, as shown in Table XII. It will be noticed that no estimates can be obtained when all cultures are positive or all negative. For intermediate dilutions, the estimates of d should tend to be proportional to concentration of virus if this procedure is valid, though this may be difficult to judge in assays involving a small number of cultures. Since this is approximately the case in the titration presented, the estimates may be expressed in terms of a single dilution and averaged. At a dilution of 10^{-7} the average number of infectious particles per inoculum would seem to be about 0.71. The average number of infectious particles in the original suspension is then about 0.71×10^7 particles per volume of inoculum.

TABLE XII

Estimates of Particle Density at Each Dilution
of the Titration Given in Table IX

Dilution of Virus	p: Proportion of Positive Cultures	d: Estimated Number of Particles Per Inoculum	Estimated Number of Particles Per Inoculum at 10^{-7}
$10^{-8.0}$	0.0		
$10^{-7.5}$	0.2	0.22	0.70*
$10^{-7.0}$	0.6	0.92	0.92
$10^{-6.5}$	0.8	1.61	0.51
$10^{-6.0}$	1.0		

* $0.70 = 0.22 \sqrt{10}$

An extension of this procedure provides a more satisfactory estimate of particle density commonly called the "most probable number."[150] Applied here it yields an estimate of 0.63×10^7 infectious particles per volume of inoculum. This approach also provides a basis for testing whether the observations conform to the assumptions made. An interesting illustration of the use of this quantity in tissue culture is given in a paper by Chang et al.[65]

Since 50 per cent of cultures will be positive, on the average, for 0.69 infectious particles per inoculum, the log ED_{50} may be readily used to determine an estimate of density. By the Kärber procedure the log ED_{50} is -7.05; this gives an estimate of density of 0.78×10^7 particles per volume of inoculum.

Plaque Method for Confluent Layers of Cells

A second and more recent means of making virus titrations in tissue culture takes advantage of the cytopathic effect and of techniques developed earlier for the study of bacterial viruses. Thus, Dulbecco and Vogt[95] were able to demonstrate that animal viruses plated on animal cells produce plaques similar to those formed when bacterial viruses are plated on bacterial cells; these consist of areas of lysed cells. These lysed areas are made visible in the animal-cell work by staining the living cells with vital dyes (for example, neutral red), which causes the plaques to stand out as colorless areas in a stained background (Figs. 76 and 77). When the technique was applied to a study of polioviruses, it was found[93] that each plaque contains a viral population stemming from a single virus particle. This was proved by the following observations: (1) The number of plaques produced by a virus sample was proportional to the amount of the sample deposited on the cell layer in dilution experiments, which meant that either a single virus particle or a clump of particles, inseparable by dilution, was sufficient to produce a plaque; and (2), because ultraviolet inactivation experiments[95] gave no suggestion of a lag at low doses, it was concluded that the virus particles were not aggregated in clumps. The plaque-forming ability of a clump would be destroyed only after destroying the plaque-forming ability of all the individual particles present in the clump. Also, since the plaque-forming titer of a virus preparation was of the same order of magnitude as the infectious titer determined by other methods, the plaque-forming particle could be identified with the infectious particle, i.e., with the virus particle. Dulbecco and his associates[94,301] have used the plaque method to advantage in quantitative studies of the growth of animal viruses in cell suspensions and in single cells and have obtained important information concerning the intracellular growth of viruses, their release from infected cells, their genetic properties, and their inactivation by antibody.

For polioviruses, Dulbecco and Vogt[93] prepared trypsin-dispersed suspensions of monkey-kidney cells in much the same manner as described on page 122. Appropriate aliquots of these suspensions were then used to seed the cultures, which were prepared in 60-mm or 100-mm Petri dishes. Because the Petri dishes were unsealed, they were incubated at 38° C in a humidified atmosphere containing sufficient CO_2 to maintain the pH of the medium at an optimal level (see p. 184). The cultures were incubated, with two changes of medium a week, until the bottom of the dishes were covered by a continuous layer of cells. The time required was from three to seven days, depending upon the inoculum.

Cultures showing a continuous cell layer were washed twice with phosphate buffer saline (see p. 58). After removal of the last washing fluid, 0.3 or 0.5 ml (depending upon the size of the Petri dish) of an appropriate virus dilution was pipetted onto the cell layer. As for titrations made by the tube method (*see* p. 250), the virus dilutions to be assayed by the plaque method were prepared in synthetic medium at optimal pH; and a minimum of two Petri dishes with confluent cell layers were selected for each dilution to be tested. After 1 hours' incubation at 38° C, to permit adsorption of the virus onto the cells, the infected cultures were covered with a nutrient medium containing melted agar (agar overlay). The cultures were kept at room temperature for about 10 min to allow the agar mixture to solidify and were finally placed in an incubator supplied with CO_2, air, and moisture. The number of plaques that appeared on each plate was determined after four or five days' incubation by counting the number of cleared areas in a stained background. The titers are expressed as the number of plaque-forming units per ml.

In estimating concentrations of virus present on agar plates containing a layer of susceptible cells, it may be assumed that each plaque results from an infectious virus particle. Also, the number of plaques is closely reproducible and proportional to the concentration of virus, provided the plates are not too crowded; to reduce the loss by overlapping, there should not be more than 40–50 plaques per plate. The method can be expected to give more precise estimations of virus concentration than end point titrations in roller tubes.

As usually happens, the original methods have been changed somewhat by workers in other laboratories. Whereas, for example, Dulbecco and Vogt[93] used especially prepared agar for the overlay, it has been found that Difco's Bacto-agar may be used without further purification. Also, it has become fairly general practice to use 6 ml of medium for 60-mm Petri dishes and 12 ml for 100-mm dishes. Usually, these volumes consist of equal parts of double-strength agar (to give a final concentration of 1 per cent) and double-strength nutrient medium. Although neutral red is sometimes added to the nutrient-agar mixture, certain preparations of neutral red are sufficiently toxic to reduce the virus titer. For this reason, many laboratories add 1:20,000 neutral red (in phosphate buffered saline) to the agar overlay for 1–2 hr at or near the end of the plaque-forming period.

Porterfield and Allison[408] found that the plaques formed by poxviruses in "monolayer" cultures of chick-embryo cells (Fig. 77) appeared earlier and were larger and more numerous when an overlay containing Tris buffer (0.05M; pH 7.6) replaced the conventional bicarbonate overlay. The titers obtained with plaque counts were of the same order as those obtained with chorioallantoic-membrane pock counts; for vaccinia, it was estimated that one plaque was produced for about ten virus particles. When plates were incubated at 39° C (instead of 35° C), plaque formation with ectromelia was suppressed completely but, although the size of plaques produced by other pox-viruses was reduced at 39° C, the number was not.

Plaque Method for Cells in Suspension

Cooper[75] developed a method for producing virus plaques in an agar overlay from cell suspensions in a manner similar to a procedure used for bacteriophage. This method, which has certain advantages over the "monolayer" method, was initially applied to vesicular-stomatitis virus growing on chick-embryo cells and on L-strain cells from the mouse, and to Type 1 poliovirus growing on HeLa and monkey-kidney cells. For the vesicular-stomatitis, chick-embryo cell system, the nutrient medium consisted of either Earle's balanced saline (see p. 57) containing 12.5 per cent chick-embryo extract or balanced saline containing 0.5 per cent lactalbumin hydrolysate, 0.1 per cent yeast extract, and 0.1 per cent crystalline bovine albumin. Replacement of bicarbonate by 0.3 per cent Tris buffer (see p. 61) made it unnecessary to incubate the cultures in an atmosphere containing CO_2. The plating procedure was as follows: (1) Three milliliters of double-strength nutrient medium was mixed with 3 ml of molten 1.8 per cent agar at 44° C, poured into flat-bottomed (pressed), Pyrex Petri dishes, and allowed to set as base layers. (2) To 10-ml Pyrex tubes were added 0.5-ml samples of a suspension of cells (1–1.5 $\times 10^8$ cells per ml) prepared from ten-day-old chick embryos. Samples (0.1 ml) of a virus or infected cell suspension containing 100–1000 plaque-forming particles per ml were added, followed by 2.0 ml of the molten agar medium at 44° C. No adsorption period was found necessary. The cell-agar suspension was mixed rapidly, poured at once onto the base layer, and spread by rotating before it set. The tube was allowed to drain as completely as possible, and the final drop was removed by contact with the agar surface. (3) After setting, the plates were incubated at 37° C for 40 hr in a humid atmosphere before staining for 1–2 hr with Earle's balanced saline containing 1:20,000 neutral red, after which the plaques were counted. In assays of free virus, the cell suspension gave 30–50 per cent more plaques than the "mono-layer" method in parallel assays from the same virus dilution. Also, as with bacteriophage, plaques could be obtained by adding virus to agar-cell suspensions after they had been allowed to set. For this purpose, it was preferable to use an agar concentration of 1.2 per cent for both layers, to dry the plate in an open and inverted position for 30 min at 37° C before adding virus, and to use a glass spreader rather than a wire loop. The plates could be stored at 4° C for at least two days before use. It should be mentioned that the suspension method of making plaque assays requires more cells per plate than the monolayer method; when chick cells are used, survival is poor if the initial population density in the agar medium is less than 1.5×10^7 cells per ml.[75]

Isolation of Virus from Plaques

As already mentioned, Dulbecco and Vogt[93] have shown that under their conditions a plaque is always initiated by a single plaque-forming particle. Pure virus lines can therefore be established by isolating the virus population produced in single plaques. The virus is recovered from a plaque by picking up, with a hand-drawn Pasteur pipette, a small cylinder of the agar (about 2 mm in diameter) from the center of the plaque. The agar cylinder is suspended in 1 ml of balanced salt solution containing 20 per cent embryo extract and frozen. Dulbecco and Vogt[93] found that 20 such suspensions from different plaques of poliovirus contained from 10^4–10^5 plaque-forming doses (a plaque-forming dose is equivalent to one plaque-forming particle). They also found that Type 1 poliovirus diffuses from a plaque to a distance of 3–4 mm from the margin of the plaque. At a distance of 10 mm or more from the margin, diffused virus is entirely absent.

Purity of the plaque is assured if the following requirements are ful-filled: (1) absence of plaques of multiple origin due to secondary over-lapping: (2) no contamination of the plaque selected by virus diffusing from a adjacent plaque, or (3) by residual, nonadsorbed seed virus. The conditions fulfilling the first two requirements consist in the use of plates having less than ten plaques and in the selection of plaques that are at least 10 mm distant from the margin of an adjacent plaque. The third requirement is met by washing the cell layer free of unadsorbed virus at the end of the adsorption period. Contaminating virus particles can also be avoided by using two or more serial plaque passages. Virus lines derived in this manner have the same morphological, serological, and pathogenic properties as the parent strain.

One-Step Growth Experiments

WITH BACTERIOPHAGE

Because quantitative procedures for studying host-virus interactions at the cellular level were first developed for bacterial viruses and then served as models for similar undertakings with animal viruses, we shall

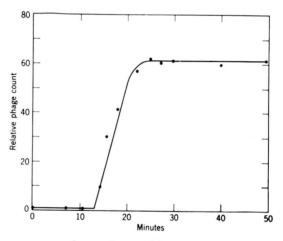

FIG. 78. A cne-step growth experiment with bacteriophage T1 on *Escherichia coli*, strain B, in nutrient broth at 37° C. Phage and bacteria, at a ratio 1:10, were mixed at time 0. The mixture was diluted after 4 min, when 45 per cent of the phage had been adsorbed. Assays were made at intervals after dilution. Average phage yield per infected cell = 62 × 100/45 = 138. (S. E. Luria.[298])

describe briefly one of the early, classic experiments devised by Ellis and Delbrück.[128] This experiment isolates in time one complete cycle of virus multiplication, i.e., virus adsorption, multiplication, and liberation, and provides information on the duration of intracellular phage development and on the amount of phage produced. Thus, sensitive bacteria under standard culture conditions are mixed with phage, and adsorption is allowed to proceed for a brief period, shorter than the minimum interval between adsorption and lysis (the *latent period*). The mixture is then diluted to such an extent that adsorption is practically stopped due to decreased frequency of phage-bacterium collisions. Platings are made at intervals for phage counts, and results of the type shown in Figure 78 are obtained. The low plateau represents the latent period; no lysis occurs and the count remains constant because each infected bacterium that is plated produces only one plaque on the solid medium, whatever its intracellular phage content at the moment of plating. The rise in plaque count corresponds to lysis (which can be checked by microscopic observation), and the final plateau is due to the fact that the newly liberated phage particles fail to adsorb to any bacterium in the diluted mixture and, therefore, remain free and do not reproduce further. This procedure isolates, then, one step or cycle of growth; but if dilutions were not made there would be a series of steps blurring into one another due to repeated, nonsynchronized cycles of adsorption and liberation until lysis is completed or until bacterial growth stops and with it phage reproduction.

With Animal Viruses

The one-step growth procedure just described for bacterial viruses was first adapted to animal viruses propagated in tissue culture by Dulbecco and Vogt[94] and can be carried out either with cells on glass or in suspension, as follows: Monolayer cultures are prepared in Petri dishes or in bottles. The cells are usually freed of media containing serum by washing them with phosphate buffered saline. A small volume (0.1–0.5 ml) of saline containing a suitable dilution of virus is then added to the cells and 1–2 hr are allowed for adsorption of virus (small volumes facilitate adsorption). Excess virus is then removed, and growth medium is added. At various times thereafter sample cultures are titrated for virus. Virus titers can be made on the medium (supernatant), on the contents of the cells themselves (by removing the medium and disrupting the cells by sonic energy, freeze-thawing, or some other means), or on cells plus medium (by disrupting the cells without removing the medium). It is also possible to determine the number of infected cells in such monolayer cultures during the latent period by removing the medium, trypsinizing the monolayer, washing the cells, and replating them for a plaque assay (*see* p. 255). As in bacterial virus work, every cell that is destined to yield some virus will produce a plaque, thus acting as an infectious center. At the end of the latent period, the virus titer will rise in the cells, or in the medium, or both. Because the volume of medium is kept large during the one-step

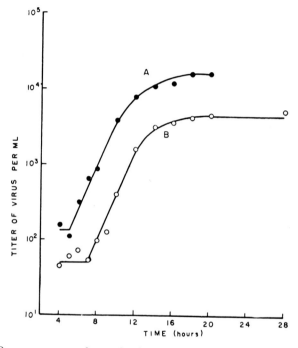

Fig. 79. One-step curves of growth of herpes-simplex (H4) virus in suspension of rabbit-kidney cells, sufficiently dilute to prevent readsorption of newly released virus. One monolayer (A) was inoculated with H4 virus in phosphate buffered saline and horse serum (10 per cent) to give a virus:cell ratio of 64; the second monolayer (B) was inoculated to give a ratio of 1.6. (A. S. Kaplan.[250])

experiment, any virus released into the medium will be adsorbed back into the cells very slowly if at all. A typical one-step growth curve is shown in Figure 79.

One-step growth experiments with suspended cells are performed in essentially the same manner. If the cells are first grown on glass, they are suspended by means of trypsin either before or after adsorption of virus, the excess virus is removed by centrifugation and washing, and the infected cells are then suspended in growth medium. Virus titrations on the infected cell suspension are then made at various time intervals, as before.

The latent period for the development of animal viruses in cell cultures varies widely. For Western-equine-encephalomyelitis (WEE) virus, for example, it is 2–3½ hr.[94] In many cases, the length of the latent period depends on the number of virus particles per cell in the original infection (multiplicity of infection), that is, the length of the latent period becomes shorter as the multiplicity of infection increases. The virus yield per cell also varies widely; for WEE virus, Dulbecco and Vogt[94] found that the yield was from 100–200 virus particles per cell for cells in suspension but was higher in cells adhering to glass. The rate of release of virus from animal cells varies with the cell-virus system being investigated. In some instances, the virus is released quickly, as soon as it is formed; in others, very little virus is released from the cells during the latent period, or the rate of release may vary between these two extremes.

Preparation of an Inactivated-Virus Vaccine
(Poliomyelitis Vaccine: Salk Type)

In 1949, Enders and his associates[130] reported the propagation of the Lansing (Type 2) strain of poliovirus in cultures of nonneural tissue from human embryos. In 1952, a Toronto group headed by Rhodes reported[167,515,552] that the Lansing strain of poliovirus could be cultivated in Erlenmeyer-flask and roller-tube cultures of human embryonic brain, cord, kidney, and monkey testis, nourished with medium 199. In the following year, the same group reported[96,168] that satisfactory virus yields could also be obtained in cultures of other monkey organs, including kidney, in medium 199. At about the same time, Salk and his associates reported[465] that polioviruses grown in tissue culture were antigenic in monkeys and that formalin-treated culture fluids were likewise capable of stimulating antibodies; and, in 1953, Salk reported[463,464] a preliminary series of inoculations of humans with a vaccine prepared from virus fluids obtained from cultures of monkey-kidney cells in medium 199. In that year also, the Connaught Medical Research Laboratories of the University of Toronto, at the request of the National Foundation for Infantile Paralysis, Inc., undertook large-scale production of virus fluids, over 3000 l of which were transferred to two commercial laboratories in the U.S.A. (Eli Lilly and Co., Indianapolis, Ind., and Parke, Davis and Co., Detroit, Mich.) for conversion into the Salk-type vaccine that was used in the 1954 field trials in the U.S.A., Canada, and Finland.[134,135,166,523] The "placebo" injections that served as controls in the field trials consisted of medium 199 alone.

Manufacturers of biological products in various countries prepare poliomyelitis vaccine by inactivating poliovirus culture fluids with formalin. The methods of testing are basically those devised for the 1954 field trials with subsequent additions and modifications that were introduced as "Minimum Requirements" and later incorporated in the "Regulations" of the United States Public Health Service. Regulations in Canada, Great Britain, and other countries have been based on those of the United States. An outline of the procedures followed by the Connaught Medical Research Laboratories, University of Toronto, is presented here through the courtesy of the Director, Dr. J. K. W. Ferguson.

Preparation of Virus Fluids*

The monkeys (usually rhesus or cynomolgus) providing the tissue are tuberculin tested before sacrificing, and an autopsy is performed on each. Cultures are prepared by either of two methods.

(a) *Cultures from chopped tissue.* Kidney cortex is finely minced, washed, and added to Povitsky (5-l) bottles with 500 ml of medium 199 or CMRL-597 (a modification of medium 199) containing antibiotics. The bottles are incubated on rocking platforms at 36–37° C for six days. After discarding bottles showing evidence of contamination or inadequate cell metabolism (high pH), three fourths of the fluid is withdrawn and replaced with fresh medium. Seed virus of a single type is added to the cultures, which are again incubated for four to five days. The virus fluids are then harvested and stored in the refrigerator in pools of 10–15 l. These pools are assayed for virus titer, tested with poliovirus antiserum of each type for identity and for the possible presence of certain simian viruses, inoculated into rabbits to detect B virus, if present, and tested for sterility. The virus strains

---

* This section was prepared by Dr. D. R. E. MacLeod, Associate Professor of Epidemiology, School of Hygiene, and Research Member, Connaught Medical Research Laboratories, University of Toronto.

employed are Mahoney (Type 1), MEF 1 (Type 2), and Saukett (Type 3).

(b) *Cultures from trypsin-dispersed cells.* Cell suspensions prepared by trypsinizing kidney cortex (*see* p. 125) are added to Povitsky bottles with 500–700 ml of medium 199 (or CMRL-597) containing antibiotics and supplemented with 1 per cent ox serum. After seven days at 36–37° C, confluent growth of healthy cells is confirmed by microscopic observation, the cell layer is washed twice with phosphate buffered saline, and fresh medium (without serum) containing seed virus is added. After two to three days' incubation, the virus fluids are harvested and tested as in (a).

Filtration

Large single-type pools of virus fluids are filtered through Seitz pads to remove cell debris and clumps containing infectious particles and to ensure sterility. The filtered pools are assayed for virus titer and tested for sterility, toxicity, and for *M. tuberculosis*, by appropriate tests in animals and culture media.

Inactivation

Filtered virus fluid is warmed to 37° C, the pH adjusted to 7.0–7.1, and formalin added to a final concentration of 1:4000. The progress of inactivation is followed by making assays of virus titer on each of the first three days. A second filtration through Seitz pads is done on the seventh day of inactivation, which is continued for a total of 12 days. Three days before completion of inactivation, and again at the end of the process, 500-ml samples are taken for "safety tests" in tissue culture. After neutralization of the formalin in these samples with sodium bisulfite, followed by dialysis to remove toxicity, the samples are inoculated into monkey-kidney cultures that are observed for 14 days. Subcultures made at 7 and 14 days are observed for a similar period. The monovalent vaccines are tested for sterility and for pyrogenicity.

Pooling of Monovalent Vaccines to Form Trivalent Vaccine

Monovalent vaccines that have passed all tests are pooled to constitute the trivalent vaccine; and the formalin is neutralized with sodium bisulfite. Before the addition of preservative, a large sample is removed for testing. A minimum of 1500 ml is tested in tissue cultures for residual, live virus. The vaccine is then dispensed into vials or ampules, and final tests are made as follows:

(a) safety test in monkeys by intraspinal, intracerebral, and intramuscular inoculation;

(b) antigenic-potency test in monkeys;

(c) toxicity tests in mice and guinea pigs;

(d) test in mice for possible presence of lymphocytic choriomeningitis;

(e) bacterial-sterility tests;

(f) pyrogenicity test;

(g) total nitrogen content; and,

(h) identity of product.

Final-container samples and bulk samples taken before the addition of preservative are also tested by the Laboratory of Hygiene, Department of National Health and Welfare, Ottawa.

XVII

Growth Measurements

GROWTH in tissue culture may be roughly defined as an increase in the number and mass of the cells. Under certain conditions, it is possible to have an increase in the number of cells without a corresponding increase in mass, and it is also possible to have an increase in mass without an increase in number; but neither phenomenon alone can proceed indefinitely. Until recent years, most tissue-culture experiments were made in media containing plasma, and growth measurements were made in various ways: (1) by making periodic measurements of the surface area of the cultures; (2) by estimating for a particular period of time the ratio of resting cells to dividing cells in a given area of the culture; (3) by weighing cells that had been separated from the plasma coagulum by chemical means; and (4) by measuring certain chemical changes taking place in the culture system. In 1940, however, Gemmill, Gey, and Austrian,[175] who were studying the metabolism of Walker rat sarcoma 319, centrifuged the cells in a hematocrit tube as a means of measuring packed cell volumes; when plasma was present in the culture medium the clot was first digested with trypsin. This was one of the first attempts to apply quantitative methods to culture work. Eleven years later, as many investigators began to cultivate cells directly on glass without plasma, Evans, Sanford, and their associates[133,467] developed methods for preparing replicate cultures from washed-cell suspensions and for estimating the size of initial cell populations and those developed from them by isolating and making hemocytometer counts of cell nuclei from representative culture flasks at various stages of an experiment (*see* p. 184). More recently, it has become common practice in many laboratories to estimate the size of cell populations by counting intact cells rather than isolated nuclei. Sometimes the cells are counted while they are still attached to glass. Otherwise, suspensions of the cells are counted. These counts are very easy to make if the cells have been multiplying in suspension (*see* Chap. XII); but cells multiplying on glass can be brought into suspension with enzymes or other agents. Although cells in suspension tend to clump, the errors involved in making such counts are probably no greater than those inherent in the culture procedures themselves. Other investigators are currently measuring cell populations in replicate culture systems by making various chemical determinations, e.g., of total protein, total purines and pyrimidines, and nucleic-acid constituents. Also, by taking advantage of the plating procedures that have been developed (*see* Chap. XIII), it is now possible to determine the number of cells in a population that are capable of division (*see* p. 207) and to determine the rate of growth of colonies (clones) derived from single cells (*see* p. 218). Examples of some of these and other methods will be described in the present chapter.

Measurement of the Growth of Cultures in a Plasma Coagulum

When freshly explanted tissue fragments and established lines of cells are embedded in a plasma coagulum, they tend to form discrete colonies, partly as the result of the migration of cells away from the explant and partly as the result of cell multiplication. The growth of these colonies may be measured in various ways, the most common of which is to make periodic measurements of the surface area of the cultures and to construct diagrams in which the increase in area is expressed as a function of time. By careful handling, reasonably homogeneous cell strains can be developed in plasma and used to prepare series of cultures that are remarkably uniform in appearance and behavior. In the author's laboratory, it was common practice at one time to develop strains of fibroblasts by repeated subculture over several weeks and then to make assays in which several sister cultures were each divided into four reasonably comparable parts that were placed in separate culture flasks (Fig. 41). At the end of an experiment, significant differences in surface area could always be detected by visual inspection without any form of measurement. As a rule, however, outline drawings were made at intervals during the experiment by means of a projectoscope; and, if diagrams or tables were to be prepared, the surface area enclosed by each successive outline was measured with a planimeter.[123] Some workers estimated increases in surface area from ocular micrometer measurements.[496] When two diameters at right angles to one another were measured, the area was estimated on the assumption that the colonies were circular.

It is obvious, of course, that this method has serious limitations, for it fails to distinguish between increases in area resulting from cell multiplication and increases due to cell migration, though both phenomena usually contribute to the ultimate size of the cell colony.[541] Nor do surface measurements take into account variations in the density of the cell population, in the general thickness of the colony, or in cell size. Still, the estimation of surface area has given significant data in many thousands of experiments. But like every other measuring device, it must be used with discretion and with a complete under-standing of the possible sources of error. Thus, the method should be used only for plasma cultures prepared in flasks or tubes from homo-geneous strains of cells that produce uniform colonies or from carefully dissected fragments of tissue that are reasonably uniform in size and morphology (e.g., fragments of buffy coat, embryonic spinal cord, or blood vessels). The method is not suitable for cells that form irregular colonies (Fig. 80) or for cultures that digest the fibrin of the coagulum too rapidly for regular compensation by "patching" (*see* p. 155).

Other investigators have attempted to distinguish between cell multi-plication and cell migration in plasma cultures. Champy[59] estimated, for a particular moment of time, the ratio of dividing cells to resting cells and expressed this ratio in terms of *mitotic coefficients*. Willmer,[542] and Willmer and Jacoby[545] described an elaboration of this method that consisted of photographing a sample of cells (100–400) from the peripheral part of a colony of cells. The photographs were taken automatically at 6-min intervals for as long as five days, and an estimate of the percentage of dividing cells, per unit of time, was expressed as a *mitotic index*. Several years ago, however, Stroud and Brues[494] suggested that considerable caution should be taken in interpreting data based on the mitotic index. In studying radiation effects in tissue

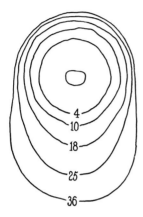

FIG. 80. Diagram showing the increase in surface area of a culture of skeletal muscle from a 14-day chick embryo, after 36 days in plasma and balanced salt solution. Note the increasing irregularity in the contour of the culture as a result of localized cellular activity. (R. C. Parker.[372])

culture, they found that certain doses resulted in a doubling of the mean duration of mitosis but that there was great variation in the length of the delay, some cells completing the process in normal time, others taking over 2 hr. It was also noted that while the number of cells entering mitosis was little affected during the first hour, the delay during mitosis resulted in a higher concentration of dividing cells than normal. Thus, if one were to judge the mitotic rate by the mitotic index, one would have concluded that there was actually a stimulation of cell division.

Some investigators have measured the dry weight of cultures that were separated from the plasma coagulum by means of alcohol,[320] pepsin,[264] or sodium hydroxide[287]; and still others have sought a direct correlation between cell multiplication and oxygen consumption,[319] aerobic and anaerobic glycolysis,[263,287] glucose utilization,[401,546] lactic-acid production,[320,543] and nitrogen metabolism.[546] And many of these approaches have been reinvestigated in recent years[185,349,421,557] with cultures propagated directly on glass without plasma or in suspension. In general, however, these procedures are too complicated for routine use.

Estimation of Cell Numbers in Cultures
with Fluid Medium

Physical Methods of Estimating Cell Numbers

Measurements of Packed Cell Volumes

As mentioned earlier, Gemmill, Gey, and Austrian[175] estimated the size of cell populations by measuring packed cell volumes in a hematocrit. More recently, Waymouth[529] has used a Van Allen microhematocrit to measure the volume of cells contained in a single culture (e.g., in a Carrel flask containing 1 ml of medium). This hematocrit consists of a capillary tube with a bulb of about 1 ml capacity near the top. The portion of the tube below the bulb is about 70 mm long with a bore of about 0.5 mm and is graduated in 100 divisions.

In preparation for the assay, the cells are detached from the glass by introducing into each flask, without removing the nutrient, 0.2 ml of a 0.25 per cent solution of trypsin (1:300) in 0.8 per cent NaCl, 0.04 per cent KCl, and 0.02 per cent Na_2HPO_4. The flask is allowed to stand for about 1 min and then shaken to detach the cells. (A longer digestion period is necessary for cells in media containing serum.) The cell suspension is transferred as completely as possible to a small siliconed shell vial and from there it is taken up in the hematocrit, which is also siliconed. (The shell-vial step is necessary only because the hematocrit cannot be inserted in a flask with a bent neck.) The hematocrit is closed with a spring clip, centrifuged at 2800 r.p.m. for 30 min (International centrifuge, size 1, model SBV, with 8-place head #225, metal shields #303, and a ½-in., Gooch rubber-tubing liner for each shield), and the length of the column of packed cells is read on the stem. The tubes are cleaned in a suction device designed especially for washing and drying blood-dilution pipettes.

A comparison of hematocrit readings with hemocytometer counts showed good agreement for limited periods (e.g., one week) or until the cells in the cultures became closely packed. But Kuchler and Merchant,[256] who have made a considerable study of cells in suspension, found that an increase in cell size during the lag phase of growth accounted for an increase in packed cell volumes in the absence of an increase in cell numbers.

Measurements of the Optical Density of Cell Suspensions

Younger[553] estimated cell numbers in suspensions of monkey-kidney cells by determining their optical density. After trypsin-dispersed cell suspensions had been prepared and washed (*see* p. 122), the packed cells from the final centrifugation were diluted 1:50 with 2 per cent horse serum in medium 199 and passed through three layers of cheese-cloth to remove connective tissue fibers. An aliquot of this suspension was further diluted to 1:200 for purposes of standardization. Four milliliters of the cell suspension were acidified (with 0.3 ml of 0.2N HCl) and optical density (negative log of transmittance) was determined in a Coleman Junior spectrophotometer at a wave-length of

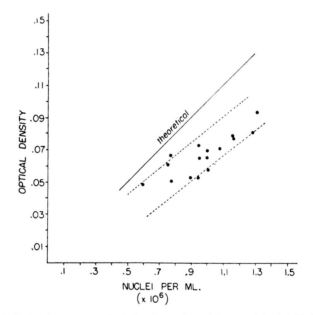

Fig. 81. Relation between optical density and nuclei per ml in 1:200 dilutions of trypsin-dispersed monkey-kidney cells. Points are based on data from 16 successive batches of cells. (J. S. Younger.[553])

590 mμ, where light absorption by acidified phenol red was least. An equal volume of acidified medium served as a blank. The relationship between optical density and cell numbers in 16 batches of cells is shown in Fig. 81. As will be noted, all measurements fell below a line that would express the theoretical relationship between optical

density and cell numbers in a uniform suspension of single cells without aggregates. It was possible, however, to use the method to advantage in estimating the extent to which the original suspension could
be further diluted for the preparation of cultures.

Measurements Made with an Electronic Cell Counter

Harris[220] and Kuchler and Merchant[256] have measured cell populations by means of an electronic device, the Coulter cell counter

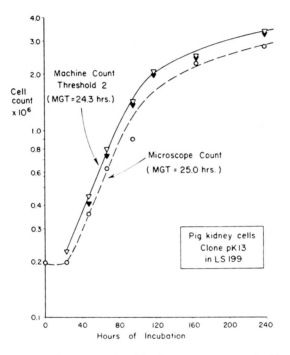

FIG. 82. Comparison of counts made with a hemocytometer and with a Coulter cell
counter on pig-kidney cells (clone pK13) that had been cultivated in Earle's T-15
flasks in 10 per cent lamb serum (LS), 50 per cent medium 199, and 40 per cent balanced salt solution (Earle's); each point represents three flasks. Solid triangles represent Coulter counts at threshold 10. MGT = mean generation time. (M. Harris.[220])

(Coulter Electronics, Chicago 40, Ill.), which was developed for
automatic blood-cell counting.[35,310] When a standard volume of a
suspension is drawn through a small (100 μ) aperture in the machine,
the passage of a cell causes a voltage drop that can be visualized in an
oscilloscope and recorded on a decade counter. Harris tested the

method with monolayer cultures of chick skeletal-muscle fibroblasts and pig-kidney cells (Fig. 82). Flask cultures to be enumerated were drained briefly and incubated for 10–15 min with 1.0 or 2.0 ml 1 per cent trypsin in Ca-Mg-free saline (chick cells) or 1 per cent trypsin containing 1 per cent sodium versenate (pig-kidney cells). The higher concentration of trypsin or trypsin-Versene gave better separation of cells and did not impair viability for subculture. After incubation, the cells in each flask were suspended uniformly and clumps were dispersed by gentle mixing with a 1.5-ml pipette. Convenient final dilutions (made with 0.85 per cent NaCl) ranged from $1-2 \times 10^4$ cells per ml. Four consecutive counts on a single suspension required about 1 min. Harris found that although higher absolute values for cell number were obtained with the electronic counter, these values could be adjusted by calibration against other standards (hemocytometer counts or DNA measurements).

Quite obviously, the use of electronic cell counting is limited to populations that can be dispersed without conspicuous damage or debris. Kuchler and Merchant[256] reported that the method is especially well suited to cells propagated in suspension. Under these conditions, counts made with the electronic device gave standard deviations that varied between 8,000 and 16,000 cells per ml, whereas the standard deviations of hemocytometer counts varied between 25,000 and 35,000 cells per ml.

CHEMICAL METHODS OF ESTIMATING CELL NUMBERS

Nucleic Acid Determinations

A method of measuring the rate of cell multiplication in cultures by determining the amount of nucleoprotein phosphorus present in the tissues was introduced by Willmer,[543] who cultivated chick-heart tissues in plasma in roller tubes and found good agreement between nucleoprotein phosphorus and the dry weight of cultures. It soon became clear, however, that estimations based on total nucleoprotein phosphorus are not too reliable inasmuch as the ribonucleic acid (RNA) portion of nucleoprotein varies with the physiological state of the cells; in contrast, the quantity of deoxyribonucleic acid (DNA) per cell is reasonable uniform. In 1945, Schmidt and Thannhauser[477] reported a method for the quantitative determination of RNA and

DNA in animal tissues. In 1949, Davidson, Leslie, and Waymouth[82] employed a modified Schmidt-Thannhauser procedure to follow changes in RNA and DNA in fibroblast cultures by making phosphorus (P) determinations of these fractions. Later, Healy and his associates[231] used a variation of this procedure for the estimation of DNAP in replicate cultures of L cells (see p. 184). According to this method, a modified Schmidt-Thannhauser separation of RNA and DNA was followed by spectrophotometric estimation of the orthophosphate. Because good correlation was found between nuclear counts and DNAP values in natural media (containing horse serum and embryo extract) and in chemically defined media, the two methods could be used interchangeably. In the meantime, Ceriotti[57] devised a new microchemical method for the determination of DNA that is based on the measurement of the density of color produced in the reaction between DNA and indole when heated in the presence of HCl. The DNA can be determined quantitatively in concentrations ranging from 2.5 to 15 μg per ml. Although slightly less sensitive than the DNAP method, it is presently the method preferred, for it is relatively simple, exceedingly rapid, and highly specific.

Kuchler and Merchant,[256] working with L cells propagated in suspension, computed the DNA, RNA, total nitrogen, and dry weight during the growth cycle and compared these measurements with cell counts and packed cell volumes. DNA was found to correlate directly with cell numbers, whereas RNA, total nitrogen, and dry weight increases during the lag phase were related to an increase in cell size.

Salzman[466] has studied fluctuations in cellular protein, RNA, and DNA during the growth of HeLa cell populations as "monolayers" and in suspension. In monolayer cultures, the lag phase was characterized by rapid synthesis of RNA, DNA, and protein. Within 6 hr after subculture, the DNA approached a level twice that found in cultures in the logarithmic phase of growth. This excess DNA disappeared by the second or third day, and the DNA per cell thereafter remained relatively constant. In contrast, the levels of RNA and protein continued to decline during the logarithmic and the stationary phase and without relationship to the rate of cell division. Suspension cultures showed a similar increase in cellular RNA and protein during the lag phase, but there was no accumulation of DNA during this period.

Protein Determinations (Colorimetric)

Oyama and Eagle[367] made protein determinations as a means of measuring the size of cell populations that are adherent to a glass surface. The method is based on the colorimetric method of Lowry and his associates[296] and involves the use of a phenol reagent (Folin-Ciocalteu[163]) for color development. The results, referred to a bovine-serum-albumin standard, may be converted to dry weight, nitrogen, or cell count by appropriate conversion factors. It must be remembered, however, that this method is based on the assumption that the protein per cell remains constant throughout the growth cycle.

Determination of Total Purines and Pyrimidines

McIntire and Smith[314] measure the size of cell populations by making determinations of the total purines and pyrimidines (TPP). The determination is made by extracting washed cultures with hot acid-salt solution and measuring the absorbance of the extract at 268 mμ. While TPP values obtained from cultures of three cell strains propagated under different conditions correlated well with cell counts, both TPP and protein nitrogen values varied somewhat and similarly with respect to DNA, which was used as a standard of reference. It was concluded that TPP values are at least as reliable as protein nitrogen values for estimating cell numbers, and they are easier to obtain.

ENUMERATION OF ISOLATED CELL NUCLEI

Enumeration of Nuclei from Cells Cultivated on Glass Surfaces in Chemically Defined Media

In 1951, Sanford, Evans, and their associates[133,467] devised short-term replicate culture procedures according to which the number of cells placed in each of a series of cultures is estimated by counting the cell nuclei in representative samples of a washed and continuously stirred cell suspension used as inoculum (see p. 184). The nuclei are isolated by treating the cells with citric acid, after which they are concentrated by low-speed centrifugation, lightly stained with crystal violet, and enumerated in a hemocytometer. At intervals throughout the experiment, the nuclei are isolated from the cells of various cultures comprising the series and are counted in the same manner. These procedures, which had been worked out with great care, were designed specifically for L cells cultivated in media containing protein. But Parker and his associates[378] modified the procedures for cells cultivated in chemically defined media. Under these conditions, a large proportion of the nuclei could not be detached from the glass by the original method of treatment, which consisted essentially of shaking the cultures vigorously during and after 1 hour's incubation at 37° C with 2 per cent citric acid. Eventually, however, it was found that a brief pretreatment with 1 per cent tannic acid coagulated the nuclei just enough to prevent gross distortion and to allow the cytoplasm to be stripped from them by subsequent treatment with 30 per cent citric acid; simultaneously, the nuclei were detached from the glass. Also, the original procedure was shortened by eliminating the period of incubation with citric acid and by eliminating a final centrifugation of the isolated, stained nuclei. The revised procedure is as follows:

(1) Five milliliters of 30 per cent citric acid are added to each of as many 25-ml, round-bottom test tubes ($\frac{3}{4}$ × 6 in., graduated in 0.5 ml) as there are cultures to be handled.

(2) Five milliliters of 1 per cent tannic acid are added to each T-15 culture flask, which is then restoppered and allowed to lie flat (with the fluid covering the cells) for not longer than 2 min. This maximum period will determine the number of flasks that can be handled simultaneously.

(3) The contents of the first flask are poured into one of the 25-ml tubes and shaken. Immediately thereafter, 5 ml of 30 per cent citric acid are placed in the drained flask, which is shaken vigorously and allowed to lie flat (with the fluid covering the cells) for 5–10 min.

(4) The contents of the flask are then added to the 25-ml tube, after which the flask is again shaken vigorously with 5 ml of 30 per cent citric acid and the contents added to the tube, which should now contain about 23 ml. (The measurements need only be approximate up to this point; hereafter, they must be exact.)

(5) The tubes are stoppered, shaken, and centrifuged for 20 min at 1100 r.p.m. (No. 2 International).

(6) After centrifugation, all but 1.0 ml of the supernatant fluid is removed from each tube by mild suction, care being taken not to disturb the cells.

(7) To each tube is added 1.0 ml of 0.1 per cent crystal violet, after which the tube is shaken and the contents poured into a 20-ml beaker.

(8) Thirty per cent citric acid (1.0 ml) is added to the drained tube, shaken, and poured into the beaker; this is repeated to give a final volume of 4.0 ml in the beaker. (If a higher dilution is desired, the final volume is increased.)

FIG. 83. Cell-counting pipette of approximately 5-ml capacity, for use in making hemocytometer counts of isolated nuclei; a model with a larger chamber holds 15 ml. (K. K. Sanford et al.[467]; Kontes Glass Co., Vineland, N.J.)

(9) The contents of the beaker are transferred immediately to a special cell-counting pipette (Fig. 83) by applying suction to the latter from a mouth tube while the beaker is being agitated by a gentle swirling motion.

Rappaport[424] modified this procedure by using smaller volumes of citric acid to obviate the necessity of concentrating the cells by centrifugation and by adding the crystal violet not later than 5 min after the citric acid in order to stop the swelling and bursting of nuclei. Her procedure is as follows:

(1) The supernatant fluid is decanted, the culture bottled drained, and the cell layer covered with 1 per cent tannic acid for 1½–2 min.

(2) The tannic acid is decanted, the bottle drained on absorbent paper, and exactly 2 ml of 10 per cent citric acid are added to the cell layer.

(3) After about 1 min, the culture bottle is shaken vigorously for 10–15 sec. (The time required to remove the cells from the glass depends on the age of the culture and whether the cells have been cultivated in a medium containing serum or one that is protein free. Young cultures and older cultures in synthetic medium may require as long as 5 min in citric acid.)

(4) The nuclei are stained by adding 0.5 ml of 0.1 per cent crystal violet in 0.1M citric acid.

The special counting pipettes (Fig. 83) should be large enough to hold at least 4 ml of cell suspension; for heavy suspensions, larger pipettes are used to accommodate higher dilutions. If the counting is to be delayed, the counting pipettes are stored at 4° C in sealing devices consisting of two brass cups fitted with rubber cushions and connected by wire springs. At the time of counting, the pipettes are clamped in Bryan-Garrey blood-cell-counting-pipette rotors (A. S. Aloe Co., St. Louis 3, Mo.) and rotated for at least 15 min to establish and maintain a uniform dispersion of nuclei before samples are taken. The angle between the axis of the pipette and the axis of the rotor shaft should be increased to 22° to increase the amplitude of motion of the modified glass bead used to agitate the nuclear suspension in the pipette bulb.* Before the hemocytometer is charged, the contents of the tip of the pipette are discarded.

The enumeration is based on the number of nuclei counted in the nine 1-mm squares comprising one chamber of the bright-line, double, improved Neubauer hemocytometer (American Optical Co., Buffalo, N.Y.). Thus, if a total of 225 nuclei are counted in nine hemo-cytometer squares or a volume of 0.9 cu mm of a suspension that has been diluted to 4000 cu mm, the number of nuclei per culture would be calculated as follows: $\dfrac{225 \times 4000}{0.9} = 1{,}000{,}000$. For greater ac-curacy, more chambers may be counted. In fact, Sanford and her associates[467] have computed that 750 to 800 nuclei must be counted in order to attain an accuracy of 90 per cent, 95 per cent of the time.

Although, in theory, blood-cell counts follow a Poisson distribution, large errors arise through faulty technique. Also, special precautions have to be taken with tissue cells that have a tendency to cluster. Rinaldini,[437] who has made a careful study of the procedures, makes the following suggestions:

A Pasteur pipette or a long tube of about 1.5 mm bore should be used for sampling and the suspension should be stirred gently before taking each sample. The tube or pipette is filled without suction, simply by dipping it about 1 cm deep in the suspension and then closing the opposite end with the finger. To load the haemocytometer, the tip of the pipette should be brought in contact with the edge of the coverslip without exerting any air pressure, allowing the cell suspension to run in by capillary attraction. The counting chamber should of course be grease-free and the graticule should be in the centre of the coverslip. If the cells are not evenly scattered, the chamber should be washed and reloaded with a fresh sample. . . . To pre-vent errors arising from cells adhering to the glass during the preparation of quantitative inocula, siliconed tubes are used.

* Earle, W. R. Personal communication.

Enumeration of Nuclei from Replicate Samples of a Cell Suspension Used as Inoculum

At the time the cultures comprising a single experiment are prepared from the washed-cell suspension, three flasks without medium are inoculated with double samples of the stirred suspension, as follows: (1) at the beginning of the culture series; (2) midway through the series; and (3) at the end of the series. The nuclei isolated from these cells are stained and enumerated as a means of estimating the size of the culture inoculum. Because these samples are not incubated with synthetic media, the original procedures devised by Sanford, Evans, and their associates[133,467] could be used without modification. In the author's laboratory, however, the samples are prepared for counting by a shortened procedure[378] that is quite similar to the one just described for the cultures. It is, as follows:

(1) Five milliliters of 2 per cent citric acid are added to each of the three flasks, which are then shaken and allowed to lie flat for 5–10 min.

(2) The contents of each flask are poured into a 25-ml graduated tube.

(3) Each of the flasks is rinsed with 5 ml of 2 per cent citric acid, and the rinsings are added immediately to their respective tubes.

(4) The graduated tubes are stoppered, shaken, and centrifuged for 20 min at 1100 r.p.m.

(5) After centrifugation, all but 1.0 ml of the supernatant is removed from each tube by suction.

(6) To each tube is added 1.0 ml of 0.1 per cent crystal violet, after which the tube is shaken and the contents poured into a 20-ml beaker.

(7) Two per cent citric acid (1.0 ml) is added to the drained tube, shaken, and poured into the beaker; this procedure is then repeated to give a final volume of 4 ml in the beaker.

(8) The contents of the beaker are transferred immediately to a cell-counting pipette, and the nuclei enumerated in the usual manner.

Enumeration of Nuclei from Cells Cultivated on Glass Surfaces in Media Containing Serum

Swim and R. F. Parker[501] enumerate cells propagated on glass in replicate cultures containing serum by the following modification of the original procedure of Sanford and her associates.[467] The medium

(4 ml) contained in each S-20 culture flask (*see* p. 18) is replaced by 2 to 4 ml of an aqueous solution containing 6 per cent citric acid and 0.01 per cent crystal violet. A uniform suspension of nuclei, free from cytoplasm, is obtained by shaking the flasks for 5 min at a rate of 120 cycles per min on a reciprocating shaker (Eberbach Corp., Ann Arbor, Mich.; variable-speed, blood-pipette shaker, equipped with a holder for S-20 flasks). Aliquots of the suspension are then placed immediately in a hemocytometer chamber for the enumeration of nuclei. The number of cells present at the beginning of the experiment is determined by applying the same procedure to duplicate flasks from the same series.

Enumeration of Nuclei from Cells Cultivated in Suspension

According to a method developed by Bryant and his associates[38] for the enumeration of nuclei liberated from cells cultivated in suspension, 4 ml of 0.1M citric acid and 1 ml of 0.1 per cent crystal violet in 0.1M citric acid are placed in a dry beaker. A 1-ml sample of the cell suspension is added and mixed with the acid and dye. Then, while the beaker is being agitated by a gentle swirling motion, the contents are taken up in a counting pipette (Fig. 83). The pipette is rotated in a Bryan-Garrey blood-cell-counting-pipette rotor for at least 15 min prior to enumerating the nuclei. The enumeration is based on the number of nuclei counted in nine 1-mm squares (0.9 cu mm) of the hemocytometer, as described on page 279.

ENUMERATION OF INTACT CELLS

In many laboratories cell populations are measured by counting intact cells in a hemocytometer. Such counts are made on cell suspensions to determine their density or the extent to which they should be diluted in setting up new experiments. Intact cells may also be counted after they have been released from glass surfaces with enzymes or chelating agents (*see* Chap. XI). If a cell suspension is combined with an appropriate dye, it may be possible to distinguish living and dead cells (*see* next section). The relative accuracy of intact-cell counts depends largely upon the manner of sampling, the total number of cells that are counted, and the extent to which cell clumping occurs. The hemocytometer procedures described on the preceding pages will serve as a guide in making the counts and in detecting sources of error.

Determination of Cell Viability
by Dye-Exclusion Tests

It is always important to know the percentage of viable cells in a population, particularly if it is one that is being measured. Schrek[478] used eosin (0.95 mg per ml) as a means of distinguishing between living and dead cells. Because of selective permeability, viable cells remain colorless whereas dead cells become diffusely stained. Hanks and Wallace,[211] who use the eosin exclusion test as a routine assay

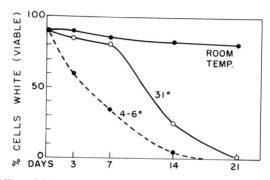

FIG. 84. Viability of dilute suspensions of L cells (5×10^5 per ml) during storage at various temperatures in siliconed tubes, without pH readjustment or renewal of medium. Fluid depth: 8 mm. Assays: Transfer of 2-mm loops of cell suspension to eosin slides (*see* text); counts after 2 min. (J. H. Hanks and J. H. Wallace.[211])

procedure, store clean slides on which 1-mm loop spots of aqueous eosion (1 per cent) are dried, usually in three horizontal rows of five spots each. To test the ability of cells to survive in a particular solution, a slide is laid in a Petri dish containing sheets of moistened filter paper in both the top and bottom sections. One or more of the eosin spots are then rehydrated with 2-mm loops of cell suspension and stirred. The slide is held in the moist chamber for 2 min before observations are recorded on 200 cells per spot (*see* Fig. 84). When the suspensions are dense, the eosin is rehydrated with a 2-mm loop of test solution (or 2 per cent serum in balanced salt solution without bicarbonate) and a 0.7-mm loop of cells is added. Cells that exclude eosin are seen to be plump and smooth, whereas those that admit the dye resemble flattened spheroids. (Standard platinum loops are available from Arthur H. Thomas Co., Philadelphia, Pa.)

Phillips and Andrews[394] distinguish between living and dead cells in making hemocytometer counts by adding erythrosin B, which is carried as a stock solution of 0.4 per cent of the dye in phosphate buffered saline. Because protein in solution binds erythrosin, a slight excess of the dye is added to solutions containing protein. For each ml of cell suspension containing dissolved protein 0.3 ml of the stock solution is used, whereas only 0.05 ml is required when the medium is protein free. The counts are completed within 2 hr. McLimans and his associates[315] distinguished between living and dead cells by mixing 1 ml of cell suspension with 0.5 ml of a 0.5 per cent water solution of trypan blue.[370]

Methods for estimating the number of cells in a culture population that are capable of forming colonies are described on pages 207 and 217.

XVIII

Preservation of Cells by Freezing

IN the study and use of cell strains derived by tissue-culture procedures, it has become increasingly important in many laboratories to preserve them by low-temperature storage for the following reasons: (1) to compare, at some future time, cells from various sources or sublines of strains at various stages of their development; (2) to reduce the danger of cells losing desirable properties or acquiring undesirable ones; (3) to reduce the danger of losing cell strains as the result of microbial contaminations or other laboratory accidents; and (4) to reduce the time and effort that would otherwise be expended in maintaining at 37° C strains not in continuous use.

Early in the century, Michaelis[329] and Ehrlich[125] made pioneer studies on the low-temperature preservation of animal tumors. But it was 30 years later before Barnes and Furth[16] made the important observation that the survival rate of frozen cells was higher if the tissue was frozen slowly, and Breedis and Furth[36] demonstrated tumor survival for over 400 days at −70° C. Although there is still considerable disagreement both as to the nature of the damage caused by freezing and thawing and how best to avoid it, it has become possible to maintain a wide variety of cells and tissues in a viable state for months and years by storing them in a cabinet cooled with dry (CO_2) ice. In this chapter, some of the problems will be discussed and successful methods will be described.

Much that is known about the effects of freezing and thawing in biological systems has been worked out empirically by various groups of investigators. Fortunately, however, the basic work of Luyet[299] on the effects of ultrarapid freezing, of Lovelock[293, 295] on the mechanism of slow-freezing injury and glycerol protection, and the more recent

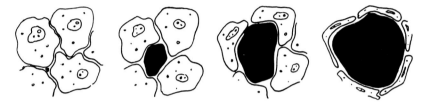

FIG. 85. Slow freezing in tissue. Crystal nuclei develop in the extracellular spaces. As they grow, water is removed from the cells and added to the crystal. Eventually, the dehydrated cells are bathed in a concentrate of their own solutes. (H. T. Meryman.[327])

discoveries of Meryman,[326, 327] Rey,[430, 431, 432] and others, have contributed to a broad foundation of theory that will continue to be tested and modified as more and more investigators develop adequate procedures for their own particular needs and take the trouble to report their experiences. The present procedures were developed mainly because of the urgent needs of animal husbandry and blood-donor services; and those working with cell strains have benefited indirectly.

General Features of Freezing and Thawing

Meryman[327] has shown that when animal tissues are frozen slowly, e.g., in air at dry-ice temperature, crystal formation is extracellular (Fig. 85). When the rate of cooling is increased by immersing the material in alcohol and dry ice, crystals form at random throughout the material and are, therefore, mostly intracellular. It was also demonstrated by Lovelock[293, 295] that when ice-crystal formation is slow and extracellular, injurious effects usually do not result from the mechanical presence of the ice crystals but from dehydration and the concentration of electrolytes that inevitably results from the removal of water to form ice crystals. In blood, hemolysis occurs rapidly when the salt concentration approaches 4.7 per cent, well before freezing has been completed. In view of this, one method of preventing injury is to freeze slowly and then, before significant injury has developed, to lower the temperature to one at which the rate of denaturation is insignificant. This is, in effect, what is done when tumor samples are maintained for long periods in dry ice. Meryman[327] feels that maintenance under dry-ice conditions (where temperatures sometimes rise to −60° C) is generally border line, however, and useful only when the survival of isolated cells fulfills the purpose.

A second means of preventing injury is to prevent a lethal concentration of electrolytes by reducing the amount of ice that forms. This is the basis for the use of glycerol. In fact, little progress was made in the freezing and thawing of normal vertebrate cells until Polge, Smith, and Parkes[397] discovered in 1949 that glycerol had the remarkable property of protecting fowl spermatozoa from the damaging effects of freezing to −79° C and thawing. Lovelock,[293, 294] working with red blood cells, showed that the effect of glycerol was to reduce the range of critical temperatures in which cell damage takes place (Fig. 86). He also demonstrated that the protective action of glycerol is exerted fully only when it is present both within and without the cell. This discovery suggested that damage from freezing results largely from the increased concentration of electrolytes within the cell and that glycerol serves to reduce this concentration. Glycerol has the ability to attach to itself considerable water, which is then unavailable to form ice but can still act as a solvent. Glycerol also passes freely through cell membranes; hence, the addition of glycerol to a specimen results in the binding of water and a reduction in the amount removed to form ice. The electrolyte concentration is therefore less and, if sufficient glycerol is added, is no longer lethal.[327] In addition, glycerol is usually nontoxic, miscible with electrolytes, alcohols, lipids, inorganic and organic compounds, does not modify the pH, and is almost incompressible.[430, 486] In fact, the advantages of freezing with glycerol are that the rates of freezing and thawing are relatively undemanding.[327]

Certain cells, notably human spermatozoa[383] and mammalian skin,[25] will survive cooling in the absence of glycerol. Lovelock[294] suggests that such cells survive because they are so completely dehydrated that insufficient water remains within them to crystallize. But there are also species differences. For example, a large proportion of bull spermatozoa (up to 90 per cent, depending on the specimen) may survive freezing to $-79°$ C and subsequent thawing when the semen is diluted with a variety of different media, e.g., with a solution of sodium citrate and egg yolk containing about 10 per cent glycerol.[395] During slow cooling to $-79°$ C, there is a critical temperature range between $-15°$ and $-25°$ C at which the greatest damage occurs.

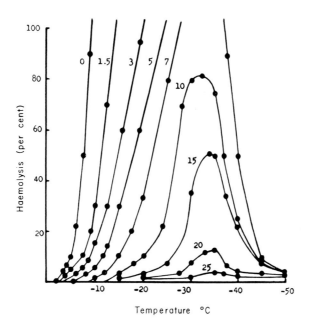

FIG. 86. The hemolysis that occurs when red blood cells in suspension in 0.16M NaCl containing various concentrations of glycerol are frozen. The curves shown are, left to right, those corresponding to glycerol concentrations of 0, 0.15, 0.3, 0.5, 0.75, 1.0, 1.5, 2.0 and 2.5M. In all experiments the cells were frozen for 10 min at the temperatures indicated. (J. E. Lovelock.[293])

The rate at which the capacity for motility is destroyed within this range is reduced by allowing the spermatozoa to stand at $2°$ C in contact with their special medium for 18 hr before freezing and by cooling the specimen at a rate of $0.25–0.5°$ C per sec between $-15°$ and $-25°$ C. When a similar procedure is adopted for rabbit spermatozoa, the proportion of cells surviving freezing is negligible.

Meryman[326] points out that not all cellular materials will withstand freezing even in the presence of glycerol. In many cases, it is the glycerol itself that becomes toxic in concentrations sufficient to protect against freezing. In the author's laboratory, a subline of L cells that has been propagated for four years in unsupplemented chemically defined media does not withstand freezing at any levels of glycerol that have been tried. Meryman also points out that additives that prevent injury during slow freezing are not necessarily identical with those useful for rapid freezing. Thus, glycerol is almost valueless in aiding the recovery of red blood cells after rapid freezing, while glucose and other hexose sugars, urea, and sodium citrate provide substantial benefit.[326] Luyet and Keane,[300] on the other hand, found glycerol to be superior to glucose in protecting chick-embryo heart from damage by rapid freezing.

The applications of rapid freezing have not as yet been very extensively investigated, except in the preservation of whole blood. With 5 per cent glucose, loss of red cells was reduced to 2 or 3 per cent.[327] More complex, nucleated cells do not survive as well; although successful transplants of both the Walker 256 and Ehrlich ascites cells have been achieved with rapidly frozen material, there is 100 per cent mortality of mammalian spermatozoa.[327]

Regardless of the manner in which glycerol exerts its beneficial effects, it is now generally agreed that rapid thawing is essential for maximum survival. Rey[430] points out, however, that because of the high caloric conductivity of ice (10 times that of water), the temperature rises rapidly until a liquid phase appears. At this point, cells that are still solid are surrounded by a hypertonic layer with a weak thermal conductivity. Here again, glycerol is effective in reducing the toxic effect of this critical phase in the process of defrosting.

Although the list of different types of cells and tissues that have remained viable after freezing, low-temperature storage, and thawing is too long to include here, it is interesting to note that it includes such diversified items as pathogenic amoeba,[170] mammalian eggs,[384,487] adrenal tissue,[486] human erythrocytes,[247] mammalian spermatozoa,[395] and the superior cervical ganglion of the rat.[385]

It is also interesting to note that serious efforts are being made to test the extent to which cells and tissues survive freezing and drying. Passey and his associates[386,387] demonstrated growth in vitro from cell suspensions of mouse sarcoma cells that had been frozen at $-79°$ C, stored for 12 hr, and desiccated for periods of 30 and 75 min. Because the cells failed to survive longer periods of desiccation, it was concluded that the degree of dehydration reached after 75 min was not complete. Also, Billingham and Medawar[24,25] found that skin grafts from the rabbit's ear, with a water content of about 70 per cent, could survive the degree of desiccation represented by a final water content of 25 per cent, though higher degrees of dehydration were fatal.

For more complete surveys of the literature on the subject, the reader is referred to a comprehensive review by Meryman[326] and to the published proceedings of discussion meetings held in London (England) in 1954[505] and 1957[506] and in New York in 1959.[328]

Freezing and Thawing of Cell Strains

In 1954, Scherer and Hoogasian[476] reported experiments in which trypsinized suspensions of Earle's strain-L cells from the mouse and Gey's human strain HeLa were preserved successfully at $-60°$ to $-70°$ C for six and seven weeks, respectively, at the time of the report. Solutions of glycerol (5 per cent for L cells, 20 or 30 per cent for HeLa cells) that were prepared in Scherer's maintenance solution,[510] in Hanks's balanced salt solution, or in serum (horse serum for L cells, human serum for HeLa) gave approximately the same results. It was also found that the preservation of L cells was slightly better when freezing was performed in 1–1.5 hr rather than 3–5 min, whereas HeLa cells withstood both methods of freezing equally well. For both strains, thawing over periods of 1–2 min was less harmful than thawing over periods of 30–60 min. More recently, Scherer[475] reported that both strains could be recovered and propagated after four to five years' storage if the glycerol diluent had contained serum. But only those HeLa cells that had been frozen slowly remained viable. Also, although balanced salt solution was effective as a diluent for glycerol for three to twelve months, it failed to keep cells viable for four to five years.

Swim and his associates[498] made a careful comparison of various methods for the low-temperature storage of a variety of established cell lines (3–16 years *in vitro*) and newly isolated lines (one to five passages *in vitro*). The established lines included fibroblasts from mouse, rabbit, and man, Gey's strain HeLa, and deBruyn's MB-13 strain from the mouse. The newly isolated lines were derived from chick muscle, foreskin of neonatal infants, and human-embryo skin muscle. Some of the cell lines had been stored for three years.

For the low-temperature storage tests, $2–6 \times 10^6$ cells per ml were suspended in 13×100-mm Pyrex tubes in medium of the same composition as that used in their propagation, except that glycerol was added at levels of 5, 10, and 20 per cent, respectively. The pH of the glycerolated cell suspension was adjusted by gassing each tube with a mixture of 5 per cent CO_2, 21 per cent O_2, and 74 per cent N_2, immediately after which the tubes were sealed in a gas-oxygen flame and placed for freezing according to one of the following procedures: (1) the tubes were placed immediately in the dry-ice chest; (2) the tubes were stored at 4° C for 18 hr or for 1–6 hours, before being placed in the dry-ice chest; or (3) the tubes were frozen rapidly by rotating them in a mixture of dry ice and alcohol prior to storage in the dry-ice chest. *To determine the number of surviving cells*, tubes were removed periodically from the dry-ice chest and thawed immediately by plunging them into a water bath at 37° C. The moment the suspension had thawed, the tubes were opened and the cells washed twice in 10 ml of the medium in which they were to be incubated. After the cultures (in T-flasks) had been incubated for 18–24 hr, the medium was removed and the cells that remained adherent to the glass after the flasks had been rinsed once with fresh medium were counted by enumerating the nuclei (*see* p. 280). The values obtained were used in calculating the percentage of cells that survived low-temperature storage. On the basis of this and earlier experiments, the following conclusions were reached:

(1) The optimal concentration of glycerol differed for different strains, and ranged from 5–20 per cent by volume. Strains that have not previously been stored should be tested in more than one concentration of glycerol and checked for survival at frequent intervals.

(2) The more rapid freezing, with a mixture of dry ice and alcohol, was of questionable value for culture populations of mammalian cells, all of which survived when they were placed directly in the dry-ice chest without pretreatment with dry ice and alcohol. Only strain HeLa, and to a lesser extent strains L and MB-13, withstood the more rapid freezing procedure.

(3) Precooling at 4° C for 18 hr prior to storage at −70° C was satisfactory for some cells but not for others. Precooling at 4° C for 1–6 hr did not appear to alter the results obtained with any of the strains tested.

(4) The best results were always achieved when the cells were thawed in a water bath at 37° C, immediately after removal from the dry-ice chest.

(5) The best results were obtained with young cultures, that is, with cell populations that had not yet reached maximum density.

(6) The medium used for low-temperature storage should be of the same composition as the medium used in propagating the cells, plus the optimal concentration of glycerol. In any event, media containing protein constituents afford better protection than those without.

(7) Variations in the ability of cells to withstand freezing and storage were observed between strains of different origin as also between nutritive variants of the same parent strain.

(8) After one to three months' storage, neither the microscopic appearance of the thawed cells nor the rapidity with which they become attached to the glass are adequate criteria in attempting to predict the effect of longer storage. When the population is reduced from $2-6 \times 10^6$ to 2×10^4 viable cells per ml, either as the result of freezing and thawing or prolonged storage, it may be difficult to continue the strain indefinitely at 37° C.

Hauschka and his associates[228] preserve tumor cells and tissue-culture strains in a dry-ice-and-alcohol-slush bank at $-78°$ C (see p. 296). Tissue-culture cells are scraped from the glass with a rubber policeman, resuspended in fresh maintenance medium (medium 199 plus calf or horse serum plus penicillin) plus 10 per cent glycerol, and 1.0-ml aliquots are placed in 1.5-ml Pyrex ampules and heat sealed with a propane torch. Solid tumors are cut into small cubes fitting a 12-gauge trocar; and about 30 such pieces are placed in each ampule and covered with balanced salt solution plus 10 per cent glycerol. Ascites tumor cells are withdrawn from the host with a syringe, about 1.0 ml is placed in an ampule together with 0.1 ml of absolute glycerol, and the ampule is rolled between the hands for 2 min for thorough mixing. The sealed ampules are clipped temporarily to a nylon rod and immersed in a dry-ice–alcohol slush in a Dewar flask, from which they are later transferred to the storage cabinet. Once the ampules have been sealed, any appreciable delay at room temperature is avoided.

Slow Freezing at a Controlled Rate

Polge and Lovelock[396] found that the best survival of bull spermatozoa after freezing in 10 per cent glycerol occurred when the rate of cooling between 0° and −15° C did not exceed 2° per minute. Below −15° C, more rapid cooling was not harmful. Slow cooling to −15° C was accomplished by surrounding the ampule with a solution of 20 per cent glycerol in water. When the vessel containing this solution was immersed in a −79° C cooling bath, the temperature dropped slowly as water was frozen out until −15° C was reached; it then dropped rapidly to −79° C.

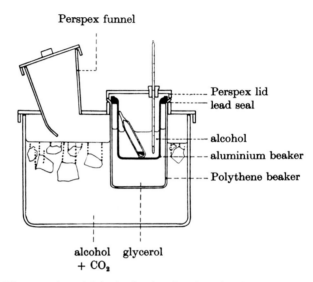

Perspex funnel

Perspex lid
lead seal
alcohol
aluminium beaker
Polythene beaker

alcohol   glycerol
+ CO₂

Fig. 87. Diagram of special device for slow freezing of cells and tissues. For description, see text. (T. Gibson.[183])

Eventually, Parkes and his associates[183] devised a system (Fig. 87) in which slow freezing could be accomplished more easily. The ampules are contained in an aluminum beaker and covered with alcohol to ensure an even transfer of heat. The aluminum beaker is supported in a plastic beaker, which contains 20 per cent glycerol solution. This double freezing vessel is tightly covered with a plastic lid and is held suspended in a dry-ice-and-alcohol bath by means of a larger lid that covers the bath. The lid covering the bath also has a port for the addition of dry ice. The freezing procedure is as follows: The freezing vessel is charged with glycerol (20 per cent) solution, placed in a refrigerator and cooled to between 2° and 5° C. Bull semen treated with glycerol (10 per cent) at the same temperature is placed in sealed ampules in the inner container of the freezing vessel. The ampules are covered with cool, clean alcohol, and the freezing vessel is suspended in the bath of alcohol and dry ice. Any time after 1 hr has elapsed, the ampules may be transferred directly to the permanent storage bath at −79° C.

Stulberg and his associates[495] tested two methods of slow freezing on nineteen human cell strains, two of which were fibroblastic, the others epithelial. According to the first method, the ampules were immersed in an ice-alcohol bath at approximately 0° C, and the temperature was lowered to −10° C over a period of 30 min. The ampules were then stored at −20° C until their contents were solidly frozen, after which they were transferred to a dry-ice chest for permanent storage at −70° C. According to the second method, use was made of a mechanical slow-freeze apparatus,* by means of which it was possible to lower the temperature at a controlled rate of 1° C per min to −25° C, at which point the temperature was lowered quickly to −70° C for permanent storage. While both methods of slow freezing gave good results for the epithelial cells, it was possible by these procedures to preserve also the fibroblast strains, which had always been killed by faster methods of freezing. In these experiments, the cell suspensions were diluted to approximately 5×10^5 cells per ml, glycerol was added to 5 per cent by volume, and 1 ml aliquots of the suspensions were heat sealed in glass ampules.

Low-Temperature Storage Equipment

There are at least five types of low-temperature storage cabinets in use: (1) conventional dry-ice boxes; (2) cabinets in which dry ice serves as the refrigerant and 95 per cent alcohol as a heat-transfer agent; (3) cabinets in which the consumption of dry ice is reduced by combining intermittent periods of electric refrigeration, regulated by a time clock; (4) electric refrigerators in which alcohol is used as a heat-transfer agent and in which dry ice may be used in the event of power failure or mechanical breakdown; and (5) electric refrigerators provided with emergency power supply and a stand-by compressor that cuts in automatically in the event of mechanical failure.

In the author's laboratory, cell strains are preserved in a conventional dry-ice box with a stainless-steel liner and three compartments

* Canal Industrial Corporation, Bethesda 14, Md.

separated by reinforced stainless-steel partitions. The end compartments are for dry ice, the middle one for the storage of cells contained
in heat-sealed, 6-ml Color-Break ampules (Neutraglass; Kimble
Glass Co., Toledo 1, Ohio). The tubes are stored in four vertical
stainless-steel drawers, each consisting of a series of bins accessible

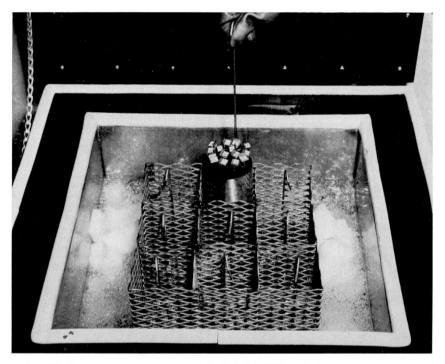

Fig. 88. Low-temperature storage unit (Model COD-A9) developed by American
Breeders Service (Chicago 10, Ill.) for use with solid CO_2 and alcohol. For more complete description, see text. (Sub-Zero Freezer Company, Madison, Wis.)

from one side of the drawer. In addition to adhesive tape label
bearing the date and identification of the sample, each tube carries
a color code consisting of one or more strips of colored plastic tape ($\frac{1}{4}$
in. wide).* All labels are fixed to the tubes as ring bands with
overlapping ends to prevent accidental removal during storage.

The American Breeders Service has developed a special cabinet
(Model COD-A9; Fig. 88) for the storage and transportation of frozen

* Available in eight colors from the Minnesota Mining and Manufacturing Company,
Minneapolis, Minn.

bull semen. The cabinet is designed for use with dry ice as the refrigerant and alcohol as a heat-transfer agent. The dry ice is confined to a space surrounding nine central sections, which are constructed of wire mesh to allow passage of alcohol. Each of the nine central sections accommodates a cylindrical canister ($2\frac{3}{4}$-in. diameter) in which the ampules of semen are stored. The ampules are affixed end to end to channeled metal strips that are referred to as "racks" and are $\frac{3}{8}$ in. wide and $11\frac{1}{2}$ in. long. Each canister accommodates 14 racks, each of which holds six ampules. The racks are identified at the top with code numbers and are slipped into individual tubes for greater protection. The size and other characteristics of the cabinet are as follows:

Dimensions of cabinet (outside)	$25 \times 25 \times 22\frac{1}{2}$ in. (high)
Stainless-steel liner (leak-proof)	$17 \times 17 \times 15\frac{1}{2}$ in. (high)
Number of ampules accommodated	756 (1.5-ml)
Amount of alcohol required for initial filling, approximately	52 l
Amount of dry ice required for initial filling, approximately	75 lb
Temperature maintained during holding time, not less than	$-79°$ C
Temperature holding time at ambient temperature 20° C, after initial filling and without refilling, approximately	6 days
Temperature holding time at ambient temperature 40° C, after initial filling and without refilling, approximately	5 days
Daily consumption of dry ice at ambient temperature 20° C, approximately	$11\frac{1}{2}$ lb
Daily consumption of dry ice at ambient temperature 40° C, approximately	14 lb

The American Breeders Service has also developed an electric refrigerator (Cincinnati Sub-Zero Model SA-120-3),* so designed that dry ice can be used as the refrigerant to provide emergency protection in the event of power failure or mechanical breakdown. Alcohol is used as a heat-transfer agent, whether or not dry ice is used. The size of the inner tank and the capacity of the racks are the same as in Model COD-A9. When dry ice is not used, the capacity of the cabinet may be increased from 756 ampules to 2100 by using the dry-ice section for additional canisters. The temperature range without dry ice is adjustable from $-57°$ to $-93°$ C.

* Supplied by Cincinnati Sub-Zero Products, Cincinnati 29, Ohio.

Craigie[80] devised a large, heavily insulated, low-temperature cabinet (for the preservation of tumor strains) that also combines dry-ice and electrical refrigeration. But instead of depending primarily on electric power, he uses intermittent periods of electrical refrigeration (2 hr in every 8), regulated by a time clock, as a means of reducing

Fig. 89. Interior view of an alcohol–CO_2-ice storage unit, with a capacity of 1800 frozen samples held by wire clips on vertically sliding canes. Note code marks on three samples raised from refrigerant. (T. S. Hauschka *et al.*[228])

the consumption of dry ice. The cabinet contains five compartments, three of which are for the storage of dry ice and, sandwiched between them, two for the storage of cells and tissues. A heavy, insulated cover, common to all compartments, is raised and lowered by means of a chain hoist, and the individual compartments are further protected by canvas-covered insulating blankets.

Hauschka and his associates[228] operate a dependable dry-ice-and-alcohol storage cabinet with a total capacity of 1800 immediately accessible, 1.5-ml ampules and a weekly dry-ice consumption of about 75 lb, or less than one quarter of that required for an ordinary dry-ice box of the same capacity. This unit (Fig. 89), which is based on the design of the American Breeders Service Model COD-A9 (*see* p. 294), consists of a glass-wool insulated, stainless-steel dry-ice storage cabinet containing a waterproof 14-gauge stainless-steel tank (16 in. wide, 28 in. long by 20 in. high) that is tightly surrounded by an insulating layer of powdered Colfoam (Colton Chemical Co., Cleveland 14, Ohio) covered with Plexiglas. The tank contains an insert, open at the top and bottom, that is fabricated of perforated stainless steel and allows about 2 in. clearance between itself and the tank wall. Commercially available dry-ice slabs fit loosely into this space all around the insert, which serves as a fence to prevent floating pieces of ice from damaging the ampules. Twenty-five gallons of 95 per cent alcohol bring the coolant level with the rim of the rectangular fence. The ampules are attached by clips to nylon rods that stand upright in ten racks, each rack sliding on two vertical tracks fixed to opposite sides of the tank. Each rack accommodates 36 of these rods to each of which five ampules may be attached. The slush has the consistency of glycerol. Occasionally, about once a month, approximately one fifth of the alcohol in the tank is siphoned off and immediately replaced with prechilled ($-78°$ C) fresh, 95 per cent alcohol. The dry ice is replenished three times a week. The storage unit is accommodated in a small room equipped with an inexpensive dehumidifier to reduce condensation and icing around the lid of the box.

Note: Investigators planning to install low temperature storage equipment are advised to give serious thought to the use of liquid nitrogen, which has many advantages over dry ice. Also, it was recently reported (H. T. Meryman, 12th Annual Meeting of the Tissue Culture Association, Detroit, Mich., 1961) that thawing from the frozen state should be as rapid as possible and that polyvinyl pyrrolidone is most effective in lessening thermal shock if it is added to the frozen material at the time of thawing.

XIX

Histological Procedures

THE present chapter is not intended as a compendium of the innumerable staining procedures that have been applied to tissue cultures. Instead, a description will be given of a few typical procedures that have been found to be satisfactory. From these, the investigator may acquire a certain degree of assurance in handling culture material and can discover some of the changes that are required in adapting the procedures of histology and histochemistry[9, 56, 74, 174, 194, 390] to particular problems.

In general, cells and tissues cultivated on coverslips or on the inner surfaces of tubes, flasks, bottles, and Petri dishes can be fixed and stained most easily *in situ*, but they can also be separated from the glass and embedded and sectioned for electron microscopy. Total preparations or serial sections can be made of cells and tissues cultivated in a plasma coagulum, and serial sections are easily made of tissue fragments cultivated in fluid medium or by the sponge-matrix procedure of Leighton (*see* pages 170, 193 and 195). Cells propagated in suspension can be concentrated, fixed, and stained with minimal distortion if slide preparations are required or if it is desired to section them for electron microscopy. Also, efficient methods have been developed for obtaining well-spread metaphase plates of cells in cultures. A brief description will be given of at least one method that has been applied in each of these situations.

Fixing Reagents

RINGER-FORMOL

	Parts
Ringer's solution	9
Neutral formalin (40 per cent solution)	1

Formaldehyde is a gas and is dispensed as a 40 per cent aqueous solution known as formaldehyde U.S.P., formalin, or formol. Four per cent formaldehyde (10 per cent formalin or formol) is the strength ordinarily recommended for fixation. It is prepared by diluting commercial formalin 1:9 with saline. Before it is diluted, the commercial material is neutralized by shaking with powdered calcium or magnesium carbonate, which is left in the storage bottle.

Cultures embedded in plasma clots may be fixed with two or three changes of *Ringer-formol* (at 37° C) for a total period of at least 1 hr. If necessary, this fixing reagent may be left on the culture for a much longer period, even for days. After fixation the cultures are washed thoroughly in running water, then in several changes of distilled water. Washing at the tap for 30 min to 1 hr is usually sufficient for the average clot. If the cells are cultivated directly on glass in a fluid medium, the period of fixation may be reduced to 10 min. Where the fixing fluid may wash away too many of the cells, the material is treated with *formalin vapor*. Thereafter the treatment is the same as with Ringer-formol except that washing at the tap is replaced by changing the water frequently with a pipette.

BOUIN'S FLUID

	Parts
Picric acid (saturated aqueous solution)	15
Neutral formalin (40 per cent solution)	5
Glacial acetic acid	1

Bouin's fluid keeps well, has considerable penetrating power, and can be followed by almost any stain. It is suitable for either whole mounts or sectioned material. Because picric acid serves as a desirable mordant, it need not be completely washed away. Plasma cultures are fixed for ½ hr, fluid cultures for a shorter period. The preparations are then passed through several changes of 80 per cent alcohol and stored in this reagent until they are stained. Prolonged seasoning (several days to several weeks) in 80 per cent alcohol improves their staining qualities.

Zenker's Fluid

Parts

Stock solution
$$\begin{cases} \text{Potassium bichromate} & 25 \ \text{Gm} \\ \text{Bichloride of mercury (crystals)} & 40 \ \text{Gm} \\ \text{Water} & 1000 \ \ \text{ml} \end{cases} \quad 19$$

Glacial acetic acid   1

(The first-named substances are brought into solution by heating. The glacial acetic acid is added just before use.)

Zenker-formol (Helly's Fluid)

	Parts
Zenker's stock solution	18
Neutral formalin (40 per cent solution)	2

(The formalin is added just before use.)

Zenker's fluid and *Zenker-formol (Helly's fluid)* should not be used for total plasma preparations. These reagents leave a large amount of precipitate on the surface of the clot and render it granular and opaque. They may be used, however, when the cultures are subsequently to be embedded and sectioned. For this purpose, Zenker-formol is preferable to ordinary Zenker's fluid. Depending upon the size and thickness of the culture, the time required for fixation in Zenker-formol will vary from 30 min to 2 hr or longer. After fixation, the cultures are washed for 1–6 hr in running water and dehydrated in the usual manner. A few drops of iodine are added to the 70 per cent alcohol to remove any bichloride of mercury that may remain in the tissues. Otherwise, crystals may form in the sections.

Acetic Alcohol Fixatives

Acetic acid preserves chromosomes and lessens the hardening effect of alcohol. Alcohol is not a fixative for chromatin and is omitted from fixatives for the Golgi complex and mitochondria, but it does not interfere with cytoplasmic staining. Formalin lessens the hardening effect of alcohol and, by neutralizing basic groups, gives proteins a particular affinity for basic dyes.[9] Formalin also preserves mitochondria and lipoids.

A mixture of acetic acid and alcohol destroys cytoplasm but does not greatly affect the nucleus; it is recommended especially for chromosome preparations. A mixture of acetic acid, alcohol, and chloroform (Carnoy's fluid) is recommended for nuclear detail; but prolonged fixation should be avoided. A mixture of acetic acid, alcohol, and formalin (Kahle's fluid) is recommended for the Feulgen stain.[97]

Acetic Alcohol

	Parts
Glacial acetic acid	1
Absolute alcohol	3

Carnoy's Fluid

	Parts
Glacial acetic acid	1
Absolute alcohol	6
Chloroform (reagent grade)	3

Kahle's Fluid

	Parts
Glacial acetic acid	1
Alcohol (95 per cent)	15
Formalin	6
Distilled water	30

Fixation and Staining of Cells Cultivated in Fluid Media

Considerable care must be taken in staining fluid cultures in which the cells are attached directly to the glass (Fig. 90). Under these conditions cells are extremely susceptible to violent treatment. As a rule it is desirable to flush out the culture containers with two or three changes of warm fixing solution (e.g., Ringer-formol) and to leave them inverted and filled with the fixative, in the incubator, so that any debris will fall away from the cells. Subsequent washing is done with a pipette

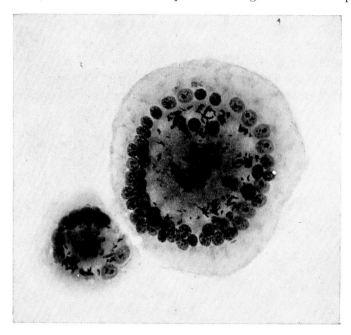

FIG. 90. Giant cells in a flask culture of chicken leukocytes in fluid medium, infected with avian tubercle bacilli. Large aggregations of ingested bacilli are completely surrounded by nuclei. Harris's hematoxylin and Ziehl-Neelson carbolfuchsin after Ringer-formol. (R. C. Parker, unpublished experiments, 1935.) × 520.

rather than with running water from the tap. Tube cultures are fixed and stained in an upright position. To retard the fading of delicate stains (such as Giemsa), flask cultures are finally filled with oil of cedarwood, Florida extra, instead of with xylene. Oil of cedarwood of the immersion type hardens on exposure to air, whereas oil of cedarwood, Florida extra, remains fluid.

HEMATOXYLIN PROCEDURE FOR FLUID CULTURES

1. Before fixation, wash culture in several changes of warm, balanced salt solution.

2. Fix overnight in Ringer-formol.

3. Rinse several times with distilled water.

4. Stain ½–1½ hr in full strength Delafield's alum hematoxylin. Overstained cultures may be destained in acid alcohol (*see* p. 314). Understained cultures may be rinsed with distilled water and stained again.

5. Wash three times in distilled water.

6. Wash with dilute ammonia water (*see* p. 313) until the tissues have become deep blue in color.

7. Wash in two changes of distilled water.

8. If cells are in a tube, flask, or bottle, fill container with 50 per cent glycerine, and close with a rubber stopper. If cells are on a coverslip or slide, dehydrate by rinsing twice, quickly but thoroughly (without allowing the preparation to dry), in each of the following: pure acetone; acetone (2 parts), xylene (1 part); acetone (1 part), xylene (2 parts); and pure xylene. Then, mount in Canada balsam or Euparal (Flatters & Garnett, Ltd., Manchester 13, Eng.).

Delafield's alum hematoxylin: Keep on hand a 10 per cent stock solution of hematoxylin in absolute ethanol so that a supply of ripened hematoxylin will always be available. To 360 ml of saturated aqueous ammonium alum, add 40 ml of the stock solution of ripened hematoxylin, close neck of container with a cotton plug, and leave in a warm light place for four to seven days. At the end of this period add 100 ml of C.P. methyl alcohol and 100 ml of C.P. glycerine, and allow the mixture to stand for another four to seven days. Store in a cool dark place, and filter each time before using. If ripened hematoxylin is not available, let the first mixture stand for two weeks and the final mixture for six to eight weeks before using.

MAY-GRÜNWALD-GIEMSA STAIN FOR FLUID CULTURES

This stain differentiates DNA-protein, which stains red-purple, from RNA-protein, which stains blue. Ribonuclease treatment (*see* p. 310) may be used for control preparations.[244]

1. Wash in three rinses of warm balanced salt solution.

2. Fix for 5 min in absolute methanol.

3. Stain for 10 min in May-Grünwald solution.

4. Stain for 20 min in Giemsa solution (diluted 1:10 with distilled water).

5. If cells are in a tube, flask, or bottle, fill container with 50 per cent glycerine, and close with a stopper. If cells are on a slide or coverslip, dehydrate (*see* p. 303) and mount in Canada balsam or Euparal.

PROCEDURE FOR FLATTENING CHROMOSOMES IN CULTURES WITHOUT MANUAL SQUASHING

Rothfels and Siminovitch[456] have devised a method for obtaining well-spread metaphase plates of mammalian cells (Fig. 91) without recourse to manual squashing. When used in conjunction with procedures developed earlier for arresting mitosis at metaphase with colchicine[276,277] and for spreading the chromosomes with hypotonic fluids,[240,241,307] preparations are obtained that facilitate rapid analyses of chromosome complements. The essential part of the treatment is the complete air drying of films of cells following conventional fixation. The drying does not impair the appearance of the chromosomes and results in flattening of dividing nuclei without chromosome scattering. Usually, the cells are cultivated on slides in 10-cm Petri dishes accommodated in a humidified incubator flushed continuously with 5 per cent CO_2 in air (*see* p. 184). Trypsinized cell suspensions from freshly explanted tissues may be introduced into the Petri dishes, or the dishes may be inoculated with cells harvested from stationary cultures or from cells propagated in suspension (*see* Chap. XII). The directions for staining follow:

(1) Dilute the medium in the Petri dish (about 12 ml) with four to six times its volume of distilled water that is introduced around the edge of the dish very slowly. (It should take about 10 min to add 50 ml.)

(2) Ten minutes after the distilled water has been added, fix in acetic-alcohol (*see* p. 301) for 10 min.

(3) Remove slide from dish, clean its under surface, and allow the cell layer to dry completely at room temperature.

(4) Stain with a few drops of acetoorcein and place coverslip on slide. If slide begins to dry out while it is being studied, more stain may be introduced under edge of coverslip; or the coverslip may be rimmed with Vaseline, Krönig's cement (George T. Gurr, Ltd., London S.W. 6, Eng.), or paraffin. The stain is prepared by boiling 4 per cent orcein (natural, G. T. Gurr, Ltd.) in 60 per cent glacial

acetic acid for ½ hr in a reflux condenser with the boiling flask immersed in a water bath.* Just before use, small amounts are filtered (Whatman No. 50 paper) as required.

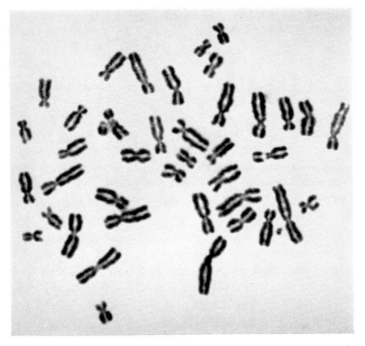

FIG. 91. A slightly imperfect metaphase plate of a nucleus from a Petri-dish culture of freshly explanted, colchicine-treated monkey-kidney cells fixed in acetic alcohol, stained with acetoorcein, mounted in Euparal, and photographed three years later. Photographed with bright-field optics on Kodak Micro-File (panchromatic) film, with a combination of filters giving a transmission of 520–560 mμ. × 2065.

If it is desired to arrest cell divisions at metaphase by means of colchicine, 0.01 ml of 0.1 per cent colchicine (crystalline, distributed in 3 ml ampules of 3 mg each, in isotonic saline, by Laboratoires Houdé, Paris X, France) may be added to the culture medium (12–15 ml) about 18 hr before the slides are to be stained. By arresting spindle formation, colchicine gives an increased number of metaphase plates;

* J. H. Tjio and A. Levan (*An. Aula Dei 3:* 225, 1954) prepare 2 per cent orcein in 45 per cent acetic acid by dissolving 2 Gm of orcein in 45 ml of boiling glacial acetic acid. When this solution has cooled, 55 ml of distilled water are added, and the solution is filtered.

and sister chromatids become separated sufficiently (Fig. 91) to disclose the position of centromeres.

If it is desired to prepare stained slides from cell populations being cultivated in suspension in test tubes rotated at 50 r.p.m. (see p. 199), colchicine (if required) should be added to the medium while the cells are still in the exponential phase of growth. Twelve to eighteen hours later, the cells are concentrated by mild centrifugation and the pellet dispersed in 10 ml of quarter-strength balanced salt solution. After 5–8 min, the cells are again concentrated by mild centrifugation, and the moist pellet is fixed with acetic alcohol. After 1 min, the pellet is broken up with a pipette and the cells are transferred to a slide, air dried, and stained.

Axelrad and McCulloch[8] took advantage of the tendency of cells to lose their attachment to glass during mitosis by shaking them free (into a hypotonic medium) 18–24 hr after the cultures had been treated with colchicine. When the loose cells were concentrated by centrifugation, fixed, placed on a slide, and stained with acetoorcein, 50 per cent or more of the cells were usually found to be in colchicine metaphase.

Harnden[214] modified the procedure of Rothfels and Siminovitch by introducing a 2-sec interval of fixation with 2 per cent osmic-acid vapor before final fixation in acetic alcohol. The osmic-acid treatment served to keep the cell membranes intact and to reduce the scattering of chromosomes, but if it was continued too long chromosome spreading was impaired.

Squash Technique for Chromosomes

Although the air-dry method just described can be applied to coverslips, such as those removed from Leighton tubes (see p. 19), it is sometimes desirable to prepare them by the squash method, as follows:

(1) Add about 3 ml of distilled water very slowly to medium (1 ml) in culture tube.

(2) After 10 min, replace fluid with acetic-alcohol fixing solution.

(3) After 10 min, decant fluid, remove coverslip from tube, and clean its under surface.

(4) Invert coverslip over small drop of acetoorcein on a slide and press gently between layers of bibulous paper.

(5) Seal for temporary study or make the slide permanent.

To Make Chromosome Preparations Permanent

(1) Quick-freeze[73] the stained preparation by placing it on CO_2-ice or by dipping it in liquid nitrogen.

(2) Remove coverslip by prying it loose with a razor blade.

(3) While the preparation is still frozen, dehydrate by placing it in 95 per cent alcohol.

(4) Drain off alcohol and, without allowing preparation to dry, mount in Euparal.

Parasynchronous Division of Cells in Culture

It is often desirable to obtain an abundance of dividing cells in cultures without resorting to the use of colchicine. Newton and Wildy[362] accomplished this with HeLa cells by incubating them at 37° C for 24 hr after subculture, placing them at 4° C for 1 hr, and then returning them to the incubator. Few if any divisions occurred during the next 17 hr, after which as many as 95 per cent of the cells divided within an hour. Although further divisions were not observed for 18 hr, the most of the cells then divided again. The term *parasynchronous* was used because the cells did not exhibit a *complete* synchrony of the events of mitosis.

Feulgen Method with Fast Green for DNA

The Feulgen stain is used as a specific test for DNA. In this reaction, a red-purple color is produced when a reduced (colorless) form of basic fuchsin is brought into contact with chromatin that has been subjected to hydrolysis with HCl. It is thought that the chromatic form is reconstituted when the reduced dye combines with the aldehyde radical freed from DNA by hydrolysis. The nucleolar core and the RNA in the cytoplasm remain unstained by the fuchsin. The method given here is recommended by Duryee.[97] Two reagents are required.

Reagent A (Schiff): Over 1 Gm of basic fuchsin, pour 100 ml of boiling distilled water, cool solution to 60° C, filter, and add 2 Gm of potassium or sodium metabisulfite and 20 ml of N HCl. After allowing the solution to bleach for 24 hr at room temperature in a dark place, add 0.3 Gm of activated charcoal. The whole is shaken vigorously for 1 min and then filtered through coarse filter paper. Store (well stoppered) in amber glass at 4° C.

Reagent B: Make up a fresh sulfurous acid solution by adding 5 ml of N HCl to a solution of 0.5 Gm of sodium or potassium metabisulfite in 100 ml of distilled water. Because this solution deteriorates rapidly, it should be prepared just before use.

Staining Procedure

(1) Fix for 30 min in Kahle's fluid (*see* p. 301).

(2) Place in 70 per cent alcohol, 1 hr; in triethyl phosphate (Eastman Kodak Co., Rochester, N.Y.), ½ min; in 95 per cent alcohol (No. 1), ½ min; in 95 per cent alcohol (No. 2), ½ min; and in distilled water until the slide is no longer streaked. (At this point, any aqueous stain may be applied.)

(3) Feulgen reaction: Place in N HCl (No. 1) at room temperature, 1 min; hydrolyze in N HCl (No. 2) at 60° C, 10 min; place in N HCl (No. 3) at room temperature, 1 min.

(4) Stain in Reagent A, 10 min.

(5) Three changes of 2 min each in fresh Reagent B.

(6) Running tap water, 5 min.

(7) Counterstain in Fast Green FCF (0.2 per cent in 95 per cent alcohol), 5 min.

(8) Dehydrate and clear as follows: 95 per cent alcohol (No. 1), ½ min; 95 per cent alcohol (No. 2), ½ min; triethyl phosphate, ½ min; xylene, 3 min; xylene (fresh), 3 min.

(9) Mount in Canada balsam, Euparal, or Permount (Fisher Scientific Co., Pittsburgh, Pa.).

For treatment with deoxyribonuclease (DNAse), Leblond and his associates (C. P. Leblond, personal communication) incubate slides for 24 hr at 37° C in a solution containing 0.05 mg crystallized DNAse (Worthington Biochemical Corp., Freehold, N.J.) per ml of Tris buffer (with a 0.2M concentration of magnesium sulfate) at a pH of 5.7. Tris buffer without magnesium has a pH of 6.1 (see Quay[422]).

Leuchtenberger and her associates[275] have shown that when very small fragments of human tissue are fixed with 1 per cent OsO_4 buffered at pH 7.3–7.5 with 0.028M Na acetate–Na veronal buffer (Palade's method[369]), the staining of paraffin sections by basic and acidic dyes results in a distinct color difference between chromatin and cytoplasm. Furthermore, the Feulgen reaction can also be carried out successfully on these sections; and OsO_4-fixed, Feulgen-stained sections are especially suitable for microspectrophotometric determinations of DNA in individual nuclei.

METHYL-GREEN–PYRONIN-Y METHOD FOR RNA AND DNA

Brachet[34] devised an indirect cytological method for demonstrating RNA, which depends on the specific depolymerization of RNA by the enzyme ribonuclease (RNAse). Material staining red with pyronin and removable by incubating the sections with RNAse is considered to be RNA; that which is not so removable is not. The staining procedure given here is one reported by Long and Taylor.[292]

Preparation of Methyl-Green–Pyronin-Y Solution[511]

(1) *Acetate buffer solution (0.2M pH 4.2).* Use analytical reagents: glacial acetic acid, M.W. 60.05; sodium acetate, M.W. 136.09. For 0.2M acetic acid: 1.15 ml acetic acid + 98.85 ml distilled water. For 0.2M sodium acetate: 2.72 Gm sodium acetate in 100 ml distilled water. Mix 75 ml of 0.2M acetic acid with 25 ml of 0.2M sodium acetate for pH 4.16. Adjust pH with sodium hydroxide or acetic acid.

(2) *Purification of methyl green in acetate buffer.* Wash 0.5 per cent methyl green (certified) in acetate buffer with chloroform in a separatory funnel until all violet color (a common impurity) has been removed, and let solution stand in an open flask overnight.

(3) *Purified methyl-green–pyronin-Y solution.* Mix 100 ml purified methyl green in pH 4.2 acetate buffer with 0.1 Gm pyronin Y (certified). Solution may be refrigerated in glass-stoppered bottles and reused for months, after bringing it each time to room temperature.

Staining Procedure

(1) Fix slide preparations in Kahle's fluid (*see* p. 301) and bring to water as directed on page 308.

(2) Stain in methyl-green–pyronin solution for 1 hr, and continue treatment by handling one slide at a time.

(3) Plunge quickly into distilled water, renewed frequently.

(4) Blot quickly with No. 1 filter paper.

(5) Plunge immediately into a mixture of tertiary butyl alcohol (3 parts) and absolute ethyl alcohol (1 part) $\frac{1}{2}$ min with continuous agitation.

(6) Rinse quickly in xylene.

(7) Xylene, two changes, 5 min each.

(8) Mount in Permount or clarite, and clean forceps carefully before proceeding with next slide.

Results: DNA stains green, bluish green, or purplish green; RNA stains red.

Confirmation of the RNA requires control slides treated with RNAse. Leblond and his associates (C. P. Leblond, personal communication) incubate slides for 4 hr at 40° C in a solution containing 1 mg crystallized salt-free RNAse (Worthington) per ml of distilled water adjusted to pH 6.1 with Tris buffer.

Fixation and Staining of Plasma Cultures

Although plasma (or fibrinogen) cultures are now used only occasionally, for particular purposes (*see* Chaps. IX and X), they are discussed here because they require special handling. Regardless of whether the cultures are originally prepared in tubes, flasks, bottles, or on coverslips, it is usually possible to fix and stain them as whole mounts (Fig. 92B) or to embed and section them before staining (Fig. 92A). Because the fibrin of the coagulum has a tendency to overstain, most histological procedures have to be modified somewhat if cultures grown in plasma or fibrinogen clots are to be stained *in situ*. Even with a thin coagulum, it is usually difficult to obtain the necessary contrast between cells and medium. Sometimes the stain is almost completely removed from the cells during the process of dehydration, which must be greatly prolonged because of the density of the coagulum. When cultures are sectioned, these difficulties are eliminated. As already indicated on page 158, it is easy to remove plasma cultures intact from the flasks prior to fixation. Or plasma cultures may be removed from the flasks during the early stages of fixation before the clot has hardened.[115]

In making whole mounts of plasma cultures grown on coverslips, it is desirable to rinse the cultures in several changes of warm, balanced

Fig. 92. (A) Stained section of 24-hr coverslip (hanging-drop) culture of fibroblasts from chick-embryo bone in homologous plasma and embryo extract; 8th passage. Hematoxylin-eosin after Zenker-formol. (A. Fischer and R. C. Parker.[159]) × 58. (B) Marginal area of a 48-hr coverslip (hanging-drop) culture of fibroblasts from chick-embryo skeletal muscle in homologous plasma and embryo extract; 12th passage. Hematoxylin after Ringer-formol. (R. C. Parker.[371]) × 175.

salt solution before fixation. The various procedures may be carried out conveniently in Columbia staining dishes in which the cultures can be rinsed, fixed, and stained while held in a vertical position (Fig. 31). The staining is improved if the preparations are stored after fixation for several days or even weeks in 80 per cent alcohol. Eventually, the stained cultures are mounted face down on a glass slide with neutral Canada balsam or some other mounting medium. When cultures are grown on mica coverslips instead of on glass, they are mounted somewhat differently, in order to reduce the optical interference of the mica. After the cultures have been stained and cleared, the mica sheets are split with a sharp knife or razor blade to leave only a thin supporting membrane. The mica surrounding the culture is then trimmed away with scissors, and the remaining square is mounted on a glass slide, culture side up, with a drop of Canada balsam between the slide and the mica. After a second drop of balsam has been placed on the culture, the preparation is covered with a thin glass coverslip. Lead weights are applied during the final stages of drying.

In making whole preparations of plasma cultures grown in flasks and tubes, both the fixing and staining may be done *in situ*. Otherwise the coagulum may be removed from its container after preliminary fixation, but before it has completely hardened. When flask cultures are stained *in situ*, the flasks are kept with the culture side up so that any precipitate formed will not settle on the cells. Fluids that do not pour readily may be withdrawn with a pipette; or the surface tension of the fluid may be altered by adding a drop or two of alcohol or acetone. Under no circumstances should the flasks be shaken. Any washing may be done at the tap by leading glass-tipped rubber tubing directly from the water line into the neck of the flask. The flow should be extremely moderate. Eventually the flasks are filled with oil of cedarwood, Florida extra, and fitted with corks. The corks are inserted very loosely to ensure against breakage resulting from expansion of the fluid with changes in temperature. For the same reason, a small air space is left just beneath the cork. Rubber stoppers are never used for this purpose.

To reduce the thickness of the preparations, Cohen and Waymouth[70] dried plasma cultures for 24–48 hr in an incubator after fixation and washing. After drying they can be stained with hematoxylin, dehydrated, cleared, and mounted. Because dried preparations are unusually thin, they can be dehydrated and cleared in less time than is usually required.

In the preparation of flask cultures for embedding and sectioning, care is taken to avoid mutilating the cells. Cultures grown in a plasma or fibrinogen clot that is unusually thin should have a fresh coagulum superimposed on the first a few hours before the cultures are fixed. As already indicated, the cultures may be partially fixed before they are removed from the flasks. Otherwise, they may be removed from the flasks before fixation (*see* p. 158). The excess plasma surrounding the culture is cut away with a sharp knife and the parts to be preserved are re-embedded in a plasma coagulum on a glass slide to facilitate handling. After the new coagulum has become firm, the slide is dropped into the fixing fluid. The subsequent treatment is the same as for coverslip cultures that are to be sectioned (*see* p. 315).

HEMATOXYLIN (HARRIS'S) STAIN FOR WHOLE PLASMA CULTURES

1. After the cultures have been fixed in Helly's, Zenker's or Bouin's fluid, and washed, fill the flasks with a very dilute solution of Harris's alum hematoxylin (2–3 drops in 10 ml distilled water) and let them stand overnight. If coverslip preparations are being stained, the hematoxylin may be placed in Columbia staining dishes. Care should be taken to stain progressively and not to overstain. With a thick clot, the removal of stain is not only difficult to control but usually renders the color unstable. The stain may be removed, if necessary, with 0.5 per cent acid alcohol; the culture is then washed thoroughly at the tap. The blue color of the hematoxylin may also be restored by treating the culture with very dilute ammonia water (one drop of the strong commercial solution in about 50 ml of water). This treatment is again followed by thorough washing at the tap.

2. Wash thoroughly in running water until both the culture and the coagulum have become bright blue in color; this may take 30–60 min, or longer.

3. When an eosin counterstain is used, rinse the culture thoroughly in distilled water, then place in a 0.5 per cent solution of aqueous eosin for 5–10 min according to the intensity desired. After formalin fixation, tissues do not stain readily with eosin, hence a higher concentration or a longer staining period is required.

4. Dehydrate with 95 per cent and absolute alcohols. Each alcohol is left on the culture until convection currents are no longer discernible. If eosin has been used, the steps should be made as rapidly as possible.

5. Clear in the following acetone-xylene mixtures:

> Acetone, 95 per cent; xylene, 5 per cent
> Acetone, 70 per cent; xylene, 30 per cent
> Acetone, 30 per cent; xylene, 70 per cent
> Pure xylene (two or three changes)

Let each mixture penetrate the coagulum thoroughly. If the alcohol steps have been abbreviated due to the presence of eosin, a prolonged treatment with acetone-xylene will be necessary to insure both complete dehydration and adequate clearing. Coverslip cultures can now be mounted; flask cultures are filled with oil of cedarwood, Florida extra, and closed with loose-fitting corks.

Harris's Alum Hematoxylin

Hematoxylin crystals	2 Gm
95 per cent alcohol	20 ml
(Dissolve the hematoxylin in the alcohol)	

Ammonium alum	45 Gm
Distilled water	400 ml

Dissolve the alum in the water by heating, and then add the hematoxylin solution. Place the mixture in a 2-l flask, and bring it rapidly to a boil. To this add 1 Gm of mercuric oxide. The solution will boil very violently and will at once assume a dark purple color. Cool immediately by plunging the flask into a basin of cold water. After cooling, filter and keep in a well-stoppered bottle. This solution, which is now ready for use, will keep for several months. Although the addition of glacial acetic acid up to about 4 per cent increases the precision of the nuclear staining, it renders the solution unstable.

Acid Alcohol

	ml
70 per cent alcohol	100
Hydrochloric acid, concentrated	5

MURRAY'S MODIFICATION OF MASSON'S TRICHROME STAIN FOR WHOLE COVERSLIP PREPARATIONS*

1. Fix in Bouin's or Zenker's fluid.

2. Treat Zenker-fixed cultures with a weak solution of iodine (e.g., 1:15 or 1:20 dilution of tincture of iodine) for 5 min, rinse with water, place for a few minutes in a 5 per cent solution of sodium thiosulfate and wash 5–10 min in running water.

3. Store as long as possible (several days to several weeks) in 80 per cent alcohol. Before staining, rinse quickly in distilled water.

4. Stain ½ hr in acid fuchsin–ponceau mixture (0.9 Gm ponceau de xylidine,† 0.1 Gm acid fuchsin, 1.0 ml glacial acetic acid, 100 ml distilled water; filtered) and rinse quickly in distilled water.

5. Differentiate in 1 per cent aqueous phosphomolybdic acid, 15 min to 1 hr.

6. Drain and stain 1 min in ½ to ⅓ strength anilin blue (2.5 per cent anilin blue in 2.5 per cent glacial acetic acid), and rinse quickly in distilled water.

7. Return to phosphomolybdic acid, 5–10 min.

8. Fix for 10 min in 1 per cent acetic acid.

9. Rinse quickly in 95 per cent alcohol, and dehydrate in absolute alcohol.

10. Clear in methyl salicylate and several changes of toluene (water free).

11. Mount in balsam or clarite.

Results: Nuclei and cytoplasm, red; collagen and bone and cartilage matrix, blue.

TECHNIQUE OF SECTIONING PLASMA CULTURES

1. As already described on page 313, flask cultures to be sectioned are removed from the flasks in the usual manner and re-embedded in a fresh plasma coagulum on a glass slide. If this is not done, the cultures will shrink and curl to such an extent that it will be impossible to obtain flat sections. The additional coagulum serves also to protect the culture from damage in subsequent handling. Plasma cultures carried as hanging drops can be fixed directly. It is sometimes desirable,

* Murray, M. R. Personal communication.
† Ponceau 2R, Colour Index Number 79, of the British Society of Dyers and Colourists.

however, to give them the protection of an additional, superficial layer of plasma.

2. Immerse the mounted culture in the fixing fluid. With Zenker-formol the time required for fixation will vary from 30 min to 2 hr or longer, according to the size and thickness of the culture.

3. Wash for 1–6 hr in running water, unless the particular type of fixation requires some other form of treatment.

4. Dehydrate and harden:
   (a) Fifty per cent alcohol, 30 min or longer.
   (b) Seventy per cent alcohol, 1 hr to overnight. If a fixative containing bichloride of mercury has been used, the cultures should be left overnight in a dilute solution of tincture of iodine in 70 per cent alcohol, followed by several changes of fresh 70 per cent alcohol. If it is necessary for the cultures to stand for a considerable length of time before embedding, e.g., over a weekend, they may be left in 70 per cent alcohol.
   (c) Eighty per cent alcohol, 1 hr.
   (d) Ninety-five per cent alcohol, 1 hr to overnight.
   (e) Absolute alcohol containing a few drops of a strong solution of alcoholic eosin in absolute alcohol, two changes, 1–3 hr each. The eosin colors the material in such a manner that the culture may still be seen after it has been embedded in paraffin.
   (f) Transfer to fresh absolute alcohol for 20–30 min.

5. Clear as follows:
   (a) Clear the culture with 2 per cent Parlodion in methyl benzoate (two changes) until both culture and clot are transparent. If a culture of average size does not clear in 1 hr or less, return it to absolute alcohol for further dehydration.
   (b) Place in two changes of benzene for a total of 5–15 min. In the first change, the culture is cut away from the slide with a thin knife or razor blade. While the culture is being detached, both the knife and the coagulum are kept moistened with benzene.

6. Impregnate and embed:
   (a) Benzene-paraffin mixture at 40° C, 5–10 min or longer;
   (b) Paraffin, melting point 50–52° C, 5–10 min or longer;
   (c) Paraffin, melting point 56–58° C, 5–10 min or longer;
   (d) Embed in fresh paraffin (56–58° C). When the paraffin has cooled, the embedded culture is ready for sectioning.

7. The paraffin block is trimmed in such a manner that flat sections of the entire culture may be obtained. With a sharp microtome knife, serial sections (5–7 μ) of the whole culture are cut. The clot, tinted with eosin, is readily distinguished from the surrounding paraffin; the tissue stains a brighter red than the clot.

8. The paraffin sections are now mounted on glass slides flooded with distilled water containing one drop of Mayer's egg-albumen mixture to about 75 ml of water. After the slides have been heated gently on a hot plate, the ribbons are stretched and flattened with fine needles. Care must be taken to avoid heating the hot plate above the melting point of the paraffin, for under no condition should the ribbon be melted. Then, without wiping away the excess water, place the flattened sections in an incubator to dry at 40° C. When thoroughly dry, the ribbons have a translucent appearance and are ready for staining.

Tincture of Iodine Solution

Potassium iodide	5 Gm
Iodine crystals	7 Gm
Distilled water	10 ml
95 per cent alcohol, to make	100 ml

Dissolve the potassium iodide and the iodine crystals in the water by allowing them to stand overnight in a well-stoppered bottle. On the following day, add the alcohol.

Parlodion-Methyl-Benzoate Solution

Parlodion	2 Gm
Methyl benzoate (pure), about 100 ml	

Parlodion is the trade name given to celloidin strips. The strips are washed with distilled water and dried. They are not readily soluble in the methyl benzoate; hence, the solution is prepared several days in advance. It is stable and may be used repeatedly.

Benzene-Paraffin Mixture

	Parts
Benzene	1
Paraffin (50 to 52° C), melted	1

This mixture solidifies at room temperature but remains fluid at 40° C.

Mayer's Egg-Albumen Mixture

	Parts
Fresh egg albumen	1
Glycerine, pure	1

Beat together, and filter through paper. Preserve with a crystal of thymol or with 1 per cent sodium salicylate. The mixture keeps for many months.

Hematoxylin-Eosin Procedure for Sections

1. After removing the paraffin from the mounted sections (with xylene, toluene, or benzene) place them in absolute alcohol, and then run them down through the graded alcohols to distilled water.

2. Stain with Harris's hematoxylin, 1–15 min or longer; overstain slightly.

3. Rinse thoroughly, first with distilled water and then with running tap water.

4. Differentiate with acid alcohol. Here the sections become pink.

5. Rinse quickly in running tap water and neutralize with a weak ammonia solution (one drop in about 200 ml of water). Here the sections become blue. If the ammonia solution is too strong, there is danger of detaching the sections from the slides.

6. Wash for at least 15 min in running tap water.

7. Stain 3 min with 0.1 per cent aqueous eosin.

8. Run the sections up rapidly through the graded alcohols, dehydrate with three changes of absolute alcohol, clear in three changes of xylene or toluene, and mount in Canada balsam or clarite.

Bodian's Silver-Impregnation Method

for Nerve Structures

Bodian[31] has found that much of the selectivity of silver stains is dependent upon the initial fixation. The most generally satisfactory fixative is formol (1 part), glacial acetic acid (1 part), and 80 per cent alcohol (18 parts). Satisfactory results have also been obtained with Bouin's fluid. Fixatives containing chrome salts are not recommended. After fixation, paraffin sections are prepared in the usual manner (*see* p. 315). The subsequent procedures may be summarized as follows:

1. Remove paraffin with xylene, and run sections through absolute alcohol and 95 per cent alcohol to distilled water.

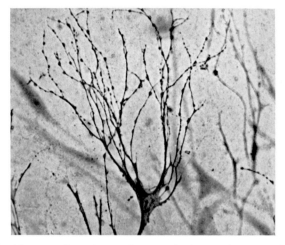

FIG. 93. Double-coverslip culture of sympathetic ganglion cell (human) from ganglioneuroma of lumbar peritoneal region, showing branching, dendritic processes. Sixteen days *in vitro;* Bouin's fixative followed by Bodian's protargol stain. (M. R. Murray and A. P. Stout.[356])

2. Place sections in a solution of 1 per cent protargol (silver albumose) containing 4 to 6 Gm of metallic copper (e.g., copper wire) per 100 ml; 12–24 hr at 37° C. (The protargol-copper bath can be used only once.) Wash in distilled water.

3. Reduce for 10 min in the following solution:

Hydroquinone	1 Gm
Sodium sulfite	5 Gm
Distilled water	100 ml

Wash in at least three changes of distilled water. If toning with gold is not desired, the sections are now dehydrated and mounted in balsam. For double impregnation (to accentuate certain structures that stain very lightly), the sections, after having been washed, are placed in a second bath of fresh protargol and copper and are subsequently reduced as before.

4. If greater contrast is desired, the washed sections may be toned in 1 per cent gold chloride containing 3 drops of glacial acetic acid per 100 ml of solution, until they are decolorized (usually 2–5 min). Wash in distilled water.

5. Place sections in 2 per cent oxalic acid until they become slightly blue or purple (usually 2–5 min). Wash in distilled water.

6. Remove residual silver salts in 5 per cent sodium thio-sulfate (hypo), 5–10 min.

7. Wash thoroughly in distilled water, dehydrate, and mount in balsam or clarite.

Note: This method may be adapted, very simply, for use with whole cultures (Fig. 93).

Preparation of Cultures for Electron Microscopy

A number of investigators, notably Porter and his associates,[402, 404, 406, 407] have made important observations on cell structure by studying electron micrographs of fixed and dried preparations of whole cells cultivated on formvar-coated glass surfaces (Fig. 94); and cells cultivated on carbon films have also been studied.[84] In the meantime, thin-sectioning techniques were developed for electron microscopy,[267, 361, 369, 403] but these were not immediately suitable for cells cultivated directly on glass. Eventually, Howatson and Almeida[239] succeeded in sectioning cells cultivated on glass, in a plane parallel to the surface to which the cells had been attached. Their micrographs have the high resolution usually associated with sectioned material and have the added advantage of presenting the cells in the aspect in which they are observed in the light microscope and in micrographs made from whole cells.

Howatson and Almeida propagate the cells on the surfaces of Petri dishes according to the procedures described on page 183. To prepare cells for simultaneous study by phase microscopy, ordinary microscope slides are laid on the bottom of the Petri dish. Cells adhering to the floor of the dish are fixed by inverting the dish over a small quantity of 1 per cent buffered OsO_4 solution[369] in a closed container for about 2 hr; or 0.25 ml of buffered OsO_4 solution can be added to a covered

Petri dish for the same period. After a brief wash in distilled water, the cells are dehydrated in successively higher concentrations of ethanol, at 10-min intervals. The ethanol is replaced by a mixture of 50 per cent ethanol and 50 per cent methacrylate (9 parts butyl and

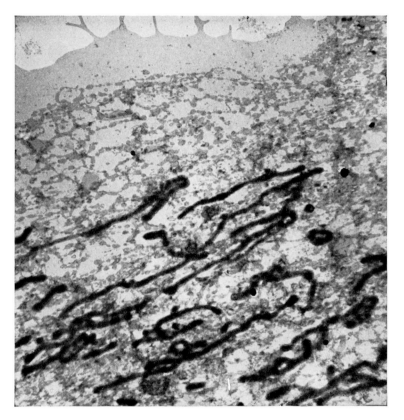

FIG. 94. Electron micrograph of the margin of a cell from a culture of rat fibroblasts. Mitochondria are evident and show some internal structure and a surrounding membrane. Vesicular bodies are seen in the endoplasm. The marginal area of the cell is free of granules. Osmic-acid fixation. (K. R. Porter, courtesy of the W. B. Saunders Company.) × 5600.

1 part methyl methacrylate) and then by several changes of pure methacrylate containing 1 per cent benzoyl peroxide. Excess fluid is poured off, and half of a gelatin capsule filled with partially polymerized methacrylate is inverted over each area of cells selected for sectioning. Cells multiplying on the slides for examination by phase

microscopy are fixed, dehydrated, and infiltrated with methacrylate in the same way, but the final step consists in applying a few drops of partially polymerized methacrylate to the slide and mounting a cover-slip over it.

Polymerization is completed by transferring the Petri dishes with capsules and the microscope slides to an oven held at 50–55° C, for 16–24 hr. When polymerization is complete the slides may be studied under the light (phase) microscope, and the Petri-dish capsules, which are firmly attached to the glass, may be removed by placing them on a block of CO_2 ice for about 2 min, after which they are easily detached. The surfaces of contact usually break cleanly, leaving the cell layer embedded at the surface of the block. A harmful condensation of water on the cooled block may be avoided by placing it in a desiccator until it has returned to room temperature. Sections for electron microscopy are cut with a Porter-Blum microtome; but because the cells extend only a few microns below the surface of the block, it must be trimmed and sectioned with extreme care.

Bloom[30] has described a simple device that makes it possible to cement a previously selected and embedded cell, while still on its coverslip, onto the center of the end of a leucite rod. The rod can be inserted into the chuck of a microtome of the Porter-Blum type after removal of the coverslip.

References

1. ADAMS, R., FAHLMAN, B., DUBE, E. W., DUBE, F. J. C., and READ, S. Control of infections within hospitals. Special reference to prevention within operating rooms. *J.A.M.A. 169:* 1557, 1959.
2. ALIVISATOS, G. P., and EDIPIDIS, T. Über die Immunisierung von Zellen in Zellkulturen. II. Mitteilung. *Ztschr. Immunitätsforsch. 119:* 344, 1960.
3. ANDERSON, N. G. The mass isolation of whole cells from rat liver. *Science 117:* 627, 1953.
4. ANDREWES, C. H. Virus III in tissue cultures. I. The appearance of intranuclear inclusions *in vitro. Brit. J. Exper. Path. 10:* 188, 1929.
5. ANDREWES, C. H. Virus III in tissue cultures. II. Further observations on the formation of inclusion bodies. III. Experiments bearing on immunity. *Brit. J. Exper. Path. 10:* 273, 1929.
6. ANDREWES, C. H. Tissue-culture in the study of immunity to herpes. *J. Path. & Bac'. 33:* 301, 1930.
7. ARNOLD, J. Ueber Theilungsvorgänge an den Wanderzellen, ihre progressiven und regressiven Metamorphosen. *Arch. mikroskop. Anat. 30:* 205, 1887.
8. AXELRAD, A. A., and McCULLOCH, E. A. Obtaining suspensions of animal cells in metaphase from cultures propagated on glass. *Stain Technol. 33:* 67, 1958.
9. BAKER, J. R. *Cytological Technique*, 3rd ed. London, Methuen & Co., Ltd., 1951.
10. BAKER, L. E. The chemical nature of the substances required for cell multiplication. II. The action of glutathione, hemoglobin, and ash of liver on the growth of fibroblasts. *J. Exper. Med. 49:* 163, 1929.
11. BAKER, L. E. Artificial media for the cultivation of fibroblasts, epithelial cells and monocytes. *Science 83:* 605, 1936.
12. BAKER, L. E. Causes of the discontinuity of growth of fibroblasts cultivated in embryo juice. *J. Exper. Med. 69:* 625, 1939.
13. BAKER, L. E., and CARREL, A. Action on fibroblasts of the protein fraction of embryonic tissue extract. *J. Exper. Med. 44:* 387, 1926.

14. Baker, L. E., and Ebeling, A. H. Artificial maintenance media for cell and organ cultivation. I. The cultivation of fibroblasts in artificial and serumless media. *J. Exper. Med. 69:* 365, 1939.

15. Balls, A. K., and Swenson, T. L. The antitrypsin of egg white. *J. Biol. Chem. 106:* 409, 1934.

16. Barnes, W. A., and Furth, J. A transmissible leukemia in mice with atypical cells. *Am. J. Cancer 30:* 75, 1937.

17. Baron, S., and Low, R. J. New maintenance medium for cell culture. *Science 128:* 89, 1958.

18. Beebe, S. P., and Ewing, J. A study of the biology of tumour cells. *Brit. M. J. 2:* 1559, 1906.

19. Bergmann, M., and Niemann, C. On blood fibrin. A contribution to the problem of protein structure. *J. Biol. Chem. 115:* 77, 1936.

20. Bernard, C. Leçons sur les phénomènes de la vie communs aux animaux et aux végétaux. Paris, 1878–9.

21. Biggers, J. D., Claringbold, P. J., and Hardy, M. H. The action of oestrogens on the vagina of the mouse in tissue culture. *J. Physiol. 131:* 497, 1956.

22. Biggers, J. D., Rinaldini, L. M., and Webb, M. The study of growth factors in tissue culture. *Symposia Soc. Exp. Biol. No. XI:* 264, 1957.

23. Biggers, J. D., Webb, M., Parker, R. C., and Healy, G. M. Cultivation of embryonic chick bones on chemically defined media. *Nature 180:* 825, 1957.

24. Billingham, R. E. The preservation of tissues. In *Biological Applications of Freezing and Drying*, R. J. C. Harris, ed. New York, Academic Press, Inc., 1954, p. 253.

25. Billingham, R. E., and Medawar, P. B. The viability of mammalian skin after freezing, thawing and freeze-drying. In *Freezing and Drying: A Symposium*, R. J. C. Harris, ed. London, Institute of Biology, 1951, p. 55.

26. Bishop, L. W. J., Smith, M. K. and Beale, A. J. An apparatus for producing trypsinized monkey kidney cell suspensions. *Virology 10:* 280, 1960.

27. Bland, J. O. W., and Canti, R. G. The growth and development of psittacosis virus in tissue cultures. *J. Path. & Bact. 40:* 231, 1935.

28. Bland, J. O. W., and Robinow, C. F. The inclusion bodies of vaccinia and their relationship to the elementary bodies studied in cultures of the rabbit's cornea. *J. Path. & Bact. 48:* 381, 1939.

29. Bloom, W. Cellular differentiation and tissue culture. *Physiol. Rev. 17:* 589, 1937.

30. Bloom, W. Preparation of a selected cell for electron microscopy. *J. Biophys. Biochem. Cytol. 7:* 191, 1960.

31. Bodian, D. The staining of paraffin sections of nervous tissues with activated protargol. The role of fixatives. *Anat. Rec. 69:* 153, 1937.

32. Borghese, E. Organ differentiation in culture. In *A Symposium on the Chemical Basis of Development*, W. D. McElroy and B. Glass, eds. Baltimore, Johns Hopkins Press, 1958, p. 704.

33. Bowman, D. E. Fractions derived from soy beans and navy beans which retard tryptic digestion of casein. *Proc. Soc. Exper. Biol. & Med. 57:* 139, 1944.

34. Brachet, J. *Embryologie Chimique*. Paris, Masson & Cie, 1944.

35. Brecher, G., Schneiderman, M., and Williams, G. Z. Evaluation of electronic red blood cell counter. *Am. J. Clin. Path. 26:* 1439, 1956.

36. Breedis, C., and Furth, J. The feasibility of preserving neoplastic cells in the frozen state. *Science 88:* 531, 1938.

37. Bryant, J. C., Earle, W. R., and Peppers, E. V. The effect of ultracentrifugation and hyaluronidase on the filtrability of chick-embryo extract for tissue culture. *J. Nat. Cancer Inst. 14:* 189, 1953.

38. BRYANT, J. C., SCHILLING, E. L., and EARLE, W. R. Massive fluid-suspension cultures of certain mammalian tissue cells. I. General characteristics of growth and trends of population. *J. Nat. Cancer Inst. 21:* 331, 1958.

39. BUCHSBAUM, R., and KUNTZ, J. A. The effects of certain stimulants and depressants on individual fibroblasts in a perfusion chamber. *Ann. New York Acad. Sc. 58:* 1303, 1954.

40. BURROWS, M. T. The cultivation of tissues of the chick-embryo outside the body. *J.A.M.A. 55:* 2057, 1910.

41. BURROWS, M. T. A method of furnishing a continuous supply of new medium to a tissue culture *in vitro. Anat. Rec. 6:* 141, 1912.

42. BURROWS, M. T. The tissue culture as a physiological method. *Tr. Cong. Am. Physicians & Surgeons 9:* 77, 1913.

43. CARREL, A. Artificial activation of the growth *in vitro* of connective tissue. *J. Exper. Med. 17:* 14, 1913.

44. CARREL, A. Present condition of a strain of connective tissue twenty-eight months old. *J. Exper. Med. 20:* 1, 1914.

45. CARREL, A. A method for the physiological study of tissues *in vitro. J. Exper. Med. 38:* 407, 1923.

46. CARREL, A. Action de l'extrait filtré du sarcome de Rous sur les macrophages du sang. *Compt. rend. Soc. biol. 91:* 1069, 1924.

47. CARREL, A. Effets de l'extrait de sarcomes fusocellulaires sur des cultures pures de fibroblastes. *Compt. rend. Soc. biol. 92:* 477, 1925.

48. CARREL, A. Some conditions of the reproduction *in vitro* of the Rous virus. *J. Exper. Med. 43:* 647, 1926.

49. CARREL, A. Maintien de la constance du milieu dans les cultures de tissus. *Compt. rend. Soc. biol. 106:* 7, 1931.

50. CARREL, A. The new cytology. *Science 73:* 297, 1931.

51. CARREL, A. Monocytes as an indicator of certain states of blood serum. *Science 80:* 565, 1934.

52. CARREL, A., and BAKER, L. E. The chemical nature of substances required for cell multiplication. *J. Exper. Med. 44:* 503, 1926.

53. CARREL, A., and BURROWS, M. T. Cultivation of adult tissues and organs outside of the body. *J.A.M.A. 55:* 1379, 1910.

54. CARREL, A., and BURROWS, M. T. Cultivation of sarcoma outside of the body. *J.A.M.A. 55:* 1554, 1910.

55. CARREL, A., and LINDBERGH, C. A. *The Culture of Organs.* New York, Paul B. Hoeber, Inc., 1938.

56. CASSELMAN, W. G. B. *Histochemical Technique.* London, Methuen & Co., Ltd., 1959.

57. CERIOTTI, G. A microchemical determination of desoxyribonucleic acid. *J. Biol. Chem. 198:* 297, 1952.

58. CHAMBERS, R., and CAMERON, G. The effect of *l*-ascorbic acid on epithelial sheets in tissue culture. *Am. J. Physiol. 139:* 21, 1943.

59. CHAMPY, C. L'action de l'extrait thyroïdien sur la multiplication cellulaire: Caractère électif de cette action. *Arch. morphol. gén. et exper.,* fasc. *4:* 1922.

60. CHANG, R. S. Continuous subcultivation of epithelial-like cells from normal human tissues. *Proc. Soc. Exper. Biol. & Med. 87:* 440, 1954.

61. CHANG, R. S. Isolation of nutritional variants from conjunctival and HeLa cells. *Proc. Soc. Exper. Biol. & Med. 96:* 818, 1957.

62. CHANG, R. S. Differences in inositol requirements of several strains of HeLa, conjunctival and amnion cells. *Proc. Soc. Exper. Biol. & Med. 99:* 99, 1958.

63. Chang, R. S., and Geyer, R. P. A serum albumin medium for the cultivation of human epithelial-like cells. *J. Immunol. 79:* 455, 1957.

64. Chang, R. S., and Geyer, R. P. Propagation of conjunctival and HeLa cells in various carbohydrate media. *Proc. Soc. Exper. Biol. & Med. 96:* 336, 1957.

65. Chang, S. L., Berg, G., Busch, K. A., Stevenson, R. E., Clarke, N. A., and Kabler, P. W. Application of the "most probable number" method for estimating concentrations of animal viruses by the tissue culture technique. *Virology 6:* 27, 1958.

66. Chen, J. M. The cultivation in fluid medium of organised liver, pancreas and other tissues of foetal rats. *Exper. Cell Res. 7:* 518, 1954.

67. Chen, J. M. The effect of insulin on embryonic limb-bones cultivated *in vitro*. *J. Physiol. 125:* 148, 1954.

68. Cherry, W. R., and Hull, R. N. Studies on the growth of mammalian cells in agitated fluid media. *Anat. Rec. 124:* 483, 1956.

69. Christiansen, G. S., Danes, B., Allen, L., and Leinfelder, P. J. A culture chamber for the continuous biochemical and morphological study of living cells in tissue culture. *Exper. Cell Res. 5:* 10, 1953.

70. Cohen, A., and Waymouth, C. A new histological procedure for whole tissue cultures grown in plasma. *Science 108:* 480, 1948.

71. Cohn, E. J., Gurd, F. R. N., Surgenor, D. M., Barnes, B. A., Brown, R. K., Derouaux, G., Gillispie, J. M., Kahnt, F. W., Lever, W. F., Liu, C. H., Mittelman, D., Mouton, R. F., Schmid, K., and Uroma, E. A system for the separation of the components of human blood: quantitative procedures for the separation of the protein components of human plasma. *J. Am. Chem. Soc. 72:* 465, 1950.

72. Cohn, E. J., Strong, L. E., Hughes, W. L., Jr., Mulford, D. J., Ashworth, J. N., Melin, M., and Taylor, H. L. Preparation and properties of serum and plasma proteins. IV. A system for the separation into fractions of the protein and lipoprotein components of biological tissues and fluids. *J. Am. Chem. Soc. 68:* 459, 1946.

73. Conger, A. D., and Fairchild, L. M. A quick-freeze method for making smear slides permanent. *Stain Technol. 28:* 281, 1953.

74. Conn, H. J., Darrow, M. A., and Emmel, V. M. *Staining Procedures*, 2nd ed. Baltimore, The Williams & Wilkins Company, 1960.

75. Cooper, P. D. A method for producing plaques in agar suspensions of animal cells. *Virology 1:* 397, 1955.

76. Cooper, P. D. Some characteristics of vesicular stomatitis virus growth-curves in tissue culture. *J. Gen. Microbiol. 17:* 327, 1957.

77. Cooper, P. D., Burt, A. M., and Wilson, J. N. Critical effect of oxygen tension on rate of growth of animal cells in continuous suspended culture. *Nature 182:* 1508, 1958.

78. Cooper, P. D., Wilson, J. N., and Burt, A. M. The bulk growth of animal cells in continuous suspension culture. *J. Gen. Microbiol. 21:* 702, 1959.

79. Coriell, L. L., Tall, M. G., and Gaskill, H. Common antigens in tissue culture cell lines. *Science 128:* 198, 1958.

80. Craigie, J. Survival and preservation of tumors in the frozen state. In *Advances in Cancer Research*, J. P. Greenstein and A. Haddow, eds. New York, Academic Press, Inc., 1954, vol. 2, p. 197.

81. Danes, B. S. Suspension cultures of strain L mouse fibroblasts. *Exper. Cell Res. 12:* 169, 1957.

82. Davidson, J. N., Leslie, I., and Waymouth, C. The nucleoprotein content of

fibroblasts growing *in vitro*. 4. Changes in the ribonucleic acid phosphorus (RNAP) and deoxyribonucleic acid phosphorus (DNAP) content. *Biochem. J. 44:* 5, 1949.

83. DAVIDSON, J. N., and WAYMOUTH, C. The nucleoprotein content of fibroblasts growing *in vitro*. 2. The effect of tissue extracts. *Biochem. J. 39:* 188, 1945.

84. DAVIES, M. C., and WALLACE, R. The use of carbon films in the culture of tissue cells for electron microscopy. *J. Biophys. Biochem. Cytol. 4:* 231, 1958.

85. DAVIS, E. V., GLOVER, F., and McLIMANS, W. F. Proliferation of human amnion cells (FL strain) in submerged culture. *Proc. Soc. Exper. Biol. & Med. 97:* 454, 1958.

86. DAY, M. F., and GRACE, T. D. C. Review of recent work on insect tissue. *Ann. Rev. Entomol. 4:* 17, 1959.

87. DEUTSCH, H. F. Fetuin: the mucoprotein of fetal calf serum. *J. Biol. Chem. 208:* 669, 1954.

88. DOANE, F., RHODES, A. J., and ORMSBY, H. L. Virological investigations in adenovirus infections of the conjunctiva, Toronto, 1955–56. *Canad. M. A. J. 77:* 675, 1957.

89. DOLJANSKI, L., HOFFMANN, R. S., and TENENBAUM, E. Stimulation de la croissance de colonies de fibroblastes *in vitro* par des extraits de tissu adulte. L'action des extraits de cerveau, de muscle lisse, d'ovaire, de poumon, de pancréas, de testicule, de moelle osseuse, de rate, de rain et de foie. *Compt. rend. Soc. biol. 131:* 432, 1939.

90. DOLJANSKI, L., and WERNER, H. Studies on the growth-promoting factor of adult tissue extracts. III. Precipitation with alcohol. IV. Action of lipid solvents. *Growth 9:* 229, 1945.

91. DRAPER, G., RAMSEY, H. J., and DUPERTUIS, C. W. Variation in behavior of buffy coat cultures among individuals of different constitution types. *J. Clin. Investigation 23:* 864, 1944.

92. DULBECCO, R. Production of plaques in monolayer tissue cultures by single particles of an animal virus. *Proc. Nat. Acad. Sci. U.S. 38:* 747, 1952.

93. DULBECCO, R., and VOGT, M. Plaque formation and isolation of pure lines with poliomyelitis viruses. *J. Exper. Med. 99:* 167, 1954.

94. DULBECCO, R., and VOGT, M. One-step growth curve of Western equine encephalomyelitis virus on chicken embryo cells grown *in vitro* and analysis of virus yields from single cells. *J. Exper. Med. 99:* 183, 1954.

95. DULBECCO, R., and VOGT, M. Biological properties of poliomyelitis viruses as studied by the plaque technique. *Ann. New York Acad. Sc. 61:* 790, 1955.

96. DUNCAN, D., FRANKLIN, A. E., WOOD, W., and RHODES, A. J. Cultivation of poliomyelitis virus in tissue culture. V. Observations on virus propagation in certain animal tissues with a synthetic nutrient medium. *Canad. J. M. Sc. 31:* 75, 1953.

97. DURYEE, W. R. Precancer cells in amphibian adenocarcinoma. *Ann. New York Acad. Sc. 63:* 1280, 1956.

98. DURYEE, W. R. The mechanism of virus-induced transformations in tubules of the frog kidney. *Acta Unio internat. contra cancrum 15:* 587, 1959.

99. DURYEE, W. R., LONG, M. E., TAYLOR, H. C., JR., McKELWAY, W. P., and EHRMANN, R. L. Human and amphibian neoplasms compared. *Science 131:* 276, 1960.

100. EAGLE, H. The specific amino acid requirements of a mammalian cell (strain L) in tissue culture. *J. Biol. Chem. 214:* 839, 1955.

101. EAGLE, H. The specific amino acid requirements of a human carcinoma cell (strain HeLa) in tissue culture. *J. Exper. Med. 102:* 37, 1955.

102. EAGLE, H. The minimum vitamin requirements of the L and HeLa cells in tissue culture, the production of specific vitamin deficiencies, and their cure. *J. Exper. Med. 102:* 595, 1955.

103. EAGLE, H. Nutrition needs of mammalian cells in tissue culture. *Science 122:* 501, 1955.

104. EAGLE, H. The salt requirements of mammalian cells in tissue culture. *Arch. Biochem. 61:* 356, 1956.

105. EAGLE, H. Amino acid metabolism in mammalian cell cultures. *Science 130:* 432, 1959.

106. EAGLE, H. The sustained growth of human and animal cells in a protein-free environment. *Proc. Nat. Acad. Sc. U.S. 46:* 427, 1960.

107. EAGLE, H., AGRANOFF, B. W., and SNELL, E. E. The biosynthesis of meso-inositol by cultured mammalian cells, and the parabiotic growth of inositol-dependent and inositol-independent strains. *J. Biol. Chem. 235:* 1891, 1960.

108. EAGLE, H., BARBAN, S., LEVY, M., and SCHULZE, H. O. The utilization of carbohydrates by human cell cultures. *J. Biol. Chem. 233:* 551, 1958.

109. EAGLE, H., FREEMAN, A. E., and LEVY, M. The amino acid requirements of monkey kidney cells in first culture passage. *J. Exper. Med. 107:* 643, 1958.

110. EAGLE, H., OYAMA, V. I., LEVY, M., and FREEMAN, A. E. *myo*-Inositol as an essential growth factor for normal and malignant human cells in tissue culture. *J. Biol. Chem. 226:* 191, 1957.

111. EAGLE, H., OYAMA, V. I., LEVY, M., HORTON, C. L., and FLEISCHMAN, R. The growth response of mammalian cells in tissue culture to L-glutamine and L-glutamic acid. *J. Biol. Chem. 218:* 607, 1956.

112. EAGLE, H., and PIEZ, K. A. The utilization of proteins by cultured human cells. *J. Biol. Chem. 235:* 1095, 1960.

113. EARLE, W. R. A study of the Walker rat mammary carcinoma 256, *in vivo* and *in vitro. Am. J. Cancer 24:* 566, 1935.

114. EARLE, W. R. Production of malignancy *in vitro*. IV. The mouse fibroblast cultures and changes seen in the living cells. *J. Nat. Cancer Inst. 4:* 165, 1943.

115. EARLE, W. R. Procedure for the fixation, staining, and mounting of whole mounts from tissue cultures grown in Carrel D-3.5 flasks. *J. Nat. Cancer Inst. 8:* 83, 1947.

116. EARLE, W. R. Long-term cultivation of animal tissue cells in large cultures. *Fed. Proc. 17:* 967, 1958.

117. EARLE, W. R., BRYANT, J. C., and SCHILLING, E. L. Certain factors limiting the size of the tissue culture and the development of massive cultures. *Ann. New York Acad. Sc. 58:* 1000, 1954.

118. EARLE, W. R., BRYANT, J. C., SCHILLING, E. L., and EVANS, V. J. Growth of cell suspensions in tissue culture. *Ann. New York Acad. Sc. 63:* 666, 1956.

119. EARLE, W. R., and HIGHHOUSE, F. Culture flasks for use with plane surface substrate tissue cultures. *J. Nat. Cancer Inst. 14:* 841, 1954.

120. EARLE, W. R., SCHILLING, E. L., and BRYANT, J. C. Influence of tube rotation velocity on proliferation of strain L cells in surface substrate roller-tube cultures. *J. Nat. Cancer Inst. 14:* 853, 1954.

121. EARLE, W. R., SCHILLING, E. L., BRYANT, J. C., and EVANS, V. J. The growth of pure strain L cells in fluid-suspension cultures. *J. Nat. Cancer Inst. 14:* 1159, 1954.

122. EBELING, A. H. Fibrin and serum as a culture medium. *J. Exper. Med. 33:* 641, 1921.

123. EBELING, A. H. Measurement of the growth of tissues *in vitro. J. Exper. Med. 34:* 231, 1921.

124. EHRENSWÄRD, G., FISCHER, A., and STJERNHOLM, R. Protein metabolism of tissue cells *in vitro.* 7. The chemical nature of some obligate factors of tissue cell nutrition. *Acta physiol. scandinav. 18:* 218, 1949.

125. EHRLICH, P. Experimentelle Studien an Mäusetumoren. *Z. Krebsforsch. 5:* 59, 1907.

126. EHRMANN, R. L., and GEY, G. O. The growth of cells on a transparent gel of reconstituted rat-tail collagen. *J. Nat. Cancer Inst. 16:* 1375, 1956.

127. ELIAS, J. J. Cultivation of adult mouse mammary gland in hormone-enriched synthetic medium. *Science 126:* 842, 1957.

128. ELLIS, E. L., and DELBRÜCK, M. The growth of bacteriophage. *J. Gen. Physiol.* 22: 365, 1939.

129. ENDERS, J. F. Bovine amniotic fluid as tissue culture medium in the cultivation of poliomyelitis and other viruses. *Proc. Soc. Exper. Biol. & Med. 82:* 100, 1953.

130. ENDERS, J. F., WELLER, T. H., and ROBBINS, F. C. Cultivation of the Lansing strain of poliomyelitis virus in cultures of various human embryonic tissues. *Science 109:* 85, 1949.

131. EVANS, V. J., BRYANT, J. C., FIORAMONTI, M. C., McQUILKIN, W. T., SANFORD, K. K., and EARLE, W. R. Studies of nutrient media for tissue cells *in vitro.* I. A protein-free chemically defined medium for cultivation of strain L cells. *Cancer Res. 16:* 77, 1956.

132. EVANS, V. J., and EARLE, W. R. The use of perforated cellophane for the growth of cells in tissue culture. *J. Nat. Cancer Inst. 8:* 103, 1947.

133. EVANS, V. J., EARLE, W. R., SANFORD, K. K., SHANNON, J. E., and WALTZ, H. K. The preparation and handling of replicate tissue cultures for quantitative studies. *J. Nat. Cancer Inst. 11:* 907, 1951.

134. FARRELL, L. N., WOOD, W., FRANKLIN, A. E., SHIMADA, F. T., MACMORINE, H. G., and RHODES, A. J. Cultivation of poliomyelitis virus in tissue culture. VI. Methods for quantity production of poliomyelitis viruses in cultures of monkey kidney. *Canad. J. Pub. Health 44:* 273, 1953.

135. FARRELL, L. N., WOOD, W., MACMORINE, H. G., SHIMADA, F. T., and GRAHAM, D. G. Preparation of poliomyelitis virus for production of vaccine for the 1954 field trial. *Canad. J. Pub. Health 46:* 265, 1955.

136. FAWCETT, D. W., and VALLEE, B. L. Studies on the separation of cell types in sero-sanguinous fluids, blood, and vaginal fluids by flotation on bovine plasma albumin. *J. Lab. & Clin. Med. 39:* 354, 1952.

137. FAWCETT, D. W., VALLEE, B. L., and SOULE, M. H. A method for concentration and segregation of malignant cells from bloody, pleural, and peritoneal fluids. *Science 111:* 34, 1950.

138. FELL, H. B. The application of tissue culture *in vitro* to embryology. *J. Roy. Micr. Soc. 60:* 95, 1940.

139. FELL, H. B. Histogenesis in tissue culture. In *Cytology and Cell Physiology,* 2nd ed., G. H. Bourne, ed. Oxford, Clarendon Press, 1951, p. 419.

140. FELL, H. B. Techniques of bone cultivation. In *Methods in Medical Research,* M. B. Visscher, ed. Chicago, Year Book Publishers, Inc., 1951, vol. 4, p. 234.

141. FELL, H. B. Recent advances in organ culture. *Science Progr. 41:* 212, 1953.

142. FELL, H. B. Morphogenesis in animal tissue cultures (discussion). *J. Nat. Cancer Inst. 19:* 601, 1957.

143. FELL, H. B., and MELLANBY, E. The effect of hypervitaminosis A on embryonic limb-bones cultivated *in vitro. J. Physiol. 116:* 320, 1952.

144. FELL, H. B., and MELLANBY, E. The effect of L-triiodothyronine on the growth and development of embryonic chick limb-bones in tissue culture. *J. Physiol.* *133:* 89, 1956.

145. FELL, H. B., MELLANBY, E., and PELC, S. R. Influence of excess vitamin A on the sulphate metabolism of bone rudiments grown *in vitro*. *J. Physiol.* *134:* 179, 1956.

146. FELL, H. B., and ROBISON, R. The growth, development and phosphatase activity of embryonic avian femora and limb-buds cultivated *in vitro*. *Biochem. J.* *23:* 767, 1929.

147. FERREBEE, J. W., and GEIMAN, Q. M. Studies on malarial parasites. III. A procedure for preparing concentrates of *Plasmodium vivax*. *J. Infect. Dis.* *78:* 173, 1946.

148. FERRY, J. D., and MORRISON, P. R. Preparation and properties of serum and plasma proteins. VIII. The conversion of human fibrinogen to fibrin under various conditions. *J. Am. Chem. Soc.* *69:* 388, 1947.

149. FINDLAY, G. M. A note on the cultivation of the virus of fowl-pox. *Brit. J. Exper. Path.* *9:* 28, 1928.

150. FINNEY, D. J. The estimation of bacterial densities from dilution series. *J. Hyg.* *49:* 26, 1951.

151. FINNEY, D. J. *Probit Analysis*, 2nd ed. London, Cambridge University Press, 1952.

152. FISCHER, A. Beitrag zur Biologie der Gewebezellen. Eine vergleichend-biologische Studie der normalen und malignen Gewebezellen *in vitro*. *Arch. f. mikr. Anat. u. Entwcklngsmechn.* *104:* 210, 1925.

153. FISCHER, A. Nature of the growth-accelerating substance of animal tissue cells. *Nature 144:* 113, 1939.

154. FISCHER, A. Die Bedeutung der Aminosäuren für die Gewebezellen *in vitro*. *Acta physiol. scandinav.* *2:* 143, 1941.

155. FISCHER, A. *Biology of Tissue Cells*. Copenhagen, Gyldendal, 1946.

156. FISCHER, A. Amino-acid metabolism of tissue cells *in vitro*. *Biochem. J.* *43:* 491, 1948.

157. FISCHER, A. The application of soybean inhibitor in tissue cultivation. *Science 109:* 611, 1949.

158. FISCHER, A., ASTRUP, T., EHRENSVÄRD, G., and ÖHLENSCHLÄGER, V. Growth of animal tissue cells in artificial media. *Proc. Soc. Exper. Biol. & Med. 67:* 40, 1948.

159. FISCHER, A., and PARKER, R. C. The occurrence of mitoses in normal and malignant tissues *in vitro*. *Brit. J. Exper. Path. 10:* 312, 1929.

160. FISHER, H. W., PUCK, T. T., and SATO, G. Molecular growth requirements of single mammalian cells: The action of Fetuin in promoting cell attachment to glass. *Proc. Nat. Acad. Sc. U.S. 44:* 4, 1958.

161. FOGH, J., and LUND, R. O. Plaque formation of poliomyelitis viruses on human amnion cell cultures. *Proc. Soc. Exper. Biol. & Med. 90:* 80, 1955.

162. FOGH, J. F., and LUND, R. O. Continuous cultivation of epithelial cell strain (FL) from human amniotic membrane. *Proc. Soc. Exper. Biol. & Med. 94:* 532, 1957.

163. FOLIN, O., and CIOCALTEU, V. On tryosine and tryptophane determinations in proteins. *J. Biol. Chem. 73:* 627, 1927.

164. DE FONBRUNE, P. *Technique de Micromanipulation*. Paris, Masson & Cie., 1949.

165. FRANCIS, M. D., and WINNICK, T. Studies on the pathway of protein synthesis in tissue culture. *J. Biol. Chem. 202:* 273, 1953.

166. FRANCIS, T., JR., and KORNS, R. F. Evaluation of 1954 field trial of poliomyelitis vaccine: synopsis of summary report. *Am. J. M. Sci. 229:* 603, 1955.

167. FRANKLIN, A. E., DUNCAN, D., WOOD, W., and RHODES, A. J. Cultivation of Lansing poliomyelitis virus in tissue culture. II. Utilization of glucose in synthetic medium. *Proc. Soc. Exper. Biol. & Med. 79:* 715, 1952.

168. FRANKLIN, A. E., DUNCAN, D., WOOD, W., and RHODES, A. J. Cultivation of poliomyelitis virus in tissue culture. IV. Further observations on virus propagation in human tissues with a synthetic nutrient medium. *Canad. J. M. Sci. 31:* 64, 1953.

169. FRISCH, A. W., JENTOFT, V., BARGER, R., and LOSLI, E. J. A human epithelium-like cell (Maben) derived from an adenocarcinoma of lung. *Am. J. Clin. Path. 25:* 1107, 1955.

170. FULTON, J. D., and SMITH, A. U. Preservation of *Entamoeba histolytica* at $-79°$ C in the presence of glycerol. *Ann. Trop. Med. 47:* 240, 1953.

171. GAILLARD, P. J. Growth, differentiation and function of explants of some endocrine glands. *Symposia Soc. Exper. Biol.*, Cambridge Univ. Press, 1948, No. II, p. 139.

172. GAILLARD, P. J. Organ culture technique using embryologic watch glasses. In *Methods in Medical Research*, M. B. Visscher, ed. Chicago, Year Book Publishers, Inc., 1951, vol. 4, p. 241.

173. GAILLARD, P. J. Growth and differentiation of explanted tissues. In *International Review of Cytology*, G. H. Bourne and J. F. Danielli, eds. New York, Academic Press, Inc., 1953, vol. 2, p. 331.

174. GATENBY, J. B., and BEAMS, H. W. *The Microtomist's Vade-Mecum*. (Bolles Lee) London, J. & A. Churchill, Ltd., 1950.

175. GEMMILL, C. L., GEY, G. O., and AUSTRIAN, R. The metabolism of tissue cultures of Walker Rat Sarcoma 319. *Bull. Johns Hopkins Hosp. 66:* 167, 1940.

176. GEY, G. O. An improved technic for massive tissue culture. *Am. J. Cancer 17:* 752, 1933.

177. GEY, G. O. Some aspects of the constitution and behavior of normal and malignant cells maintained in continuous culture. *Harvey Lect. 50:* 154, 1954–55.

178. GEY, G. O., COFFMAN, W. D., and KUBICEK, M. T. Tissue culture studies of the proliferative capacity of cervical carcinoma and normal epithelium. *Cancer Res. 12:* 264, 1952.

179. GEY, G. O., and GEY, M. K. The maintenance of human normal cells and tumor cells in continuous culture. I. Preliminary report: Cultivation of mesoblastic tumors and normal tissue and notes on methods of cultivation. *Am. J. Cancer 27:* 45, 1936.

180. GEYER, R. P., and CHANG, R. S. Meso-inositol requirement of HeLa and human conjunctival cells. *Proc. Soc. Exper. Biol. & Med. 95:* 315, 1957.

181. GEYER, R. P., and CHANG, R. S. Bicarbonate as an essential for human cells *in vitro. Arch. Biochem. 73:* 500, 1958.

182. GIARDINELLO, F. E., MCLIMANS, W. F., and RAKE, G. W. The apparent toxicity of metallic materials of construction and antifoam agents for mammalian cell lines. *Appl. Microbiol. 6:* 30, 1958.

183. GIBSON, T. Viability of cartilage after freezing. *Proc. Roy. Soc., London, s.B. 147:* 528, 1957.

184. GIFFORD, G. E., ROBERTSON, H. E., and SYVERTON, J. T. Application of manometric method to testing chemical agents *in vitro* for interference with poliomyelitis virus synthesis. *Proc. Soc. Exper. Biol. & Med. 86:* 515, 1954.

185. GIFFORD, G. E., ROBERTSON, H. E., and SYVERTON, J. T. Metabolism of HeLa

cells: methodology and media evaluation. *J. Cell. & Comp. Physiol. 49:* 367, 1957.

186. Ginsberg, H. S., Gold, E., and Jordan, W. S., Jr. Tryptose phosphate broth as supplementary factor for maintenance of HeLa cell tissue cultures. *Proc. Soc. Exper. Biol. & Med. 89:* 66, 1955.

187. Goldhaber, P., Cornman, I., and Ormsbee, R. A. Experimental alteration of the ability of tumor cells to lyse plasma clots *in vitro*. *Proc. Soc. Exper. Biol. & Med. 66:* 590, 1947.

188. Goldstein, M. N. A method for more critical isolation of clones derived from three human cell strains *in vitro*. *Cancer Res. 17:* 357, 1957.

189. Gomori, G. Buffers in the range of pH 6.5 to 9.6. *Proc. Soc. Exper. Biol. & Med. 62:* 33, 1946.

190. Graff, S. On the nature of cancer. *Tr. New York Acad. Sc., Ser. II, 21:* 505, 1959.

191. Graff, S., and McCarty, K. S. Sustained cell culture. *Exper. Cell Res. 13:* 348, 1957.

192. Graham, A. F., and Siminovitch, L. Proliferation of monkey kidney cells in rotating cultures. *Proc. Soc. Exper. Biol. & Med. 89:* 326, 1955.

193. Grand, C. G. Cytoplasmic inclusions and the characteristics of Hodgkin's diseased lymph nodes in tissue culture. *Cancer Res. 9:* 183, 1949.

194. Gray, P. *The Microtomist's Formulary and Guide.* New York, McGraw-Hill Book Company, Inc., Blakiston Division, 1954.

195. Grob, D. Proteolytic enzymes. I. The control of their activity. *J. Gen. Physiol. 26:* 405, 1943.

196. Grobstein, C. Trans-filter induction of tubules in mouse metanephrogenic mesenchyme. *Exper. Cell Res. 10:* 424, 1956.

197. Grobstein, C. Some transmission characteristics of the tubule-inducing influence on mouse metanephrogenic mesenchyme. *Exper. Cell Res. 13:* 575, 1957.

198. Grobstein, C., and Dalton, A. J. Kidney tubule induction in mouse metanephrogenic mesenchyme without cytoplasmic contact. *J. Exper. Zool. 135:* 57, 1957.

199. Gwatkin, R. B. L., and Siminovitch, L. Multiplication of single mammalian cells in a nonbicarbonate medium. *Proc. Soc. Exper. Biol. & Med. 103:* 718, 1960.

200. Gwatkin, R. B. L., Till, J. E., Whitmore, G. F., Siminovitch, L., and Graham, A. F. Multiplication of animal cells in suspension measured by colony counts. *Proc. Nat. Acad. Sc. U.S. 43:* 451, 1957.

201. Haagen, E., and Theiler, M. Untersuchungen über das Verhalten des Gelbfiebervirus in der Gewebekultur. *Zentr. f. Bakt., 1. Abt., Orig. 125:* 145, 1932.

202. de Haan, J. Einige Verbesserungen in der Methode der Gewebezüchtung mittels Durchströmung. *Arch. exper. Zellforsch. 7:* 275, 1928.

203. Haberlandt, G. Culturversuche mit isolierten Pflanzenzellen. *Sitz. ber. Akad. Wiss. Wien, Math.-naturw. Klasse, Abt. I, 111:* 69, 1902.

204. Haff, R. F., and Swim, H. E. The amino acid requirements of rabbit fibroblasts, strain RM3-56. *J. Gen. Physiol. 41:* 91, 1957.

205. Haff, R. F., and Swim, H. E. Minimal vitamin requirements of rabbit fibroblasts, strain RM3-73. *Proc. Soc. Exper. Biol. & Med. 94:* 779, 1957.

206. Hallauer, C. Über das Verhalten von Hühnerpestvirus in der Gewebekultur. *Ztschr. Hyg. 113:* 61, 1931–32.

207. Hanks, J. H. The longevity of chick tissue cultures without renewal of medium. *J. Cell. & Comp. Physiol. 31:* 235, 1948.

208. HANKS, J. H. Inorganic aging of the plasma layer of tissue cultures. *Proc. Soc. Exper. Biol. & Med. 71:* 313, 1949.

209. HANKS, J. H. Calcification of cell cultures in the presence of embryo juice and mammalian sera. *Proc. Soc. Exper. Biol. & Med. 71:* 328, 1949.

210. HANKS, J. H. Balanced salt solutions, inorganic requirements and pH control. In *An Introduction to Cell and Tissue Culture*, W. F. Scherer, ed. Minneapolis, The Burgess Publishing Co., 1955, p. 5.

211. HANKS, J. H., and WALLACE, J. H. Determination of cell viability. *Proc. Soc. Exper. Biol. & Med. 98:* 188, 1958.

212. HANKS, J. H., and WALLACE, R. E. Relation of oxygen and temperature in the preservation of tissues by refrigeration. *Proc. Soc. Exper. Biol. & Med. 71:* 196, 1949.

213. HARDING, H. G., and TREBLER, H. A. Detergents for dairy plants and methods of their evaluation. *Food Technol. 1:* 478, 1947.

214. HARNDEN, D. G. A human skin culture technique used for cytological examinations. *Brit. J. Exper. Path. 41:* 31, 1960.

215. HARRIS, M. Growth factors in alcoholic extracts of chick embryos. *Growth 16:* 215, 1952.

216. HARRIS, M. The use of dialyzed media for studies in cell nutrition. *J. Cell. & Comp. Physiol. 40:* 279, 1952.

217. HARRIS, M. Partial purification of growth factors in the dialyzable fraction of chick embryo extract. *Growth 17:* 147, 1953.

218. HARRIS, M. The role of bicarbonate for outgrowth of chick heart fibroblasts *in vitro. J. Exper. Zool. 125:* 85, 1954.

219. HARRIS, M. Selective uptake and release of substances by cells. In *A Symposium on the Chemical Basis of Development*, W. D. McElroy and B. Glass, eds. Baltimore, Johns Hopkins Press, 1958, p. 596.

220. HARRIS, M. Growth measurements on monolayer cultures with an electronic cell counter. *Cancer Res. 19:* 1020, 1959.

221. HARRIS, M. Essential growth factor in serum dialysate for chick skeletal muscle fibroblasts. *Proc. Soc. Exper. Biol. & Med. 102:* 468, 1959.

222. HARRIS, M., and KUTSKY, P. B. Utilization of added sugars by chick heart fibroblasts in dialyzed media. *J. Cell. & Comp. Physiol. 42:* 449, 1953.

223. HARRIS, M., and KUTSKY, R. J. Synergism of nucleoprotein and dialysate growth factors in chick embryo extract. *Exper. Cell. Res. 6:* 327, 1954.

224. HARRIS, M., and KUTSKY, R. J. Growth rates of fibroblasts from chick skeletal muscle in cultures supplemented with homologous nucleoproteins. *Cancer Res. 18:* 585, 1958.

225. HARRISON, R. G. Observations on the living developing nerve fiber. *Proc. Soc. Exper. Biol. & Med. 4:* 140, 1907.

226. HARRISON, R. G. The outgrowth of the nerve fiber as a mode of protoplasmic movement. *J. Exper. Zool. 9:* 787, 1910.

227. HART, D., and SHARP, D. G. Surgery: Asepsis. In *Medical Physics*, O. Glasser, ed. Chicago, Year Book Publishers, Inc., 1944, p. 1497.

228. HAUSCHKA, T. S., MITCHELL, J. T., and NIEDERPRUEM, D. J. A reliable frozen tissue bank: viability and stability of 82 neoplastic and normal cell types after prolonged storage at $-78°$ C. *Cancer Res. 19:* 643, 1959.

229. HAWN, C. v. Z., and PORTER, K. R. The fine structure of clots formed from purified bovine fibrinogen and thrombin: A study with the electron microscope. *J. Exper. Med. 86:* 285, 1947.

230. HAYFLICK, L. Decontaminating tissue cultures infected with pleuropneumonia-like organisms. *Nature 185:* 783, 1960.

231. HEALY, G. M., FISHER, D. C., and PARKER, R. C. Nutrition of animal cells in tissue culture. VIII. Desoxyribonucleic acid phosphorus as a measure of cell multiplication in replicate cultures. *Canad. J. Biochem. Physiol. 32:* 319, 1954.

232. HEALY, G. M., FISHER, D. C., and PARKER, R. C. Nutrition of animal cells in tissue culture. IX. Synthetic medium No. 703. *Canad. J. Biochem. Physiol. 32:* 327, 1954.

233. HEALY, G. M., FISHER, D. C., and PARKER, R. C. Nutrition of animal cells in tissue culture. X. Synthetic medium No. 858. *Proc. Soc. Exper. Biol. & Med. 89:* 71, 1955.

234. HEALY, G. M., MORGAN, J. F., and PARKER, R. C. Trace metal content of some natural and synthetic media. *J. Biol. Chem. 198:* 305, 1952.

235. HECKE, F. Züchtung des Maul- und Klauenseucheerregers. *Zentralbl. Bakt., 1 Abt., Ref. 102:* 283, 1931.

236. HERBST, C. Über das Auseinandergehen von Furchungs- und Gewebezellen in kalkfreiem Medium. *Arch. Entwcklngsmechn. Organ. 9:* 424, 1900.

237. HINZ, R. W., and SYVERTON, J. T. Mammalian cell cultures for study of influenza virus. I. Preparation of monolayer cultures with collagenase. *Proc. Soc. Exper. Biol. & Med. 101:* 19, 1959.

238. HOLYOKE, E. A., and BEBER, B. A. Cultures of gonads of mammalian embryos. *Science 128:* 1082, 1958.

239. HOWATSON, A. F., and ALMEIDA, J. D. A method for the study of cultured cells by thin sectioning and electron microscopy. *J. Biophys. Biochem. Cytol. 4:* 115, 1958.

240. HSU, T. C. Mammalian chromosomes *in vitro*. I. The karyotype of man. *J. Hered. 43:* 167, 1952.

241. HUGHES, A. Some effects of abnormal tonicity on dividing cells in chick tissue cultures. *Quart. J. Micr. Sc. 93:* 207, 1952.

242. HUNGERFORD, D. A., DONNELLY, A. J., NOWELL, P. C., and BECK, S. The chromosome constitution of a human phenotypic intersex. *Am. J. Human Genet. 11:* 215, 1959.

243. IRWIN, J. O., and CHEESEMAN, E. A. On an approximate method of determining the median effective dose and its error, in the case of a quantal response. *J. Hyg. 39:* 574, 1939.

244. JACOBSON, W., and WEBB, M. The two types of nucleic acid during mitosis. *J. Physiol. 112:* 2P, 1951.

245. JACOBY, F., TROWELL, O. A., and WILLMER, E. N. Studies on the growth of tissues *in vitro*. V. Further observations on the manner in which cell division of chick fibroblasts is affected by embryo tissue juice. *J. Exper. Biol. 14:* 255, 1937.

246. JOLLY, J. Sur la durée de la vie et de la multiplication des cellules animales en dehors de l'organisme. *Compt. rend. Soc. biol. 55:* 1266, 1903.

247. JONES, N. C. H., MOLLISON, P. L., and ROBINSON, M. A. Factors affecting the viability of erythrocytes stored in the frozen state. *Proc. Roy. Soc., London, s.B. 147:* 476, 1957.

248. KAHN, R. H. Effect of oestrogen and of vitamin A on vaginal cornification in tissue culture. *Nature 174:* 317, 1954.

249. KAHN, R. H. Organ culture in experimental biology. *Univ. Michigan M. Bull. 24:* 242, 1958.

250. KAPLAN, A. S. A study of the herpes simplex virus-rabbit kidney cell system by the plaque technique. *Virology 4:* 435, 1957.

251. KATZ, S. L., MILOVANOVIC, M. V., and ENDERS, J. F. Propagation of measles virus in cultures of chick embryo cells. *Proc. Soc. Exper. Biol. & Med. 97:* 23, 1958.

252. KAZAL, L. A., SPICER, D. S., and BRAHINSKY, R. A. Isolation of a crystalline trypsin inhibitor-anticoagulant protein from pancreas. *J. Am. Chem. Soc. 70:* 3034, 1948.

253. KOOREMAN, P. J., and GAILLARD, P. J. Therapeutic possibilities of grafting cultivated embryonic tissues in man: the parathyroid gland in cases of post-operative tetany. *Arch. chir. neerl. (II), fasc. 4:* 326, 1950.

254. KOPAC, M. J. Micrurgical studies on living cells. In *The Cell,* J. Brachet and A. E. Mirsky, eds. New York, Academic Press, Inc., 1959, vol. 1, p. 161.

255. KUCHLER, R. J., and MERCHANT, D. J. Propagation of strain L (Earle) cells in agitated fluid suspension cultures. *Proc. Soc. Exper. Biol. & Med. 92:* 803, 1956.

256. KUCHLER, R. J., and MERCHANT, D. J. Growth of tissue cells in suspension. *Univ. Michigan M. Bull. 24:* 200, 1958.

257. KUNITZ, M., and NORTHROP, J. H. Isolation from beef pancreas of crystalline trypsinogen, trypsin, a trypsin inhibitor, and an inhibitor-trypsin compound. *J. Gen. Physiol. 19:* 991, 1936.

258. KUTSKY, R. J. Stimulating effect of nucleoprotein fraction of chick embryo extract on homologous heart fibroblasts. *Proc. Soc. Exper. Biol. & Med. 83:* 390, 1953.

259. KUTSKY, R. J. Nucleoprotein constituents stimulating growth in tissue culture: active protein fraction. *Science 129:* 1486, 1959.

260. KUTSKY, R. J., and HARRIS, M. Effects of nucleoprotein fractions from adult and juvenile tissues on growth of chick fibroblasts in plasma cultures. *Growth 21:* 53, 1957.

261. KUTSKY, R. J., TRAUTMAN, R., LIEBERMAN, M., and CAILLEAU, R. M. Nucleo-protein fractions from various embryonic tissues. A comparison of physico-chemical characteristics and biological activity in tissue culture. *Exper. Cell Res. 10:* 48, 1956.

262. LANDSTEINER, K., and PARKER, R. C. Serological tests for homologous serum proteins in tissue cultures maintained on a foreign medium. *J. Exper. Med. 71:* 231, 1940.

263. LASER, H. Der Stoffwechsel von Gewebekulturen und ihr Verhalten in der Anaerobiose. *Biochem. Ztschr. 264:* 72, 1933.

264. LASER, H. Flächengrösse und Wachstum von Gewebekulturen. *Ztschr. Krebsforsch. 39:* 384, 1933.

265. LASFARGUES, E. Y. Cultivation and behavior *in vitro* of the normal mammary epithelium of the adult mouse. *Exper. Cell Res. 13:* 553, 1957.

266. LASNITSKI, I. The influence of hypervitaminosis on the effect of 20-methyl-cholanthrene on mouse prostate glands grown *in vitro*. *Brit. J. Cancer 9:* 434, 1955.

267. LATTA, H., and HARTMANN, J. F. Use of a glass edge in thin sectioning for electron microscopy. *Proc. Soc. Exper. Biol. & Med. 74:* 436, 1950.

268. LEIGHTON, J. A sponge matrix method for tissue culture. Formation of organized aggregates of cells *in vitro*. *J. Nat. Cancer Inst. 12:* 545, 1951.

269. LEIGHTON, J. The growth patterns of some transplantable animal tumors in sponge matrix tissue culture. *J. Nat. Cancer Inst. 15:* 275, 1954.

270. LEIGHTON, J. Studies on human cancer using sponge matrix tissue culture. I. The growth patterns of a malignant melanoma, adenocarcinoma of the parotid gland, papillary adenocarcinoma of the thyroid gland, adenocarcinoma of the pancreas, and epidermoid carcinoma of the uterine cervix (Gey's HeLa strain). *Texas Rep. Biol. & Med. 12:* 847, 1954.

271. LEIGHTON, J. Plasma, serum, other body fluids and derivatives. In *An Introduction to Cell and Tissue Culture*, W. F. Scherer, ed. Minneapolis, The Burgess Publishing Co., 1955, p. 9.

272. LEIGHTON, J. Cultures in sponge and other special matrices. In *An Introduction to Cell and Tissue Culture*, W. F. Scherer, ed. Minneapolis, The Burgess Publishing Co., 1955, p. 36.

273. LEIGHTON, J. and KLINE, I. Studies on human cancer using sponge matrix tissue culture. II. Invasion of connective tissue by carcinoma (strain HeLa). *Texas Rep. Biol. & Med. 12:* 865, 1954.

274. LEIGHTON, J., KLINE, I., BELKIN, M., LEGALLAIS, F., and ORR, H. C. The similarity in histologic appearance of some human "cancer" and "normal" cell strains in sponge-matrix tissue culture. *Cancer Res. 17:* 359, 1957.

275. LEUCHTENBERGER, C., DOOLIN, P. F., and KUTSAKIS, A. H. Buffered osmium tetroxide (OsO_4) fixation for cytological and Feulgen microspectrophotometric studies of human rectal polyps. *J. Biophys. Biochem. Cytol. 1:* 385, 1955.

276. LEVAN, A. Colchicine-induced c-mitosis in two mouse ascites tumors. *Hereditas 40:* 1, 1954.

277. LEVAN, A. Chromosome studies on some human tumors and tissues of normal origin grown *in vivo* and *in vitro* at the Sloan-Kettering Institute. *Cancer 9:* 648, 1956.

278. LEVINE, S. Effect of manipulation on ^{32}P loss from tissue culture cells. *Exper. Cell Res. 19:* 220, 1960.

279. LEWIS, M. R., and LEWIS, W. H. The cultivation of tissues from chick embryos in solutions of NaCl, $CaCl_2$, KCl and $NaHCO_3$. *Anat. Rec. 5:* 277, 1911.

280. LEWIS, W. H. Rat malignant cells in roller tube cultures and some results. *Carnegie Inst. Washington, Pub. No. 459, Contrib. Embryol. 25:* 161, 1935.

281. LEWIS, W. H. Malignant cells. *Harvey Lect. 31:* 214, 1935–36.

282. LEWIS, W. H. Pinocytosis by malignant cells. *Am. J. Cancer 29:* 666, 1937.

283. LIEBERMAN, I., LAMY, F., and OVE, P. Nonidentity of fetuin and protein growth (flattening) factor. *Science 129:* 43, 1959.

284. LIEBERMAN, I., and OVE, P. Purification of a serum protein required by a mammalian cell in tissue culture. *Biochim. et biophys. acta 25:* 449, 1957.

285. DES LIGNERIS, M. J. A. Studies on cell growth. I. Serum cultures of young and adult mammalian tissues and their relation to growth processes *in vivo*. *Publ. S. African Inst. M. Res. 3:* 257, 1928.

286. LINDBERGH, C. A. A culture flask for the circulation of a large quantity of fluid medium. *J. Exper. Med. 70:* 231, 1939.

287. LIPMANN, F. Stoffwechselversuche an Gewebekulturen, insbesondere über die Rolle der Glykolyse im Stoffwechsel embryonaler Zellen. *Biochem. Ztschr. 261:* 157, 1933.

288. LJUNGGREN, C. A. Von der Fähigkeit des Hautepithels, ausserhalb des Organismus sein Leben zu behalten, mit Berücksichtigung der Transplantation. *Deutsche Ztschr. Chir. 47:* 608, 1897–98.

289. LLOYD, W., THEILER, M., and RICCI, N. I. Modification of the virulence of yellow fever virus by cultivation in tissues *in vitro*. *Tr. Roy. Soc. Trop. Med. & Hyg. 29:* 481, 1936.

290. LOCKE, F. S. Die Wirkung der Metalle des Blutplasmas und verschiedener Zucker auf das isolierte Säugethierherz. *Centr. Physiol. 14:* 670, 1901.

291. LOEB, L. On the growth of epithelium in agar and bloodserum in the living body. *J. Med. Res. 8:* 109, 1902.

292. LONG, M. E., and TAYLOR, H. C., JR., Nucleolar variability in human neoplastic cells. *Ann. New York Acad. Sc. 63:* 1095, 1956.

293. LOVELOCK, J. E. The mechanism of the protective action of glycerol against haemolysis by freezing and thawing. *Biochim. et biophys. acta 11:* 28, 1953.

294. LOVELOCK, J. E. Biophysical aspects of the freezing of living cells. In *Preservation and Transplantation of Normal Tissues*, Ciba Foundation Symposium. London, J. & A. Churchill, Ltd., 1954, p. 131.

295. LOVELOCK, J. E. Biophysical aspects of the freezing and thawing of living cells. *Proc. Roy. Soc. Med. 47:* 60, 1954.

296. LOWRY, O. H., ROSEBROUGH, N. J., FARR, A. L., and RANDALL, R. J. Protein measurement with the Folin phenol reagent. *J. Biol. Chem. 193:* 265, 1951.

297. LU, K. H., and WINNICK, T. The roles of the nucleic acids and free nucleotides in chick embryonic extract on the growth of heart fibroblast. *Exper. Cell Res. 9:* 502, 1955.

298. LURIA, S. E. *General Virology.* New York, John Wiley & Sons, Inc., 1953.

299. LUYET, B. J. Survival of cells, tissues and organisms after ultra-rapid freezing. In *Freezing and Drying; A symposium*, R. J. C. Harris, ed. London, The Institute of Biology, 1951, p. 77.

300. LUYET, B. J., and KEANE, J. F., JR. Comparative efficiency of ethylene glycol, glucose and sodium chloride in protecting tissues against freezing injury. *Biodynamica 7:* 119, 1952.

301. LWOFF, A., DULBECCO, R., VOGT, M., and LWOFF, M. Kinetics of the release of poliomyelitis virus from single cells. *Virology 1:* 128, 1955.

302. MADIN, S. H., ANDRIESE, P. C., and DARBY, N. B. The *in vitro* cultivation of tissues of domestic and laboratory animals. *Am. J. Vet. Res. 18:* 932, 1957.

303. MADIN, S. H., and DARBY, N. B., JR. Established kidney cell lines of normal adult bovine and ovine origin. *Proc. Soc. Exper. Biol. & Med. 98:* 574, 1958.

304. MAGEE, W. E., SHEEK, M. R., and SAGIK, B. P. Methods of harvesting mammalian cells grown in tissue culture. *Proc. Soc. Exper. Biol. & Med. 99:* 390, 1958.

305. MAITLAND, H. B., and MAITLAND, M. C. Cultivation of vaccinia virus without tissue culture. *Lancet 215:* 596, 1928.

306. MAITLAND, M. C., and MAITLAND, H. B. Cultivation of foot-and-mouth disease virus. *J. Comp. Path. & Therap. 44:* 106, 1931.

307. MAKINO, S., and NISHIMURA, J. Water-pretreatment squash technic. *Stain Technol. 27:* 1, 1952.

308. MARGOLIASH, E., and DOLJANSKI, L. The mitosis stimulating effects of fresh adult chicken heart extract and of chick embryonic extracts. *Growth 14:* 7, 1950.

309. MARTINOVITCH, P. N. A modification of the watch glass technique for the cultivation of endocrine glands of infantile rats. *Exper. Cell Res. 4:* 490, 1953.

310. MATTERN, C. F. T., BRACKETT, F. S., and OLSON, B. J. Determination of number and size of particles by electrical gating: blood cells. *J. Appl. Physiol. 10:* 56, 1957.

311. MAXIMOW, A. Über die Entwicklung argyrophiler und kollagener Fasern in Kulturen von erwachsenem Säugetiergewebe. (Nach des Verfassers Tode geschrieben und veröffentlicht von W. Bloom.) *Ztschr. f. mikr. anat. Forsch. 17:* 625, 1929.

312. MAYYASI, S. A., and SCHUURMANS, D. M. Cultivation of L strain (Earle) mouse cells in bacteriological media combined with horse serum. *Proc. Soc. Exper. Biol. & Med. 93:* 207, 1956.

313. McILWAIN, H., and BUDDLE, H. L. Techniques in tissue metabolism. I. A mechanical chopper. *Biochem. J. 53:* 412, 1953.

314. McINTIRE, F. C., and SMITH, M. F. A new chemical method for measuring cell populations in tissue cultures. *Proc. Soc. Exper. Biol. & Med. 98:* 76, 1958.

315. McLIMANS, W. F., DAVIS, E. V., GLOVER, F. L., and RAKE, G. W. The submerged culture of mammalian cells: the spinner culture. *J. Immunol. 79:* 428, 1957.

316. McLIMANS, W. F., GIARDINELLO, F. E., DAVIS, E. V., KUCERA, C. J., and RAKE, G. W. Submerged culture of mammalian cells: the five liter fermentor. *J. Bact. 74:* 768, 1957.

317. MEDAWAR, P. B. Sheets of pure epidermal epithelium from human skin. *Nature 148:* 783, 1941.

318. MEDEARIS, D. N., JR., and KIBRICK, S. An evaluation of various tissues in culture for isolation of Eastern equine encephalitis virus. *Proc. Soc. Exper. Biol. & Med. 97:* 152, 1958.

319. MEIER, R. Zur Methodik der Stoffwechseluntersuchungen an Gewebekulturen. I. Atmungsmessung an Gewebekulturen. *Biochem. Ztschr. 231:* 247, 1931.

320. MEIER, R. Zur Methodik der Stoffwechseluntersuchungen an Gewebekulturen. II. Gewichtsbestimmung an einzelnen Gewebekulturen. Gewichtszunahme und Flächenzunahme. *Biochem. Ztschr. 231:* 253, 1931.

321. MELNICK, J. L. Tissue culture techniques and their application to original isolation, growth, and assay of poliomyelitis and orphan viruses. *Ann. New York Acad. Sc. 61:* 754, 1955.

322. MELNICK, J. L. Problems associated with viral identification and classification in 1956. *Ann. New York Acad. Sc. 67:* 363, 1957.

323. MELNICK, J. L., HSIUNG, G. D., RAPPAPORT, C., HOWES, D., and REISSIG, M. Factors influencing the proliferation of viruses. *Texas Rep. Biol. & Med. 15:* 496, 1957.

324. MELNICK, J. L., and OPTON, E. M. Assay of poliomyelitis neutralizing antibody in disposable plastic panels. *Bull. World Health Organ. 14:* 129, 1956.

325. MELNICK, J. L., and RIORDAN, J. T. Poliomyelitis viruses in tissue culture. IV. Protein-free nutrient media in stationary and roller tube cultures. *Proc. Soc. Exper. Biol. & Med. 81:* 208, 1952.

326. MERYMAN, H. T. Mechanics of freezing in living cells and tissues. *Science 124:* 515, 1956.

327. MERYMAN, H. T. Physical limitations of the rapid freezing method. *Proc. Roy. Soc., London, s.B. 147:* 452, 1957.

328. MERYMAN, H. T., ed. *Freezing and Drying of Biological Materials. Ann. New York Acad. Sc. 85:* 501, 1960.

329. MICHAELIS, L. Experimentelle Untersuchungen über den Krebs der Mäuse. *Med. Klin. (Berlin) 1:* 203, 1905.

330. MILOVANOVIC, M. V., ENDERS, J. F., and MITUS, A. Cultivation of measles virus in human amnion cells and in developing chick embryo. *Proc. Soc. Exper. Biol. & Med. 95:* 120, 1957.

331. MOEN, J. K. The development of pure cultures of fibroblasts from single mononuclear cells. *J. Exper. Med. 61:* 247, 1935.

332. MOORE, S., and STEIN, W. H. Chromatography of amino acids on sulfonated polystyrene resins. *J. Biol. Chem. 192:* 663, 1951.

333. MORANN, G. L., and MELNICK, J. L. Poliomyelitis virus in tissue culture. VI. Use of kidney epithelium grown on glass. *Proc. Soc. Exper. Biol. & Med. 84:* 558, 1953.

334. MORGAN, J. F. Tissue culture nutrition. *Bact. Rev. 22:* 20, 1958.

335. MORGAN, J. F., CAMPBELL, M. E., and MORTON, H. J. The nutrition of animal tissues cultivated *in vitro*. I. A survey of natural materials as supplements to synthetic medium 199. *J. Nat. Cancer Inst. 16:* 557, 1955.

336. MORGAN, J. F., and MORTON, H. J. Studies on the sulfur metabolism of tissues cultivated *in vitro*. I. A critical requirement for L-cystine. *J. Biol. Chem. 215:* 539, 1955.

337. MORGAN, J. F., and MORTON, H. J. Studies on the sulfur metabolism of tissues cultivated *in vitro*. II. Optical specificities and interrelationships between cystine and methionine. *J. Biol. Chem. 221:* 529, 1956.

338. MORGAN, J. F., and MORTON, H. J. The nutrition of animal tissues cultivated *in vitro*. IV. Amino acid requirements of chick embryonic heart fibroblasts. *J. Biophys. Biochem. Cytol. 3:* 141, 1957.

339. MORGAN, J. F., MORTON, H. J. and PARKER, R. C. Nutrition of animal cells in tissue culture. I. Initial studies on a synthetic medium. *Proc. Soc. Exper. Biol. & Med. 73:* 1, 1950.

340. MORGAN, J. F., MORTON, H. J., and PARKER, R. C. Nutrition of animal cells in tissue culture. IV. Inhibition of cell activity by cobalt and the protective action of L-histidine. *Growth 15:* 11, 1951.

341. MORGAN, J. F., and PARKER, R. C. The use of antitryptic agents in tissue culture. I. Crude soybean trypsin-inhibitor. *Proc. Soc. Exper. Biol. & Med. 71:* 665, 1949.

342. MORTON, H. J., MORGAN, J. F., and PARKER, R. C. Nutrition of animal cells in tissue culture. II. Use of Tweens in synthetic feeding mixtures. *Proc. Soc. Exper. Biol. & Med. 74:* 22, 1950.

343. MORTON, H. J., MORGAN, J. F., and PARKER, R. C. Nutrition of animal cells in tissue culture. V. Effect of initial treatment of cultures on their survival in a synthetic medium. *J. Cell. & Comp. Physiol. 38:* 389, 1951.

344. MOSCONA, A. Cell suspensions from organ rudiments of chick embryos. *Exper. Cell Res. 3:* 535, 1952.

345. MOSCONA, A. Morphogenesis in animal tissue cultures (discussion). *J. Nat. Cancer Inst. 19:* 602, 1957.

346. MOSCONA, A. The development *in vitro* of chimeric aggregates of dissociated embryonic chick and mouse cells. *Proc. Nat. Acad. Sc. U.S. 43:* 184, 1957.

347. MOSCONA, A., and MOSCONA, H. The dissociation and aggregation of cells from organ rudiments of the early chick embryo. *J. Anat. 86:* 287, 1952.

348. MOSCONA, H., and MOSCONA, A. The development *in vitro* of the anterior lobe of the embryonic chick pituitary. *J. Anat. 86:* 278, 1952.

349. MUNYON, W. H., and MERCHANT, D. J. The relation between glucose utilization, lactic acid production and utilization and the growth cycle of L strain fibroblasts. *Exper. Cell Res. 17:* 490, 1959.

350. MURRAY, M. R. Comparative data on tissue culture of acoustic neurilemmomas and meningiomas. *J. Neuropath. & Exper. Neurol. 1:* 123, 1942.

351. MURRAY, M. R. Tissue culture procedures in medical installations. In *Methods in Medical Research*, M. B. Visscher, ed. Chicago, Year Book Publishers, Inc. *4:* 211, 1951.

352. MURRAY, M. R., and STOUT, A. P. Demonstration of the formation of reticulin by Schwannian tumor cells *in vitro*. *Am. J. Path. 18:* 585, 1942.

353. MURRAY, M. R., and STOUT, A. P. Characteristics of a liposarcoma grown *in vitro*. *Am. J. Path. 19:* 751, 1943.

354. MURRAY, M. R., and STOUT, A. P. Distinctive characteristics of the sympathicoblastoma cultivated *in vitro:* A method for prompt diagnosis. *Am. J. Path. 23:* 429, 1947.

355. MURRAY, M. R., and STOUT, A. P. The classification and diagnosis of human tumors by tissue culture methods. *Texas Rep. Biol. & Med. 12:* 898, 1954.

356. MURRAY, M. R., and STOUT, A. P. Tissue culture in tumor classification and diagnosis. In *Treatment of Cancer and Allied Diseases*, G. T. Pack and I. M. Ariel, eds. New York, Paul B. Hoeber, Inc., 1958, p. 124.

357. NELSON, J. B. (editor) Biology of the pleuropneumonialike organisms. *Ann. New York Acad. Sc. 79:* 305, 1960.

358. NEUMAN, R. E., and McCOY, T. A. Dual requirement of Walker carcinosarcoma 256 *in vitro* for asparagine and glutamine. *Science 124:* 124, 1956.

359. NEUMAN, R. E., and McCOY, T. A. Growth-promoting properties of pyruvate, oxalacetate, and α-ketoglutarate for isolated Walker carcinosarcoma 256 cells. *Proc. Soc. Exper. Biol. & Med. 98:* 303, 1958.

360. NEUMAN, R. E., and TYTELL, A. A. Purine stimulation of Walker carcinosarcoma 256 in cell culture. *Exper. Cell Res. 15:* 637, 1958.

361. NEWMAN, S. B., BORYSKO, E., and SWERDLOW, M. New sectioning techniques for light and electron microscopy. *Science 110:* 66, 1949.

362. NEWTON, A. A., and WILDY, P. Parasynchronous division of HeLa cells. *Exper. Cell Res. 16:* 624, 1959.

363. NOWELL, P. C. Differentiation of human leukemic leukocytes in tissue culture. *Exper. Cell Res. 19:* 267, 1960.

364. OSGOOD, E. E., and BROOKE, J. H. Methods developed for culture of human leukocytes. In *Methods in Medical Research*, J. V. Warren, ed. Chicago, Year Book Publishers, Inc., 1958, vol. 7, p. 156.

365. OSGOOD, E. E., and KRIPPAEHNE, M. L. The gradient tissue culture method. *Exper. Cell Res. 9:* 116, 1955.

366. OWENS, O. v. H., GEY, G. O., and GEY, M. K. A new method for the cultivation of mammalian cells suspended in agitated fluid medium. *Proc. Am. Assoc. Cancer Res., 1:* 41, 1953.

367. OYAMA, V. I., and EAGLE, H. Measurement of cell growth in tissue culture with a phenol reagent (Folin-Ciocalteu). *Proc. Soc. Exper. Biol. & Med. 91:* 305, 1956.

368. PAINTER, J. T., POMERAT, C. M., and EZELL, D. The effect of substances known to influence the activity of the nervous system on fiber outgrowth from living embryonic chick spinal cords. *Texas Rep. Biol. & Med. 7:* 417, 1949.

369. PALADE, G. E. A study of fixation for electron microscopy. *J. Exper. Med. 95:* 285, 1952.

370. PAPPENHEIMER, A. W. Experimental studies upon lymphocytes. I. The reactions of lymphocytes under various experimental conditions. *J. Exper. Med. 25:* 633, 1917.

371. PARKER, R. C. Physiologische Eigenschaften mesenchymaler Zellen *in vitro*. *Arch. exper. Zellforsch. 8:* 340, 1929.

372. PARKER, R. C. The races that constitute the group of common fibroblasts. I. The effect of blood plasma. *J. Exper. Med. 55:* 713, 1932.

373. PARKER, R. C. The races that constitute the group of common fibroblasts. II. The effect of blood serum. *J. Exper. Med. 58:* 97, 1933.

374. PARKER, R. C. The cultivation of tissues for prolonged periods in single flasks. *J. Exper. Med. 64:* 121, 1936.

375. PARKER, R. C. Studies on the production of antibodies *in vitro*. *Science 85:* 292, 1937.

376. PARKER, R. C. Cultivation of tumor cells *in vitro*. In *Canadian Cancer Conference,* R. W. Begg, ed. New York, Academic Press, Inc., 1955, vol. 1, p. 42.

377. PARKER, R. C., CASTOR, L. N., and McCULLOCH, E. A. Altered cell strains in continuous culture: A general survey. *Spec. Publ. New York Acad. Sc. 5:* 303, 1957.

378. PARKER, R. C., HEALY, G. M., and FISHER, D. C. Nutrition of animal cells in tissue culture. VII. Use of replicate cell cultures in the evaluation of synthetic media. *Canad. J. Biochem. Physiol. 32:* 306, 1954.

379. PARKER, R. C., and HOLLENDER, A. J. Propagation of Theiler's GD-VII mouse virus in tissue culture. *Proc. Soc. Exper. Biol. & Med. 60:* 88, 1945.

380. PARKER, R. C., and HOLLENDER, A. J. Propagation of rabies virus in tissue culture. *Proc. Soc. Exper. Biol. & Med. 60:* 94, 1945.

381. PARKER, R. C., MORGAN, J. F., and MORTON, H. J. Nutrition of animal cells in tissue culture. III. Effect of ethyl alcohol on cell survival and multiplication. *J. Cell. & Comp. Physiol. 36:* 411, 1950.

382. PARKER, R. C., MORGAN, J. F., and MORTON, H. J. Toxicity of rubber stoppers for tissue cultures. *Proc. Soc. Exper. Biol. & Med. 76:* 444, 1951.

383. PARKES, A. S. Preservation of human spermatozoa at low temperatures. *Brit. Med. J.* II: 212, 1945.

384. PARKES, A. S. Viability of ovarian tissue after freezing. *Proc. Roy. Soc., London, s.B. 147:* 520, 1957.

385. PASCOE, J. E. The survival of the rat's superior cervical ganglion after cooling to $-76°$ C. *Proc. Roy. Soc., London, s.B. 147:* 510, 1957.

386. PASSEY, R. D., and DMOCHOWSKI, L. Freeze-drying of tumour tissues. In *Freezing and Drying: A Symposium,* R. J. C. Harris, ed. London, Institute of Biology, 1951, p. 63.

387. PASSEY, R. D., DMOCHOWSKI, L., LASNITZKI, I., and MILLARD, A. Cultivation *in vitro* of frozen and desiccated mouse tumour tissues. *Brit. M. J. 2:* 1134, 1950.

388. PAUL, J. A perfusion chamber for cinemicrographic studies. *Quart. J. Microscop. Sc. 98:* 279, 1957.

389. PAVLOV, I. P. *The Work of the Digestive Glands,* 2nd ed., Trans. by W. H. Thompson. London, Charles Griffin & Co., Ltd., 1910.

390. PEARSE, A. G. E. *Histochemistry, Theoretical and Applied,* 2nd ed. Boston, Little, Brown & Company, 1960.

391. PEDERSEN, K. O. Ultracentrifugal and electrophoretic studies on fetuin. *J. Phys. Colloid Chem. 51:* 164, 1947.

392. PERKINS, J. J. *Principles and Methods of Sterilization.* Springfield, Ill., Charles C Thomas, Publisher, 1956.

393. PETERSON, E. R., DEITCH, A. D., and MURRAY, M. R. Type of glass as a factor in maintenance of coverslip cultures. *Lab. Invest. 8:* 1507, 1959.

394. PHILLIPS, H. J., and ANDREWS, R. V. Some protective solutions for tissue-cultured cells. *Exper. Cell Res. 16:* 678, 1959.

395. POLGE, C. Low-temperature storage of mammalian spermatozoa. *Proc. Roy. Soc., London, s.B. 147:* 498, 1957.

396. POLGE, C., and LOVELOCK, J. E. Preservation of bull semen at $-79°$ C. *Vet. Rec. 64:* 396, 1952.

397. POLGE, C., SMITH, A. U., and PARKES, A. S. Revival of spermatozoa after vitrification and dehydration at low temperatures. *Nature 164:* 666, 1949.

398. POMERAT, C. M. Action of chemical agents on living cells. In *Methods in Medical Research*, M. B. Visscher, ed. Chicago, Year Book Publishers, Inc., 1951, vol. 4, p. 260.

399. POMERAT, C. M. Perfusion chamber. In *Methods in Medical Research*, M. B. Visscher, ed. Chicago, Year Book Publishers, Inc., 1951, vol. 4, p. 275.

400. POMERAT, C. M., DRAGER, G. A., and PAINTER, J. T. Effect of some barbiturates on tissues *in vitro*. *Proc. Soc. Exper. Biol. & Med. 63:* 322, 1946.

401. POMERAT, C. M., and WILLMER, E. N. Studies on the growth of tissues *in vitro*. VII. Carbohydrate metabolism and mitosis. *J. Exper. Biol. 16:* 232, 1939.

402. PORTER, K. R. Observations on a submicroscopic basophilic component of cytoplasm. *J. Exper. Med. 97:* 727, 1953.

403. PORTER, K. R., and BLUM, J. A study of microtomy for electron microscopy. *Anat. Rec. 117:* 685, 1953.

404. PORTER, K. R., CLAUDE, A., and FULLAM, E. F. A study of tissue culture cells by electron microscopy. Methods and preliminary observations. *J. Exper. Med. 81:* 233, 1945.

405. PORTER, K. R., and HAWN, C. V. Z. The culture of tissue cells in clots formed from purified bovine fibrinogen and thrombin. *Proc. Soc. Exper. Biol. & Med. 65:* 309, 1947.

406. PORTER, K. R., and PAPPAS, G. D. Collagen formation by fibroblasts of the chick embryo dermis. *J. Biophys. Biochem. Cytol. 5:* 153, 1959.

407. PORTER, K. R., and THOMPSON, H. P. Some morphological features of cultured rat sarcoma cells as revealed by the electron microscope. *Cancer Res. 7:* 431, 1947.

408. PORTERFIELD, J. S., and ALLISON, A. C. Studies with poxviruses by an improved plaque technique. *Virology 10:* 233, 1960.

409. POTTER, V. R., and ELVEHJEM, C. A. A modified method for the study of tissue oxidations. *J. Biol. Chem. 114:* 495, 1936.

410. PROP, F. J. A. Organ cultures of total mammary glands of the mouse. *Nature 184:* 379, 1959.

411. PUCK, T. T. Quantitative studies on mammalian cells *in vitro*. *Rev. Modern Phys. 31:* 433, 1959.

412. PUCK, T. T. The action of radiation on mammalian cells. *Am. Naturalist 94:* 95, 1960.

413. PUCK, T. T., CIECIURA, S. J., and FISHER, H. W. Clonal growth *in vitro* of human cells with fibroblastic morphology. Comparison of growth and genetic characteristics of single epithelioid and fibroblast-like cells from a variety of human organs. *J. Exper. Med. 106:* 145, 1957.

414. PUCK, T. T., CIECIURA, S. J., and ROBINSON, A. Genetics of somatic mammalian cells. III. Long-term cultivation of euploid cells from human and animal subjects. *J. Exper. Med. 108:* 945, 1958.

415. PUCK, T. T., and FISHER, H. W. Genetics of somatic mammalian cells. I. Demonstration of the existence of mutants with different growth requirements in a human cancer cell strain (HeLa). *J. Exper. Med. 104:* 427, 1956.

416. PUCK, T. T., and MARCUS, P. I. A rapid method for viable cell titration and clone production with HeLa cells in tissue culture: the use of X-irradiated cells to supply conditioning factors. *Proc. Nat. Acad. Sc. U.S. 41:* 432, 1955.

417. PUCK, T. T., and MARCUS, P. I. Action of X-rays on mammalian cells. *J. Exper. Med. 103:* 653, 1956.

418. Puck, T. T., Marcus, P. I., and Cieciura, S. J. Clonal growth of mammalian cells *in vitro*. Growth characteristics of colonies from single HeLa cells with and without a "feeder" layer. *J. Exper. Med. 103:* 273, 1956.

419. Puck, T. T., Morkovin, D., Marcus, P. I., and Cieciura, S. J. Action of X-rays on mammalian cells. II. Survival curves of cells from normal human tissues. *J. Exper. Med. 106:* 485, 1957.

420. Pumper, R. W. Adaptation of tissue culture cells to a serum-free medium. *Science 128:* 363, 1958.

421. Quastel, J. H., and Bickis, I. J. Metabolism of normal tissues and neoplasms *in vitro*. *Nature 183:* 281, 1959.

422. Quay, W. B. Experimental cyanine red, a new stain for nucleic acids and acid mucopolysaccharides. *Stain Technol. 32:* 175, 1957.

423. Rappaport, C. Trypsinization of monkey-kidney tissue: an automatic method for the preparation of cell suspensions. *Bull. World Health Organ. 14:* 147, 1956.

424. Rappaport, C. Colorimetric method for estimating number of cells in monolayer cultures without physiological damage. *Proc. Soc. Exper. Biol. & Med. 96:* 309, 1957.

425. Rappaport, C. Studies on properties of surfaces required for growth of mammalian cells in synthetic medium. II. The monkey kidney cell. *Exper. Cell Res. 20:*479, 1960.

426. Rappaport, C., and Bishop, C. B. Improved method for treating glass to produce surfaces suitable for the growth of certain mammalian cells in synthetic medium. *Exper. Cell Res. 20:*580, 1960.

427. Rappaport, C., Poole, J. P., and Rappaport, H. P. Studies on properties of surfaces required for growth of mammalian cells in synthetic medium. I. The HeLa cell. *Exper. Cell Res. 20:*465, 1960.

428. von Recklinghausen, F. D. Ueber die Erzeugung von rothen Blutkörperchen. *Arch. mikroskop. Anat. 2:* 137, 1866.

429. Reed, L. J., and Muench, H. A simple method of estimating fifty per cent endpoints. *Am. J. Hyg. 27:* 493, 1938.

430. Rey, L. R. Aspects physico-chimiques de la congélation des tissus et de leur conservation par les basses températures. *Ann. Nutr. Aliment. 11:* 103, 1957.

431. Rey, L. R. Studies on the action of liquid nitrogen on cultures *in vitro* of fibroblasts. *Proc. Roy. Soc., London, s.B. 147:* 460, 1957.

432. Rey, L. R. Physiologie du coeur le l'embryon de Poulet *in vitro* après congélation à très basse température. *J. Embryol. Exp. Morphol. 6:* 171, 1958.

433. Richter, K. M., and Woodward, N. W., Jr. A versatile type of perfusion chamber for long-term maintenance and direct microscopic observation of tissues in culture. *Exper. Cell Res. 9:* 585, 1955.

434. Rigas, D. A., and Osgood, E. E. Purification and properties of the phytohemagglutinin of *Phaseolus vulgaris*. *J. Biol. Chem. 212:* 607, 1955.

435. Rinaldini, L. M. A quantitative method for growing animal cells *in vitro*. *Nature 173:* 1134, 1954.

436. Rinaldini, L. M. J. The isolation of living cells from animal tissues. *Internat. Rev. Cytol. 7:* 587, 1958.

437. Rinaldini, L. M. An improved method for the isolation and quantitative cultivation of embryonic cells. *Exper. Cell Res. 16:* 477, 1959.

438. Ringer, S. Further observations regarding the antagonism between calcium salts and sodium, potassium and ammonium salts. *J. Physiol. 18:* 425, 1895.

439. Rivers, T. M., Haagen, E., and Muckenfuss, R. S. Development in tissue cultures of the intracellular changes characteristic of vaccinal and herpetic infections. *J. Exper. Med. 50:* 665, 1929.

440. Rivers, T. M., Haagen, E., and Muckenfuss, R. S. A study of vaccinal immunity in tissue cultures. *J. Exper. Med. 50:* 673, 1929.

441. Rivers, T. M., and Ward, S. M. Jennerian prophylaxis by means of intradermal injections of culture vaccine virus. *J. Exper. Med. 62:* 549, 1935.

442. Robbins, F. C., Enders, J. F., and Weller, T. H. Cytopathogenic effect of poliomyelitis viruses *in vitro* on human embryonic tissues. *Proc. Soc. Exper. Biol. & Med. 75:* 370, 1950.

443. Robbins, F. C., Enders, J. F., Weller, T. H., and Florentino, G. L. Studies on the cultivation of poliomyelitis viruses in tissue culture. V. The direct isolation and serologic identification of virus strains in tissue culture from patients with nonparalytic and paralytic poliomyelitis. *Am. J. Hyg. 54:* 286, 1951.

444. Robbins, F. C., Weller, T. H., and Enders, J. F. Studies on the cultivation of poliomyelitis viruses in tissue culture. II. The propagation of the poliomyelitis viruses in roller-tube cultures of various human tissues. *J. Immunol. 69:* 673, 1952.

445. Robertson, H. E., and Boyer, P. D. Orthophosphite as a buffer for biological studies. *Arch. Biochem. 62:* 396, 1956.

446. Robertson, H. E., Brunner, K. T., and Syverton, J. T. Propagation *in vitro* of poliomyelitis viruses. VII. pH change of HeLa cell cultures for assay. *Proc. Soc. Exper. Biol. & Med. 88:* 119, 1955.

447. Robinson, L. B., Wichelhausen, R. H., and Roizman, B. Contamination of human cell cultures by pleuropneumonialike organisms. *Science 124:* 1147, 1956.

448. Rose, G. A separable and multipurpose tissue culture chamber. *Texas Rep. Biol. & Med. 12:* 1074, 1954.

449. Rose, G. G. Evidence for intercellular exchange of cytoplasmic components between associated cells in tissue culture. *Texas Rep. Biol. & Med. 18:* 103, 1960.

450. Rose, G. G., Pomerat, C. M., Shindler, T. O., and Trunnell, J. B. A cellophane-strip technique for culturing tissue in multipurpose culture chambers. *J. Biophys. Biochem. Cytol. 4:* 761, 1958.

451. Rose, W. C. The nutritive significance of the amino acids. *Physiol. Rev. 18:* 109, 1938.

452. Rosenberg, S., and Kirk, P. L. Tissue culture studies. Identification of components and synthetic replacements for the active fraction of chick embryo extract ultrafiltrate. *J. Gen. Physiol. 37:* 239, 1953.

453. Rosenberg, S., Zitcer, E., and Kirk, P. L. Tissue culture studies. Isolation of the active components in the ultrafilterable portion of the chick embryo extract. *J. Gen. Physiol. 37:* 231, 1953.

454. Rothblat, G. H., and Morton, H. E. Detection and possible source of contaminating pleuropneumonialike organisms (PPLO) in cultures of tissue cells. *Proc. Soc. Exper. Biol. & Med. 100:* 87, 1959.

455. Rothfels, K., and Parker, R. C. The karyotypes of cell lines recently established from normal mouse tissues. *J. Exper. Zool. 142:*507, 1959.

456. Rothfels, K. H., and Siminovitch, L. An air-drying technique for flattening chromosomes in mammalian cells grown *in vitro*. *Stain Technol. 33:* 73, 1958.

457. Rous, P., and Jones, F. A. A method of obtaining suspensions of living cells from the fixed tissues, and for the plating out of individual cells. *J. Exper. Med. 23:* 555, 1916.

458. ROUX, W. Beiträge zur Entwicklungsmechanik des Embryo. *Ztschr. Biol. 21:* 411, 1885.

459. RUBIN, H., BALUDA, M., and HOTCHIN, J. E. The maturation of Western equine encephalomyelitis virus and its release from chick embryo cells in suspension. *J. Exper. Med. 101:* 205, 1955.

460. SABIN, A. B. The mechanism of immunity to filterable viruses. II. Fate of the virus in a system consisting of susceptible tissue, immune serum and virus, and the role of the tissue in the mechanism of immunity. *Brit. J. Exper. Path. 16:* 84, 1935.

461. SABIN, A. B. Coxsackie viruses (discussion). *Ann. New York Acad. Sc. 67:* 250, 1957.

462. SABIN, A. B. Present status of attenuated live virus poliomyelitis vaccine. *Bull. New York Acad. Med. 33:* 17, 1957.

463. SALK, J. E. Recent studies on immunization against poliomyelitis. *Pediatrics 12:* 471, 1953.

464. SALK, J. E., BENNETT, B. L., LEWIS, L. J., WARD, E. N., and YOUNGER, J. S. Studies in human subjects on active immunization against poliomyelitis. I. A preliminary report of experiments in progress. *J.A.M.A. 151:* 1081, 1953.

465. SALK, J. E., LEWIS, L. J., BENNETT, B. L., and YOUNGER, J. S. Immunization of monkeys with poliomyelitis viruses grown in cultures of monkey testicular tissue. *Fed. Proc. 11:* 480, 1952.

466. SALZMAN, N. P. Systematic fluctuations in the cellular protein, RNA and DNA during growth of mammalian cell cultures. *Biochim. et biophys. acta 31:* 158, 1959.

467. SANFORD, K. K., EARLE, W. R., EVANS, V. J., WALTZ, H. K., and SHANNON, J. E. The measurement of proliferation in tissue cultures by enumeration of cell nuclei. *J. Nat. Cancer Inst. 11:* 773, 1951.

468. SANFORD, K. K., EARLE, W. R., and LIKELY, G. D. The growth *in vitro* of single isolated tissue cells. *J. Nat. Cancer Inst. 9:* 229, 1948.

469. SANFORD, K. K., WALTZ, H. K., SHANNON, J. E., JR., EARLE, W. R., and EVANS, V. J. The effects of ultrafiltrates and residues of horse serum and chick-embryo extract on proliferation of cells *in vitro*. *J. Nat. Cancer Inst. 13:* 121, 1952.

470. SANFORD, K. K., WESTFALL, B. B., FIORAMONTI, M. C., McQUILKIN, W. T., BRYANT, J. C., PEPPERS, E. V., EVANS, V. J., and EARLE, W. R. The effect of serum fractions on the proliferation of strain L mouse cells *in vitro*. *J. Nat. Cancer Inst. 16:* 789, 1955.

471. SANTESSON, L. Characteristics of epithelial mouse tumour cells *in vitro* and tumour structures *in vivo*. A comparative study. *Acta path. et microbiol. Scand. Suppl. 24:* 1, 1935.

472. SATO, G., FISHER, H. W., and PUCK, T. T. Molecular growth requirements of single mammalian cells. *Science 126:* 961, 1957.

473. SCHABERG, A., and DEGROOT, C. A. The influence of the anterior hypophysis on the morphology and function of the adrenal cortex *in vitro*. *Exper. Cell Res. 15:* 475, 1958.

474. SCHERER, W. F. Tissue extracts and derivatives. In *An Introduction to Cell and Tissue Culture*, W. F. Scherer, ed. Minneapolis, The Burgess Publishing Co., 1955, p. 11.

475. SCHERER, W. F. Effects of freezing speed and glycerol diluent on 4–5 year survival of HeLa and L cells. *Exper. Cell Res. 19:* 175, 1960.

476. SCHERER, W. F., and HOOGASIAN, A. C. Preservation at subzero temperatures of mouse fibroblasts (strain L) and human epithelial cells (strain HeLa). *Proc. Soc. Exper. Biol. & Med. 87:* 480, 1954.

477. SCHMIDT, G., and THANNHAUSER, S. J. A method for the determination of desoxyribonucleic acid, ribonucleic acid, and phosphoproteins in animal tissues. *J. Biol. Chem. 161:* 83, 1945.

478. SCHREK, R. Studies *in vitro* on the physiology of normal and of cancerous cells. II. The survival and the glycolysis of cells under aerobic and under anaerobic conditions. *Arch. Path. 37:* 319, 1944.

479. SHAFFER, B. M. The culture of organs from the embryonic chick on cellulose-acetate fabric. *Exper. Cell Res. 11:* 244, 1956.

480. SHARP, J. A. A modification of the Rose perfusion chamber. *Exper. Cell Res. 17:* 519, 1959.

481. SIDMAN, R. L. The direct effect of insulin on organ cultures of brown fat. *Anat. Rec. 124:* 723, 1956.

482. SIMINOVITCH, L., GRAHAM, A. F., LESLEY, S. M., and NEVILL, A. Propagation of L strain mouse cells in suspension. *Exper. Cell Res. 12:* 299, 1957.

483. SIMMS, H. S. The effects of physiological agents on adult tissues *in vitro*. *Science 83:* 418, 1936.

484. SIMMS, H. S., and SANDERS, M. Use of serum ultrafiltrate in tissue cultures for studying deposition of fat and for propagation of viruses. *Arch. Path. 33:* 619, 1942.

485. SIMON, D. Sur la localisation des cellules germinales primordiales chez l'embryon de Poulet et leur mode de migration vers les ébauches gonadiques. *Compt. rend. Acad. sc. 244:* 1541, 1957.

486. SMITH, A. U. Effects of low temperatures on living cells and tissues. In *Biological Applications of Freezing and Drying*, R. J. C. Harris, ed. New York, Academic Press, Inc., 1954, p. 1.

487. SMITH, A. U., and PARKES, A. S. Storage and homografting of endocrine tissues. In *Preservation and Transplantation of Normal Tissues*, Ciba Foundation Symposium. London, J. & A. Churchill, Ltd., 1954, p. 76.

488. SMITH, H. H., CALDERÓN-CUERVO, H., and LEYVA, J. P. A comparison of high and low subcultures of yellow fever vaccine (17D) in human groups. *Am. J. Trop. Med. 21:* 579, 1941.

489. STEINHARDT, E., ISRAELI, C., and LAMBERT, R. A. Studies on the cultivation of the virus of vaccinia. *J. Infect. Dis. 13:* 294, 1913.

490. STEWART, D. C., and KIRK, P. L. The liquid medium in tissue culture. *Biol. Rev. (Cambridge) 29:* 119, 1954.

491. STONE, H. B., OWINGS, J. C., and GEY, G. O. Transplantation of living grafts of thyroid and parathyroid glands. *Ann. Surg. 100:* 613, 1934.

492. STRANGEWAYS, T. S. P., and FELL, H. B. Experimental studies on the differentiation of embryonic tissues growing *in vivo* and *in vitro*. I. The development of the undifferentiated limb-bud (a) when subcutaneously grafted into the postembryonic chick and (b) when cultivated *in vitro*. *Proc. Roy. Soc., London, s.B. 99:* 340, 1925–26.

493. STRANGEWAYS, T. S. P., and FELL, H. B. Experimental studies on the differentiation of embryonic tissues growing *in vivo* and *in vitro*. II. The development of the isolated early embryonic eye of the fowl when cultivated *in vitro*. *Proc. Roy. Soc., London, s.B. 100:* 273, 1926.

494. STROUD, A. N., and BRUES, A. M. Radiation effects in tissue culture. *Texas Rep. Biol. & Med. 12:* 931, 1954.

495. STULBERG, C. S., SOULE, H. D., and BERMAN, L. Preservation of human epithelial-like and fibroblast-like cell strains at low temperatures. *Proc. Soc. Exper. Biol. & Med. 98:* 428, 1958.

496. SWIFT, H. F., MOEN, J. K., and VAUBEL, E. A comparison of ocular micrometric and projectoscopic methods of estimating growths in tissue cultures. *J. Exper. Med. 60:* 419, 1934.

497. SWIM, H. E. Microbiological aspects of tissue culture. *Ann. Rev. Microbiol. 13:* 141, 1959.

498. SWIM, H. E., HAFF, R. F., and PARKER, R. F. Some practical aspects of storing mammalian cells in the dry-ice chest. *Cancer Res. 18:* 711, 1958.

499. SWIM, H. E., and PARKER, R. F. Nonbicarbonate buffers in cell culture media. *Science 122:* 466, 1955.

500. SWIM, H. E., and PARKER, R. F. Vitamin requirements of uterine fibroblasts, strain U12-72; their replacement by related compounds. *Arch. Biochem. 78:* 46, 1958.

501. SWIM, H. E., and PARKER, R. F. The amino acid requirements of a permanent strain of altered uterine fibroblasts (U12-705). *Canad. J. Biochem. Physiol. 36:* 861, 1958.

502. SWIM, H. E., and PARKER, R. F. The role of carbon dioxide as an essential nutrient for six permanent strains of fibroblasts. *J. Biophys. Biochem. Cytol. 4:* 525, 1958.

503. SWIM, H. E., and PARKER, R. F. Stable tissue culture media prepared in dry form. *J. Lab. & Clin. Med. 52:* 309, 1958.

504. SYKES, J. A., and MOORE, E. B. A new chamber for tissue culture. *Proc. Soc. Exper. Biol. & Med. 100:* 125, 1959.

505. Symposium: *Preservation and Transplantation of Normal Tissues.* Ciba Foundation. London, J. & A. Churchill, Ltd., 1954.

506. Symposium (under the leadership of A. S. Parkes): *A Discussion on Viability of Mammalian Cells and Tissues after Freezing. Proc. Roy. Soc., London, s.B. 147:* 423, 1957.

507. SYVERTON, J. T., and McLAREN, L. C. Human cells in continuous culture. I. Derivation of cell strains from esophagus, palate, liver, and lung. *Cancer Res. 17:* 923, 1957.

508. SYVERTON, J. T., and McLAREN, L. C. Stable and pure line cell strains: derivation and comparative viral susceptibility. *Texas Rep. Biol. & Med. 15:* 577, 1957.

509. SYVERTON, J. T., and SCHERER, W. F. The application of mammalian cells in continuous culture for assays in virology. *Ann. New York Acad. Sc. 58:* 1056, 1954.

510. SYVERTON, J. T., SCHERER, W. F., and ELWOOD, P. M. Studies on the propagation *in vitro* of poliomyelitis viruses. V. The application of strain HeLa human epithelial cells for isolation and typing. *J. Lab. & Clin. Med. 43:* 286, 1954.

511. TAFT, E. B. The problem of a standardized technic for the methyl-green-pyronin stain. *Stain Technol. 26:* 205, 1951.

512. TENBROECK, C. A simple grinder for soft tissues. *Science 74:* 98, 1931.

513. THEILER, M., and SMITH, H. H. The effect of prolonged cultivation *in vitro* upon the pathogenicity of yellow fever virus. *J. Exper. Med. 65:* 767, 1937.

514. THEILER, M., and SMITH, H. H. The use of yellow fever virus modified by *in vitro* cultivation for human immunization. *J. Exper. Med. 65:* 787, 1937.

515. THICKE, J. C., DUNCAN, D., WOOD, W., FRANKLIN, A. E., and RHODES, A. J. Cultivation of poliomyelitis virus in tissue culture. I. Growth of the Lansing strain in human embryonic tissues. *Canad. J. M. Sc. 30:* 231, 1952.

516. THOMAS, W. J., ZIEGLER, D. W., SCHEPARTZ, S. A., and McLIMANS, W. F. Use of arginine to eliminate medium changes in tissue culture systems. *Science 127:* 591, 1958.

517. THOMSON, D. Some further researches on the cultivation of tissues *in vitro. Proc. Roy. Soc. Med. 7* (Marcus Beck Lab. Rep.): 21, 1914.

518. TIMOFEYEVSKI, A. D. Tumor origin as determined by tissue culture. *Am. Rev. Soviet Med. 4:* 106, 1946.

519. TROWELL, O. A. The culture of mature organs in a synthetic medium. *Exper. Cell Res. 16:* 118, 1959.

520. TROWELL, O. A., and WILLMER, E. N. Studies on the growth of tissues *in vitro*. VI. The effects of some tissue extracts on the growth of periosteal fibroblasts. *J. Exper. Biol. 16:* 60, 1939.

521. TYRODE, M. V. The mode of action of some purgative salts. *Arch. internat. pharmacodyn. 20:* 205, 1910.

522. VALLEE, B. L., HUGHES, W. L., JR., and GIBSON, J. G., 2ND. A method for the separation of leukocytes from whole blood by flotation on serum albumin. *Blood, Spec. Issue No. 1:* 82, 1947.

523. VAN RIPER, H. E. Progress in the control of paralytic poliomyelitis through vaccination. *Canad. J. Pub. Health 46:* 425, 1955.

524. VOGELAAR, J. P. M., and ERLICHMAN, E. A feeding solution for cultures of human fibroblasts. *Am. J. Cancer 18:* 28, 1933.

525. WALTER, C. W. *The Aseptic Treatment of Wounds.* New York, The Macmillan Company, 1948.

526. WARREN, J., WITTLER, R. G., and VINCENT, M. The cultivation of tissues in small sealable dishes. *J. Lab. & Clin. Med. 46:* 144, 1955.

527. WAYMOUTH, C. Proteins with growth-promoting action on tissue cells *in vitro. Proc. Soc. Exper. Biol. & Med. 64:* 25, 1947.

528. WAYMOUTH, C. The nutrition of animal cells. *Internat. Rev. Cytol. 3:* 1, 1954.

529. WAYMOUTH, C. A rapid quantitative hematocrit method for measuring increase in cell population of strain L (Earle) cells cultivated in serum-free nutrient solutions. *J. Nat. Cancer Inst. 17:* 305, 1956.

530. WAYMOUTH, C. A serum-free nutrient solution sustaining rapid and continuous proliferation of strain L (Earle) mouse cells. *J. Nat. Cancer Inst. 17:* 315, 1956.

531. WAYMOUTH, C. Rapid proliferation of sublines of NCTC clone 929 (strain L) mouse cells in a simple chemically defined medium (MB 752/1). *J. Nat. Cancer Inst. 22:* 1003, 1959.

532. WAYMOUTH, C., and WHITE, P. R. Filtration of embryo extract for tissue cultures. *Science 119:* 321, 1954.

533. WEINSTEIN, H. J., ALEXANDER, C., YOSHIHARA, G. M., and KIRBY, W. M. M. Preparation of human amnion tissue cultures. *Proc. Soc. Exper. Biol. & Med. 92:* 535, 1956.

534. WEISS, L. P., and FAWCETT, D. W. Cytochemical observations on chicken monocytes, macrophages and giant cells in tissue culture. *J. Histochem. 1:* 47, 1953.

535. WELLER, T. H., ENDERS, J. F., ROBBINS, F. C., and STODDARD, M. B. Studies on the cultivation of poliomyelitis viruses in tissue culture. I. The propagation of poliomyelitis viruses in suspended cell cultures of various human tissues. *J. Immunol. 69:* 645, 1952.

536. WELLER, T. H., WITTON, H. M., and BELL, E. J. The etiologic agents of varicella and herpes zoster. Isolation, propagation, and cultural characteristics *in vitro. J. Exper. Med. 108:* 843, 1958.

537. WESTWOOD, J. C. N., MACPHERSON, I. A., and TITMUSS, D. H. J. Transformation of normal cells in tissue culture: its significance relative to malignancy and virus vaccine production. *Brit. J. Exper. Path. 38:* 138, 1957.

538. WHITE, P. R. Cultivation of animal tissues *in vitro* in nutrients of precisely known constitution. *Growth 10:* 231, 1946.

539. WHITE, P. R. Prolonged survival of excised animal tissues *in vitro* in nutrients of known constitution. *J. Cell. & Comp. Physiol. 34:* 221, 1949.

540. WHITMORE, G. F., TILL, J. E., GWATKIN, R. B. L., SIMINOVITCH, L., and GRAHAM, A. F. Increase of cellular constituents in X-irradiated mammalian cells. *Biochim. et biophys. acta 30:* 583, 1958.

541. WILLMER, E. N. Studies on the growth of tissues *in vitro.* I. Some effects of the mechanical properties of the medium on the growth of chick heart fibroblasts. *J. Exper. Biol. 10:* 317, 1933.

542. WILLMER, E. N. Studies on the growth of tissues *in vitro.* II. An analysis of the growth of chick heart fibroblasts in a hanging drop of fluid medium. *J. Exper. Biol. 10:* 323, 1933.

543. WILLMER, E. N. Carbohydrate metabolism of chick fibroblasts *in vitro. J. Exper. Biol. 18:* 237, 1942.

544. WILLMER, E. N. *Tissue Culture*, 3rd ed. London, Methuen & Co., Ltd., 1958.

545. WILLMER, E. N., and JACOBY, F. Studies on the growth of tissues *in vitro.* IV. On the manner in which growth is stimulated by extracts of embryo tissues. *J. Exper. Biol. 13:* 237, 1936.

546. WILSON, H., JACKSON, E. B., and BRUES, A. M. The metabolism of tissue cultures. I. Preliminary studies on chick embryo. *J. Gen. Physiol. 25:* 689, 1942.

547. WINNICK, R. E., and WINNICK, T. Utilization of amino acids, peptides, and protein by cultures of embryonic heart. *J. Nat. Cancer Inst. 14:* 519, 1953.

548. WOLFF, E. Potentialités et affinités des tissus, révélées par la culture *in vitro* d'organes en associations hétérogènes et xénoplastiques. *Bull. Soc. zool. France 79:* 357, 1954.

549. WOLFF, E., and HAFFEN, K. Action féminisante de la gonade droite de l'embryon femelle de canard en culture *in vitro. Compt. rend. Soc. biol. 146:* 1772, 1952.

550. WOLFF, E., and HAFFEN, K. Sur le developpement et la differenciation sexuelle des gonadés embryonnaires d'Oiseau en culture *in vitro. J. Exper. Zool. 119:* 381, 1952.

551. WOLFF, E., and SCHNEIDER, N. La culture d'un sarcome de souris sur des organes de Poulet explantés *in vitro. Arch. Anat. microscop. Morphol. exper. 46:* 173, 1957.

552. WOOD, W., FRANKLIN, A. E., CLARK, E. M., DUNCAN, D., and RHODES, A. J. Cultivation of poliomyelitis virus in tissue culture. III. Synthetic medium in roller tube cultures. *Proc. Soc. Exper. Biol. & Med. 81:* 434, 1952.

553. YOUNGER, J. S. Monolayer tissue cultures. I. Preparation and standardization of suspensions of trypsin-dispersed monkey kidney cells. *Proc. Soc. Exper. Biol. & Med. 85:* 202, 1954.

554. ZEIDMAN, I. Chemical factors in the mutual adhesiveness of epithelial cells. *Cancer Res. 7:* 386, 1947.

555. ZIEGLER, D. W., DAVIS, E. V., THOMAS, W. J., and McLIMANS, W. F. The propagation of mammalian cells in a 20-liter stainless steel fermentor. *Appl. Microbiol. 6:* 305, 1958.

556. ZITCER, E. M., FOGH, J., and DUNNEBACKE, T. H. Human amnion cells for large-scale production of polio virus. *Science 122:* 30, 1955.

557. ZWARTOUW, H. T., and WESTWOOD, J. C. N. Factors affecting growth and glycolysis in tissue culture. *Brit. J. Exper. Path. 39:* 529, 1958.

558. ZWILLING, E. Dissociation of chick embryo cells by means of a chelating compound. *Science 120:* 219, 1954.

Index

Acetic alcohol fixatives, 300, 304, 306, 308, 309

Acetoorcein stain, 304, 306

Acid alcohol, 303, 314

Albumin-flotation method, for separating leukocytes from blood, 135

for separating malignant cells from serosanguineous fluids, 131

Alterations, cellular, prevention of, 176

Amino acids, in chemically defined media, 64, 69, 72

uptake of, 239

Amnion, human, cells from, 127

Amniotic fluid, bovine, 108, 110

Amphibian cells, 62, 148

Antibiotics, 8, 9, 10, 47, 69

sensitivity discs, 48

Antibody formation, 193

Anticoagulants, 89

Antiseptics, 48, 50, 51

Antitryptic agents, 168

Ascitic fluid, 2

Assay procedures, with cell suspensions, 184, 187, 219

with fibroblast strains, 161

with fresh tissues, 118, 138

with leukocytes, 134, 165, 191

Auto-burets, for storing medium, 15

Bacteriological preparations, in culture media, 109, 113

Balanced salt solutions. *See* Salt solutions

Blood cells, 191

See also Leukocytes

vessels, 269

Blood-forming organs, cells of, 191

Bone formation, 238

Bouin's fluid, 299

Bovine amniotic fluid, 108

plasma albumin, 132, 135

serum albumin, 98, 110, 113

Buffered saline, phosphate, 58

phosphite, 58

Buffy-coat cultures, 134, 165, 190, 269

Cabinets, safety, 12

with controlled atmosphere, 184

Carbohydrates, in chemically defined media, 71

Carbon dioxide, for adjusting pH, 59

and bicarbonate buffer, 59, 73

cabinet for cultures, 184

solid, for low-temperature storage, 284

Carnoy's fluid, 301

Cartilage, constituents of, in chemically defined media, 68

development of, 238

Cell aggregates, cultivation of, 242

Cell leakage of P³², 57
Cell lines, established, 4, 5, 161, 175, 176, 197
Cell migration and mitosis, 236, 269
Cell multiplication, and differentiation, 236
   high speed, 178
   parasynchronous, 307
Cell nuclei, isolated and counted, 185, 276
Cell nutrition, 62, 81, 91, 99, 109, 113, 211
Cell strains, development of, 209
Cell suspensions, density of, estimated
   by counting intact cells, 281
   by counting isolated nuclei, 276
   by determining protein colorimetrically, 276
   by determining purines and pyrimidines, 276
   with electronic counter, 273
   from nuclei acid determinations, 274
   from optical density, 272
   from packed cell volumes, 271
Cell types, 5
Cell viability determined by dye-exclusion tests, 282
   by ability to form colonies, 207, 215
Cellophane, 225
   perforated, 16, 188, 195
Cells, capable of division, estimation of, 207, 215
   dissociated, reaggregation of, 242
   in fluid medium, cultivation of, 174
      methods of harvesting, 187
   genetic characteristics of, 209
   intact, counted in hemocytometer, 281
   malignant. See Malignant cells
   packed, measured in hematocrit, 271
   parasynchronous division of, 307
   plating efficiency (Puck) of, 208, 217
   prepared for cultivation, 115
   preserved by freezing, 284
   propagated in suspension, 197, 306
   released from tissues by chelating agents, 131
      by enzymes, 6, 119, 130
   single, isolation of, 209
   trypsinized, from human amnion, 127
      trom monkey kidney, 122
      from newborn-mouse brain, 129

Cells (Continued)
   trypsinized (Continued)
      from slaughterhouse material, 126
      from whole chick and mouse embryos, 128
Cellular adaptation, 178
Cellular attachment to glass, 98
Cellulose-sponge cultures, 170
Chelating agents, 25, 27, 131, 189, 274
Chemical analysis, cells harvested for, 189
Chemically defined media, 62, 81, 229, 237, 288
   amino acid levels (millimoles) of 5 media, 72
   growth of L cells (Earle) in, 10, 76
   ingredients (mg per l) of 10 media, 74
   preparation of CMRL-1066, 77
   prepared from mixed ingredients stored in solid form, 80
Chemo-turbidostat (Cooper et al.), 205
Chlorazene solution, 117
Chondrosarcoma, mouse (S180), 229
Chromosomes, 165, 221
   flattened without squashing, 304
   squash technique, 306
   permanent preparations, 307
Citrate, sodium, as anticoagulant, 90
   in harvesting cell cultures, 188
Cleansing procedures, 25
Clones, isolated from single cells, 209
   mutant, 220
Coenzymes, in chemically defined media, 68, 69
Colchicine, 304, 305, 306
Collagen (rat-tail), as substitute for plasma, 172
Collagenase, 130
Conditioned medium (Earle), 211, 212, 215
Connective tissue cells. See Fibroblasts
Contaminated materials, disinfection of, 48
Cornwall syringe (automatic), for preparing replicate cell cultures, 186
Coverslip cultures, 138
   for assay purposes, 118
   with double coverslips, 145, 223
   as hanging drops, 139
   with perforated cellophane, 148
   with perforated slides, 151

Coverslip cultures (*Continued*)
  with plasma, 139
  without plasma, 144
  with ring supports, 16, 145
  with Romicron slides, 148
Coverslips, glass, 16, 138
  mica, 16, 139
  with stained cultures, 312
Crystal violet, 276, 278, 280, 281
Culture bottles, milk dilution, 17, 183
  Povitsky, 183, 264
  prescription, 17, 27, 183
Culture chamber (Trowell) for tissue
      fragments, 238
Culture dishes (Petri), 17, 183, 212, 234,
      256, 304
  plastic, 28
  sealable, 17
Culture flasks (Carrel), 17, 128, 183,
      215, 222, 312
  (Earle), 18, 183
  (Erlenmeyer), 193, 263
  (Lindbergh), 222
  (Porter), 18
  (Swim), 18, 183
Culture slides, micro, 18, 138, 242
  Romicron, 19, 148
Culture tubes, Leighton, 19, 182
  observation track for, 19
  screw-capped, 19
Cultures, agitated by various means, 197
  for embryological studies, 227
  fixed and stained, 298
  fluid, for cells in suspension, 197
    on coverslips, 144, 148, 182
    in flasks and bottles, 174, 183
    with perforated cellophane, 148, 195
    with perfusion of medium, 222
    in Petri dishes, 183, 212, 215
    in roller tubes, 182, 199
    in stationary tubes, 179, 250
    for virus studies, 245
  incubated at lowered temperatures,
      161
  parabiotic (Eagle), 71
  plasma, 139, 152
  preserved by freezing, 284
  replicate, 66, 182, 184
  from single cells, 209
  sponge-matrix, 170, 195
  stationary, 174, 182, 222

Cytogenerator (Graff and McCarty), 204
Cytopathic effects (CPE) of virus multi-
      plication, 247

Dakin's solution, 116, 117
  preparation of, 51
Deoxyribonuclease (DNAse), 308
Detergents, 30
Differentiation, cellular, 236
Disinfectants, 48, 50, 51
Dissociated cells, reaggregation of, 242
DNAP values, 67, 186, 275
Double-coverslip cultures, 145
Dry ice (solid CO_2), for low-temperature
      storage of cells, 284
  and alcohol, 291, 296

Earle's salt solution, 57
Eggs (fowl) for culture work, 19, 103
Electron microscopy, cultures for, 320
  methyl methacrylate, 321
  Porter-Blum microtome, 322
Embryology, experimental, 2, 227
Embryonic induction (Grobstein), 232
Enzymes, in cell nutrition, 68, 76
  diluting agents for, 59, 128
    Puck's saline A, 59, 128
    Rinaldini's solution, 59
  to release cells from glass, 120, 188, 274
    from plasma coagulum, 120, 165,
      267, 270
    from tissues, 119
  in selecting particular cell types, 130
Epithelium, 164
Equipment, special, 15
Erlenmeyer-flask cultures, 193, 263
Extract, embryo tissue, 62, 92, 110, 111,
      139, 154, 234
  and cell division, 99, 102
  dialyzed, 64, 65
  frozen and dried, 106
  nucleoprotein fractions of, 65, 100
  preparation of, 102
  ultrafiltrate of, 100

Fatty acids, in chemically defined media,
      69
Feeder cells, 111, 208, 211, 215
Fermenter vessels, for cells cultivated in
      suspension, 203
Fetuin, 99

Feulgen stain, 307
Fiberglas cloth, for protective pads, 42
Fibrinogen cultures, 159, 168, 169
Fibroblasts, one year without subculturing, 153
    strains, development of, 162
    34-year-old strain (Carrel), 4, 162
Filters, for air, 11
    for fluids, 42
        cleansing of, 29, 32, 33
        sterilization of, 41
    membrane (Millipore), 46, 232
    steam (Selas), 34
Filtration, 42, 232, 265
Fishes, bony, cells of, 62
Fixation and staining of cells, 298
    in fluid media, 301
    in plasma, 310
Fixing reagents, 299
Flask and bottle techniques. See also Culture flasks
    and adjustment of pH, 59, 155
    for cells in suspension, 197
    for continuous circulation of medium, 222
    for fluid cultures, 183
    for plasma cultures, 152
    for virus studies, 245
Flasks. See also Culture flasks
    for sterilizing fluids (Pour-O-Vac), 41
    trypsinization (Rappaport), 24, 122
Formalin, neutral, 265, 299
Formvar, 320
Freeze-drying (cells and tissues), 288
    (media), 83, 106
Freezing, cells preserved by, 284
    estimating percentage of survivors, 290
    glycerol protection, 285, 286
    ice-crystal formation, 285
    polyvinyl pyrrolidone, 297
    rapid freezing, 288, 290
    slow freezing, 285, 289, 291
    thawing, speed of, 288, 297
    ultra-rapid freezing, 285
Freezing-point (cryoscopic) determinations, 53

Gas burner, micro, 19
    Touch-O-Matic, 13
Gas mixtures for pH adjustment, 60, 155, 180, 184

Gelfoam (Upjohn) particles in cultures, 195
Germicidal lamps, 11, 12, 13
Gey's salt solution, 57
Glands, cultivation of, 229, 231, 235
Glassware, cleansing, 25
    contaminated, disinfection of, 48
    special items, 15
    sterilization, 39
    surface properties, 26
Glucose utilization, 242, 270
Glycerol protection during freezing of cells, 285, 286
Glycolysis, 270
Gonads, development of, 229
Gradient method (Osgood) for cultivation of blood cells, 191
Grafts (endocrine) prepared for transplantation, 231, 235
Growth, cycles, 197
    factors (accessory), 66
    measurements, 267
    organized, 227

Hands, antibacterial treatment of, 50
Hanging-drop cultures, 138
"Hanks-Simms" medium, 110
Hanks's salt solution, 57
Harvesting cells and tissues from fluid cultures, 187
Helly's fluid (Zenker-formol), 300
Hematocrit for measuring packed cell volumes, 267, 271
Hematoxylin (Delafield), 303
    (Harris), 314
    stain, for fluid cultures, 302
        for sections, 318
        for whole plasma cultures, 313
Hemocytometer, for cell counts, 279, 281
Heparin, 89
Histological procedures, 298
History of tissue culture, 1
Hodgkin's disease, 151
Homogenizers for preparing tissue extracts, 104
Homoiografting, 231
Hormones, 63, 229, 231
Hyaluronidase, in filtration of embryo extract, 107

Inclusion bodies, 246, 248
Incubators, with controlled atmosphere, 19, 184
  walk-in, 13, 19
Inorganic requirements of cells, 73
Insect tissues, 62
Instruments, 20
  cleansing, 33
  sharpening, 236
  sterilization, 40
Insulin, 63, 229
Iodine, tincture of, 317
Irradiated cells as feeder layers (Puck), 215
Irradiation effects, assessment of, 220, 270
Isotonic solutions, 53
Isotopes, radioactive 57, 102, 239, 242

Joint formation, 227

Kahle's fluid, 301, 308, 309
Karyotype, 177, 221
Knives made from razor blades, 118, 119

Laboratory arrangements, 8
  Carrel's, 8, 9, 49
  Pavlov's, 8
Lactalbumin hydrolysate, 110, 112, 113
Lactic-acid production, 270
Leukocytes, as assay material, 134
  in fluid media, 190
  normal and pathological, in various sera, 191
  in plasma coagulum, 165
  separated from blood, by albumin flotation, 135
    by buffy-coat method, 134
    with phytohemagglutinin, 137
Limb-bones (embryonic), 227, 234, 238
Low-temperature storage of cells, 284
  equipment for, 293
Lymph, clotted, as used by Harrison, 3
Lymphocytes, 193
Lymphosarcoma, 2

Macrophages. See Leukocytes
Malignant cells, 2, 6, 146, 160, 164, 171, 195, 216, 219, 220, 284, 289, 291, 296
  from frog (renal), 148
  human, classification of, 151

Malignant cells (Continued)
  invasive properties, 229
  separated from serosanguineous fluids, 131
Mammary gland, cultivation of, 130, 229
Masks and gowns, 49
Masson's trichrome stain, 315
Mayer's egg albumen mixture, 318
May-Grünwald-Giemsa stain for fluid cultures, 303
Measurements, growth, 267
  metabolism, 270
  plating efficiency (Puck), 208, 217
  virus infectivity, 251
Media, balanced salt solutions, 53
  conditioned (Earle), 211, 212, 215
  dialyzed, 64, 65, 76, 92
  chemically defined, 62, 81, 229, 237, 288
  containing bacteriological preparations, 112, 113
  containing naturally occurring ingredients, 81
  gaseous atmosphere, 60, 184, 213, 215
  heterologous, 167, 193, 236
  osmotic pressure, 53
  perfused, 222
  pH control, 59
  plasma, 82
  serum, 91
  tissue extracts, 99
Metabolites, intermediary, 66
Metals, toxicity of, 21
  trace, 69
Methylcellulose (Methocel), 203
Methyl-green–pyronin-Y stain, 309
Micrometer, ocular, measurements, 269
Microscopy, electron, 320
Milk (skim) as supplement for synthetic media,111
Millipore filters, 41, 46, 232
Mitosis and differentiation, 236
Mitotic coefficients, 269
Mitotic index, 270
Monocytes. See Leukocytes
Mutants, isolation of, 218

Nerve fibers, origin of (Harrison), 2
Neurilemmoma, 151
Nitric acid, as cleansing agent, 31

Nitrogen, liquid, for low-temperature storage, 297
  metabolism, 270
Nuclei (isolated), enumeration of, 276
Nucleic-acid constituents, in chemically defined media, 66, 67
Nucleic-acid phosphorus, 67
Nucleoproteins, 65, 100
Nutrition. *See* Cell nutrition

Oil, of cedarwood, Florida extra, 302
  spindle, for dust prevention, 12
Organized growth, 227
Organs, cultivation of, 4, 5, 63, 109, 227
Osmic-acid fixative, 306, 308, 320
Osmotic pressure, 53

Pancreatic extract, dialyzed (Eagle), 76
Paper, cover tubes for pipettes, 21, 39
  sulfur-free, for sterilizing, 21, 38, 40
Paraffin, for coverslip cultures, 141
  for embedding, 316
  for plasma storage tubes, 83
Parathyroid grafts, human, 231, 235
Patching, to compensate for digestion of coagulum, 155, 172, 269
Peptones, 63, 113, 114
Perforated cellophane, for coverslip cultures, 16, 148
  for flask cultures, 195
  used in harvesting cells, 188
Perforated slides, for coverslip cultures, 151
Perfusion chambers, 222
Petri-dish cultures, 183
  controlled atmosphere for, 184
pH control, 59, 184
  with CO₂-bicarbonate buffer, 59, 73, 184
  with other buffers, 58, 61, 73, 203
Phenol red, as pH indicator, 60, 154, 168
Phosphate-buffered saline (PBS), 58, 117
Phosphite-buffered saline, 58
Phytohemagglutinin, for separating leukocytes from blood, 137, 193
Pipettes, Pasteur, 21
  serological, 21
Placental-cord serum (Gey), 97, 177, 231, 235
Planimeter, 269

Plasma, albumin, 131, 135
  coagulum, lysis of, 155, 167
    opacity of, 153
    washed, to remove foreign protein, 168
  cultures, of blood leukocytes, 165
    on coverslips, 139
    for embryological studies, 234
    of epithelial cells, 164
    of fibroblasts, 161, 269
    fixation and staining, 310
    in flasks, 152
    harvested with trypsin, 120, 165
    with heterologous plasma, 166, 236
    preparation of subcultures, 141, 157
    sectioning, 315
    with sponge matrix, 170
    in tubes, 158
  frozen and dried, 83
  preparation of, 82
Plastic culture containers, 28
Plates, glass, 22
Plating efficiency (Puck), of cells in suspension, 207, 217
Plating procedures, in assessing irradiation damage, 220
Pleuropneumonialike organisms (PPLO), 47
Poliomyelitis vaccine (Salk type), preparation of, 263
Polyvinyl pyrrolidone, 297
Prescription bottles as culture containers, 17, 27, 183
Projectoscope, for surface measurements, 269
Proliferation and differentiation, 236
Protein degradation products, 63, 99
Proteins, serum, origin of, 193
Pure strains from single cells, 209

Racks, for coverslip cultures, 23, 148, 151
  for flask cultures, 23
  for pipettes and instruments, 22
  for tube cultures, 23, 159, 179
Reducing agents, in chemically defined media, 67
Replicate cultures, 66, 184
Ribonuclease (RNAse), 309, 310
Rinaldini's solution, for enzymes, 59
Ring-slide cultures, 145
Ringer-formol, 299

Ringer-Locke solution, 55
Ringer's solution, 55
Roller-tube cultures, with plasma, 158
  without plasma, 66, 182, 199
Rubber, cleansing and sterilization, 33, 40
  pipette bulbs, 23
  toxicity of, 226

Saline A (Puck), for enzymes, 59, 128
Salt solutions, balanced, 53
  composition of, 55, 57
  for diluting enzymes, 59
  osmotic pressure of, 53
  "particle" concentration of, 58
  phosphate buffered (PBS), 58
  phosphite buffered, 58
  preparation of, 56
  with serum albumin, 57
Schiff reagent, 307
Serum, albumin, 57, 98
  dialyzed, 64, 65, 76
  fetal calf, 177
  fractions, 92, 98
  frozen and dried, 83
  heated, to reduce clot lysis, 170
    to reduce toxicity, 96, 193
  heterologous, 193
  horse, 96
  individual variations in, 191
  placental-cord (Gey), 97, 177, 231, 235
  preparation of, 93
  as supplement for chemically defined
    media, 69, 76, 92
  for complex media, 109, 112, 113
  ultrafiltrate (Simms), 92, 110
Silver-impregnation stain (Bodian), 318
Single-cell isolation, 209
Skeletal rudiments, 227, 238
Skin, prepared for cultivation, 117
Skin grafts, human, 2
Slide cultures. See Coverslip cultures
Soap, for cleansing glassware, 30
  for cleansing hands, 50
Solutions, sterilization of, 41, 42
Spatulas, platinum, 23, 154, 187
Spinal cord (chick embryo), 119, 269
Spleen, 193
Sponge-matrix cultures, with fluid
    medium, 195
  with plasma, 170

Staining procedures, 298
Steam for autoclaves, cleansed by filtra-
    tion, 34
  generated from distilled water, 34
Sterilization, 34
  by filtration, 42
  of fluids, by steam, 41
  indicators, 36
  special paper for, 21, 38, 40
Stoppers for cultures, 23, 24
Subculturing, from bottles and flasks,
    157, 187, 197
  from coverslips, 141
Surface area of cell colonies in plasma,
    measurement of, 268
Suspended-cell cultures, 197
Sympathicoblastoma, 150, 151
Synthetic media. See Chemically defined
    media

Test tubes for cultures, 179, 199
Thrombin, 170, 235
Tissue extracts, 99, 110, 111
Tissue fragments, discrete, in fluid
    medium, 193
Tissue homogenizers, 104
Tissues, prepared for cultivation, 115
  by chopping and dissection, 117
  by treatment with enzymes, 119,
    130
  from slaughterhouse material, 116, 126
  from surgery, 116, 119
Transplantation (grafting) of tissues, 231
Tris buffer, 61, 73, 110
Trypsin, for detaching cells from glass,
    120, 188, 274
  for releasing cells from tissues, 121
  for releasing cultures from plasma, 120,
    165, 267
Tube cultures, with fast rotation (50
    r.p.m.), 199
  with slow rotation, 182
  without rotation, 179
Tyrode's solution, 55
  modifications of, 57
  preparation of, 56

Ultrafiltrate, of embryo extract, 100
  of serum, 92, 110
Ultrasonic energy, for cleansing glass-
    ware, 28

Versene, 27, 31, 131, 189, 274
Viruses, bacterial, 260
  identification, 249
  inactivation, 265
  infectivity, estimation of, 251
  isolation, from plaques, 259
  multiplication, 246
  one-step growth experiments, 260
  plaque counts, 257
  poliomyelitis vaccine, 263
  titrations, 250
    tube method, 250
    plaque method, 255, 258
  ultraviolet inactivation of, 256
  yellow-fever vaccine, 245

Vitamins, in chemically defined media, 63, 66, 69, 71
  in organ culture, 229

Watch-glass cultures, 234
Water, demineralized, 29, 31, 32, 77
Weight (dry) of cultures, 270

Yeast extract, 110, 112, 113
Yellow-fever virus, 245

Zenker-formol (Helly's fluid), 300
Zenker's fluid, 300